建设工程管理中英文双语丛书
Construction Management Series

建 筑 工 程 危 机 管 理

Grisis Management in Construction Projects

Martin Loosemore, PH.D.

尚 梅 译

中国建筑工业出版社

著作权合同登记图字:01－2003－1859 号

图书在版编目(CIP)数据

建筑工程危机管理/(英)罗斯茂编著;尚梅等译.

北京:中国建筑工业出版社,2003

(建设工程管理中英文双语丛书)

ISBN 7－112－06029－X

Ⅰ.建… Ⅱ.①罗…②尚… Ⅲ.建筑工程—风险

管理—汉、英 Ⅳ.F407.9

中国版本国书馆 CIP 数据核字(2003)第 083514 号

　　本书由美国土木工程协会出版公司正式授权我社在中国翻译、出版、发行中英文版

　　责任编辑：常　燕

建筑工程危机管理

Martin Loosemore

尚　梅　译

中国建筑工业出版社出版、发行 (北京西郊百万庄)

新　华　书　店　经　销

广东省肇庆市科建印刷有限公司

开本:787×1092 毫米 1/16 印张:19

2003 年 10 月第一版　　2003 年 10 月第一次印刷

定价:**36.00 元**

ISBN 7－112－06029－X

F·483(12042)

建筑工程危机管理 旨在阐明如何防止建筑工程中的危机,以及对于无法避免的危机,如何利用它。基于数十年的危机管理研究工作以及在施工建筑业的咨询工作经验,马丁·罗斯茂为我们提供了大量的来自高风险企业的经验教训。在这本书中,以反应和预防为中心,把危机看成是一种发展的机遇——这对把危机看成是管理上的失败,应该不计一切代价来避免和压制的观点来说是一个挑战。

危机管理 要求读者用当代危机管理,风险管理,心理学及行为科学等研究成果,用一种新的思路来看待工程。案例研究给读者提供了绝好的工具来吸取他人的经验,洞察在实际的危机过程中人们的行为方式。

讨论的主题包括:

* 危机计划
* 危机管理的动态性
* 建筑工程中的应急计划
* 危机管理者作为社会建筑师
* 危机管理者的教训
* 创建乐观性的组织

马丁·罗斯茂: 哲学博士,澳大利亚·悉尼·新南威尔士大学建筑环境系副教授。他曾在多种杂志上发表过文章,是建筑工程人力资源的作者之一。马丁·罗斯茂博士同时也作为顾问和学术研究者。

"数百万盎司投资的预防措施不足以医治工程的所有隐患。尽管我们有设计精良的计划,但有时潜在的带有极大破坏性的危机会突然降临。罗斯茂博士为您的组织对危机做出准备以及有效的处理危机提供了一个很好的工作框架……"

布莱恩 A. 戴利,P.E.
副会长
HARRIS & ASSOCIATES

致 谢

赫斯，谢谢你无尽的耐心和支持。也谢谢我的三个孩子，如果没有他们，这本书会容易得多，但就没有这么大的价值了。

我还要对其他许多人表示感谢，比如教给我许多东西的我的父母、约翰和安妮塔；帮助我形成我的观点的同事们。特别要感谢彼得·希伯德、威尔·休斯、特福·弗兰斯、丹尼·麦克乔治、高兰·罗逊、麦里萨·托以及德瑞克·沃克等给我的友谊、批评和支持。

最后，感谢新南威尔士大学我的同事们给我提供了写这本书的合作、支持的环境。在一个有利于研究工作的团队中工作是那样的令人愉快。

前　言

政治、经济和社会的不稳定性；自然资源的耗竭；日益激烈的全球性竞争以及技术的突飞猛进使得商业活动日益的难以预测。无法预料的问题已经成为正常现象而不再是例外了，诸如 1981 年堪萨斯城．海特．雷金斯宾馆人行道坍塌事故这样影响力较大的工程灾难也只不过是冰山一角了。风险理论认为，对应每一个报道过的危机，都有不计其数的没有报道的事故。例如，斯密斯（1996）指出航空公司的每一起死亡事故中，就有 10 起重伤，30 起轻伤和 600 起准事故一起发生。本书中严格地区分了常伴管理者身边的日常问题和偶然性的危机。危机管理工作需要给予特别的重视，因为它过度扩展了组织系统和人员间的关系，强加给管理者大量的复杂问题，而且这些问题若不迅速处理很快就会演变成全方位的危机。本书旨在阐述如何防止这种现象的发生。

本书的特点之一就是把注意力集中在预防和反应上。这一点和传统的建筑管理书籍形成明显的对比。传统的建筑管理只注重预防措施而不重视危机发生以后的应对策略，虽然说"防优于治"，但管理者能够创造一个没有危机的环境的可能性已经越来越小了。这就要求组织要具有对不可预料的事件做出反应的能力。

本书的另一个独特之处在于它很注重人。这一点也和传统的建筑管理书籍形成明显的对比。传统的建筑管理书籍解决问题的方法在本质上是很科学的，其特点是采用大量的条线图、网络图、现金流量图等。传统的建筑管理书籍强调措施、控制和通用的降低不确定性的方法，而本书却强调周全的考虑，灵活性和对不确定性的适应。从这个角度去研究建筑管理是难能可贵的，因为在这方面，对人力方面的研究几乎还是没有的。正如巴特费德（1975）认为的那样，"对一个只会拿着直尺做计量工作的人，你就别指望他能把什么思想安排得井井有序了"（第一页）。

本书为什么人而写：危机并没有职业的界限，这使得这本书适合所有的工程管理者。虽然它偏向于建筑方面，但所举的例子来自各行各业，所以应该能够引起广泛读者的兴趣。

虽然这本书面对实践者，对传统的认为理论和实践不能兼容的观点来说是个挑战。沃森（1994）向我们展示了管理实践者是如何凭直觉，在日常生活中发展、更新和利用复杂的理论思想的。虽然它们可能不是正规的管理理论，管理者们从本质上说却是"实践－理论家"，他们大多数人都认识到了把这些理论作为他们行动指南的价值。因为这个原因，本书把应用、战略及基础研究结合在一起。

本书的与众不同之处：经验在处理危机时非常重要，但取得这样的经验是困难的，也是痛苦的。最好的方法是通过对过去危机管理案例的研究重温别人的经验。但是，在建筑施工环境中能够详细记录危机管理过程的资料是很有限的。为了补偿这个不足，本书分析了四个实际的工程危机。这些案例的研究能为读者提供良好的重温他人经验的工具，它所提出的深刻见解几乎是无边无际的。特别是，它能帮助我们理解在危机过程中，人们的行为是怎样的，又为什么是那样的，从而对一定的行为对危机管理的结果造成的影响做出判断。

　　从教育的意义上来说，所研究的案例为我们提供了能作为分析和讨论资料的有趣的教学题材。管理的内容包括问题的解决，决策的制定，领导，沟通，风险管理，灾难管理，健康和安全，冲突和变更管理，组织设计和协作。

马丁·罗斯茂，哲学博士，M.ASCE,MXIOB

副教授

新南威尔士大学

悉尼.澳大利亚

目 录

第一章

简　介

　　本章对反冲突价值系统提出了挑战。反冲突价值系统使大多数人将危机看成是一种威胁而不是机遇。本章旨在说明：危机，通过适当的管理，可以使工程得到加强而不是受到损害。

我们的反冲突价值观

　　用整本书来讨论危机管理似乎显得有点否定和失败主义者的味道。在诸如全面质量管理、联营体及生产机构重组这样的商业潮流中，这是不难理解的。这种潮流在建筑业日益明显，它告诫经理们：预防重于治理，危机是管理失败的标志，任何形式的不和谐和冲突都是一种浪费和损害。

　　反冲突价值观起源于一种习惯，这种习惯在我们最易受影响和最易形成性格的年龄阶段给我们灌输了这种观点。比如，在家里，我们被教导"父母是无所不知的"，"我们不应该顶撞"，"我们应该多做少说"。教堂文化告诉我们，"幸福存在于一致性、和谐性、和平性和安定性"。在学校，"老师说的总是对的，是不可质疑的"。而且，传统的教育方式趋向于压抑孩子所可能拥有的一切创造性和带有批判性的疑问，教导他们成功的秘诀在于我们所给出的答案和老师认可的真理是相符的。事实上，当我们已长大成人，这种遵守习惯的压力并没有减少。例如，进入一个行业通常需要通过很严格的考试并且要同意遵守一套严格的职业准则。这种体系的设置就是为了维持每种职业为自己开辟的区别于其他职业的传统角色的持久性，这种传统的角色把其成员和其他职业的成员区分开来，并为之在社会中定位。

　　这种习惯抑制我们的思维方式的最生动的例子可见于现代科学的发展史中，在这个进程中，教堂文化阻止了思维的发展。例如，中世纪基督教会的大学里，人们都相信应该把追求真理从日常事务中分离出来；教会对才智、发明、知识、科学和推测具有最高的保护权。虽然认为教会经常性的惩罚和折磨那些对他们的学说提出批评的人们的说法是一种谬误，但他们确实希望科学家（其中多数为僧侣），能够压抑他们直接和明确地质疑教会权威的欲望。比如，虽然有函件证明教会曾鼓励哥白尼出版他的关于太阳而不是地球是宇宙的中心的学说，亦有事实证明，迫于无法避免的来自于同僚们批判的折磨（凯斯特勒1975），他推迟30年出版他的学说。事实上，在1633年，当伽里略出版他支持哥白尼早期学说的研究成果时，他被迫在教堂法庭前撤回他的研究成果。难以置信的是，直到最近教皇才废除了对他的指控。

　　虽然从中世纪至今我们又经历了很长的一段历程，现代的习惯仍操纵着我们的生活，在这种环境下，对人类知识发展进程最具深远意义的两大理论——相对论和进化论——出现于这种影响的范围之外也就不足为奇了。非常有趣且值得指出的是，爱因斯坦和达尔文都是业余工作者，他们不属于任何大学或教会。这种强烈的个性意识在当代最有影响的政治家中也表现得很明显。例如，马格里特·萨奇尔因"没有这种像社会的东西"的言论而著名，亚历克山大·赫泽尔发展了 Glasnost 思想，这种思想后来被麦克哈尔·戈贝奇所采纳，亚历克山大·赫泽尔一生的大部分时光都过着流放生活，他拒绝任何形式的、可能导致他信念妥协的集体生活。看来不和谐并不像我们被教导的那样不受欢迎，创造力常常来自那些敢于对充满整个社会、塑造我们行为的强有力的反冲突价值观提出质疑的人们。

需要——创造力之母

在主流管理系统中反冲突价值观日益受到重视，但在建筑管理中，这种现象值得忧虑，因为它导致那种以缓和而不是以最优作为战略的机构的产生。这种机构不能充分发挥他们的潜力。虽然初看起来这本书有点持否定观点，但它的目的是想通过发展一种乐观的机构来挑战这种悲观的思想模式。和悲观的组织机构相比较，乐观的组织机构将危机看成是一种潜在的机遇而不是威胁。危机，如果妥善管理，能够使工程得到加强而不是受到损害。

或许从我们的历史课本中，能够找到最活生生的有关乐观派的例子，其中记载了大量人们在危机前、危机中以及危机后所表现出来的强大的创造力的例子。例如，黑死病促成检疫制度的诞生，天花病促使种痘技术的发展，霍乱病是第一个公共卫生权威机构诞生的推动力。严重的灾难也一样刺激了我们的创造力。例如，1666 年伦敦的大火给诸如克里斯托福·雷恩和尼古拉斯·霍克斯茂提供了许多建造诸如圣保罗大教堂等美丽壮观的大教堂的机遇，也促使了英国第一部建筑法规的诞生。同样的道理，芝加哥 1870 年的大火给建筑师和工程师们提供了建造世界上第一座钢骨架摩天大楼的机会。事实上，当今芝加哥仍然以其独具创新和令人振奋的建筑而举世闻名。

在当今世界，发明创造最重要的刺激物莫过于两次世界大战了，第二次世界大战为雷达、DDT、青霉素、喷气式飞机、联合国、世界银行和国际货币基金组织的诞生创造了机遇。近些年来，冷战给我们带来了核能和太空竞赛，太空竞赛又为我们带来了第一颗通讯卫星和载人的宇宙飞船。

逆境中也产生了许多管理领域的革新。例如，早期工业革命中的掠夺、剥削和社会动乱现象促使像查理斯·巴比杰和罗伯特·欧文这样的先驱者做家长式统治和社会责任管理制（谢尔德克 1996）的实践尝试，刺激了诸如分享管理制、工作组制、利润分享方案、雇员的教育和福利设施等观念的产生。在近代，我们在建筑行业中所遇到的许多当代管理动态的起源都可追溯到那个充满问题的年代。例如，二战时，为了应付严重的材料缺乏问题，生产商被迫鉴定出生产过程中的多余费用，用新的具有可替换性的原材料做替换性试验。令人吃惊的是，结果通常是价廉而又高质量的产品的出现（麦尔斯 1967）。全面质量管理（TQM）也可追溯到相同的起源。全面质量管理的动力来源于二战时期日本经济的毁灭。据 Tsurumi（1982），日本经济的毁灭激发了人们对全面质量管理原则探讨的热情，而且很庆幸地在一定程度上，这种原则和日本传统的文化价值相适应。正如戴明在提到美国全面质量管理频频失败的原因时所指出的那样："只有身处危机之中，才能真正的关注某事"。

20 世纪 70～80 年代，日本对美国的竞争优势不断增强，这导致了由 Rank Xerox 公司提出的水准基点这个现代观念的诞生。面对日本竞争对手能够以低于美国厂商的价格出售复印机，Rank Xerox 公司解体了日本的产品，将它的元件作为自己生产标准的模型（坎普

1989)。后来，通用汽车公司和福德对日本生产的变速箱做了同样的事情，这种变速箱远比他们所生产的变速箱的运行要平稳得多，他们发现竞争对手所使用的允许公差远比美国工业所采用的允许公差要小得多。这些原则现在已扩展到世界上大多数主要机构的所有商业活动领域中。

抛弃过去的谬见——未来的挑战

如果危机为人类社会的巨大进步提供了舞台，那么管理者们的未来应该是令人兴奋的。在 1970 年，阿尔文·托夫勒所著写的未来冲击一本书中描绘了主要由人口变动、资源枯竭、全球化、技术进步和世界范围内的政治经济改革所导致的混乱、易变和危机四伏的商业环境。事实上，他的这种预测趋向于保守，因为我们的前辈在发展的进程中所采用的是尝试和检测过的技术，而现代工程管理者正面临着不断增长的新的、大部分未经测试的技术流，他们很少有时间去理解这些技术的性能和相容性。这种技术的复杂性导致了组织机构的复杂性，这反映在对不同种类专家的大量需求上和复杂的难以理解的相互关系上。为了解决这些问题，人们逐渐意识到建筑业对雇员的健康和福利、对公众、对环境是一种威胁，这导致了对建筑业外部管理法规标准的提高。虽然人们可以以过去的工程为例，证明这些压力总是存在的，但严密的检查表明，建筑管理者从来不是必须与众多的压力、需求和规章的制约做斗争。例如，在 1931 年承建 102 层高的帝国大厦时，工期计划只有 14 个月，建筑工艺相对来说是经过充分试验和测试过的，但建筑规章制度比当今的要宽松得多，而且安全被置于第二重要的地位(西奥多 1975)。

所以，对建筑业来说，未来的挑战不像过去那样只在于纯粹的规模上，而在于工程的复杂性和多变性上。就像丹特(1983)指出的那样，那里有更多的竞争，有更多的活动需要组织，更重要的是，由于资源是有限的，我们只能成功不能失败。这里也有新的机遇，为了充分运用它，需要从传统的管理方式转换到富有思想的、灵活的、响应的和以人为中心的管理模式上。这是因为，在日益不确定和竞争的环境中，缺乏弹性的体制变得具有局限性并且使劳动生产率降低，在这种情况下，组织机构利用人们创造性的能力就成了该机构生命力和成功的基础(帕斯卡尔 1991)。未来的挑战在于更有效地利用人力资源，去寻找更好的方法，充分利用可能出现的令人兴奋的机遇。

不幸的是，像在其他行业一样，在建筑业迎接这种挑战也是非常困难的，因为管理方法不断的被 20 世纪初由弗雷德里克·泰勒所倡导的科学的价值观(布洛克雷 1996)所加强。就像比(1994)在船舶结构事故调查中所发现的那样，大多数工程师依然对人力资源和不确定性感到极为不安。这是一种近来被工程界普遍关注的无能的表现，现在越来越多的工程师逐渐认识到他们职业的兴旺发展将依赖于他们能否将自己的关注点从"只关注客观事物扩展到同样娴熟地运用人力资源"(约翰 1999)。人们认为这样能使工程师得到更好的装备，使之能最大限度的发挥多种劳动力的潜能，最终提高建筑物结构的可靠性。

当你看见一个危机时，鉴别出它

相信世界上充满了日益增加的复杂性和不确定性的人，就是那种认为在未来的发展进程中，会不时地出现突然的、不可预料的、潜在的、需要当机立断做出决策的事件。这种相对比较强烈的事件就叫危机，它不同于常伴管理者身边的日常问题，大多数人会期望在自己的职业生涯中至少遇上一次这样的事件。管理者处理这类事件的方法关系到公司的生死存亡，在建筑工程施工环境中，人们自然会联想到诸如火灾、破产、严重的争执、严重的事故、坍塌、罢工还有像自然现象的洪水等鲜活的事故。然而，在工程施工过程中可能出现的危机是大量的、多种多样的。最近，美国在一次调查中，工程师把危机按频率从大到小排列如下：施工延误；设计错误；费用超支；管理的连续性；当地对工程的对抗性；竞争对手对雇员的突然行动；第三方诉讼；雇员的不满；机构合并或收购及其他事故。

危机，无论它本身多么精确，通常都被认为是一种低概率的、不可预料的、有较大影响的事件且没有被包含在应急计划内(波斯 1993)。危机给优先级别较高的目标系统带来瞬间的、严重的威胁，要求管理者在极短的时间压力下，做出非常规的决策。这种决策通常有极为广泛的经济、政治、文化和社会影响，它的结果常受到广大公众、媒体和政府的检查(皮尔逊和克莱尔 1998)。不足为奇，这些极端的特性趋于强调组织内不可预测的力量及其分歧，过度扩展的人们之间的联系，测定人们的极限，在组织内不同的利益集团间产生压力和忧虑感。从这个意义上来说，危机对管理者提出了和他们日常所遇见的问题截然不同的挑战。

区分灾难和危机

就像我们上面所讲的那样，危机是复杂的、无情的，将高级决策者引入未知的领域，展现出在通常情况下不易显露的弱点和力量。许多机构和这些复杂的、大量的事件所带来的挑战搏斗，和日常的问题相比较，不当的管理可能造成"灾难"的后果。灾难和危机的区分是十分重要的，但因它们常作为同义词使用，很容易造成混淆。从本质上说来，灾难是由于危机处理不当而造成的，本书就拟阐述危机的管理，以防灾难的发生。

易发生危机的施工过程

在工程的整个生命期中，潜在的危机是很大的。一方面的原因是普遍存在于各个行业的技术和组织不断的复杂化；另一方面的原因是建筑业特殊的文化和管理实践。

文化问题

职　业

讨论建筑业最重大的问题，一个好的出发点就是研究各职业团体之间制度化的分工。为了充分理解这些分工的特征和重要性，我们应该回首 19 世纪，那时工业化进程抚育了职业化和以建筑业及工程师为其顶端的社会等级结构的发展(欣德利和马勒 1996)。随着专业化的发展，出现了独特的专业亚文化，这种专业亚文化体现在它独一无二的信仰、价值观、态度、语言、宗教仪式、行为准则、着装习惯、期望、规范和实践上。这种亚文化的出现不但损害了建筑业内部的交流，而且为强烈的专业化陈规的发展打下了基础，这种专业化陈规已经深深地植根于现代建筑业的社会组织机构中，影响人们彼此之间的行为方式。例如，罗斯茂和切·切(2000)发现，其他行业往往把承包商和消极的旧框框联系在一起，但对工程师的评价却非常有利，认为他们富有效率、有系统性、有信心而且沉着冷静。这种根深蒂固的观念给管理者带来了许多麻烦，特别是在相对较短的工程建设期内。解决这种问题最有效的办法，是采用招标法，比如设计招标和施工招标，它对传统的权力对比提出了质疑，便于人们更多的参与，要求人们在跨职业的团队内共同工作。

设计管理

许多施工中的问题都源于设计中未解决的问题；所以，一个好的设计管理能明显地降低施工中的危机倾向性。例如，1994 年，比的关于工程事故的调查中发现，大部分危机源于设计中甚至设计前，但其中 98% 都是在施工后(施工结束)甚至运行阶段才被检测出来。事实上，历史上有无数的例子都能证明，蹩脚的设计管理导致了灾难的发生。或许最古老的证明文件算是有关 1907 年奎柏克大桥灾难的例子。拟建的大桥将是世界上最长的大桥，单跨 1800 英尺。然而，施工过程中灾难发生了，结构坍塌，导致 82 名施工人员死亡。1908年出版的皇家调查委员会的报告中指出，迫于时间和费用的压力，设计者在设计方案上作了妥协，在设计图纸还没有最终完成时就已火速上场，并且发现，在施工过程中，设计者已经注意到承重 4 000t 的悬臂梁的负荷已超出了它的设计极限。令人惋惜的是，这些问题被忽视了，桥梁断裂的最后期限也来临了。

1995 年 6 月，导致 501 人死亡、900 人受伤的南朝鲜购物商城坍塌事件的主要原因也是设计管理的失误。调查表明，有许多非法的设计变更，设计者受贿，没有充分在现场对承包商进行监控和管理。设计组的大部分人员，包括委托人和地方政府官员皆因重大过失而入狱。作为反应，许多国家通过立法使设计队伍对他们设计的长期效果负责。然而，立法毕竟不能代替良好的管理，从这种事实，我们吃惊的发现建筑业花了那么长时间，才把注意力放在了设计管理上(格雷·埃特·奥尔 1994)。毫无疑问，高效的设计管理对降低工程危机的倾向性有重大的贡献。

市场问题

和上面所述的文化问题相比较，一种强烈的经济观点认为，建筑队伍的发展超过其市场需求是导致建筑市场危机倾向性的主要原因。虽然人们推测，随着时间的推移，建筑队伍自然会和建筑市场相适应，一代代建筑公司受时走时停的政府方针的影响，已经变成知晓幸存方法的专家了。在下一个繁荣期再一次反转建筑市场趋向之前，建筑业很少有足够的时间去适应这种变化。这就意味着建筑队伍规模的变化总是不可避免的和建筑市场的变化不同步，而且往往比建筑市场要大一些。在这种僧多粥少的环境下，市场迫使建筑公司降低利润和不可预见费用，去承担自己没有能力承担的风险，这不但导致了豆腐渣工程而且为肆无忌惮的建筑公司的繁荣创造了条件。这种对立的环境鼓励平凡，将建筑队伍的行为降低到它最低的水准。

在上述的环境中，委托方的角色是至关重要的，因为他们决定了建筑市场的特征。除了少数最开明的委托人外，大多数委托人都屈服于低价的诱惑，产生了源源不断的问题。在 9900 万英镑预算基础上超支 2600 万英镑的卡德社千年橄榄球体育馆工程，就能够很好地阐述这种传统的、受费用驱使的思想的危险，在高风险工程中，这种现象更为明显。承建本馆是为了迎接 1999 年 10 月的威尔士世界杯橄榄球赛。许多因素导致了工程费用超支、尖锐的争执以及严重的工期延误，这种延误简直是一种灾难，它几乎可以严重到迫使事件的举行地点改变。然而最重要的因素却是与总承包商签订的受保障的最高价格合同，这个合同签订时，设计工作正在进行之中。这种问题在建筑市场上的频频发生，促使人们呼吁建立一种明智的承包商及其咨询单位选择系统，这种系统以综合的全面的准则来进行选择，而不是以价格作为唯一的标准(哈特舍和斯凯特茂1997)。此外，有很多人提倡合同谈判和合伙经营，以减少在选择过程中对价格过分的强调(Latham 1994)。遗憾的是，很多建筑商采纳上述建议的步伐很慢，价格依然是选择施工队伍的主要因素。

人为的问题

合　同

上面我们讨论了由文化和经济条件所导致的建筑业中的冲突和不信任。这种现象活生生的表现在长篇的、复杂的、合法的合同文件中，这种合同文件以下列假设为基础：合同授予的合法权威人士能准确的控制人们的行为，存在一种最好的管理方法，不信任人们能做正确的事情，人们总是喜欢别人告诉自己应该做什么，合同起草者知道所有应该知道的东西。建筑施工中许多破坏性的冲突都源于没能符合合同系统这种强制性的要求。现在出现了一种学派，主张通过培养一种相互信任和共同的责任感来更好的管理工程。构想这种文化的基础是：大多数冲突都是偶然的，源于项目成员间的误解，通过简化语言和合同结构，使他们带有更少的惩罚性，更多的灵活性和平等性，以此创造这种文化氛围。联合王国土木工程协会印发的建筑工程合同(1995)就建立在此基础之上，然而，它的有效性却依赖于能否消除传统的招致不和的文化，而这种文化在传统的施工合同中是永存的。这一点做起来很困难或者不被管理者们所欣赏，结果导致了一连串很有影响力的争执。

分　包

建筑业中的大部分争执都出现在总承包商和分包商之间。事实上，许多研究已经发现了工程业绩和分包间的直接关系(NEDO 1983；Kumaraswamy 1996)。分包是应日益复杂的技术和日益缩短的工期要求而产生的，它同时使工程变得零碎、不稳定，导致短期行为，削弱了以顾客为中心的指导思想，使工程复杂化，导致不公平竞争，带来信息流通、动机和质量控制等方面的问题。

1981年堪萨斯城·海特·雷紧斯宾馆的悬吊式人行道坍塌，造成113人死亡、186人重伤，这一事故就能充分说明由分包商的管理问题所引起的灾难隐患。后来国家标准局的调查结论表明，坍塌是由未被发现的结构变更引起的，变更是钢结构厂为了生产方便，擅自改变了原设计而做出的(NBS 1982)。这种变更导致构件的承载力严重减弱，达到了人行道连自身重量都无法承受的程度，更不用说承受额外的行人的重量了。

生产问题

不确定性

建筑物的范围和复杂性变幻无穷，比起许多工业产品，可以说，建筑产品是在相对无法控制的环境中建成的。例如，有多少其他行业的管理者必须考虑秃鹰的繁殖习惯？这看起来似乎有点可笑，但美国怀俄明州穿过蛇谷的高速公路承包商必须停工六个月，因为工地是这种鸟至关重要的栖息地。这意味着承包商必须在冬期施工，那么，在低于 0℃环境中适用的特殊的施工方法就成为必需的了。然而，此种特殊情况通过环境学家的参与是可以预测的，还有许多自然事件却是无法预测的，那么，工程施工中出现问题也就不足为奇了。

人

虽然有人致力于建筑生产过程的工业化尝试，许多工程构件的生产，特别是建筑物的施工，实质上仍然是以工艺为基础的、小批量的、户外生产过程，和许多工业生产过程相比，它的一个个产品包含相对较少的重复性、常规性和机械化的生产过程。从这种意义上说，建筑业实际上是一种以人为主的施工管理过程，受人们不可预言的个性风格的影响很大。许多工程方面的灾难都可以证明建筑工程很易受人们错误的影响。例如，我们已经提到1907 年奎伯克大桥的坍塌事故，皇家专派员将事故归咎于管理工程的工程师的判断失误。人为错误才是许多其他大桥坍塌事故的重要原因，例如 1940 年雄心勃勃设计的谭克马·南倍斯大桥；1967 年导致 46 名摩托司机死亡的俄亥俄希尔弗大桥事故；1976 年澳大利亚墨尔本的西门大桥事故。西门大桥坍塌事故的起因是一名工程师移动了一个螺栓的位置，其目的是修正中跨中出现的错位问题，然而没注意到由此引起的大桥结构变化。实际上，在研究了美国在 1975～1986 年间的 604 起建筑事故后（埃尔度凯尔和阿伊博 1991）发现，其中大多数事故都是由于工程师和承包商知识贫乏、无知、粗心和失职而引起的。有趣的是，虽然许多导致事故的失误从本质上说是技术性的，但仍有 40% 的失误是和责任心及信息流通有关的。

工程组织机构

和工程结构相适应的工程组织机构通常被认为是一种临时的多边组织机构，因为它定义了开始和结束时间，由具有顾问和承包性质的独立的专家机构的代表组成（切尔斯和布兰特 1984）。在人员方面这种组织机构具有很高的临时性，因为工程施工过程中涉及的活动和人员是随着时间而变动的。而且，由于摆脱不了以竞争方式选择施工队伍的传统，不同的工程通常使用截然不同的施工队伍，这就保证了工程施工组织是由一种经常变动的劳动力组成的，且不同的组织忠于他们不同的集团利益。这同时也保证了与急剧升降的知识曲线相适应的不断变动的人事关系曲线，特别是在工程的最终状态定义不当或根本无从知道的工程早期阶段。1973 年 8 月 2 日，导致联合王国 50 人死亡的萨姆兰德娱乐中心的火灾事故，就能生动的阐述这种组织机构潜在的问题。根据特纳和皮杰（1997）报道，"一个小规模的建筑公司首次承接了这种大规模的工程，使用一些新的建筑材料，冒着发生火灾的风险设计一种新型的建筑物。除此之外，期望的建筑物运行条件在设计阶段又有了重大的变更"（p.46）。这就导致了一系列的人为错误、蹩脚的信息流通系统、误解、冲突和无知，所有这些又都被时间的压力所激化。

管理者是危机倾向性的源泉

虽然建筑业趋于接受开放的、灵活的、以人为导向的管理风格，相当的证据证明，建筑业的管理思想本质上还是具有科学性的。这点在建筑管理文化中得到了最好的体现，它预示着人们日渐热衷于主流管理系统中流行的商业风尚，比如全面质量管理(TQM)、水准基点、供应链管理和价值工程。

近来在建筑业，吸引管理者注意力的两个词汇是"营业过程重组工程"和"精简施工"，这在日渐高涨的组织机构转换过程中得到了集中体现。"营业过程重组工程"和"精简施工"的方法，是通过赋予工人决定他们最终命运的权力来克服规模生产带来的问题，然而事实表明，他们无情的只关注生产率、生产工艺的改进和生产效率的提高的做法，导致了组织机构中人性化的降低和创造力的匮乏，这种组织机构更易受危机的影响(理查逊1996；格林1998；卡米切埃尔1999)。虽然营业过程重组工程并不需要精简机构，但实际上，他们常常是这样做的，就如霍尔·埃特·奥尔(1993)所说，他们经常被当成管理的一个方面，使机构精简计划合法化，使人们多做少得，且对这种重大的变化只给予象征性的关注。支持这种观点的事例是令人信服的。例如，Xerox，世界上最大的营业过程重组工程的倡导者之一，三年内耗资7亿美元解雇1万名雇员，美国Fortune的500个工业公司在20世纪80年代花费320万美金来解雇劳动力，联合王国的四个私有企业(英国电信、英国燃气、英国航空和约克舍电力)通过机构重组，在使产量提高24%的同时使劳动力下降32%。这种现象值得忧虑，因为，澳大利亚西门大桥坍塌，联合王国罗纳点式塔坍塌和美国的挑战号空中灾难无不是由劳动力过渡使用的压力所致。实际上，精简的机构不但提高了危机的倾向性，而且降低了对危机的反应力，因为机构被剥夺了它所赖以用来应付不测事件的备用劳动力资源。

除了劳动力队伍日渐缩小、压力逐渐增大外，新的商业趋势又使劳动力雇佣制度无情的朝着更灵活的方向发展。

今天，许多机构的劳动力核心组织比起五年前减少了许多，他们依赖于那种唯利是图的劳动力组织，这种组织冷漠的从一种工作变换到另一种工作，除了自己，他们缺乏对任何人的诚意，他们的主要目标是保证最大的经济回报(罗斯茂1999)。这就导致了一种充满恐惧和自私的环境，而这种环境对工地相对较高的事故发生率、歧视、种族主义和争执负有不可推卸的责任，这也是世界各地建筑业的基本特色。

可靠性高的组织机构

令人啼笑皆非的是，正当商业环境需要灵活性时，建筑业却试图建立一种刚性较大的组织机构。桑根指出(1993)，所有高可靠性(低风险)组织机构的主要特点都是过剩性和重复性。他通过一些研究有效处理高风险环境的组织机构的事例来阐明这个观点。例如，在美国航天业中，人们很重视技术(备用计算机、天线等)和人员(后备人员和重复责任制)的过剩。在当今的商业社会中，重复责任制显得缺乏效率，但在航天业，这种做法可以保证，如果事故隐患没有被一个人检查出来，就有机会被另一个人发现，这已经就是生与死之间的区别了。同样的道理，在核电站的管理上，设计时就已经把独立的外部能源和一些冷却管道纳入系统中，以防现存的系统出现故障。最后，桑根指出，我们的免疫系统内也有多余的组织，这就是为什么在我们的部分组织严重受伤后，我们依然能够幸存的原因。例如，如果把一个肾从人的体内摘除，另一个可以来补偿，继续工作。如果摘除了脾，我们的骨髓可以承担起制造红细胞的工作。这些事例说明，在充满了潜在风险的环境中，过剩对组织的生存来说是必要的。

危机管理的艺术

虽然现代管理的革新似乎帮助管理人员跟上了瞬息万变的世界的步伐,但由于降低了机构的灵活性、创造性和反应性而产生了负效应。看起来,以当代管理潮流自居的管理科学,其实很少能为当今的工程管理者提供帮助。当今的商业世界,要求人们把管理看成是一种艺术,而不是像传统的做法那样,把它当成是一种计算科学。这就意味着,我们应该少强调通过常规的制度来控制不确定性,约定俗成的过程,缺乏弹性的等级结构,专业化,以及处罚的威胁。取而代之,我们应该把不确定性看成是一种机遇而不是威胁,我们应该去适应它而不是去压制它。这种目标可以通过具有弹性的组织机构来实现,这种组织机构的特点是:开放性、敏感性、集体责任心和相互信任感。今天,人们的个性化作风和创造性就是组织机构的生命力,如果充分利用,可以变平庸为杰出,最终,变失败为成功。

结 论

相对于日常问题来说,危机带来了特殊的管理问题。本章所举事例说明,在管理领域内,危机将越来越普遍。遗憾的是,传统的管理价值观没有将注意力放在在管理系统内建立恢复机制,以便来处理不测事件这件事情上。为了做好应付危机的充分准备,管理者应该采取一种更积极的态度来对待他们,应该选择更周全、开放、信任和雇员导向型的管理模式。这种做法不仅能降低灾难发生的概率,还能充分释放未被开发的潜力和能量,尽管这种潜力还没有被传统的管理实践所开发。

然而,这种以雇员为中心的管理模式是不是更具吸引力、更合伦理、更适应未来的发展还依赖于管理工作的环境。如果管理学发展的思想曾教给我们什么东西的话,那就是不存在一种能适应各种环境的解决问题的最好方法。而且,最合适的管理方法的选择依赖于所承担任务的特征、生产技术的特征、环境的不稳定性和所管理的人员的特征。实质上,以任务为中心的管理模式适用于那些常规的、没有创造性的、重复性的工作,这种工作在稳定的、高机械化的环境中由没有高度自治欲望的人来承担。相反的,以雇员为中心的管理模式适用于那些非常规的、具有创造性的工作,这种工作在无法预料的环境中进行,由具有高度自治欲望的人来承担。所以,虽然有足够的理由来软化统治建筑管理业的科学态度,但成功的关键还在于对环境的敏感性和响应性。遗憾的是,负责高风险工程的管理者不愿意在思维方式上做大的改变,因为身处危险环境的人们趋向于在类似的事物中寻找安全感。在建筑业,这意味着数字、制度和过程,这正是建筑工程危机管理的困境。

第二章

危机计划

计划是有效管理危机的基础。本章讨论了建筑和工程施工中可能出现的各种类型的危机，并给出了相应的处理办法。

简　介

为了有效的应付危机，准备工作是至关重要的，有充分准备的组织机构应该是这样的：他们花时间去搞清楚他们将面临的危机的种类。这种机构为危机建立档案，对他们的优先权进行排序，并对他们应该计划的危机提出解决措施。当然，他们也经常对所有可能遇到的风险类型进行重新评价，如果它落在现存的目录之外，就应该提出新的、对付他们的策略。正如米特罗夫和皮尔逊发现的那样，灾难性事故一般的起因都是人们只关注那些存在于特定的工业或组织中的常见危机。

建筑工程危机的种类

现已建立的建筑工程风险模型是非常有限的。一个很好的模型是佩里和海斯所建立的模型(1985)，见表 2-1。虽然在理解风险暴露方面，这个模型是非常有用的，但它对建筑危机的不同种类，特别是对危机管理的结果的洞察是很有限的。它的焦点只集中在危机的起源上。所以，人们对于不同种类的危机出现时如何做出反应的理解很有限。然而，主流危机管理的研究已经发展出了基于对起因和结果两方面研究的危机类型学，从实用的观点看，这是非常有用的。

主要危机类型

按照危机的起因和后果，危机管理研究将危机分为五大类，即：技术的、自然的、政治的、社会的和组织的。技术上的危机定义了它们人为的根源和潜在的可能并由之引起的对人类健康和环境可能造成的重大的损失。在建筑施工之外，这样的例子包括 1982 年印度博帕尔·卡柏德联合发电厂的燃气泄漏事故，这起事故造成 3500 人死亡 10000 多人受伤(谢里范斯达范 1992)。在建筑施工业内部的例子包括 2000 年 5 月伦敦施工现场的塔吊坍塌事故。这起事故死亡 3 人，且本来有可能使更多人受伤，包括行人和摩托车司机(艾肯莱德 2000)。堪萨斯城·海特·雷金斯宾馆(NBS 1982)坍塌事故、澳大利亚墨尔本的西门大桥坍塌事故(贝格奈尔 1977)都是属于这一类的例子。和技术危机相比较，自然危机具有相同的人事结果，但起因却不是人为的，这一点和技术危机截然不同。这一类例子包括 1999 年土耳其毁灭性的地震及同一年内袭击澳大利亚悉尼的雹暴，这起事故造成大约 1.4 亿美元的财产损失(克莱奈尔 1999)。比较起来，政治危机起源于政治系统、战争及公共事业的改革。例如，1991 年，乔治分析了国际范围内的一系列冲突，包括古巴导弹危机、阿拉伯和以色列的战争以及海湾战争，在分析时，他将可能加速美国和苏维埃之间偶然战争的因素分离了出来。在施工业，一个很好的例子就是关于联合王国在伦敦的城堡吊闸包层施工中的合同纠纷，该纠纷涉及的合同既昂贵又麻烦且持续了长达 7 年之久。1999 年幕墙承包商以投标阶段，下议院利用特权把工程包给了报价极高的承包人为由，成功地起诉下议院，结束了这场纠纷。另一个例子是联合王国的威姆布莱体育馆工程，该工程被威胁要延迟开工，原因是如果开发商不捐资 30 万英镑作为地方发展基金，地方政府计划负责人就拒绝批准该计划。与社会危机有关的事件有洛杉矶的罗德尼·金暴乱(夸尔安特利 1993)和 20 世纪 90 年代初联合王国道路工程带来了严重损害及工期的延误的环境保护方面的抗议。最后，和组织危机有关的有些危机事件涉及到很有影响力的公司，诸如贝尔银行丑闻和英特尔奔腾 IV 芯片缺陷(宫泽来兹和普朗特 1995;斯菲利戈杰 1997)。在建筑业，一个很好的例子是联合王国的千年体育馆工程，公众信心危机给莱因带来了极大的麻烦。组织危机还包括与劳动力有关的危机，这种危机使伦敦的朱柏莉地下铁路延长线工程深受磨难，首期工程工期延误 14 个月，费用超支 1.5 亿英镑。

表 2-1　典型的施工风险模型(来源:佩里、海斯 1985)

种　类	事　例
自然的	火灾、地震、洪水、塌方引起的损失和损害
环境的	生态环境方面的破坏、污染、废物处理、公共调查
设计的	新工艺、创新的应用、可靠性、安全性;技术规范的详细性、准确性和适应性;变更的可能性;设计和施工方法的互动性
后勤的	材料、设备运输过程中的损失和损害;特殊资源的可获得性—专家、设计者、承包商、供应商、设备、匮乏的施工技术、材料;便道和交通;组织界面
财务的	资金的可获得性、保险的全面性;流动资金的充足性;承包商、供应商的失误造成的损失;汇率变动、通货膨胀、税收
法律的	对其他人行为的责任、直接责任;地方法律;供应商、承包商及设计者之间所使用的法律的区别
政治的	业主、供应商、承包商所在国政治上的风险——战争、革命
施工的	施工方法的可行性、安全性;产业间关系;变更程度;气候;管理和监督的质量和有效性
运行的	产品或服务市场的波动性;保养的需要;目标的合理性;运行的安全性

特种危机的种类

从实用的观点来说，以上概括性的危机种类划分法的使用范围是很有限的，因为，没有迹象表明。比如说，技术危机是否需要对组织危机或自然危机做出不同的反应，这就导致了了很有实用价值的类型学的产生。

徐进的、突然的、周期性的危机

贾曼和蔻斯明(1990)对徐进性危机、周期性危机和突然性危机进行了区分。这些危机之间的区别在于它们发生的时间上:突发性危机表现为灾难性事件。而徐进性危机是随着时间的推移、一系列事件间相互作用相互加强,逐渐升级为全方位的危机。在建筑业,突发性危机最普遍的例子是工人的死亡事件。例如,在欧洲,建筑业通常雇佣不超过 10% 的社会劳动力,但它的死亡率却占所有行业工作场所死亡率的30%多。仅1996～1997年,联合王国的工地死亡人数就达90人,非重伤事故发生率为每天15起(安德逊1998)。实际上在2000年,欧洲引进CDM制度后的第五年,每年死亡人数仍为70人,主要事故发生率上升了73%(库特2000)。

　　徐进性危机的例子可见于不断的性骚扰和种族冲突,随着时间的推移,最终会导致诉讼事件。像新加坡和澳大利亚这样的国家,施工组织之间的文化差异很大,种族歧视常常是一种最严重和管理最不当的问题。在联合王国也存在类似的问题,随着越来越多的东欧移民进入建筑市场,这种问题变得日益显著起来(卡维尔1999)。事实上,在美国,追求平等机遇的诉讼案件是如此频繁,以至于福坦的500家工业公司用收入的2%来处理性骚扰案件。

　　为拓宽这种类型学说,布斯(1993)指出,存在着一种被他称之为周期性危机的间歇型危机。这种危机经常间歇性的发生,但它的属性却变化不定。能够引起间歇性危机的事件有:年度预算消减、管理方式的变化、政府的变动及其他。布斯指出,机构趋向于对徐进的、突发的和周期性的危机做出不同的反应。例如,对于徐进型危机,组织机构常趋向于更加信任经过试验和检测的过程,合理的把它排除掉或干脆忽略它。相反的,周期性的危机能够刺激常规化的反应,表现为刚性的应急计划,这些计划由互相竞争的利益集团经过内部协商而达成。最后,突发性危机常产生防御性的反应,特别是在没有应急计划的环境里。当最初的震撼逐渐消失后,这当然需要一段时间,围攻计划开始运作,在这个阶段,机构变成零散的利益集团。布斯的分析对管理人员制定合适的反应措施是有益的,因为它能提高他们的预见力,使他们控制有方,减少潜在的破坏性行为。

感性的和异乎寻常的危机

　　许多危机受公众感性认识的影响,而这种感性认识在很大程度上为媒体所塑造。所以,这种影响很大程度上决定于行业和媒体彼此间的相互理解,或者更常见的,彼此的不理解。艾文(1997)给出了一个有关"感性的"和"异乎寻常的"危机的类型系统,它的产生原因与媒体有关。对艾文来说,感性危机是指那种相对不重要的问题,却被反面媒体报道给大肆渲染了的。异乎寻常的危机是指那种由媒体制造出来的危机。公众监督在建筑工程管理中变得日趋重要,特别是那些对国家具有重大意义或对环境有较大冲击的工程。公共关系在本书的后半部分给出了较详细的讨论,为了阐明它的重要性,我们可以用联合王国内的一系列工程作为事例。令许多人惊奇的是,受媒体报道的影响,在这些工程甚至还没有开始时,就被看成是一些灾难,其中包括新皇家剧院、航道、赫斯罗5号终点站(公共调查的第三年)、英国图书馆及航道连线工程。公共关系在这些工程中至关重要,因为反面媒体报道可以产生巨大的思想冲击,最终影响施工队伍的执行情况,使得饥不择食的媒体实现了他们自我实现的预言。或许,最能说明这种观点的例子是伦敦的朱柏莉地下铁路延长线工程,从一开始它就是一种政治工具,在第三次保守党会议上被提出。但那时,就像盖伊(1998)指出的那样"这是一个胜利纪念碑工程,不要期望真相或者同情。你只要低着头想象着执行简单的合同,赚取中等的利润,所有这些都与公众眼中的印象相差甚远。"(P.29)

触发机制

　　本逊(1998)将危机按它的触发机制进行了分类,艾格尔胡夫和塞恩(1992)指出,这些事件可能在组织的相关环境或间接环境内出现。相关环境和间接环境的区别在于该环境内事件对组织影响的直接性。从本质上来说，组织的相关环境包括那些对组织带来直接影响的因素，且对间接环境中的事件来说，它相当于一个过滤器。间接环境中的因素被从组织中的日常活动中分离出来，它们仅通过相关环境发生作用。对管理人员来说，这种区别至关重要，因为间接环境中潜在的危机更难被检测到，而且它们的影响也相对的具有间接性、渐进性和难预料性。20 世纪 80 年代末的股票市场崩溃所引起的财产危机就是一个例证。一夜之间，它影响了财政局势，降低了许多工程生存的可能性，迫使它们搁置起来。相反的，相关环境内的危机更容易被检测到，它所导致的冲击也相对具有突然性。1998 年伦敦的朱柏莉地下铁路延长线工程危机就是由组织的相关环境引起危机的一个很好的例证。该工程中由于工资和工作环境的争执而导致了 600 名电气技术人员的罢工。

事件链

另一种区分不同类型危机的方法是研究引起这些危机的事件链。这种方法常用于安全性的研究中，它基于这样的假设：一系列可追溯其根源的事件，能加速事故的发生。通常被称作"故障树"的事件链图为我们更加深刻的理解危机的发展和管理奠定了基础。我们可以说所有的危机都被事件链所激化，事件链有三个特征因素，即：长度、复杂性和显著性。长度指链内事件的数量，复杂性指事件间相互关系的多样性，显著性指事件的明显性和易检测性。这方面的例证是一个设计阶段就出现的，由长的、复杂的、非显性的事件链所导致的严重的工地事故危机，危机的起因是在设计阶段采用了带有危险性的规范。这些事件和最终事故间的联系是如此的间接和模糊，以至于在随后的多次设计决策中都没被发觉，直到后来，在工地上，它终于显现出来了。然而，对管理人员来说，最大的挑战是应付那些由短的、非显性的、复杂的因果链引起的危机，因为它们有广泛的影响、难以检测、对各级组织都会造成一系列的冲击，具有突发性，因而，对之进行干预的机率很小。而且，事件链的复杂性可能会产生以下困难：创建响应系统的困难，为不同利益集团提供机会来定义自己不同的危机的困难。从这一点来说，这种危机引起冲突的可能性很高。相反的，长的、显性的、简单的事件链常导致渐进型的危机，它们的定义和效果都很明显，外部干预的机率也很大，引起冲突的可能性却很小。

结　论

现代建筑工程风险模型没有为管理人员提供处理不同类型风险的知识。本章在建筑工程之外，考察了一系列分类系统，该系统对建立适当的危机反应系统是很有益的。不同种类的危机需要不同的处理方式，在确定了组织的风险以后，管理人员可以运用这些知识，事先拟定一系列适当的策略方案。然而，本章提到的类型学研究，只提供了处理不同种类风险的最基础的知识，这个领域中的许多研究工作还有待我们去做。而且，通过对风险分类，类型学趋向于把每种具有复杂性和唯一性的危机过分的简单化。对危机标准化的反应可能提供了一种有益的最初的反应模式，但从长远来讲，为了有效的应付这些危机，管理人员必需详细了解危机的动态性。这些内容将在以下各章中讨论。

第三章

危机管理的动态性

在这一章的讨论中,我们把危机管理划分为以下几个阶段:检测、诊断、决策、应用、反馈、修正和学习。为了取得危机管理的成功,对每一阶段都应进行有效的管理。遗憾的是,在危机中,人们的处事方式使这一点很难办到,我们对这种破坏性的行为方式的原因进行了讨论。

简 介

任何危机管理的目标都是为了在出现可能引起较大偏离的事件发生时,鉴定它并对它做出反应以保证组织目标和行为间的一致性。这一体系,聚焦于对非常风险的研究,应把它看成是全面风险管理的专业性的组成部分,它对组织的重要性依赖于诸多因素,其中,最明显的是所面临的风险的级别。对风险做一些准备工作是必不可少的。

检测——危机管理的第一阶段

对危机迅速的反应依赖于早期对它的检测,这个目的是由监控潜在风险、获得有关信息来达到的。

什么是危机?

危机是在执行特定的活动过程中,由于不确定性所导致的财务损益、人体伤害、损害或拖延的可能性(库珀和查普曼 1987)。这种定义比许多其他定义都有用,因为它不但强调了危机的威胁性,而且强调了它的机会性。遗憾的是,许多关于危机的定义常常过分强调它的威胁性,把危机和冒险或危险联系在一起,由此加强了人们的反冲突价值观。库珀和查普曼定义的优越之处还体现在,它把不确定性和危机严格地区分了开来。它们的区别是,只有在组织以充分的责任心接受了它发生后可能产生的损益结果时,不确定性才转变为组织危机。这一点非常重要,因为它指出,好的危机管理的责任落在那些可以承担危机、转移危机的人们的手中。一个好的做法就意味着,不能把危机转移到不能控制危机、无力承担危机、没有机会给危机标价的一方(阿伯郎汉姆森 1984)。这种相互责任制没有引起建筑业管理文化的足够重视,这也可能是低效率危机管理的主要原因,并有可能继续成为建筑业中的主要问题。

建筑工程中危机的广度

建筑工程中危机处理的容量很大但范围很窄。危机处理的主要问题是将它的重点置于何处,通常把它们完全置于由立法、习惯法(不成文法)和约束双方的劳务合同所带来的危机上。然而,盖伯伦茨(1972)还鉴别出了那些带有道德和政治色彩的危机远比合同责任范围内的危机多得多。这些责任的每一类在施工组织内都是可辩别的。道德责任大体上由专业和社会的行为规则引发而来,而政治责任由建筑业的文化和单个工程的组织结构而产生,莫里斯(1998)为这个论证提供了一个很好的例子。一个开发商雇佣了一个建筑设计师为他设计了一个购物中心的框架结构,合同对该建筑设计师在施工过程中去不去工地设有规定,这省去了开发商大量的费用。然而,合同要求建筑设计师对工程装备进行监控,这些装备在另外一份合同中,由另外一个公司为未来的承担人设计。1993年7月,一场大火烧毁了购物中心。调查表明,建筑缺陷导致了火灾。而法庭调查却表明,不存在导致火灾的设计上的缺陷,但建筑师有义务关照开发商,在框架施工过程中,检查设备装备时,发现问题应及时汇报,但这些都不在合同规定的范围之内。

建筑承包商的危机范围比合同责任范围要宽的另一个原因是他们之间的相互依赖性。联合王国拉姆斯盖特工程事故鲜活地阐述了这个观点。该事故死亡6人、重伤7人。在这个工程施工中,委托人完全依赖设计和承包合同,而且按照合同,没有干预任何工作。然而,事故发生后,承包商和委托人都承担着犯罪行为,前者承担损失100万英镑,后者承担损失40万英镑。这个事例说明,虽然有合同存在,工程的参与各方都和工程的命运紧紧地联系在一起,把自己独立出来的做法是愚蠢的。这个事例还说明,工程的各参与方都暴露在自发的和非自发的危机环境中。建筑业的危机管理文化忽视了这种区别,尽管大量的事实证明,由于不公平、不明确的危机分配办法,工作不胜任、无知和时间的压力导致了危机的发生,那种把非自发危机看成是造成建筑业冲突的主要原因的想法是一种误解(Barnes 1991;Uff 1995)。非自发危机的问题在于,各责任方都没有意识到或不愿意接受它们。

内部和外部危机

总的说来,所有的危机,要不存在于组织之内,要不存在于组织之外。这就意味着,为了提高效率,必需对组织的内部和外部都进行监控。

外部危机

那些对危机负有外部监控责任者应监控工程的边界,审视环境,查找隐患。第二章讨论了间接的和相关的环境因素,得出了这样的结论:比起其他危机来,有些危机并不明显,它的影响来得更慢。由此可以得出,为了完全涵盖所有的危机,外部监控必需包括间接的、相关的、长期的和短期的监控活动。建立间接性的外部监控活动的重要性在影响力很大的公共事业工程上表现得尤为突出,政治策略能对这类工程的决策施加重要的影响。例如,联合王国的航道连线工程,这项议案必需在国会上通过,是英国历史上最大的一次计划应用的协商,它必需考虑大约258个反对这个议案的团体的意见。如盖伊(1998)所述,"与其说需要一个项目管理者,不如说需要一个项目复苏器……"(P.29)。同样的,海明斯雷(1998)强调了建立长期性外部监控活动的重要性。他指出,20世纪90年代,联合王国困扰许多公司的问题都是因为没有预测到工商业的急剧衰退。对大多数建筑业的公司来说,衰退是一个完全的意义,结果"人们发现自己处在这样的一种境地:他们的工作依赖于少数几个市场,而所有这些都在接缝处完全解体"(P.33)。

内部危机

和外部危机相反,内部危机更具相关性和短期性,基本上是由于行业的组织、合同和雇佣制度没有被很好的执行而导致的。就因为这个原因,内部监控活动集中在执行过程的反馈上,它穿过管理信息系统(MIS),在组织机构内竖向流动。

许多机构都设有一些管理信息系统,每个系统专为一定范围内的目标而设置。许多建筑工程有五个主要的信息系统专门用来处理费用、时间、质量、范围和功能方面的信息(欧伯伦得 1993)。每个系统都应该由具备这方面专门知识的专家来管理,他必须能正确的解释信息的含义。例如,在联合王国,工程一旦开工,计量员必需对费用信息负主要责任,建筑师、工程师必须对功能、范围和质量负责;主承包商必须对工期信息系统负责。无论他们是什么专业,以及每个专业的相对重要性如何,信息系统必须反映委托人目标系统的优先权和工程目标系统之间的相互依赖性,这就意味着他们之间有十分复杂的信息反馈流。也就是说,上面提到的各方,应经常性的互相交流,互相通报发现的事故隐患。这一点非常重要,因为大多数危机对目标系统的影响面都很广。例如,近来,在澳大利亚墨尔本,在工程施工过程中发现了土著人古墓,要求设计变更,这种变更对工期、费用、工作范围、功能和质量都产生了影响。为了形成一套全面的反映系统,所有发生的事件在组织内充分交流是十分必要的。

监控问题

令人遗憾的是,即使隐患被检测出来,且很快得到了交流,对该危机的监控也可能并不敏感。如果隐患没有被检测出来,就无法对它进行监控,这时管理者必须明白,为什么会出现这种情况。

缺乏集中点

组织受危机困扰的最普遍的原因常常是没有人意识到组织易被这种危机所影响。贝尔银行危机能很好的阐明这个观点。银行官员被警告,如果李桑的这种不独立的贸易组织继续它目前的活动,大的灾难就可能产生。即使 1994 年内部审计后又重申了这种担忧,贝尔银行依旧批准李桑既担任主贸易商又担任内部审计员。这使得他能够继续他削弱经济的活动。谢弗尔·埃特·奥尔(1998)发现,这种灾难性疏忽的主要原因是银行界面活动状态的混乱和不同部门之间的内部冲突,它使得责任界限及其对隐患的可说明性乱成一团。强大的时间压力和李桑合法的压倒一切的控制权加剧了这种混乱状态,最后导致了在某些区域无法控制的危机。同样的问题也存在于没有充分反馈系统的建筑工程中,造成这种不完备的反馈系统的原因是合同内时间的压力、利益的冲突、武断性和不明确的危机分配。

对风险管理的无知

在建筑业,由于对风险管理技术普遍的无知状态,使得问题的隐患常常不能被检测出来(斯密斯 1999)。风险管理是很关键的,因为它能预见潜在的危机并事先找出能够防止和处理它的办法,变幻无穷的建筑工程常常使这点很难做到。例如,最后在澳大利亚悉尼的码头改建工程中,出现了非常规的、工人感染 B 型肝炎的危机。这种肝炎病是由冲到悉尼海港的紫丁香花传染的。这种危机被预测到了,且组织了医疗队伍,对 B 型肝炎进行常规的检查、预防性注射,使危机降到了最低程度。

另一个问题就是将危机管理看成是施工阶段的事情。最后,一项美国的调查表明,只有16%的设计人员考虑到施工工人的安全问题,29%的人偶尔为之,45%的人从来没有考虑这方面的问题,10%的人在将来可能会考虑这个问题(盖木贝提斯 2000)。许多事实说明,很多设计阶段出现的危机是可以检测出来并消除掉的。例如,位于悉尼的剧院后面,引起争论的、外号"烤面包机"的居民住宅楼工程的工程师在施工过程中,给结构物设计了安装防护栅栏的临时突椽,这些突椽在完工后都被烧掉了。其他提高施工安全的设计措施包括梁的尺寸能够给施工人员留充足净空高度,不使用危险材料,使用标准化部件,使施工和制造过程合理化,以减少材料的工地储备及处理。

当使用新的、非常规的材料,新的或复杂的设计标准,而且有较大的时间和费用压力时,最容易出现设计危机。包含以上诸多因素的例子是伦敦的泰晤士截流大坝工程。建该工程的目的是避免反复出现的灾难性洪水,1953 年的洪灾造成 300 人死亡,64750 公顷耕地、24000 座房舍、200 座工业厂房、320 公里铁路、12 座汽化公司和 2 座电力发电站被淹。很明显,这一工程,对环境潜在的危机是很大的,但通过科学的设计,通过相当大的努力让当地居民和环境学家参与到工程的设计过程中,使施工危机降到了最低(墨利斯和豪夫 1987)。然而,通过这个工程也说明,对这样大型的工程项目,如果前期准备不充足,所冒的风险是很大的。在技术和环境保护方面,毫无疑问截流大坝工程是成功的,但从工程管理方面来说,却是失败的,四亿四千万英镑的结算价是原预算价的 4 倍(然而没考虑通货膨胀的影响),实际工期 7 年半,几乎是计划工期的 2 倍。

失败的原因基本上与不注意鉴别与工程实施有关的管理危机有关,这一点与详尽无遗的调查工程的技术风险,以判别工程的可行性形成明显的对比。比如,很少有人考虑河流水位变化和河流通航状况对工程计划的影响。而且,低估了当地和中央政府间根深蒂固的政治紧张关系,它影响了委托人管理工程的积极性,使各种关系更加恶化。考虑到工程所处的位置和年代,具有战斗力的劳动力队伍是不可缺少的,在工程的早期阶段就应做更大的努力以达成一个有约束力的、综合的有关工地支付和工作条件方面的协议。

工程目标间的竞争

除了组织不当的监控问题,在许多建筑工程中,还存在不同系统之间复杂的信息反馈问题。贝克森戴尔(1991)发现时间和费用管理信息系统之间的关系最为复杂,因为如果解决了时间问题,就会产生费用问题,反之相反。如果在一个系统中发现问题,而没有及时的通报给其他系统,就会产生低效率问题,从而阻止平衡的、综合的危机反应系统的形成。

投资 9900 万英镑的卡德福千年体育馆工程可以用来生动地阐述组织内不同的、相互关联的系统目标之间的竞争所导致的潜在危机。承建该体育馆是为了迎接 1999 年在威尔士举行的世纪杯橄榄球赛。据承包方董事长马丁莱茵先生所说,该工程 2600 万英镑的损失是由一种他们土木工程部门的"地方贵族"哲学和匮乏的管理所导致的(巴罗 1999)。克服这种问题的一种方法是危机共担。伦敦的千年大厦就是这样一个例子,在这个工程中,咨询机构同样承担着费用超支和工期延误的危机。就像工程现场指挥长特论旗评论的那样,这样加快了反馈速度,使人能凭直觉知道什么时候会出事(库特 1998)。

施工队伍的变动

施工队伍的频繁变动,使项目管理人员在监控工程危机时面临着特殊的问题,因为他们必须依靠勤奋的施工队伍。人员在工程内部和工程之间变动,会造成很大的危险,这可以通过下面的事例来说明。1999 年,在进行爆破试验时,斯雷普奈尔 A 油田平台降到挪威 200m 深的斯坦范戈尔峡湾外的海底。事故调查发现,这 1 亿美元损失的事故的起因与施工队伍的完全更换有关,原施工队伍有类似平台的施工经验,有全面的问题检测系统和简单的处理办法。

缺乏忠诚

工程管理人员面临的更进一步的问题是不断变动的,而且常常是冲突性的利益关系,这是建筑工程的一个特点。这就意味着,为委托人监控危机的人员,可能并不时时把委托人的利益放在心上。为了克服这个问题,建筑工程合同常要求工程参与各方对一定范围内指定的业主的危机进行监控,并在他们出现时,按指定的方式进行处理。这里没有必要来引述单个合同条款,但值得指出,工程施工合同(ECC)在这方面做了很大的努力来克服这些潜在的问题。例如,EEC 赋予顾问工程师比常规更大的监控责任,使得监控系统更完整,范围更广。而且,如果发现工程隐患,要求各参与方应及早提出预警。这种条款在美国施工合同中具有普遍性,但联合王国的合同却不是这样的,在那儿,合同条款常常被解释为只有"实际存在的"问题需要报告,这为施工延误和简单问题逐渐升级而导致大范围的危机提供了合法的基础。虽然早期预警制度实施起来有一定的难度,但最近美国法院表现出他们乐意去做此事。例如,纽约住房建筑当局授予普林斯顿 v 城的 A.H.A. 综合承包公司两个价值 4.7 百万美元的工程,要求他们及时预警事故隐患,而且有权得到额外支付。然而,A.H.A. 综合承包公司直到工程收尾时才要求得到价值 906000 美元的额外款项,当局予以拒绝,只付给他极少的额外款。1998 年 7 月 23 日,得克萨斯州上诉法院(CE/02/M)对这起案件进行了审理,他们认为,A.H.A. 综合承包公司没有及时通报的行为阻止了业主采取措施减少损害,而且妨碍了他们试图复原的计划。

费用和时间压力

对组织所面临的每一种潜在危机都进行监控,从经济的观点来说是不合理的,实际上也是不可能的。因为这个原因,人们趋于对效益和费用进行敏感性分析。例如,当费用敏感性很高时,保守的"再想一想"的做法就派上了用场,它导致了对危机的预警落后于它的发生。

兢兢业业工作和费用间的矛盾使工程管理人员在建立折衷的、可接受的决策参数时,处于精神和经济两难的境地。当考虑安全事件时,精神上的压力尤为明显,因为需要对人的健康进行标价。伦敦的朱柏莉地下铁路延长线工程中电器工程师的纠纷就能说明:在极端的时间和费用压力下,道德问题是怎样被遗忘的,以及像诸如安全这类问题出现时,转换点的决策怎样变得高度敏感。虽然导致这种激烈争执的因素是多方面的,电器工程师坚信,主要的问题在于管理人员为了提高劳动生产率,乐意让工人来冒险(格莱肯和巴利 1998)。格莱肯和巴利列举了一些可怕的安全失误,比如,用铝制梯子,在 220kV 的火线上进行工作;一名电器工程师被指令在 415V 的配电盘上进行工作,却没接到隔断电源的命令;操作人员没有接受安全教育,当一名操作人员被电源绊倒时,另一名钻机操作人员因钻机失控而被截去一个手指。

防御性

因为监控不可避免的产生威胁现状的信息,组织趋向于利用一些规范来惩罚这些人(阿迪瑞斯 1984)。而且,比起提出现存期望和假设的人,(进行监控的)人被要求提出更高标准的证据。这一点,在智能信息要求决策者做出他不想做或不准备做的决策时,表现得尤为突出。许多诸如联合王国的希尔斯博罗夫足球场灾难及美国的挑战号宇宙飞船灾难,可以生动地阐明由这种防御性所产生的潜在危机。在每一个事件中,迫于外部压力,主要决策人筛出并最终忽略了日渐逼近的灾难兆头(扎曼和寇斯明 1990;瑞查德孙 1993)。例如,在挑战号灾难中,几次发送失败,引来媒体的嘲讽,这使得决策者和领导们很难堪。发射前的晚上,工程师预警,预计发射时的温度低于油箱封的安全温度极限。然而,事实表明,迫于让同事们重新分析他们关于油箱封的计算结果,并进行比常规更严格的检测的压力,工程师怀疑他们原始的计算结果,对第二道密封寄予了比常规更大的希望,并同意发射。

优越感

特纳和皮古(1997)指出,当外界的信息对现存的思维方式产生挑战时,防御性问题就显得尤为重要。例如,他们分析了 1996 年威尔士南部导致 144 人死亡的阿波范煤矿灾难事故,指出组织的排他性使他产生了一种对非组织人员的优越感。在阿波范,地方委员会的一名成员预见到了问题,但却被说成是"怪念头"并不断地用雄心勃勃的但却是错误的诸如"我们时常的检查那些隐患"的言论来摒弃这些预警。就像特纳和皮古(1997)指出的那样,他们认为"内行比外行更知道他们所处环境的危机"(P.49)。

在那些年营业额超过许多公司的大型建筑公司,这种对外界的防御意识产生的问题更为突出。产生于这种工程的压力、凝聚力、忠诚心、重点及动力变得如此强烈,以至于他们把自己从外界隔离开来,把外界看成是分散他们注意力的因素,甚至有时掩盖问题,隐藏弱点。然而,就像特纳和皮古(1997)的例子所指出的那样,不熟悉工程情况的局外者偶然的参与往往是最有效的检测隐藏问题的方法。组织的排他性只能增加工程的危机倾向性。

闭关性

现在新兴起的一种名为"死亡学说"的行为科学,研究人类面对死亡威胁时的心理状态,指出人类在面对死亡的威胁时,趋向于关闭除了求生最必要的意识以外的其他所有意识(布罗克 1999)。为了阐明这一点,布罗克引用了美国的一起操场枪杀事件。在那儿,2 名男生枪杀了 15 名师生。在枪杀事件后的调查会上,直接受影响者回忆起在当时情况下,他们是如何关闭了自己的听觉和视觉器官。被第一枪震惊的不知措的人们中,大多数人的眼睛成了他们的主要的感觉器官——他们看得见所有的事情,除了最初的枪声,却听不见任何声音。相反的,那些确实被射中的人们,似乎看不见但却听得见进行中最细节的东西。

这一项研究对管理人员的重要性在于,它说明在危机发生时,有些监控系统可能会关闭,使组织处于一种更无力抵抗危机的状态。这意味着,当组织中某些地方出现危机时,监控系统就可能产生问题,危机管理的挑战就是通过对未来危机的预警信号保持警惕,以防混淆视界。

时间性

所有的危机并不是都具有相同的可见性,这也能导致监控系统出问题。正像我们在第一章中所指出的那样,有些危机是剧烈的、突然的和具有自显性的,而另外一些危机却是渐进的、浮现的、模糊的。例如,由于不好的监控系统,使得渐进性危机的早期预警信号不易检测,从而使它能够不断的发展,最后导致灾难的发生。1998 年 7 月 6 日的欧森登特·皮珀·阿尔弗灾难就是这个观点的例证。一系列复杂的导致最终火灾的元凶却是一个简单的、未完成的气体压缩组件的保养工作(DOE 1990)。更异乎寻常的例子是麦当劳热咖啡危机,在这个事件中,由于被由杯中溢出的热咖啡烫成三级烧伤,顾客得到 290 万美元的赔偿(高泽莱兹和普拉特 1995)。麦当劳的记录表示出,在这起风靡全球且被盲目模仿的法庭事件之前,就已有 700 多起与咖啡烫伤有关的诉讼案件。

因为管理人员常被相互矛盾的信息的海洋所淹没,很难从中抽出有意义的信息,使得即使属于突发性事件,也很难被检测出来。由于精力所限,人们不得不从信息的海洋里"选择性地觉察出"即将来临的事件的信号。令人遗憾的是,人们在做这样的选择时,本能地以自己的期望和需求为出发点。结果可能是不可避免的自我实现的预言,而且往往筛去了即将降临的危机的早期预警信号。

战无不胜性

帕斯卡尔(1991)强调指出世界上最大和最成功的公司都有自我破坏性的特征。根据帕斯卡尔所说,"没有什么东西比成功更能导致失败",因为成功的历史趋于产生一种战无不胜的意识和一种"这对我们是不可能的"的态度,这种态度是组织成员对问题的隐患视而不见。而且,伴随着成功的脚步,组织的监控责任体系变得混淆不清,并且激发了官僚作风的增长,使得他们对已诊断出的问题隐患反应缓慢。实际上,正是这种由于过去的成功所产生的"强烈和不利的反应"构成了导致挑战号航天飞机灾难的一个因素,在那儿 NASA 的"能对付"文化忽视了日益逼近的、问题隐患的早期信号(皮尔逊·埃特·奥尔 1997)。

不信任、恐惧和不说出来

本书第一章列举出了建筑工程中不信任感和恐惧感的源泉。莱恩和奥斯特伦奇(1998)发现,在这种环境下,最危险的副作用是因为害怕惩罚而犹豫着不说出来,这就产生了一种无可辩论的阴云密布的工作关系。这些都是秘密,每个人都知道,但都只在私下讨论。这种问题越长时间不进行讨论,就越难谈论,造成的损失也就越大。非常有趣的是,莱恩和奥斯特伦奇发现,某些类型的问题尤其容易成为无可辩论的问题。这些问题汇总在表 3-1 中。

营造一种让人不敢发言的环境的影响是很深刻的。莱恩和奥斯特伦奇给出了一个很好的例子来证明这种观点。这个例子说的是中西部一个小软件公司由于这种现象所导致的财务危机。雇员常常把该公司的 CEO 称作暴君。他通过侮辱雇员,公开指责他们,不经协商而武断的设置最后期限,无理地期望每个人延长工作时间,蓄意地给大家设计陷阱营造出了这种充满恐惧的环境。其结果是发行了有缺陷的软件包,造成公司 6 百万美元的损失,丢掉了公司的声誉、顾客和一些骨干雇员。讽刺的是,有一个雇员已经检测出了问题并在会上阐述了她的观点。她得到的报酬就是被解雇和当众受到侮辱。就像一个雇员所透露的那样，"这个程序是个灾难，软件不做我们认为它应该做的。因为没有所有权，也不想以此产品为傲。人们并没有被要求要投入多少。大量的时间和精力没有用在提高程序的质量上，而用在了掩盖自己的笑柄上"。

谢尔石油公司是另一个好的例子，他认识到指责文化不能带来高效的生产和公平的结果。便开发了一件管理程序，来营造一种没有指责的、合作的、安全的企业文化。有趣的是，自从它20世纪70年代末引入这种文化后，谢尔的油箱船队以伤亡率为指标的事故发生率大大降低(郝力科·约翰1996)。

早期预警信号的可见性

早期预警信号的可见性是决定人们对它敏感性的另一个因素。从本质上说来，早期预警信号的可见性由它的强度、持续时间和微妙性决定。强度是指信号的力量；持续时间指信号可以检测到的时间段；微妙性指检测它所需调查工作的复杂性和显现程度。潜在的发出强度低，持续时间短，信号微弱的诸如设计阶段出现的危机比强度高，持续时间长，信号明显的诸如施工阶段的危机更难检测出来。使设计阶段出现错误的问题在于，设计人员之间具有高度的相互依赖性，经过一系列迷宫似的相互依赖的活动，使得问题被很快的掩盖或模糊化。从这点说来，建筑工程管理者必须特别关注设计阶段的潜在危机，传统上，这一阶段的监控工作是比较弱的。

表 3-1　组织中无可辩论的问题

种　类	反应百分率
管理工作	49
合作工作情况	10
利润和补偿费	6
平等受雇的机遇	6
变更	4
支付以外的人力系统	4
个人的感受	2
执行情况反馈	2
坏消息	2
冲突	2
个人问题	2
改进的建议	2
其他	9

诊断——危机管理的第二阶段

检测出潜在的问题后,组织应该对它进行进一步的调查,进入诊断阶段,提出适当的反应方式。用控制系统的术语来表达,负责这种工作的人被称为"比较员",因为这个角色需要专业知识,这些人必须是合格的专业人才,诸如结构工程师、建筑师、计量员、成本工程师、现场经理。虽然监控员和比较员有区别,最理想的方法就是让一个人担任这两个角色,因为收集到专业方面信息的人最有权力评估它的重要性,强调它潜在的问题,从而保证能做出一个快速的、适当的反应。若把两者分开,潜在的信息就会产生流通方面的问题,对危机的反应就会失真或减慢。

诊断中的问题

诊断的过程从本质上来说就是一个数据收集的过程,在监控阶段遇到的所有问题都会影响诊断过程。然而,诊断阶段也有一些特殊的问题。

目标不明确

为了能估量出问题可能对工程目标造成的潜在影响,比较员必须对所评价的专业性工作的履行情况的标准有一个清晰的概念。令人遗憾的是,如凯立·埃特·奥尔(1992)指出的那样,即使最称职的顾问工程师在识别履行情况的标准时也会碰到困难,这是由委托人缺乏经验,委托人团体难以鉴别,委托人组织的内部政策,不了解委托人经营过程的前期策略,不完备的信息流通,不充足的总结时间等因素导致的。更进一步的问题可能由工程生命期内目标的不断变动所致。实际上,正是这个问题困扰着新伦敦图书馆工程,该工作比预算超支400%,提供的藏书空间只有1200万册,而原计划为2500万册。在这儿,对工程要求的变化是负责监控该工程的政府政策和结构变化的结果(斯平 1998)。如建筑师所述,"如果你想设计一个愚蠢的方法来进行一个工程,你应该看看政治家是怎么做的。当撒切尔夫人到来时,工程就不断地停停干干,这样做的代价是十分昂贵的。每18个月,他们建起高楼,砍掉一部分,再从地面重新建起"。其他涉及该工程的人的评论也支持该建筑师对工程变更的评价"他们不断地变换工程负责部门,每次负责部门变动,都会导致人员的变动";"你无法依靠每年变动的财政拨款来进行一个长工期的工程,因为拨款是变动的,而且下一年可能就不被通过。这就意味着工程应该在可偿还贷款的基础上进行,这样,顾问工程师和承包人就没有限制费用的财务激励了"。

实际上,这个问题存在于许多重要的公共事业工程上。比如,始于1995年投资两亿八千四百万美元的拉斯维加斯洪水控制工程就是这样的一个例子。该工程在2007年前不会完工,比计划工期滞后6年(阿格瑞斯 1990)。该工程以控制水害,保护拉斯维加斯为目标,对工程师来说,这似乎是一种魔术,他必须不断地追逐联邦基金,只要有钱,就时时刻刻准备继续工作。

防御性行为

诊断阶段也可能因为"防御性行为"而出现问题。防御性行为是一种防止个人或组织陷入困境或遭受损失的行为。这种行为在危机阶段尤为明显,因为它潜在的后果很严重,如果有责任人与此后果相关,这种现象就更为明显了(阿格瑞斯 1990)。按照森克莱尔和海尼斯(1993)所说,责任不明确也能导致防御性行为,因为通过把问题转移给其他人,一个人可以很容易不去理会这个问题。这在建筑工程中尤为明显,因为许多建筑合同起草得模棱两可,在很大程度上很难将它们解释清楚。

典型的防御性行为是通过绕过问题或用诡秘的包含不连续的和令人沮丧的辩论来掩盖问题而实现的。力威特和巴赫雷米(1998)用术语"压制"来描述这种否定不受欢迎的现实性的过程,并指出,这是面对极端的聚变或危机时的一种求生机制。令人遗憾的是,这个过程产生了一种"组织阴影",直到被压制的问题发展到了必须处理的程度之前,这个黑暗面一直萦绕在组织周围。1994 年的英特尔事件可以生动地阐明这种现象所产生的灾难性后果。在发现自己芯片上的缺陷后,英特尔拒绝撤回订货单或通知客户。通过"没有芯片永远是完美无缺的"这样典型的防御性行为来淡化问题(宫泽来兹和普朗特 1995)。实际上,英特尔公司一直在营销该芯片,直到 IBM 拒绝在他们的计算机内使用这种芯片,这导致英特尔芯片的市场占有量骤然下落,造成了公司内的财务危机。

防御性行为的研究是在受问题影响者利益基本相同的环境下进行的。所以,所报告的防御性行为基本上是相同的和普遍的。然而,建筑工程中人们的行为趋向于多样化,因为工程中涉及多种而且常常是冲突的利益集团,有的通过掩盖问题来保护自己的利益,其他的却可能通过充分的交流甚至把问题扩大化来保护自己的利益。结果是危机承担者采用多种策略来强制局势朝着有利于自己的方向发展,这也是建筑危机管理变化多端的一个原因。

决策——危机管理的第三阶段

如果诊断结果表明,检测出来的问题的影响在容许的范围内,危机管理过程就此终止。然而,如果比较员认为,威胁超出了容许的范围,则危机管理进入下一阶段,包括提出一套反应方案。这一责任由有权做决策的人承担,尽管有可能采纳很多人的意见,这个决策必须由他一人做出,保证实际的履行状况与工程的目标相一致。

决策中的问题

监控和诊断中的问题都会对决策过程产生影响,但决策过程中也有一些特殊的问题。

冲突的意见

从本质上说,决策过程的任务就是在一系列备选的行为过程中做出选择。这些决策可能是自己做出的,但大多数是由专业比较员推荐的,这些专业比较员比其他人更有资格做出判断。决策的挑战性在于危机的多样性和复杂性,这就意味着它不可避免地影响工程的整个目标系统。这就需要将众多比较员们提出的、有时是冲突性的意见综合起来——一个需要由大量的经验、敏感性、政治权利和正确理解业主目标优先性的能力做基础的行为过程。例如,在解决一个工程超支的危机问题时,若工程费用有最高的优先级,一个昂贵的,提高建筑物外形效果的详细设计就应该被牺牲掉,以保证工程回到原设计预算范围内。

决策的另一个挑战是资源的限制,因为超出这个限度的决策不会得到上级领导的支持。例如,如果预算是固定的,对委托人说来,就没有什么争取额外资金的渠道了。当所有的委托人都有资源上的限制时,在政府筹资的工程上,资源限制的不可变性和尖锐性就尤为明显。公共监督保证了在做出延长工期和增加资金的决策之前,必须对它进行审计。在危机的情况下,或许没有时间履行这个过程,这时最大的困难可能就是必须确定目标更灵活、更具不明显性的临界点。福德·皮尼特事件(哈罗 1999)或许是能够说明组织在不同的目标间进行权衡的最有名的例子。在 20 世纪 60 年代,对亚紧凑型轿车的需求量上升,皮尼特是第一批生产新一代重量轻、费用低的轿车的厂家。规范是不容折衷和不具可变性的,所生产出来的轿车重量不得超过 2000 磅,价格不得高于 2000 美元。为了使销量最大化,在皮尼特的历史上,它的轿车也比其他品牌的轿车要更快地出现在陈列室里。然而,在设计和生产过程中,撞击试验的检测结果表明,当车速为 25 英里/小时时,油箱破裂,燃油漏到地面。当车速为 40 英里/小时时,车门卡住,乘车者被关在里面。然而,生产还是继续进行,皮尼特决定忽略这个问题。考虑到每年对大约 360 起死亡和严重烧伤事故的赔偿几乎占到卡车销售收入用的三分之一,停止生产,重新设计油箱已经是必要的了。

集中决策的权力

组织的各个阶层中都存在决策人,危机的重要性部分决定着决策权应由组织的哪个级别来做出。危机是重要性极高的事件,它常常牵动着诸如项目经理,偶尔也有委托人等高层领导的注意力。然而,决策级别也常常依赖于决策权力的下放程度。一个决策权下放的机构有利于做出级别较低的决策。这种等级制的决策机制对危机管理极具重要性,因为决策者越邻近威胁,他对威胁的反应就越迅速,这是因为各级组织间信息流通的需求量大幅度降低。高集权组织以对变化的反应缓慢而出名,而且这常常引起基于个人局限性的不明智的决策。为了能对危机做出迅速的反应,监控员、比较员和决策员这三个角色由一人承担是最理想的。但在危机的极端时期,高级领导人员想要参与,做出一种决策,可能就意味着进行一趟穿越不同的组织级别、充满厌烦感、挫折感和具有潜在损害性的旅程。

德麦奇埃尔·埃特·奥尔(1982)分析了煤矿工业的事故,发现事故发生率低的煤矿,是那些赋予管理者更多决策空间,采纳工人提出的经过慎重考虑的改进意见并将之付诸实施的企业。多年来,许多公司的灾难说明,当具有官僚作风的企业主管者控制着公司的决策权时,灾难发生的可能性最高。例如,导致 20 世纪 80 年代布伦特·沃克帝国崩溃的部分原因就是有着势不可挡的说服力的董事长乔治·沃克做出了以 689 百万英镑收买威廉·希尔赌博连锁店的决策。如韦尔(1994)指出的那样,如果曾经有值得信赖的指示物表明公司将最终陷入危机,这个指示物就应该是拒绝接受建议、具有超凡魅力、注目形象的公司总裁乔治·沃克。毫无疑问,这种结论在建筑业也是正确的。

处理好与外部利益集团的关系

危机的特点之一就是它影响高层决策者。然而,有较大影响力的危机很可能突破组织界限影响到其他诸如金融家、保险公司、用户、工会、政府部门等外部利益相关者及其他和工程与相关的团体如分包人、供应商等。至少,在做决策时应把这些团体纳入考虑的范围,告知他们拟定的解决方案,在极端环境下,授予他们处理危机的全部责任。例如,在工地死亡事故发生后,安全卫生检查部门或工会领导在调查后,可能会要求在改进工作落实之前关闭工地。同样的,在银行破产事件中,合法的公司管理人员、清算人或会计师可暂时承担起公司的管理责任。

处理外部利益集团权力问题的过程是一个复杂的,细致的具有高度政治性的过程,有潜在的巨大的加剧危机和延误对危机做出反应的可能。所以,必须事先明确如何将这些利益相关者纳入到决策过程中。威尔士的橄榄球协会世界杯千年体育馆工程,可以生动地阐明没有考虑外部利益相关者的权力所带来的后果。在施工过程中,威尔士橄榄球协会和它的邻居卡德神足球俱乐部之间的不良关系使得后者不允许前者的塔吊在他们的上空操作,也不允许施工中的斜柱扫过他们的地面。这导致了后来对支承馆顶的柱的重新设计和整个结构荷载的重新计算。

建筑工程之外,导致230人死亡的TWA航班800事故,是一个很好的能阐明外部团体利益所带来的问题的事例。事后对灾难的分析强调了危机管理人员在尽最大努力处理好危机的同时,考虑心神错乱的家属,迫切的记者,情绪化的公众和外部急救设施时所遭遇的问题(芬奈尔1996)。

在建筑施工企业,外部利益一体化问题在将来会变得越来越重要。一个可能的阻碍这种趋势的组织是不断发展的绿色运动,它的成员把建筑业看成是主要的垃圾生产者,例如,美国25%的固体垃圾由建筑活动所产生,而且,多数严重危害环境的垃圾是可以消除或被重新利用的(明克斯1996)。实际上,在欧洲,很有影响力的道路工程的土建工程部门已经开始感受到环境运动潜在的力量,这些运动对他们计划的实施带来严重的延误,对承担工程的公司的声誉造成损害。当新的房地产业围绕着这些基础设施不断崛起时,房屋建设产业受到冲击是不可避免的。实际上,即使那些市内再开发工程的建筑者也会受到影响,因为,除了满足日益增长的垃圾处理的要求以外,许多城市的重居住工程要求对重住区域居民的生活质量给予极大的关注。例如,在澳大利亚悉尼市中心,一座55层高的商业开发工程中,当地居民被纳入到工程管理机构中,在制定施工计划时,征求他们的意见,以决定能否延长工作时间弥补工期延误。悉尼当局想在市中心工业区推出重居住工程,当地居民的力量是如此强大,以至于他们要跟政府签订一份250000美元的契约,该契约规定,如果在规定时间之外,工程产生噪音,这些保证金就会无条件地牺牲掉。

不合理性

决策者的任务是做出决策,布郎切尔(1997)认为,决策者可以遵循一系列可选择的路径。例如,当决策者在过去遭遇过类似的问题时,他或她会遵循一种在那种环境中发展成熟的程序来解决问题。也就是说,决策者会依赖事先已决定的反应模式来自动地做出决策。相反的,当问题是不寻常的,非常规的,为人们熟悉的模式所没料到的时,人们倾向于评估每种选择的效益和费用来做出选择。最后,当问题是唯一的、复杂的、充满不确定性,很难用效益和费用标准来衡量时,布郎切尔提出了一种可知性模式,它的基本原理是基于纯粹的感觉,人们可以做出直观性的决策。

令人遗憾的是,在危机的压力下,决策者遵循布郎切尔给出的模式进行决策的可能性并不大。例如,奈特和麦克丹尼尔(1997)发现在危机中,人们倾向于遵循一种不合适的"走着看"的决策路径,来处理那些非常规的、需要做出分析的环境中的问题。在危机中,人们进入一种自动状态的原因是很多的。例如,奈特和麦克丹尼尔认为,很难对危机所产生的非常规的信息进行分类,为了搞清这一点,还需要很长时间,付出昂贵的代价。原因很简单,危机时刻并不是收集信息的适当时刻,特别是当危机管理系统没被重视时,而危机管理系统能在适当的时候给人们提供适当的信息。其他研究人员的研究成果也表明,在危机过程中,自动决策的能力是人类能幸存的重要技巧(布洛克 1999)。例如,对战士在火灾发生时生理状态的研究结果表明,他们的心律升高到 300 次/分钟,这种状况对人的机车驾驶技巧,周边视力和听力都会造成一定的损害。因为这个原因,培养人杀人能力的军队,试图建立一种条件反射,使士兵在战斗中,能按预先决定的方式进行战斗。在极端的危机环境中,组织也应具备类似的能力。

不愿改变工作标准

一个决策,无论它是自动的、分析的或直觉的都需要对执行过程和目标系统进行重新组合。以这个目标为出发点,如果偏差能及时地自我调整过来,决策人可以合法的什么都不做。然而,在大多数情形下,必须做点什么,或者调整计划目标,或者调整执行过程的标准。例如,如果问题是由于地方政府计划官员拒绝同意设计变更,这个问题可以通过和他辩论或协商来解决或者诉诸舞弊情况于调查官员。

阿迪瑞斯(1984)认为,决策人员不愿做目标变更的选择,因为"团体准则"会逐步显现,对组织目标的挑战会受到指责。可以想象,那些影响力大的里程碑工程,就像悉尼奥林匹克体育馆、伦敦千年大厦工程,预算或设计的任何变更都会受到媒体强烈的批评和监视。例如,我们可以再回头看看威尔士的千年体育馆工程,该工程的承建是为了迎接 1999 年 10 月的橄榄球世界杯的到来。橄榄球世界杯的观众收视率在世界所有正规体育运动事件收视率中排名第三,整个国家都会以圆满的完成该工程为荣。所以,当严密监视工程施工情况的媒体透漏出工程可能不会按期完成时,承包商约翰·莱因 PLC 受到媒体强大的压力。那种把世界杯放在别的国家举行的说法是不可忍受和无法想象的,也使威尔士国家的尊严受到了严重的侮辱,总裁马丁·莱因先生被迫公开的向威尔士公众承诺"我们非常高兴,一定能按期完成这项该死的工程"(巴罗 1999)。

对主要的公共工程来说,变更目标比变更实施过程压力要大,但对建筑工程来说,情况正好相反。赫尔曼(1963)认为,在危机的压力下,以前合理的标准变得无法达到了,并且因为它的缓和效果可能变得不再严密了。实际上,许多委托人,比如英国财产联邦(1983)常常抱怨项目管理人员只要求他们降低目标,而不努力提高自己的工作水平,为达到目标而奋斗。

实施——危机管理的第四阶段

从定义上说,危机对社会、技术和资金都有着深远的影响,而且任何决策都需要组织在这些方面做出明显的变更。技术影响和工程自然过程的变更有关;社会影响和执行工程的成员改变他们已建立的关系模式有关;资金影响和实现这些变更所需的额外资源有关。在像建筑工程那样联系紧密的组织中,这种变更通过信息系统来实现,这种信息系统由决策者设计,把组织的各个部分联系在一起。例如,在澳大利亚墨尔本的一项工程建设中,发现了土著古墓,建筑物的上部结构要求设计变更,这项变更反过来又影响了结构工程师、设计人员、维修工程师、承包商、分包商、供应商以及诸如媒体,考古学家,土著利益集团等。

实施中的问题

实施中出现问题有许多原因。

不健全的信息流通系统

如果通过信息系统在项目成员间执行变更决策,那么,信息系统的任何问题都会降低危机管理的有效性。我们已经讨论过了在突发性危机时,由于信息超载及人们本能的趋向于恐慌,变得失去理性,而且关闭有些感官而使得信息系统受到损害。然而,除了这些自然现象,建筑业的特征对信息系统在危机时出现故障也负有一定的责任。信息流通方面的困难一致被认为是由于建筑专业间历史的划分所致,由于分包而导致的过程的零碎;一连串的采购过程,它将整个过程分割成设计、施工等阶段;由于招标和合同所导致的利益争执。这些问题是构成所有建筑工程紧张局势的基础,在危机的压力下,它们趋向于被加剧,且通过损害人们之间相互沟通的有效性体现出来。

抵抗变更

从定义上说,人们趋于对包括技术、资金和社会方面的变更采取一种本能的抵抗态度。这是因为所有的变更都需要放弃过去的一些劳动成果,还需要一些返工。而且,当危机没有公平分配时,这在建筑合同中很常见,变更不可避免的产生了赢家。虽然赢家有可能和支持变更,马奇维里提醒我们,和输家强烈的防御意识相比,赢家只表示出了不热心的支持。

外部利益集团

在危机管理的决策阶段已经考虑了将外部利益集团纳入到管理系统内的问题,在实施阶段是对这个问题的进一步反映。实际上,在实施阶段这个问题更加尖锐,因为对组织成员来说,比起决策阶段,这个阶段持续的时间更长,覆盖的范围更广。1987年的泽布拉格摆渡灾难生动地阐明了这个观点。当时的应急计划并没有考虑到媒体的大量涌入会导致通讯线路的堵塞,堵塞的程度是如此严重,以至于海岸和海底营救队伍无法相互联系(维金纳1996)。另一个没有预料到的问题是由好奇的公众引起的海口交通混乱状态,在现场,需要很多的应急设施。

在建筑工程的临时环境中,由于能用于建立长期工作关系的时间很短,就使得把外部利益集团纳入系统内的困难尤为明显。这就是为什么在建筑工程中,那种可持续发展的关系非常少见,很多单位和诸如消防队这样的应急服务单位之间存在这种可持续发展的关系。例如,模拟的火灾演习,即使在发生火灾可能性很大的单位也很少进行。另一个引起把外部利益集团纳入系统内困难的原因是工程劳动组织的临时性。以分包商为例,干完这个工程,他可能转移到另一个由另一个委托人投资的工地,受雇于另外一个主承包商,你可以想象一下把该分包商纳入系统内的困难。

反馈——危机管理的第五阶段

在整个工程的执行阶段,了解每一个过程的执行结果对保证计划和实际相符非常重要。这种信息被称作"反馈",组织的内部监控系统应负责收集有关执行情况的信息。不断地和目标进行对比,并对反馈回来的执行情况进行评估,直到实际执行情况和计划相符。这可能需要一段时间,从这个意义上说,危机管理过程是一个循环的过程,一个过程结束,组织返回其正常轨道后,再开始另一个循环。

令人遗憾的是,在实际的工程施工中,由于受诸如有关系不良的信息流通,利益冲突,时间压力,目标系统鉴定和评估的困难等监控因素的影响,使得执行情况的反馈成为一个问题。从因变更而蒙受损失的一方获得反馈情况就更成为问题了,而这种信息对危机管理却更为重要。危机管理必须要能辨认出潜在的蒙受损失的一方,最好能够产生一种风险共担机制,来消除这种利益冲突。

恢复——危机管理的倒数第二阶段

灾难所造成的心灵和物质上的伤害大小依赖于对危机的处理方式,对这种伤害必须进行弥补和修正。这一阶段的重点应该是恢复,尽快地使组织回到正常轨道上。由于可能有一些内部和外部的调查会伤害拟改善的关系,使得恢复需要一些时间和敏感性。而且,由于被事故所伤的人们,可能会下意识的隐藏不愉快的记忆,这使得心灵的伤害不会立刻表现出来。为了释放这种危机后的伤痛,危机管理所面对的主要问题是人们本能的希望往前看,不愿意回想不愉快的事情。然而,这个问题必须彻底解决,不仅是因为伦理上的原因,而且是因为情绪的烦乱,可能在将来某时重现,引起更进一步的危机。如布洛克(1999)指出的那样,心理学的基本原理是人因为有秘密而痛苦,从危机中完全恢复依赖于人们对他们痛苦的分担。对一个组织,这一点也是正确的。

学习——危机管理的最后阶段

管理人员不能把返回正常轨道看成是危机管理的最后阶段。如宫泽来兹和普朗特(1995)指出的那样,危机为人们提供了有深远意义的学习机会,因为它提供了对未来危机管理应用方面重要的改进。而且,通过它可以展示出在常规情况下不会显露出来的组织内的弱点。从这点说,它可以通过抛弃那些可能永远根植于组织内的、会引起危机的行为和过程而提高组织的效率。

在许多情况下,学习和抛弃是危机管理很重要的两个方面,因为我们今天用来建造、生产和运行工程的很多知识都是从分析失败中得到的。例如,卡珀(1989)指出,在欧洲哥特式教堂建筑时期,像法国比弗范斯教堂那样的螺旋塔式结构不断地失败,引起了人们的质疑,从而扩展了建筑者的技术知识。普莱特兹克(1989)引用一个更近期的例子,纽约一个新建旅馆的火灾事故导致了建筑法规和标准的变化,新的法规和标准能保证在施工中为雇员提供更好的保护。

令人遗憾的是,建设工程组织的时间压力、临时性、过渡性、零碎性和分割性并没有鼓励人们要有远见,要用学习和抛弃的态度对待过去的经验和失败。现在兴起的设备管理文化就是这种观点的一个证明,它反映出很少有企业对其产品的效果进行评估,更不用说生产过程中出现的危机了(巴瑞特 1995)。尽管存在这些潜在的问题,研究的愿望,无论多么的困难和痛苦,是防止重犯错误和提高执行效果的关键。这给我们带来了辩证管理者这个角色——一个负责调查事故、总结教训的人。

辨证管理的过程

除了内部调查总结经验外,由于政府的强制性调查或由于受害方赔偿的需要,工程还无意的被外界所调查。无论调查的原因和动机是什么,每一个工程参与者都会受到影响,简单考虑一下所涉及的过程以及如何通过最好的管理方法来产生积极的效果是很有用的。

虽然每种争端调查各不相同,但它们都包括数据的收集和分析。通常,调查者从事故发生时起追溯到它的根源。第一步是识别事故发生和调查开始之间所发生的变化(亨德瑞1989)。例如,调查一场火灾事故时,营救人员可能因为砍断大梁以便工人逃生而扰乱了案发现场。第二步是运用诸如故障树法的分析技术,分析出导致事故发生的一系列事件及它们之间相互关系。例如,如果工地上一种化学溢出物引起了工地上的有毒气体,使工人生病,调查过程应该是这样的:最初的泄漏位置在何处? 化学物品是如何释放出来的? 释放了多少? 释放物流往何处? 化学物品中包含什么成分? 应急方法有哪些? 紧跟着采取安全措施了吗? 分析的最后阶段是对以前存在情况的评估,使事故动态化。例如,设备很关键的部件丢失了吗? 对雇员进行充分的培训了吗? 雇员是在"闹着玩吗"?

争端调查的信息收集渠道通常有采访、观察、调查、照片及对文件的检查。通常,对文件的检查和对关键人员的采访需要重复进行。从这点上来说,为了使调查负有成效,调查队伍必须接近现场,接触当事人,接近文件记录。调查过程可能包括对材料进行检测的实验室工作甚至包括对导致事故的周围环境的完全模拟。以上任何一种选择都意味着对现场的暂时关闭。

很清楚,信息收集的方法依赖于所调查事件的特征。例如,对由于结构故障所致的,就像对 1981 年堪萨斯城海特人行道坍塌事故进行调查时,对结构件的测试是至关重要的。相反的,在对最后一起澳大利亚悉尼涉及逃税漏税的价值 400 万美元的工程的调查重点应放在对人的调查上。在随后的调查中,税务官员采访了所有的分包商,提出补交 30000 美元税金的要求,这对工地上的士气、对工程的进度都造成了极大的混乱。工会人员和管理者随后对主承包商的调查最终解决了这个问题,但也引起了相当的混乱。

很清楚,必须对调查工作进行高敏感性的组织以防止造成物质上和心灵上严重的伤害。做好这项工作的一种方法是,让每个人都知道调查过程所涉及的东西,如果有必要,给予被调查者心理上的帮助。如果调查过程需要人们唤起不愉快的记忆或给出可能使同事受到牵连的证据时,心理上的支持就显得尤为重要。

调查队伍

由于大多数危机是由技术的、自然的、程序的及人为的因素造成的,争端调查管理者的任务就是在一些具有调查所需的专业知识的人们之间做协调工作。这些专业人员可能包括管理顾问、心理学家、警察、火灾侦察员、各种类型的工程师、工会官员、律师、交通事故调查员、会计师、生产商、勘探员和理论科学家。争端调查面对的一个危险是不同利益集团可能按自己的利益来决定调查方向。这是因为大多数调查都发生在具有很高政治性的环境里,从行为的合法性和保险的支出方面来说,调查结果对于人们及其组织有着深远的财务意义。需要财务补偿的一方最容易接受这方面的劝说,同样的因事故遭到人身伤害或需要一些补偿来重建生活的人们也最容易接受这方面的劝说。然而,争端调查管理者必须不被个人感情、同情心和外部压力所左右,因为过程的公平性和人们对它的信任对调查结果的价值有极大的影响。例如,亨德里(1989)描述了一起事故,从中可以看出,商业压力。个人的同情心及从受害方所得的歪曲事实的信息都非常容易影响调查过程。在这个事件中,有一个人斜靠在塔吊上,当塔吊接触到上面的电缆时,此人受到严重的电击。受害方要求赔偿胜诉的原因如下:从提供给司机的视力范围说来,司机室设计不当,司机和塔吊的地面指挥员都没有过失。然而,通过检查发生事故时拍摄下来的效果极佳的照片,对塔吊进行检查,采访目击者,调查结果指出,塔吊不存在缺陷,厂商也没有任何责任。

　　为了保证调查过程的公正性和调查结果能广泛的被人们所接受,最好的办法是指定一名受各方尊敬的"局外者"来进行调查工作。可能被指责的潜在的各方涉及到的各方代表的专家也应该被包括进去。很明显,这种由多种专业人才和不同利益集团组成的复杂的调查队伍,要求极高的管理艺术,如果争端调查管理者很称职,能够做出高难度的决策,提出适时的建议,对他所得到的零碎的、冲突的信息能进行客观的分析,问题就变得简单了。另外,如果队伍成员不但是他所在的领域的专家,而且有类似的经验,喜欢现场工作,值得信任,讲道德,做事有决心,能够处理模棱两可的和充满挫折的事情,善于交际,有极大的耐心,对调查工作将是很有帮助的。这些特征是不可缺少的,因为没有一种专门的知识,能使得调查人在许多危机发生的现场,有能力分析和观察由之而起的身体和精神的混乱状态。

有争端的调查报告

　　很明显,进行一场严密的事故调查需要相当的时间和资金,且调查工作应该在事故之后尽快的开始,因为在营救或清理过程中,证据可能会被毁坏,而且,过失方故意的毁坏行为也可能造成重要的证明文件的毁坏;重要的目击者可能离开工程;目击者对事故的记忆可能会衰退。调查的最后结果应该是对事故原因的报告,而不是责任的归咎。然而,调查人经常被要求突出报道非法的和不适当的行为或对损害进行评估,而且,不可避免的,有些调查报告确定使有些人受到谴责,这时,如果调查负责人具备有关法定程序方面的知识是很有帮助的。虽然因调查导致有些人受到谴责是不可避免的,但调查过程绝对不能沦为寻找替罪羊的"政治迫害",在危机引起强烈的心灵震撼时,这种反应很普遍(赫雷瑞克·约翰 1996)。虽然找出过失方并对之进行一些惩罚,可能有防止类似事故再次发生的作用,但谴责别人很容易引起事与愿违的后果,也防碍人们从事故中吸取重要的教训。埃克逊·凡尔德兹石油泄漏事故就是这样一个例子,在危机过后,埃克逊把主要精力放在谴责海岸警卫队上,而不是用在灾难后经验教训的总结上,这种谴责使得埃克逊不但没能从事故中吸取重要的教训,而且使他陷入进一步的公共关系问题中,这反过来又加重了原始危机的代价。谴责主义者也在1989 年 3 月 4 日伦敦的珀里铁路碰撞事故的事后调查中表现出来。该事故导致 5 位乘客死亡,88 位严重受伤(郝力科·约翰 1996)。事故发生后,政府调查员将事故归咎于火车司机中的一人。结果此人以杀人罪被判处 18 个月的监禁。报告和法庭都没有考虑有关行为方面调查的结果,这种调查结果认为,重复的监控预警信号的工作,使人产生一种相信自己已经执行了任务的思想模式,即使他确实没有执行。这种判决引起了强烈的抗议,铁路工会进行了示威游行,认为对工人适用一种法律,而对管理人员适用另外一种法律。

　　虽然最好的调查报告要坚守客观性原则,但有时候你只是无法找出危机的起因。在这种情况下,调查不能变成一种猜测,因为调查负责人时时都得保护被调查各方的专业信誉。

虽然许多争端调查队伍受理的是一些涉及法律的事件,但除了那些涉及人身伤害和损失的事件,很少有提到法庭上去处理的。因为这个原因,报告应该写得具有建设性,为潜在的危机涉及到的各方之间建设性的协商打下基础。从这点说来,这样的报告如果是在各方合作下做出的,它将是一个处理第三方争端的有益方法。

结 论

这一章讨论了危机管理的各个阶段,说明为了能对危机做出成功的反应,应该对每个阶段都进行有效的管理。这些阶段包括:检测、诊断、决策、应用、反馈、修正和学习。他们之间的相互关系见图 3-1。这个模型把危机管理过程分成了一系列具有独特性但又相互联系的行为阶段,为了取得全面危机管理的成功,应该对每个阶段都进行有效的管理。该模型还定义了人们在检测、诊断、决策阶段所担任的任务。这些任务可以由一个来承担,也可以由一个人负责的团体来承担,看来,危机管理的有效性部分地与这些责任的划分有关。整个过程中每一阶段的问题都会影响危机管理的效率。实际上,危机有一种令人遗憾的产生诱发问题的环境的趋势,这种趋势提示我们低效率的危机管理不是"可能的"而是"很可能的"。

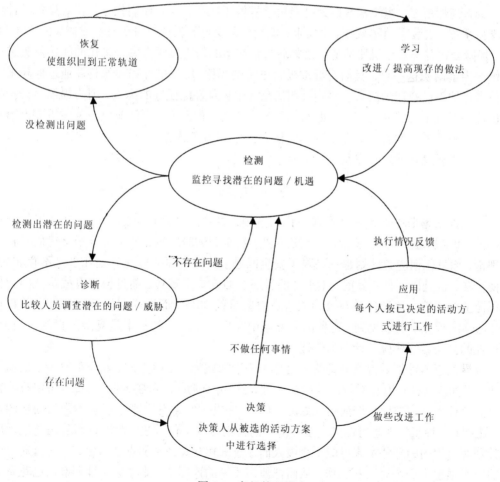

图 3-1 危机管理模式

第四章

建筑工程中的应急计划

前几章中讨论的主要问题都是缺乏准备性的问题。计划是有效的危机管理的"基石"，因为它可以帮助我们避免作为危机前期阶段特征的损害性的混乱。

简　介

无论怎么强调一个构思良好的危机管理计划的重要性都是不过分的。这一点已经被强调过无数次了，它也是引起欧森登特·皮珀·阿尔弗灾难的原因之一，在那儿，操作手册上几乎没有提及如何防止潜在灾难的方法（比 1994）。

令人遗憾的是，组织常常以为已经对危机做了准备，因为他们投了保险，配备了计算机支持系统，安装了消防系统。事实上，保险公司支付的款项只占危机造成损失的 1/8，而且，保险公司并不对危机所造成的诸如雇员精神上的伤害及顾客关系恶化的间接损失进行赔偿。为了阐明这一点，我们看看被极力诽谤的福德·皮特事件和福德打算通过保险来支付他潜在的诉讼费用的决策。事实证明这是一个灾难性的误导的决策，因为福德不得不收回价值一百五十万美元的汽车并赔偿比预计高三倍多的损失。而且他成为美国历史上第一家被指控犯杀人罪的公司。在 1980 年，差不多有 10 年汽车生产历史的福德汽车公司因安全方面的声誉是如此之差以至于它不得不停止汽车的生产（哈罗 1999）。

应急计划

应急计划越来越受到危机管理文化的重视，尽管许多公司不愿进行这个过程的研究（米特芬和皮尔逊 1993）。实际上，在建筑业，特奥（1998）发现，公司哲学不支持危机管理的理论，而且任何应急计划都只局限于安全问题。其他方面的应急计划几乎是不存在的，即使存在，也是以一种狭隘的，不正规的和随意的方式出现的，而且很少有战略上的指导和资源上的支持。这种现象在公司数量占总数量的 90%，而所雇佣员工数量只占总数量 10%那样的行业中可以见到。特奥的研究集中在世界上最大的从事最复杂工程的公司上，在这样的公司做一些应急计划是合理的。

世界上应急计划做得最完备的公司是一些诸如航海业、核电站、化学处理业、机场管理业、石油业这样具有相对较高风险的企业，这一点倒是不足为奇的。例如，谢尔石油公司将应急计划作为他们长期战略计划的一部分，并发现它常常会带来意想不到的间接的好处，比如，一种新的观念可能产生多种富有创新精神的工作方法。谢尔石油公司还发现应急计划使组织内的那些本来可能不会被人们注意的相互关系和弱点显露出来，而且通过极端的方案强迫人们去思考和工作，从而把他们紧紧的连在了一起。应急计划部门已花费了相当长的时间来从事这项研究工作，它建议人们采用这种计划，建筑业也可以得益于这种积累的经验。这对那些从事具有国内和国际重要意义的、受公众严密监视的、有引起大量伤亡事故可能的、有许多外部利益集团涉入的高风险工程尤其重要。

应急计划的目的

应急计划应该在工程开工之前就拟定好，它应包括施工过程中所有阶段的主要风险。应急计划通过快速的反应来缓和由危机造成的潜在损害。它能做到这一点是因为它是在没有压力的情况下设计出来的，这压力正是导致人们破坏性行为的元凶，而人们的破坏性行为在危机过程中趋于发展和扩大它的影响。有一个提前设计好的、可以自动执行的计划能消除与危机前期相联的那种最初的压力和震惊。这就产生了一种对人们来说十分珍贵的"喘气的空间"，在这段时间内，人们可以对问题进行调查，对合适的反应方式达成一致。危机管理应该有一个好的开始，这一点再强调都不过分。危机过程中，每一秒钟都是重要的，开始的几个小时更为关键。如果有外部集团涉入，这一点就更是无可置疑的了，因为最初印象能在很大程度上影响人们对一个人是能胜任工作还是应该受到谴责做出判断的结果。如果一个公司留给人们的最初印象不好，这个公司就会被认为是有过失的，直到它的清白得到证明，在大多数情况下，这能加剧危机的强度和加速危机的发展。这一点可以用威尔士的橄榄球协会世界杯千年体育馆工程来阐明。当约翰·莱恩 PLC 发布由该工程严重的亏损而导致的利润警告时，如马丁·莱恩先生所述（巴罗 1999）"我们一发布利润警告，很明显，建筑业的每个新闻工作者都很感兴趣，但也有少数可能是故意对问题曲解的、更具有点积极性的观点"（P.24）。

应急计划的准备

高风险企业的许多组织都有一个常设的灾难控制委员会，它负责支持危机管理工作的需要，鉴别目前的准备情况和危机倾向性，策划灾难控制计划，在灾难过程中对人们进行协调（库纳 1996）。委员会的成员是影响他们工作能力的重要因素，应该由高级管理人员、各功能部门的经理和来自外部的有危机管理、公共关系、法律、身体和精神健康问题方面有经验的专家组成。组织中的高层领导作为委员会的成员，对提高委员会工作受重视的程度和提高其成功的概率尤其重要。下面讨论这些活动的各个方面。

进行危机审计，建立危机档案

危机审计工作评价组织的抗危机能力，辨别出环境、内部活动、技术、基础设施和文化中内在的危机因素，并对他们进行分析和分类，以提高对危机的准备性（米特罗夫和皮尔逊 1993）。这个过程的第一步是从组织的观点出发对危机进行定义、辨别，然后按发生的可能性和产生的后果，对组织可能遇到的危机类型进行分类分级。这需要从过去的事件中学习经验，吸取教训，预测将来可能发生的事件，探索事件间看似不可能、但组合起来却会产生严重危机的不寻常的组合。对危机分级需要对建立一个危机管理计划所需的费用和效益做出适当的判断，因为对每种危机都作出计划从经济上说是不合理的。

澳大利亚保险公司，曼彻斯特分部 1993 年所遭遇的经济不断衰退的危机，就很好地说明了探索组织危机倾向性的重要性和困难性。危机的根源是例行的维修保养工作所引起的一场火灾，它毁坏了整栋建筑物的能源供应系统。因为保险公司基本上是计算机依赖型的，瞬息之间，整个经营机制被切断了生命的血液来源。虽然曼彻斯特分部也已经开始搞应急计划了，但它的计划只处理诸如爆炸事故和严重的火灾这类危机。没有人想过一座没有现代通信方式的完好无缺的建筑物是个什么样子，而这现代的通信方式正好是经营活动的中心。后来，经营工作已很难维持，于是决定在一个当地旅馆建立临时通信中心，将总部人员转移到郊区的分部。虽然公司对危机处理得很好，毫无疑问，如果这些情况事先被预料到，并且通过采取备用一些就像手动打字机和档案保存系统这样的简单措施，危机就会被处理的更好。

建立监控系统和标准的操作过程

灾难控制委员会的工作之一就是建立监控系统，检测潜在危机，而且形成一种标准化的过程来准确的定义，谁应该承担对危机做出反应的工作，他们应该做那些工作，什么时候做以及如何做。实际上，这个过程就是建立一个预先定义好的危机控制流程系统，该系统要求在非常关键的危机的早期，被发生的事件所误导的人们必须遵循这个模式做出反应。这样做的目的是给组织"买"来一些时间和所发生的事件做些妥协，允许人们重新适应环境，保证适当的和危机规模相适应的资源被很快地调动起来。为达到这一点，过程应该是可行的、简单的、灵活的、容易被内部和外部相关者所理解的。例如，在澳大利亚和新加坡，工地上有许多移民工人，这就可能需要项目手册用不同的语言来书写。

在许多有危机准备系统的组织里，清楚明白容易实施且为每个人都熟悉的应急过程都写在了操作手册里。通常，这些过程是一层一层进行的。第一层是危机发生初期的前几个小时，属于教导阶段。在这一阶段，由于可得到的信息非常少，有必要尽可能地使这些最初的过程标准化。例如，许多危机需要撤离现场，也有一些危机可能因为牵扯到公共健康问题需要急救处理。把危机分成特定的种类能使应急过程简单化，保证快速地做出反应，把事故蔓延的可能性降到最低。然而，由于不同种类的危机需要不同种类的快速反应，使得这种通用过程的有效性受到了限制。随后，当危机的种类已经鉴别出来，而详细的反应还没有形成，就进入了过程的第二层，拟定详细的反应过程。例如，消防部门常常根据火灾的严重程度把它分为渐进的四个级别1、2、3、4。一系列应急计划就根据以上分类投入相应的人力、时间和资源来适应上述各类危机的要求(戴维斯 1995)。再一次，这些过程被设计出来，只是作为一种暂时的反应来减少施工队伍所承受的压力，最终，为满足眼前危机独特需求的战略的发展买来时间。过分依赖于标准化的过程，几乎没有例外地导致对危机反应的低效率。

建立一个指挥中心

在危机过程中，信息不断地从大量的信息源产生出来，把这些信息在正确的时间以可理解的格式"实况转播"到正确的地点是至关重要的(戴维斯 1995)。从这个意义上说，灾难控制委员会工作的一个重要方面就是确定一个明确的对决策和信息管理全权负责的指挥中心。这种指挥中心是一个至关重要的有利于整个危机管理过程一体化的协调机制，因为危机过程中最大的问题之一就是人们各行其事。例如，出现火灾后，指挥中心对联系应急服务，协调一定区域内清理工作负责人间的关系负全部责任。在诸如主要分包商发生经济危机的情况下，指挥中心应负起重新组织工作，重新雇佣另一个分包商的责任。除了在危机中，起到实际的重要作用以外，指挥中心还扮演着一个有重要象征意义的角色。尼克德姆斯(1997)给出了一个例子，一个公司把他们在危机时的指挥中心称作"作战室"，他们在那儿向问题宣战。

安　全

安全是灾难控制委员会工作的另一个重要因素，因为不必要因素的干涉可能加速危机，或者至少影响危机管理的有效性，所以这项工作也包括鉴别出那些认为自己与危机的后果有关但又对它的解决无能为力的外部集团。那些具有破坏作用的因素必须从危机管理中分离出来，以便人们能集中精力解决问题。

有时，把发生危机的场所从这些因素中隔离开来是很重要的，特别是当它对公众仍然代表着一种危机时。在这种情况下，撤离过程或许是必要的，撤离的消息清楚的传达给工地上的每一个人是非常重要的，并应该通过定期的训练和模拟来加强它。例如，用于公共信息传递系统的警报器和喇叭，若放置在人人都能听得见的位置，就可用来通知人们事件的发生。无论使用什么信号，这种信号必须尽可能的清晰和没有二意性。它们的使用责任也必须是清晰的，而且就像莫菲的法律要求的那样，必须做适当的准备以防事件发生时负责人正好不在或主要设备出现故障。撤离的一个重要方面就是从工地的每一部分标出清晰的撤出路线。另外，人们应该知道起重机不能用来做撤离工作，撤离路线附近的有潜在危险性的设备的电源应该切断。因为工地是一个不断变化的自然环境，应该经常检查标记的位置及它的保养状况。另外，撤离路线应该设计得尽可能短，宽度应足以保证人们能有次序的从建筑物内撤出。在市中心时，这种路线可能就是一条街道，撤离活动对公众，对交通，对现场工人的危害必须通过与诸如警察这样的公共事业单位联系评估出来。

1977年5月导致164人死亡的泊维里·希尔·萨泊俱乐部的火灾事故就能证明没有考虑周全的撤离计划和明确地标注撤离线路潜在的危险。政府调查报告指出，俱乐部没有撤离计划，雇员没有受到火灾发生时如何行事的教育或训练。撤离的方法没有标记，撤离的线路是如此之窄以至于在那个特殊的时刻它不能容纳建筑物里的人们(百思特1977)。

发展一种集体责任文化

把执行对危机做出反应的队伍从不必要因素中分离出来的做法并不意味着这些队伍可以变成思想内向型的队伍。非危机管理活动也应该给予一定的重视以保证组织内其他人员能尽可能的发挥其作用。不可避免的，危机需要从组织内其他功能区域吸取能量，并要求处理它的人们付出极大的努力。很清楚，没有相当程度的周边友好关系和集体责任意识，危机的影响就会扩展到组织的其他区域。如果危机以前不存在这种友好关系，危机中就不能指望它的存在，从这个意义上说，危机管理过程应该是连续的。

发展这种集体责任文化的一种方法就是交流在危机中每个人之间的相互依赖性，并且，理想的说，明确地划分风险承担责任。许多风险需要注入外部资源，如果灾难控制委员会没有事先确定这些资源，危机就有会引发拖延对之做出反应的协商和潜在的冲突。

风险分配方法的决策对经济危机的影响尤其明显，前面的章节中我们已经指出，它是引起工程纠纷的主要原因，我们也鉴别出了一系列指导风险决策的原则。这些原则在合同链的每一点无论是对承包人还是对顾问工程师都是适用的。还有一点是非常重要的，那就是委托人最初的风险管理实践不可避免的沿着合同链往下传递。例如，如果一个承包人受雇于一个高风险的合同中，但却没有被赋予处理风险的权力，承包商就会试图沿着合同链运用"一前一后"的方法把这些风险转移到分包商那里。实际上，分包商也会对它的下一级采用同样的做法，直到后来，工程的风险被转移到了合同的最后一个环节。令人遗憾的是，这最后一个环节正是最易受危机影响的组织所在之处，当问题出现且需要外部资源时，这种联式的、强烈的、不利的、沿着合同链传递的冲突是不可避免的，因为各参与方都极力否定对其负有责任。

公共关系

公共关系是危机管理的一个重要方面，因为大多数危机的影响范围都超越了组织的边界。实际上，危机管理中涉及到的"公共"关系有以下三种：没有直接受到影响的雇员，外部和准外部利益集团及一般公众。前两种我们已经讨论过了，忽视第三种的做法是愚蠢的。正如埃斯普瑞(1993)所说，"危机，如果是在一种已经建立起来的、赋予人们很好的自我保护机会的公共关系上交流的，即使在困难的时刻，公司的声誉也会得到提高。如果一个公司在危机时才想起来要建立公共关系进行交流，它的可信性就太小了"(P.18)。

令人遗憾的是，建筑公司并不注意和媒体之间建立良好的关系，视它为一种不能创造价值的活动，认为大多数记者都是危险的、不可信任的和不负责任的(穆迪莱和普瑞斯1996)。这种对媒体的排斥倾向在危机时表现得尤为明显，这时组织是内向的、有意识的在公众面前隐藏自己，认为他们是不必要的、分散营救活动注意力的因素。然而，在这个时候忽视媒体，正是最危险的时候，因为危机之后，正是人们趋向于进行大肆谴责的时候。这对有较大影响力的社会投资项目尤为明显，因为公众认为，他们有权来谴责这些以他们的税收来投资的项目。如郝力科·约翰(1996)指出的那样，"因为取消了死刑，英国公众趋向于用那些耸人听闻的灾难的负责人来满足他们惩罚的欲望。找出某人来谴责，聚众生事，围着百厅，要求供出某人，并对之以私刑处死"。实际上，在这本书中，我们提供了很多例子来阐明不良的公共关系是如何导致许多组织垮台的，这些组织低估了媒体在形成"危机被处理的如何"这样的公众舆论上的力量。能阐明这种现象的最好的一个例子是 1991 年联合王国杰拉尔德·雷特纳珠宝帝国的崩溃事件。这个事件是由雷特纳在伦敦管理者协会上的一篇言论引起的，雷特纳扬言他能把一个纯粹是"废物"的细颈葡萄酒瓶卖上 15 英镑。第二天，媒体向公众披露了他是怎样用这种愚蠢的不忠实的行为来聚集自己的财富，一夜之间，人们抛弃了它的商店(韦尔 1994)。

媒　体

建筑业非常容易受媒体反面报道的影响，因为这会造成它消极的公众形象。1997 年联合王国的民意测验可以证明这一点，在这次测验中，只有石油业不受十几岁的青少年的欢迎(建筑 1997)。而且，由于建筑业对现存建筑物和自然环境的影响日益受到人们的重视，人们对建筑业的监视也越来越严格(穆迪莱和普瑞斯 1996)。这种趋势，再加上公众对环境保护运动的同情，在公众中引起了一系列不断增加的对立情绪，这一点在道路和房屋建设业尤为明显。很明显，在许多这些不断增加的普通公众的对立情绪中，媒体进行了没有同情心的大肆渲染，毫无疑问，将来许多工程的可行性都会受这种报道的影响。从这个意义上说，媒体是被传统建筑业所忽视，而现在应该引起足够重视的一个因素。工程管理人员不想依靠媒体来处理问题，仍然不愿意和媒体进行交流的做法几乎毫无例外地导致媒体对活动的消极报道。相反地，坦率地与媒体交流，关注环境问题能使管理人员塑造良好的公众形象，也能使危机中媒体能公正地报道事实。

危机中和媒体建立良好沟通关系的方法之一是建立一天24h新闻发布办公室，负责为媒体和雇员提供最新的、现场的消息。如果组织得好，这种办公室通过主动接近而不是被动地反应收音机和电视机的新闻报道，从而把媒体的调查变成一种机遇而不是问题。受过正规培训的、有能力对付媒体的政府发言人能把这样的公共关系处理的很好。对一个没有经过培训的、显得有些不在意、慌张和不自信的员工的电视采访会损害人们对公司能力的信心，而采访一个有这方面经验的人，却能为公司树立一个正面的形象。WTA 800航班坠毁事故的处理就能很好地说明这样一个人的重要性。那些惊慌失措的家属、迫切的媒体和感兴趣的公众由一个总票务代理人来组织管理，该代理人为了表示他没有任何过错，发布了不准确的消息，激起了更大的不确定性、忧虑感和对这件事处理的错误猜测（鲍勃1997）。这是事后TWA因这种无所谓的态度而倍受公共关系顾问，受害者家属及媒体谴责的主要原因。

危机后管理

危机过后，灾难控制委员会应该随后组织会议，以便总结经验教训，为将来的危机管理打下基础。任何一个受到危机影响的人都应该参与到这个过程中去。除了组织灾难后的学习以外，灾难控制委员会还应该把注意力转移到恢复过程上去。这是一个可能受危机管理好坏影响的漫长而又敏感的过程。例如，它可能包括很难应付的诸如事故原因调查，受损害的关系的修复，重新组织工程计划，解决不断发展的争端以及重估工程需求这样的挑战。同时，还必须关注危机的长期效应，比如对环境损害采取的矫正方案的长期效果，处理和政府间的关系以及和合法调查组织间的关系。很清楚，危机管理得越没有效率，危机后的恢复过程就越艰难。

为建筑工程拟定一个应急计划

为建筑工程拟定应急计划需要些时间，它依赖于前期的计划工作情况和那些将受到危机影响的组织内外有关人员的参与情况。对建筑工程来说，由于时间和费用的压力，特别是建筑施工队伍特有的、临时性的特征，使得这项工作进行起来非常的困难。应急计划必须时时反应工程中人员的变化，而这种人员的变化又反过来影响培训工作的效率，因为计划的任何变动都必须清楚地传达给每个变更相关者。解决这个问题的最好方法是举行每个人都参加的定期的危机管理专题研讨会，对新进入工程的各个级别的人员举行入门教育会。应急计划的复杂性，以及最终做这种计划所需要的时间和费用是建筑工程应急计划发展的主要障碍。尽管存在这些现实的问题，再怎么强调计划的重要性都是不过分的。没有计划，危机可能会导致无法控制的混乱，最终无法避免的导致时间、资源和精力的浪费，陷入更深的危机之中。

结　论

尽管应急计划能缓和许多潜在的、危机管理过程中出现的问题，在本章结束之前，应

该预警管理人员：不能过分依赖危机管理计划。这是因为，首先，危机计划需要不断的支持和努力，以保证人们对他们总是熟悉的。而且，危机计划不可能包括所有的不测事件，在危机中，危机计划可能被曲解、忽视甚至故意的歪曲。最后，无论一个应急计划做得是多么周全，投入的资源是多么庞大，在危机过程中，人是决定组织力量的最终因素。虽然有些人可能是自私的，但另一些人却可能会表现得有勇气、有智慧和守信用。危机中，好的人们和具有反应性的管理是不可替代的。

第五章

危机管理者——社会建筑师

建筑工程危机刺激了工程内外部利益相关者信息流通网络的建立。这一章讨论这些网络更详细的情况，认为最好的危机管理者是社会建筑师，他设计、创建和维护工程参与者各方之间适当的社会关系。

社会建筑学的概念

本尼斯（1996）引入了社会建筑学的概念，来概括当时流行的有关社会建筑学的概念，认为组织是一种自我组织起来的社会系统，由很多相互依赖，有着不同的文化背景和不同的、变化着的利益的人们组成。文化的多样性，从职业和地区的角度来说，保证了这些人会对他们自己世界里的东西赋予独特的定义和解释，并且对管理行为作出不同的、不可预料的反应（Tsoukas 1995）。从这点来讲，管理不再被看成是机械的、有规律的用来控制一些客观的、静止的场面的活动，而被看成是一种社会活动，用来协调那些根植于复杂的、不断变动的社会网络中的有着不同目的的人们。这种网络把组织内不同的部分通过一种渠道结合成一个连贯的整体，这种渠道是用来传递信息和传播新观点的。从这种意义上说，它们是活动的中心机制，通过它们，管理者必须尽最大努力创造完整、协调、合作的工作环境。从实用的观点说来，对组织的这种看法预示着管理人员应该注重人们之间相互关系的研究而不是单个人的研究，他们必须懂得这些社会关系的动态性和结构性，以及他们是怎样影响组织达到目标的能力的。

社会结构和危机管理的效率

支持人们之间联系的结构形式和危机管理效率之间有联系的最早的证据是贝维勒斯（1950），里维特（1951）和肖（1954）这些该领域的先驱们提出的。他们组织了一些小的集团，要求他们解决一个简单的，但需要各方面信息的问题。这些人被相互隔离开来，而且只能按预先制定好的渠道进行联系。见图 5-1

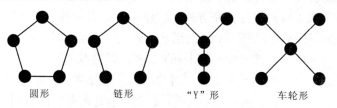

圆形　　　　链形　　　"Y"形　　　车轮形

图 5-1　里维特的经验图形

通过观察、采访和分析各集团的交流方式，研究人员发现，信息流通模式不同，解决问题的效率就大不相同。当问题比较简单时，解决问题最快的方式是链型结构方式，其次是

"Y"形，车轮形，最后是圆形。从领导的角度来说，圆形被认为是活跃的、无领导的、无组织的、无规律的，但受组织成员欢迎的组织形式。相反的，车轮形被认为是相对不活跃的，组织良好的，变动性不大的，但不受组织成员欢迎的组织方式。研究人员用"集中度"的概念来解释这种结果。集中度是指"在信息流通网络中，信息集中在一个人或少数几个人周围的程度"。低集中度组织的特征是无领导，高的活跃性，低的问题解决效率和高的组织成员满意度。然而，每种网络组织结构解决问题的效率依赖于他们所面临的问题的特征。随着问题复杂性的增加，各种组织解决问题的效率和上面的排序正好相反。圆形组织最有效率，最后是车轮形的。处于车轮形中心位置的人信息负荷量太大，周围的人也不愿意只是接受他提出的问题的解决方案。

虽然里维特和肖在是在人为的，删掉了实际生活中其他方面的环境里进行了这种试验，但他们的试验结果表明，管理组织控制人们之间信息流通结构模式的能力，能大大的影响危机管理的效率。所以，值得花时间去研究其他结构形式的信息流通网络，它们似乎对危机管理的影响很大。

正式的和非正式的沟通方式

按大多数基本标准，沟通可以分为正式沟通和非正式沟通。危机过程中的正式沟通主要由把工程的参与各方联系在一起的合同决定。合同规定了参与工程的组织成员间相互作用的模式，这样，当组织控制在自然情况下受到威胁时，就可按照合同做出事先预定好的反应。合同也可通过摒弃非相关信息和定义可接受的行为界限来保证对危机的快速反应。从这个意义上说，在危机过程中，似乎建设工程合同对参与工程的各成员的行为有很大的影响。然而，塞根(1991)认为在危机时，合同中规定的规则和步骤的影响力已经大大的减小了。他的研究指出，标准化的步骤在任务比较简单时很有帮助，然而，当任务复杂性和时间压力增大时，它因为剥夺了人们的自主权而变得有局限性和低效率性。而且，贝克斯·埃特·奥尔(1998)指出在危机过程中，工人认为合法的、有效的处理眼前问题的方法往往和合同指定的方法之间有一定差距。如果工人没有参与合同指定方法的制定过程，这种现象发生的可能性就更大。就像罗斯茂和休斯(1998)所发现的那样，在这种情形下人们通常绕过规定的步骤，使人们的沟通围绕着共同的利益集团和友谊进行。

用合同作为控制手段的危险

为了对建筑工程危机做出反应而出现的沟通网络中包括非常重要的非正式因素，如果管理人员过分的依赖于合同作为控制方式，这种非正式因素就可能是非常危险的。合同，无论起草得多么好，都不能代替一个好的组织。而且，工程管理人员面对危机时，必须认识到正式的步骤只是对非正式系统的一个补充，并认识到最后的成功可能依赖于他们是否愿意把人们从潜在的限制性的条条框框里解放出来。这需要一些勇气，因为人在危机中总是本能地倾向于求助于合同，重新用合同进行控制。它还需要对同事们有一定程度的信心和信任，但是，就如我们在第一章中讲的那样，由于组织的实践和历史的划分，使得这种信心和信任可能根本就不存在。实际上，在遍及许多工程传统的、充满对立的环境里，突然转入一种更灵活的方式可能是一种灾难，因为这种行为方式和他已经养成的、非常理想的、适用于那种充满不信任的环境的行为方式格格不入。很可能的结果是人们把这种文化的转变看成是一种牟取私利的机会而不是一种提高内聚力的手段。这正是许多工程采用由联合王国土木工程协会颁布的更灵活的建设工程合同(1995)的原因，但结果不像他们希望的那样成功。

因此，看起来，那种大容量的、刚性的和具有指定性的传统的建筑工程合同，对那些遍及许多工程的、传统的、充满对立和不信任感的环境是非常必要的。讽刺的是，正是这种合同保证了这种环境的永久性，使得建筑工程的不信任感和控制过程呈螺旋下降趋势，而且这种趋势越来越难制止。这个问题使罗斯茂和休斯(1998)提出将"应急选择"作为一种过渡的方式，使传统的合同更加灵活且被利用的风险最小。实际上，"应急选择"是一个单独的条款，它可以合法地合并到传统的建筑工程条款中去，使得参与各方都同意在特定时期为了应付危机放弃常规的合同选择权。如果一方滥用这种信任感，其他任何一方都可以单方面地使合同回到原来正式的模式上。

小组、派别和小集团

人是一种社会动物，大部分时间都是在正式和非正式的有着自己独特的准则(期望的行为标准)、议事日程、倾向性和文化的集团中度过的。集团能行使很多重要的功能，比如使人们能够解决比起单个人来说更大、更重要的问题，这个特点在危机时表现得尤为明显。集团还能提供人们所需的交际环境、身份证明和所有物，在人们协商时它能代表一种重要的力量源泉。集团结构的意识是危机管理的一个重要方面。然而，太奇·埃特·奥尔(1979)认为人们所扮演的集团内和集团外的角色对项目管理者来说也很重要。例如，一个"联系人"是指一个不属于集团的、但能把两个或更多集团联系在一起的人，一个"桥梁"是指属于多个组织的一个人。联系人和桥梁在组织中起着重要的联系功能，去掉它们会使和它相关联的集团受到损失。管理人员能够鉴别出这些联系是至关重要的，因为它可用来防止沟通的中断，并在利益冲突的集团之间出现误解和冲突之前起调节作用。第三种对危机管理非常有价值的，集团之间的角色是不属于任何一个集团的"独立者"。独立者是可以被管理者所利用的、独立性的重要源泉，但危险在于，在危机的高潮中，强有力的集团能够控制信息流通，并把人们的注意力从他们身上转移开。所以，管理人员应尽力把独立者一体化到组织管理过程中。实际上，通过提高独立者力量的基础或对独立者予以重视，管理人员可以把具有不同利益的竞争集团之间潜在的冲突最小化。

集团的危险

虽然在危机中集团可以发挥许多功能，他们也同样可能呈现出他们最危险的状态。例如，霍恩斯旦(1986)提醒人们，那种信奉"集团"而不是"个人"是创造力的源泉，以及和家庭一样，把成为集团的正式成员作为个人的最终需求的社会伦理，会对危机管理造成损害。以霍恩斯旦的观点来看，集团能产生一种特殊的、恶毒的、微妙的专制，这种专制能防碍沟通，使决策过程减慢，导致折衷的决策结果，压抑创造性和革新性。马希·埃特·奥尔(1978)也强调了集团对它的成员所施加的强大压力。他们调查足球流氓事件后总结出：集团的准则能使人们盲目地表现出一种部落行为，使他们的个性和社会活动范围常常受到抑制。珍妮斯(1988)把集团强调一致性和同意性的趋势称为"集团思想"。它的效果依赖于集团对它的成员的吸引力、自我巩固力、自我生存力、给予成员的利益、使它的过程简单化的能力、以及表达它的主导思想和价值的能力。挑战号航天飞机灾难能生动地说明集团思想的潜在危险。发射的前一天晚上,工程师清楚地知道预计发射时的温度低于安全温度,但迫于同僚们的压力而批准了发射。看起来,在有效的沟通,思想开阔,创造性和灵活性都非常重要的危机过程中,集团思想是最危险的。

组织上的等同性

和危机相关的社会结构的另一个方面是人们组织上的等同性。在一个组织中,如果两个人有一模一样的联系方式,他们就具有组织上的等同性。起初,人们认为这样的人在组织内起相同的作用,具有可替换性。然而,这种组织上等同的观点只考虑了两人之间内部作用模式上的相似性而忽略了人们个性的不同。这就是说,和不同人们之间的联系具有相同的模式使得人们之间具有了组织上的等同性。斯科特(1991)认为,这并不意味着他们充当同样的社会角色,并倡导使用"规则性等同性"的概念。

规则性等同性

两个人,如果他们以同样的方式和同样的人们相联系,则这两个人就有规则性等同性。规则性等同性的高低对危机管理者非常重要,因为,如果组织具有很高的规则性等同性,我们就有理由认为沟通和组织管理会更有效。这种集团成员间有共同的邻居,较短的沟通路线和较高级别的沟通性。

虽然看起来具有很高的规则性等同性的集团是我们所期望的,但他们极易受集团思想的影响。很清楚,社会关系的多样性对产生解决危机所需的创造性很重要。所以,为了在规则性等同性的高低和他们所鼓励的独立性之间进行权衡,危机管理者似乎需要走"绷索"。

集中性

组织的集中性是指信息集中在一个人或少数几个人周围的程度。集中度的概念对危机管理者很重要,因为大量的事实证明它和危机管理的效率紧密相关。里维特(1951)和肖(1954)发现,集中度的影响依赖于组织所面对的问题的特征,就像危机一样,如果问题具有复杂性和非常规性,就需要低集中度的结构来缓解信息超载的潜在危机。然而,敏特滋勃格(1976)发现在危机过程中,人们趋向于加紧控制,结果导致机能失调性行为。危机管理的一个似是而非的现象是:如果运用不当,集中管理能导致混乱,但混乱最终又能带来秩序。

所以,对于必须控制组织的信息在一个人或少数几个人周围的集中程度的工程管理者来说,集中度的概念是非常重要的。为了能把这点做得更好,了解现存的不同种类的集中度是非常重要的。弗里曼(1979)对这个领域内的这个问题进行了澄清。他把集中度分为集中度、紧密度和之间集中度,对于危机管理,每种集中度都有着截然不同的寓意。

集中度

集中度指组织内的人们作为信息的发送者和接受者的角色。一个充当相对较高的信息发送角色的人,对其他人来说是一个明显的信息源,处在一种"事情成堆"的位置上,是沟通网络内活跃性很高的人，而且是指令和领导关系的焦点。这些人通过提供组织所需的像它的命根子一样重要的信息来保证组织持续运行。从这个意义上说，组织对他们的依赖性很高。这就使他们处在一个强有力的地位，这一点在危机中，当人们对信息的需求量很高的情形下表现得尤为突出。相反，一个充当相对较高的信息接受者角色的人，对其他人来说是一个明显的信息的海洋，似乎在组织内充当着一个非常重要的信息存储和处理的角色，在危机过程中，它的地位举足轻重，因为这时会产生大量的、不同的信息，需要对之进行处理、转换和浓缩从而得到易管理的、有意义的和连续的信息。

之间集中度用来度量组织内一个人处在其他人之间的程度，反映他们充当"信息守门员"角色的程度，具有较高程度的之间集中度的人们有很重要的作用，因为他们能对在人们之间流通的信息进行操纵或者过滤。从这个意义上说，他们具有强大的力量，在网络中发挥着像阀门一样的作用，对保证信息流通的自由性和开放性具有重要的作用。从本质上说，这些人像胶水一样，把组织内的各个部分粘结在一起，而这个关键点上的薄弱环节可能会导致组织的崩溃。

所以，组织的之间集中度，是衡量人们不把信息处理当成是满足自己目标的手段的诚实性的标准，也是衡量人们处理经由他们手中的信息的能力的重要标准。在危机过程中，之间集中度受危机影响的程度被自然强化，因为高的赌注使人们更执著地去追求它们的利益，也因为在压力很大的同时又被信息所吞没，能使人们处理信息的能力大幅度的降低。

紧密集中度

如果人们被置于和组织中其他人距离很近的位置（用中间人的数量来衡量），这些人就具有很高的紧密集中度。一个人的紧密集中度反映他或她的独立程度，因为高的紧密集中度使人们难以在其他人不知道的情况下独立行事。相反的，具有高的紧密集中度的人们有直接监视和控制其他人的能力，也能迅速地将他们的观点基本上原模原样展现给其他人。在有极大压力的危机情况下，对管理者来说，他们代表着一个重要的信息流通渠道。

危机行为

在危机过程中，管理者必须控制人们之间信息流通的模式，因为这种模式决定着组织内信息流通的难易程度，从而决定了不确定性，误解性和由此而起的冲突性。在这一节，我们讨论危机中令人遗憾的，使人们的行为方式使得这一点很难做得的趋势。这种行为基本上由两种因素所致：危机时人们处理压力和紧张的困难以及他们处理危机所产生的巨大变动的困难。

心理的压力和紧张

从定义上说，危机是那种在极端压力下，需要采取具有独创性的办法来解决的潜在的严重事件。这就使被影响者感觉到一定程度的紧张和担忧———一种能导致积极和消极行为的条件。例如，当一些人认为这种感觉能产生一种能有效解决问题的决定时，另一些人指出它能导致可疑性并降低信息流通的有效性。产生这两种矛盾的解释的原因在于压力和紧张之间的区别。罗伯逊和库珀（1983）认为压力是作用于一个人身上的按某一特定的方式行事或取得某一特定结果的力量，它可能是不安和忧虑的源泉，但同时也可能是令人兴奋的，有挑战性的提高生产率的源泉。而紧张却只有消极的效果，因为它产生于一种对问题无法处理的无能状态，它会导致防御性和不适应性的行为。

紧张对危机管理结果的影响

根据乔治(1991)所说，紧张是一种"能对危机管理造成严重威胁的一般问题"(P.559)。和危机相关的紧张起源于：对以前所持观点的剧烈的挑战，打乱了正常的社会秩序以及所造成的自然方面的挑战。紧张也可起源于危机所造成的即刻显现出来或以后遗症形式显现出来的心理震撼。例如，工作场所的死亡事件就能引起这种类型的震撼。一个工人在工作场所死亡对组织的雇员们有很大的震撼力。然而，紧张的冲击所产生效果从来都是不一致的。身体上或思想上比较接近死者的人似乎会体验更难的处境。而且，在这样的危机中，只有组织中的高级领导阶层才有作出这种巨大决策的权力。这就意味着压力的重担会落在他们肩上，居于负有这种责任的位置上的人受这种紧张折磨的危险尤其大。

由紧张所导致的行为正好是处理危机所不必要的。赫曼(1963)指出因这种行为，可以导致人们丧失解决问题的注意力，不断增加决策中的错误，在探索备选的执行方案时表现出更大的刚性、恐惧、忧虑和撤退。斯图尔特(1983)发现人们紧张的表现包括焦虑、注意力广度缩小、旷工、生病、过激行为、冲动性行为、压抑、对风险的容忍度降低以及对其他人的不同意见的容忍度降低等。题·哈特(1993)认为，紧张还能增加人的不安全感和易受伤害感，且有可能使那些受影响者的自信心和自尊心下降。最后，在极端环境下，紧张不但可以严重的损害人们的心理健康而且可能提高人们心理上的易受伤害性和模棱两可性的趋势(乔治1991)。

从这个意义上说，管理者必须明白，危机的代价不光是自然的，身体上的，通过对雇员的伤害所造成的心理上的冲击也能使组织处于瘫痪状态。实际上，库纳(1996)指出，与紧张有关的机能丧失性赔偿占工人要求赔偿总额的14％，是平均身体伤害赔偿的两倍。很清楚，管理者必须对组织内所谓的"紧张点"给予特别的关注。为了减少潜在的制造问题的行为，给予占据这些紧张点位置的人们的个性和能力给予特别关注和大力支持是至关重要的。这个过程应该是一个延续的过程，应该延续到危机解决之后，因为，紧张所产生的冲击具有滞后性，并且，紧张点是处在不断的变动中的。

对付变更

危机不可避免的产生使人们不安于重大的社会，资金和自然方面的变化，因为它意味着对过去努力的放弃和对目前现状的威胁。这些常常会产生变更的抵抗力，这种抵抗力可以多种连续变化的，从消极的不同意到积极的对抗的形式出现。对抗的程度依赖于变更的程度，人们利益受损的程度，利益受到损失者所拥有的权力的状况，以及变更引入的方式。安索夫(1979)认为，虽然变更最终会导致抵抗力，它的出现可能会被危机内在的严重性所延误。例如，如果一种危机已经严重到威胁到组织的存亡了，对这种危机最初的反应可能是不顾各个不同集团的利益，集中精力对付危机以保证组织的生存，因为组织的生存是每一个人的利益所在。

冲突的发展

　　抵抗力或许是对变更自然的反应，存在于大多数组织内的利益冲突使人们的行为复杂化。变更对一方来说是威胁，而对另一方可能就是机遇。管理者可以用潜在的同盟者来支持那种必须贯彻的变更。管理者还必须处理潜在的收益方和受害方的紧张关系，因为这是冲突的源泉。

　　冲突是逐渐发展的，从一些简单的异议、争论、纠纷、有限度的小规模冲突逐渐升级到各方全力以付不惜血本的大规模冲突(菲利浦斯 1988)。危机本能的产生冲突的倾向使斯尼德(1972)把危机描绘成和平与战争之间的过渡地带，变迁的速度依赖于诸如对立集团之间的分歧，过去和现在的关系，对折衷的态度，以及谈判的组织方式等。因为谈判是最初和非正式的解决人们之间分歧的方法，对谈判过程的理解是危机管理战略的基础。通过很好的运用这个过程，应该能减小冲突发展的可能性并防止这些冲突朝着更正规、更昂贵、更暴露于公共眼目之中，更耗时的诸如采用仲裁或诉讼的解决办法的方向发展(CME 1997)。正如皮奈尔(1999)认为的那样，无论工程的复杂性和规模如何，冲突管理的技巧就像对灾难损失采取保险的措施一样。近来的两起施工纠纷案很好的阐述了这个观点。亚利桑那一个简单的价值 600000 美元的污水处理工程合同最终使原告得到 300000 美元的损失赔偿，而且双方都支付了 257000 美元的费用。在另一个复杂一点的案例中，律师的费用就超过了5 百万美元。

谈判过程

　　"谈判"是指把人们的利益、目标和期望之间的差异进行协调，达到一个共识。更精确地说，谈判就是"不同的集团之间为了分配稀缺的资源、金钱、地位和权力而进行的协商过程"(莫里 1981，P.113)。实际上，这个过程就是敌对双方通过争斗，试图一步一步地达成一种按照自己的利益重新分配资源的协议。在这种争斗中，就像国际象棋和扑克比赛一样，人们采用一系列的战术来达到目的，在建筑工程中，这种争斗可能是由复杂的人际关系网和组织间的相互作用力导致的。这是因为谈判者属于并代表不同的利益集团，这就决定了他们的态度和行为不但被他们自己的价值，而且被他们的业主的价值以及任何他所附属的非正式利益集团和联盟的价值所决定。实际上，有些业主在谈判桌上给谈判员决策的权力和自主权强加了许多限制条件，给快速解决问题造成了一定的困难。

谈判的策略

　　谈判过程的实质就是谈判者利用策略相互影响。罗杰(1991)认为人们谈判时采用的策略依赖于他们的"谈判准则"——他们自己的一套有关对手的信条，这种信条影响他们对对手信息的解释和反应。根据罗杰的观点，对谈判至关重要的信条与对手的目标，纠纷的动力学，以及谈判策略中强迫、协商和劝服的最优组合有关。在这个基础上，罗杰把谈判的准则分为四类：A、B、C、D。他们的特征见表5-1的描述，根据各类的不同特征，使用不同的策略。

战术上的失误和事故的逐渐升级

表 5-1 说明在谈判过程中，谈判员根据不同的信条选择不同的战术。令人遗憾的是，在危机的压力下，谈判员被迫在信息不完全的情况下做出决策，结果，如果决策失误，可能会无意中加速纠纷的升级。在国际关系领域，有许多可以说明这种危险的例子。例如，1941 年美国和日本的战争是由美国的石油禁运政策和其不可动摇的要求日本撤销其对亚洲的行政主权的政策所导致的。这把日本逼到了死角，别无选择，只能通过珍珠港事件，先发制人地发动了战争。近代 20 世纪 50 年代的南北朝鲜战争，20 世纪 80 年代的福尔克兰兹战争，20 世纪 90 年代的海湾战争都是因为决策失误而导致了战争的例子。在每种情况下，侵略者都给其对手一个既成事实，没有预料到对手反击的特征和强度。

表 5-1　谈判准则和策略(摘自罗杰 1991)

准则	信　条
A	**对手**:具有侵略性。**纠纷动力学**:只有国际范围内的战争是可能的。不需要多考虑对手的反应及其战争升级对它的冲击，任何(战争的)升级都是比较容易控制的。**策略**:公开性的侵略战争，既成事实或高度的强制性行为是解决纠纷的最好办法。谈判的成功取决于军事力量而不是外交策略
B	**对手**:更容易采用侵略性而不是防御性策略。**纠纷动力学**:只有非故意的战争升级的纠纷具有可控性。了解战争升级的动力学以便于避免失控点的出现是可能的。**策略**:一小步一小步逐渐升级的战争被看成是胆怯和软弱，这容易导致战争的升级。不坚定的表现是导致战争的普通原因 **B－1 型** **对手**:愿意也有能力利用任何软弱的表现。**纠纷动力学**:战争的升级被认为是由没能充分表达他将不惜任何代价保护自己的根本利益所致。**策略**:强迫性外交(例如:口头上威胁采取极端行为和发动全面战争)，吓唬是解决争端的最好方法。不使出最后威胁的一着是危险的 **B－2 型** **对手**:被看成是不可预测的。**纠纷动力学**:吓唬和威胁是危险的，因为他们可能无意地引发抵抗性的侵略反应。**策略**:使用有限的武力防止全面战争比威胁发动全面战争要好
C	**对手**:很难断定对手是侵略型的还是防御型的。**纠纷动力学**:两种战争升级的可能——没能表现出坚决果断，没能对可觉察出来的挑衅做出螺旋性上升的反应。有许多难以预料的战争升级的途径，很难避免滑坡，事先很难辨认出战争的边缘。**策略**:谨慎地根据当时的环境制定策略而不能采用自动化的方式。只有对部分纠纷的控制是可能的，采取威胁或其他武力的方法是危险的。小心行事，限制战争升级和折衷的方法比较实用。许诺而不兑现和欺骗是最好的可以用来操纵对手的方法
D	**对手**:认为对手处于防御状态。**纠纷动力学**:即使适当的使用强制性措施，如果不是不可能，纠纷的控制也是很成问题的。为了防止触发不可控制的战争升级，必须小心行事。**策略**:容忍和折衷是最好的解决问题的方法。所有努力的重点应放在防止导致谈判发生的时局上

南北朝鲜战争能很好的说明，即使具有很好的情报系统，预测对手将会做出什么反应的困难也是很大的，因为美国很快改变了它不参与的政策，转而支持南朝鲜。

就如狄克逊(1988)在他的军事不胜任的心理学分析中指出的那样，策略失误导致纠纷升级的危险日益增加，这就意味着，一旦开始，他们便不断的获得发展的动力，这是因为人们对其他人的看法变得越来越缺乏理性，越来越被情绪所左右。最可怕的一触即发的冲突的例子发生在 1962 年 10 月 25 日，当装备好的美国核轰炸机整齐的排列在跑道周围，准备和苏联作战时的情形。飞行员们被告知，在这种高度紧张的危机时刻，没有军事演习。

当一个军事基地的看守发现有一个人正趴在防护墙上时,他怀疑是苏联破坏者,就吹响了警笛,这个所谓的闯入者实际上是一个棕色的熊,但在一个基地上,错误的警报发出了,飞行员们被派遣到各自的飞行岗位上,完全相信一场核战争就要开始了。只有当基地指挥官认识到这是一个错误时,飞机才返回跑道没有起飞,避免了这次对苏联的核战争。

除了缺乏理性能导致纠纷外,不断增加的不可动摇性也是一个问题。随着不断增加的资源投资,人们折衷的意愿大大减小,越来越坚持自己的观点。在这种情况下,不计一切代价取得胜利变得越来越重要了,并且人们被卷入一种不断的螺旋型循环的冲突中不能自拔,这吞没了大量不该占有的资源。越南战争能很生动地说明这个观点。在这场战争中,军事指挥官们执行作战方针,耗费掉了美国 300 亿美元,从战略的角度来说,没有得到任何东西。这场战争导致 200 万人死亡,1300 万吨的炸药被消耗掉(是二战时数量的 6 倍多)。

冲突的动力——运用引诱而不是威胁

在冲突的解决过程中,集团之间通过协商或其他手段,迫使对方回到谈判桌上,接受符合他们利益的让步或协议。第三方也可通过支持其中一方,或者在他们中间进行调解,或者使用策略来影响谈判进程,保护自己的利益。试图影响对手的过程依赖于一系列的威胁和引诱。例如,在建筑工程中,威胁可以是扣留支付,引诱可以是抛掉另一个悬而未解的纠纷。在许多建筑工程中,使用威胁的几率远远大于引诱,然而,如果引诱能满足对手的需求并鼓励能转变谈判局势的互相款待,它将是一种非常有效的方法。1977 年印度国家主席 Anwar Sadat 访问耶路撒冷时的情形就是这样一个例子。访问中,Anwar Sadat 在接受以色列的地位问题上意外地作出了让步,期望他们能有所回报。这种做法的动机是把一个看来无法解决的冲突转变成一个新的、有建设性的、能够和平解决僵局的关系。这就像凯勒曼(1997)指出的那样,虽然从眼前看来,把重点放在积极的引诱上比放在消极的威胁上风险更大,但长期看来,它有潜在的更大的积极性。然而,要有效地运用积极的引诱,仅仅只为对手提供现成的回报或承诺是远远不够的,还必须提出能解决对手最根本的需求和恐惧而且是他们所愿意接受的互相款待的引诱方法。

令人遗憾的是,这个过程所需要的高度的理解,无私和信任随着冲突的升级和第三方的介入而快速消失。担任这个角色的人工作的一个很关键的方面就是促进相互之间消除疑虑,这可以由对双方很敏感的事实的确认,象征式的表示和建立信心等措施来达到。这个表示不需花费任何一方很大的代价。例如,它可能只是很简单地要求一方承认过去的错误,或同意会谈。这种表示在心理上对协商的进行奠定了重要的基础,即使它不能立即付诸行动。这是因为大多数的冲突都源于历史上一方对另一方的经历,真实性和合法性的谴责和否定。例如,在 Sadat 访问耶路撒冷开始时,Sadat 就做出了一个让对方谈判人员十分吃惊的举动:他同对方握手。以前的官员们拒绝这样做,表明阿拉伯人不接受以色列的合法地位以及他们的人民。然而,积极的鼓励,如果是真诚的和经过深思熟虑的,比用威胁来解决冲突有更大的好处,因为它为建立一个新的,建设性的关系奠定了基础。这个过程一旦开始,为了保持和发展这种友好的关系,各个集团都倾向于满足对方的期望。如果这种关系兴旺发展,对手们常常会用有难同当的方法来处理冲突,这样往往能达成一个富有成果的解决方案。

冲突作为一种积极的力量

在建筑业,用传统的眼光来看,冲突是一种应该避免的或不计代价来消灭的破坏力量。然而,从第一章我们可以看出,组织中的冲突是不可避免的,但经过有效的管理,它可能转变成有积极意义的因素。一个管理良好的冲突能使危机解决过程中的调查工作范围更广,还可充当累积的、本来还会隐藏下来的、紧张关系的释放阀。从这个意义上说来,不能把危机过程中潜在的冲突看成是完全破坏性的。然而,罗斯茂·埃特·奥尔(1999)发现建设性地管理冲突的技巧和态度在建筑业还是不存在的。从这个意义上说,对冲突积极性的鼓励看来还有些为时过早。然而,现在建筑业不计一切代价来减少施工中冲突的做法无论如何也是不合适的。这可能使建筑业丧失大量的机会成本,因为有效管理施工中的冲突可能会带来效益。从长远看来,一个更明智、更有益的方法应该是改变人们的态度,为积极的冲突管理打下基础。建筑业的问题不是冲突存在的必要性问题,而是如何管理冲突的问题。

危机过程中人们行为的阶段性

前面我们重点讨论了危机过程中人们可能有的行为的种类。然而,没有确定在危机的整个过程中,一定类型的行为是如何逐渐发展变化的。例如,西森和克拉克(1962)提出了一个三阶段的行为发展模型,即,冲击、反应和恢复阶段。在冲击阶段,人们对危机所做的处理是非常有限的。人们行为的目的只是为了生存,愚蠢的行为明显地能导致对个人以及对集团重大的损失。反应阶段是破坏性最大的阶段,这一阶段的特点是信息流通非常困难,人们的行为异常多变。这是一个损失估计阶段,充满了忧虑和混乱,人们的行为往往是非理性的和不合适的。组织过程中最主要的一个问题是把那些按自己的方法各行其是的不同的人们协调起来。最后,恢复阶段是对损害进行修复,返回正常工作轨道的开始。

芬克·埃特·奥尔(1971)提出了一个更详细的模型,阐明了一个可预言的行为变化模式。他认为,一开始,危机会产生一种使人迷失方向的效果,导致一种恐慌,无组织和混乱状态。当这种震撼的阶段被平息下来以后,人们的思想转入一种自我保护状态,从而进入了防御性撤退阶段,在这个阶段,人们想要做的就是保护自己的利益和维持现状。更进一步,随着人们趋向于保护他们的集团利益,人们间的关系内向化。令人遗憾的是,这种行为使现存的分歧更加深化,害怕失去控制,领导者们趋于使决策权和信息流通集中化。然而,这么做的效果仅仅是把组织分成了不同的派别,使得信息流通只留于形式,没有任何实际的意义。当危机不能通过这种方式来解决的趋势变得越来越明显时,就进入了一种承认阶段,人们进行自我检查,并承认相互之间的对立状态。在这个阶段中,心里的紧张和压力非常大,信息流通有沦为相互谴责和指控的危险,这可能把组织带回到防御性撤退阶段。然而,最终为了解决问题,人们会自动解决他们之间的分歧,进入一个更具建设性的适应和变化阶段。在极端环境下,这也许需要第三方的介入,其目的是寻找更好的能真正达到理解和分享信息的沟通途径。当这种情况出现时,领导们变得更加放松,也更加注重运用集体决策的方法了。再下来,人们进行相互之间联系更加密切的工作,抛开了那种代表早期阶段特征的机能性失调的行为。最终,集团之间的关系变得协调起来,组织再一次回到了正常的状态。

最后,西皮克和斯密斯(1993)提出了一个三阶段的模型。第一阶段是危机管理阶段,在这个阶段，组织文化使危机不断发展，到了无法忍受的地步时，一个触发事件会把组织推向以会聚和高活力水平为特点的操作阶段。在试图处理危机的过程中，随着信息流通复杂度的增加，混乱状态盛行。最终，组织进入到恢复策略不断运用的正规化阶段。

这些模型的价值不在于它对危机过程行为详细的描述上，而在于他们所描述的行为的动力学上。这说明危机管理策略应该和它想要控制的行为一样，是动态化的。

结　论

这一章讨论了在危机过程中人们的行为特征。所介绍的不同的原理将被用来分析以后各章中所列举的四个真实的工程危机管理案例。每个案例所收集的数据来源如下：以前工程人员所记录的有关危机前，危机中和危机后的情况，工程会议的记录，工程检查记录文件，以及对工程参与者的回访。他们既有趣又令人震惊，展现了典型建设工程的真实画面。

在继续本书的学习之前，必须指出构成以下所研究的案例基础的危机都是在人们记忆中最萧条的施工阶段出现的，这无疑影响了人们的行为。而且，所研究的案例没有描述引人注目的危机后的状况。该书是想通过对危机管理技巧更好的理解，从而达到帮助项目管理者避免这些灾难的目的。所研究的案例描述了四个工程危机的发展过程，这对以后许多同类工程的可行性是个极大的威胁。它们是许多工程生命期的一定阶段都经历过的典型的危机，虽然它们并不引人注目，但却是建设工程时间拖延和费用超支的主要原因。

第六章

案例研究 Ⅰ

简　介

接下来的四章是有些人可能不熟悉的专业方面的研究。例如，计量师(QS)负责工程各个阶段的预算和预算控制工作。在大多数工程中，顾问计量师代表委托人的利益，主承包商的计量师代表主承包商的利益。传统上，在工程的合同前期阶段，顾问计量师做出拟建工程按工程项目分类的工程量清单。该工程量清单由投标人标价，作为评标的基础。工程一旦开始，作为支付的依据。

驻地工程师可能是另一个不熟悉的概念。该人在施工过程中负责监控工地上的活动并定期的向建筑师汇报。实际上，虽然只有有限的合同权力，驻地工程师是建筑师在工地上的眼睛和耳朵。

工　程

该案例所涉及的工程是现存娱乐中心的扩建工程，该娱乐中心地处施工条件困难，受限制并与主要公路交界的地带。工程的主要承包商和所有的顾问工程师都是通过竞争性招标按最低合同报价确定下来的，而且碰巧他们都在最近刚完成的一个工程上共同工作过。在这个工程中，他们之间的关系已经变得紧张起来，而且在顾问工程师眼里，承包商以具有"索赔意识"而闻名。

危　机

在地基开挖过程中，主承包商碰到了没有预料到的问题，一个渐进性的危机开始了。在承包商看来，在邻近公路的这个地段，在地下室墙的施工过程中，永久性土方支护措施是必要的，但工程量清单中却只报了临时性土方支护的价格。承包商认为，计量师应该把永久性土方支护列入工程量清单的暂定金里，因而，他们有权得到额外支付。顾问工程师不同意。两极化的主张再加上承包商停止了关键线路上的活动导致了长达 10 个月的激烈纠纷，最终导致严重的工期延误和费用超支以及承包商工地施工队伍的全部替换。

危机管理过程叙述

以下是按时间顺序对危机管理过程进行的叙述。为了突出危机管理的动态性，把危机管理的活动划分成了不同的阶段。

承包人陈述了额外支付的索赔意向

在现场会议上，承包人的计量师陈述了对土方工程永久性支护额外支付的索赔意向。

并警告如果索赔得不到批准，受影响的区域将停工直到索赔批准为止。

承包商使用这一策略的理由是基于他对建筑师的不信任感。这种不信任感也延误了工程量清单差异通知单的发出，一段时间以来这种差异对承包商已经很明显了，但被承包商扣留了下来直到最后一分钟，以此来给顾问工程师施加压力以加快决策速度。承包商与顾问工程师的不信任是相互的。因为投标人特别低的投标报价，雄心勃勃的计划和出名的索赔意识，使得委托人的计量师对他们索赔的动机予以怀疑，而且以前投标人曾对顾问工程师过低的开挖单价表示过担忧。

顾问工程师拒绝承包人的索赔

建筑师正式拒绝了承包人额外支付的索赔，理由很简单，存在承包人所建议的永久性土方支护方案的替代方案，这种方案和原始工程量清单中的描述相符合。虽然顾问工程师还没有拟定该备选方案，他最初的策略就是先做一个"赤裸裸"的这个方案存在的陈述，其目的是"给承包商发送一个清晰的该索赔是无法容忍的信息"并且"测试承包商坚持该索赔的决心"。

顾问工程师建立反索赔例证

在等待承包商反应的同时，委托人的计量师和工程师建立了一个论证来反驳承包商所提议的永久性支护方案。委托人的计量师承认"指导工程师寻找替代方案，因为只要存在替代方案，不管多昂贵，就都已经包括在工程量清单之内了"。承包人的现场经理被告知了这个策略，因为工程师对被迫做出不合理的备选方案感到极不舒服，而且出于对承包人的同情心，向承包人泄了密。这暴露了顾问工程师队伍中的分裂现象，也更坚定了承包人索赔的决心。

委托人的项目经理对不断发展的纠纷保持警惕

委托人的项目经理对不断发展的纠纷保持警惕，但顾问工程师一再保证这种索赔已经被拒绝。

承包人使纠纷正式化

承包人的现场经理最终写信给建筑师，抱怨不断发展的纠纷，警告不断积累的延误，并威胁会采取进一步的行动。这是使纠纷正式化的关键的一步，然而，在下一次的现场会议上，并没有提供讨论这个问题的机会，建筑师只作了一个正式的陈述说"工程师正在对备选方案进行调查"。建筑师不对纠纷进行讨论的理由是这个会议不是一个合适的讨论会。承包人的项目经理给出了一个更加讽刺的能反应他们之间关系不断恶化的解释"（建筑师）没有特别地想把它列入会议议程中，他感到没有能力也不想谈论它。我要继续跟他讨论这件事情就没有意义了，因为如果你想和某人谈论一些事情，那你必须通过一种相当有建设性的方法来做"。承包人的现场经理再一次写信给建筑师，重申他关于工地上不断积累的延误的警告。

承包人绕过了建筑师

承包人的现场经理通过直接给工程师打电话讨论土方支护系统的备选方案问题而绕过了建筑师。工程师建议使用"地面冻结"法施工，但双方都认为把这种方法划归为符合原工程量清单中所描述的临时土方工程支护系统是不合理的。除了这一点，承包人的索赔在下一次会议上因为有地面冷冻方法这一可行的方案又一次被拒绝。

第二个问题出现

委托人第一次介入该事件，因为大雨破坏了因开挖而暴露在外又因纠纷而无人照管的主水管。这要求对主水管进行分流，用截水管为使用中的娱乐中心供水。

纠纷升级

承包人区域监督员的突然介入加剧了纠纷的升级。这是承包商驻地项目经理感到"关系已经恶化到如此程度以至于问题在工地这个级别已无法解决了"时所使用的孤注一掷的策略。区域监督员立刻给建筑师，委托人的项目经理打电话，且以诉讼相威胁。这使得顾问工程师口头上批准额外支付。

支付被拒绝

委托人的计量师请求委托人的项目经理正式批准额外支付，但被他拒绝了，他要求考虑所有的土方工程支护系统备选方案。他一直以为索赔已经被拒绝，非常吃惊这个纠纷还一直进行着。他还为被排除在以前的信息流通之外而感到恼火，并且怀疑他的伙伴顾问工程师是故意这么做的："据我所知我被告知索赔已经被拒绝，而这期间又没有任何变化。这是一个讽刺的观点，但是我想幕后一定一直进行着一些工作来掩盖它。我们应该反过来向顾问工程师收那些因为他们的失职而导致的额外费用。"

委托人的计量师所提供的证据无法使委托人的项目经理满意，他要求对事件的过程进行口头上的解释。这使得索赔的批准更加延误，而且使委托人的计量师受挫，因为他感到建筑师正试图从问题中解脱自己。

尽管委托人的计量师和工程师之间还在不断的进行着有关备选的土方工程支护方案的讨论，最后，委托人的项目经理还是批准了额外支付。

第三个问题变得明显起来了

一场大雨造成了未支护开挖部分的坍塌，使承包人已被批准的土方工程支护方案变得不再可行。经过各方之间一段时间相对激烈的交涉后，承包人提出了另一种较原支护方案更经济的土方工程支护方案。虽然委托人的计量师拒绝同意按重新商定的较承包人原始过低报价高得多的单价来计价而使承包人受益，支付单价还是以很和睦的方式得到了认可。

承包人第二次对损失、费用及工期延误进行索赔

承包人准备以索赔批准的延误来进行第二次对损失、费用及工期延误提出索赔。这点已经计划了一段时间了，因怕伤及到原始索赔，一直没有发出。

建筑师不受理索赔

建筑师对承包商的第二次索赔的最初反应是不去理会它，这使得承包人的计量师把该索赔又提出了一次。除了在接下来的一次工地会议上宣布了他的拒绝令以外，建筑师还是没有做出正式的反应。没有讨论的机会也没有给出理由。建筑师解释道："在我眼里所有的问题已经解决了，他们除了不断地一再提出新的要求外不会再做别的，如此等等，这种状态会一直持续到工程结束，到最后结算，然后，他们才会离开"。委托人的项目经理抱怨因承包人做出索赔在时间上的延误，使得工程进度的监控工作异常困难："也许我有点玩世不恭，但我确实感觉到，问题被刻意地压制下来，以便他将来能隆隆做响，使人们知道确实发生了一些事情"这使得这次会议变得更加紧张。这种抱怨又引来承包人计量师防御性的反应，他坚持说按合同的规定，他们只负责报告现存的问题，没有义务通知潜在的问题。

第二次索赔被正式拒绝

没有详细的解释，建筑师正式拒绝了承包商的第二次索赔。两个月后，承包人区域监督员再一次介入。这是由于建筑师写信给承包商的总经理抱怨他们施工队伍的"非专业性行为"。这在承包人区域监督员和建筑师之间引起了一场激烈的争论。

僵局的打断

承包人的项目经理再一次给建筑师写信，要求对第二次索赔的拒绝做出解释。建筑师即刻将信的内容传达给了委托人的项目经理，委托人的项目经理即刻联系承包商的项目经理并承诺立刻会有所行动。委托人的项目经理又一次没有意识到进行中的危机，委托人的计量师也是如此，直到他和承包人的现场经理的一次与本纠纷无关的交谈中才有所发现。在接下来的两次会议上，第二次索赔被讨论过，但由于对工期延误的程度没能达成一致而没有什么进展。

承包人区域监督员第二次介入

承包人的区域监督员又一次介入，给委托人的项目经理写信抱怨进行中的索赔。委托人的项目经理给委托人的计量师写信，对问题只能解决到这种程度表示遗憾。这促使顾问工程师们举行会议并建议对该工程中未解决的索赔采用一揽子的方法进行解决。这是损害限制策略的应用："过去的一切一笔购销，留点面子好进行下一阶段的工作"。越来越关注这个问题的委托人催促着问题的解决方案，一揽子的解决方法就被在会议上提了出来。这种方案得到了不确定的回应，因为本来想控制局势的承包人的区域监督员，已经把决策权从承包人的手里交了出去。

危机的解决

最终，委托人的计量师与承包人的计量师对第二次索赔进行了评估，协商出了一个可接受的方案，并同意对工程中未解决的索赔采用一揽子的解决方案来解决，这样，第二次索赔就被委托人正式的接受和批准了，工程的工期也相应的延伸了。

行为阶段

这一个渐进的危机历时大约 10 个月，耗费了大量的资源、时间和精力，危机所导致的正式会议 29 次，电话联系 68 次，来往信件 42 封。还有多次非正式会议没有计算。

最原始的有关土方开挖支护问题的危机具体在哪一点开始已经不是很确定了，但可以肯定地说它不应该导致一场危机，但后来，它确实给工程的可行性带来了严重的威胁，不但是费用的增加和工期的拖延，而且严重损害了相互之间的关系。这一点的证明就是承包商在第二期的工程施工过程中对施工队伍中的大部分人员进行了更换，因为他们之间的关系已经恶化到了这样一种地步，以至于无法再和顾问工程师一起有效地进行工作。

接下来的部分讨论危机过程中行为的主要阶段，解释关系的恶化是什么时候出现的，又是怎样出现的。

第一阶段

在危机的早期，很少能觉察出危机发展的动力。沟通过程中的特点是存在一种反对和对抗的意识。这体现在承包商决心要得到他们认为按照合同他们应该得到的索赔，而顾问工程师却拒绝同意。这个过程也有很高的策略性。承包商停止了存在土方开挖支护问题的工作段的施工，顾问工程师称承包商在吓唬人。在顾问工程师"松散结合"的队伍中，建筑师试图从危机中解脱开来，委托人的计量师迫使工程师寻找土方支护方案的替代方案，这些都是运用策略的体现。承包人反击的方法是表示出索赔的意向及对工地延误的警告。接下来，顾问工程师在做出反应时采用了拖延的策略，最终，第二次直率地拒绝了承包人的索赔。总的说来，这种行为导致了一个充满挫败，忧虑和对抗的阶段。这体现在人们的沟通模式上，其特点是：集团很多，他们之间的沟通却很少。如图 6-1 所示，每个集团用一个圆圈表示，圆圈线的粗细代表该集团与周围集团之间相互作用的平均次数。这是他们相对力量和内聚力的指示。连接集团之间的线表示沟通路线，它们的粗细根据沟通的频率而变化。这是集团之间联系强度的指示。

图 6-1 表示出了三个有联系的集团和两个孤立的集团。从被相对孤立起来的委托人的项目经理可以看出他被排除在围绕索赔的协商之外。他的错误在于仅仅依赖建筑师作为他和工程队联系的唯一路径，这就使得他特别易受建筑师这种在经济上有特权的既得利益集团的影响，由建筑师不愿把问题公开化这一点可以明显的反应出这个问题。非常明显的是，建筑师和委托人的计量师分属不同的集团，这种结构特点支持建筑师从问题中开脱自己。虽然建筑师和委托人的计量师分属两个集团，但他们之间确实有非常密切的联系，建筑师主要充当一个信息接受者的角色，依靠委托人的计量师进行反应协调工作。实际上，和承包商的驻地项目经理一起作为工程上最强大的集团的建筑师，似乎在利用委托人计量师的建议在顾问工程师和承包商之间起着一种重要的沟通作用。这使他拥有控制时局的能力却又可以不直接参与其中。另一点，工程师是他所在集团里力量最弱的一个成员，只以信息接受者的角色与委托人的计量师联系。这一点由他被迫建立承包商所提土方开挖支护方案的备选方案可以得到验证。然而，他同建筑师所属集团内的承包人现场经理的紧密联系使得他对承包人的处境产生了同情心，最终使他向承包人透漏信息，这把承包人和建筑师之间的信息差异又给等同了起来，所以，削弱了建筑师在谈判中的地位。

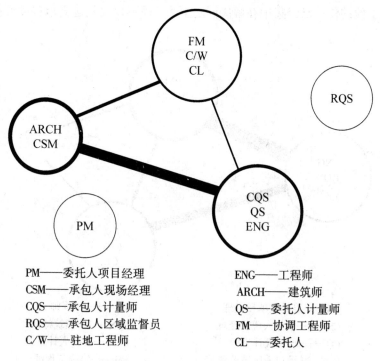

图 6-1　第一阶段集团间联系模型

对于信息流通的集中度来说，这个案例里没有明显的信息"源"与信息"海"，所以在这一阶段也就没有明显的领导核心。然而，建筑师和委托人的计量师占据着主要的信息守门员的位置，因此，对信息流通有着举足轻重的控制作用。这使得危机管理过程依赖于他们与承包商之间的关系，在这个案例中，他们之间关系的特点是互相的怀疑和不信任。实际上，似乎最初阶段信息流通的结构模式是造成危机管理过程易受组织内几个关键成员之间不良关系影响，进而造成组织无效率的重要原因。

第二阶段

和第一阶段相比，第二阶段一开始危机发展的动量就骤然增高。其原因如下：承包人区域监督员的突然介入，危机的升级，更过分的策略的突然采用和更情绪化的表现。为了对这种情况做出反应，顾问工程师的策略由第一阶段的反对和压抑变为第二阶段的更关心问题的解决。对立的局面缓和了，参与各方都表现出了更多的忍让，对承包商的索赔问题进行了更高级别的讨论。实际上，承包人区域监督员的干预使危机发展进入了一个更富有成效的、互相协作的阶段，在那儿，公开讨论代替了代表第一阶段主要特征的操纵性、强迫性的策略。

总的说来，这些条件使得人们的情绪化、受挫感和忧虑感逐渐降低，这体现在工程参与各方富有成效的沟通方式上。如图 6-2 所示，该图表明，委托人的项目经理连同建筑师和委托人的计量师位于工程中最强大的集团内。委托人的项目经理对工程更深入的参与是出于他对承包人区域监督员干预工程而导致的危机突然升级的一种防御性反应。工程师现在和承包人的现场经理及承包人的区域监督员在一个集团内，他从顾问工程师的集团内分离出来反应了他的作用已经集中在解决问题上了，而不仅仅是建立承包商开挖支护方案的替代方案。

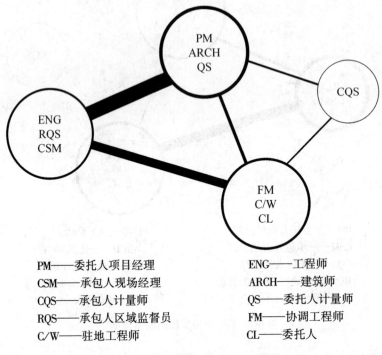

PM——委托人项目经理　　　　　　　ENG——工程师
CSM——承包人现场经理　　　　　　　ARCH——建筑师
CQS——承包人计量师　　　　　　　　QS——委托人计量师
RQS——承包人区域监督员　　　　　　FM——协调工程师
C/W——驻地工程师　　　　　　　　　CL——委托人

图 6-2　第二阶段集团间联系模型

和第一阶段对比最明显的一个特点就是人们之间高级别的直接接触和人们之间信息交流高级别的等同性。这表明类似信息普遍的可获得性和人们在协商中对对方处境充分的理解。在第一阶段，冲突的利益使得人们趋向于保护他们的信息源，从而引起混乱、误解、受挫和不信任。

除了更加直接和开放外，信息也更加集中于几个特定的人之间，这表明联系更加紧密的团队已经形成。处于最中心位置的人是承包人的现场经理和委托人的计量师，他们在纠纷处理中处于主导地位。相反的，建筑师的集中度较第一阶段有所下降，证明了建筑师依然希望委托人的计量师能承担起对问题的责任。信息流通守门员结构和第一阶段相似，但它对信息流通没有反作用，因为顾问工程师和承包商都采取了更积极的态度。

第三阶段

第三阶段恰好与承包人的第二次索赔同时发生，同第二阶段相比，它的特点是前进的动量骤减。导致这种结果的绝大部分原因是建筑师的不理会策略，这促使承包商做出了如下的反应：警告延误情况，威胁，使出使危机升级的最后一招——让承包人区域监督员再一次进行干涉。

这种不断增加的分裂和对立反应在组织上，就是组织由两个结合松散的集团控制，其中一个由建筑师和承包人的现场经理组成，另一个由协调工程师和驻地工程师组成，如图6-3所示，后者的主要任务是解决主水管坍塌的技术问题，前者的主要任务是解决承包人的第二次索赔问题。

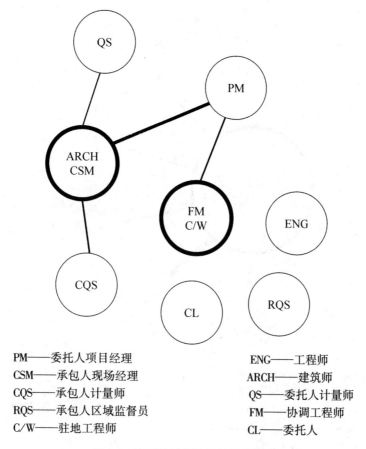

PM——委托人项目经理　　　　　　　　ENG——工程师
CSM——承包人现场经理　　　　　　　　ARCH——建筑师
CQS——承包人计量师　　　　　　　　　 QS——委托人计量师
RQS——承包人区域监督员　　　　　　　 FM——协调工程师
C/W——驻地工程师　　　　　　　　　　 CL——委托人

图 6-3　第三阶段集团间的联系模型

在这一阶段，信息流不断的集中在建筑师和承包人的现场经理周围，表明他们比项目中的其他成员都更明白发展中的纠纷。这种普遍的不理会不断发展的纠纷的做法被信息流通系统内扮演守门员角色的，除了建筑师和承包人的现场经理以外的人们给加剧了。这使得他们有相当的能力控制人们之间的信息流，使得危机管理过程易受到他们之间不良关系的影响。和第一阶段很相似，似乎这个阶段所形成的作为这个阶段特点的信息流通的结构模式对系统缺乏前进的动力和尖锐的纠纷有很重要的影响。

第四阶段

同第三阶段相比，最后一阶段行为的特点是：前进的动力骤增，合作的，折衷的和支持的气氛不断增加。这是由承包人区域监督员的第二次干预引起的，是专门用来打破围绕承包人索赔所形成的僵局的策略。在解决问题的过程中更注意使用公开讨论和协商的办法，这反应在人们采用更平静的，更知足的和不许空头愿望的信息交流方式上。信息流通中的分裂现象也大大缓解，表现在只有一个起主导作用的集团，该集团由建筑师，委托人的计量师，承包人的计量师，以及委托人的项目经理组成。如图 6-4。

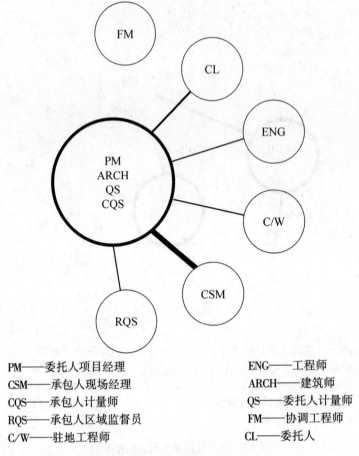

PM——委托人项目经理　　　　　　　ENG——工程师

CSM——承包人现场经理　　　　　　　ARCH——建筑师

CQS——承包人计量师　　　　　　　　QS——委托人计量师

RQS——承包人区域监督员　　　　　　FM——协调工程师

C/W——驻地工程师　　　　　　　　　CL——委托人

图 6-4　第四阶段集团间的联系模型

　　从图 6-4 可以看出，一个联系紧密的集团控制着危机管理过程的最后一个阶段，密切合作，为共同目标而奋斗。虽然承包商的现场经理被从上述集团中分离了出来，但他和该集团之间依然有着非常密切的联系。

　　这个阶段的主角是承包人的计量师，委托人的项目经理，建筑师和委托人的计量师。这反应出在前三阶段所形成的承包商、顾问工程师之间的对立已经被打破，而且建筑师也为问题的解决注入了大量的精力。和第三阶段比较起来，这个阶段建筑师在信息发放方面起着主导的作用，预示着他保持沉默的策略阶段已经结束，进入了尽力推动过程的发展，得出最后结论的阶段。

　　一个非常有趣的变化就是委托人的项目经理移向具有更高"之间集中度"的位置，这使得他能够对危机管理过程发挥更大的控制作用。实际上，他自己充当着承包人信息沟通的备选路径，从而克服了第三阶段中承包人现场经理和建筑师之间不良关系所带来的主要不良后果。

　　最后，和第三阶段再做进一步的比较可以得出，人们在信息沟通网络中的等同性也大为提高。这预示着一个富有效率的广泛的信息沟通阶段的到来，它能使人们对问题建立一种共同的谅解从而得出大家都同意的解决方案。总的说来，比起第三阶段，这种沟通模式使人们之间的信息交流更富效率，使人们的活动更富积极性。

结 论

结论部分采用图 3-1 的危机管理模式，来讨论本案例过程中危机管理的效率。

这个危机是因为没有妥善管理系统内自己产生的相对比较简单的问题而导致的。导致该危机的问题在系统内潜伏了相当一段时间，是由于构建工程量清单时的错误引起的。虽然承包人意识到这个问题已经有好长一段时间了，但因为和建筑师之间的冲突和内在的对建筑师的不信任感，使他拖延对发现的问题发出通知，其理由是把发出通知拖延到最后一分钟，能使建筑师所做决策有利于他们的可能性增大。

所以，早期的无效率性不像表面上给人的感觉那样，好像是由监控问题引起的，而是由监控员和比较员之间利益冲突而导致的不良的信息流通系统引起的。当承包人一旦提出了存在的问题，作为比较员的顾问工程师认为那个问题是承包商自己的问题。实际上，他们试图把危机管理过程终止在它刚刚出现的阶段，迫使工程队伍返回到原来的监控模式上。这一系列事件可以用图 6-5 描述。

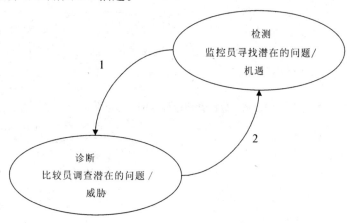

图 6-5　最初终止危机管理过程的尝试

这种策略属于一种由自身利益所驱动的、用来防止问题出现的自我保护机制，把承包商的警告称为吓唬，测试承包商的决心，并反过来又把过失压到承包商的肩上。实际上，通过既作为比较员又作为决策者，顾问工程师是想把问题限制在他们自己的权力范围内。事实上，为了防止引起由高级决策机构做出决策的必要，顾问工程师努力在委托人的项目经理面前隐藏问题。为了加强这种策略的效果，他们变得更加内向，给集团特别是工程师强加了一种集团准则，从他们自己的观点，给问题下了一个很有偏见的定义。

面对日益两极化的态度，承包人求助于威胁顾问工程师工期拖延和纠纷升级的强制性策略。虽然这种纠纷升级策略使他们的索赔成功引起了人们的注意，顾问工程师却做出了一个超越他权限的决策。这虽然使短期紧张关系得到了缓和，长期的紧张关系却又产生了，因为在这件事上有决策权的委托人的项目经理拒绝这样做。在批准顾问工程师的决策前，委托人的项目经理坚持要评估替代的土方开挖支护方案，这种做法把危机管理过程又推向了诊断阶段，延长了这个过程并使每一个相关的人都有一种受挫感。

这一系列事件可以用图 6-6 描述，其中，点线记录了危机管理过程前一阶段的活动。

委托人的项目经理最终批准了索赔，但因采用引起纠纷的土方开挖支护方案进行施工

的土方开挖部分坍塌，使得已批准的索赔变成无关的事件了，把危机管理过程又推向解决
新问题的诊断阶段。这一系列事件可以用图 6-7 描述。

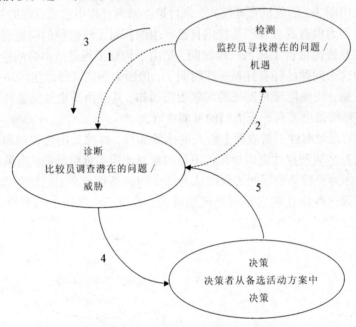

图 6-6　危机管理过程返回到诊断阶段

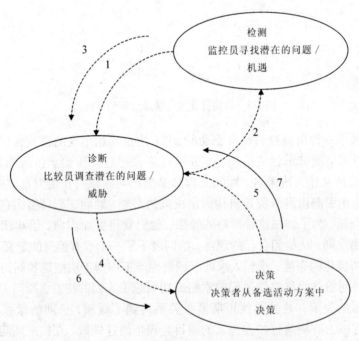

图 6-7　危机管理过程再一次返回到诊断阶段

　　在这一点上，一个似是而非的现象出现了，这种突然的亚危机使工程队内各方的利益
暂时的一致起来而且增强了各方的凝聚力，因为承包商提出了一个造价较低的土方开挖支

护方案，并及时得到了顾问工程师的批准。这一系列事件可以用图 6-8 描述。

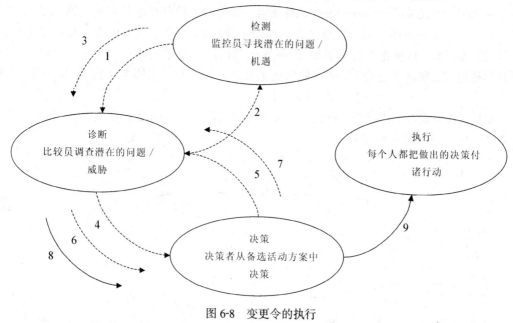

图 6-8　变更令的执行

　　到目前为止，图 3-1 所描述的危机管理过程并不是一个平滑的循环过程，而是一个相当没有效率的过程。特别是在不同的危机管理阶段，危机管理过程有明显的重复性和拖延性。这种现象一直延续的原因是，在变更的土方开挖支护方案执行过程中，承包人要求延长工期的第二次索赔把危机管理过程又推回到第二个循环周期中。这一系列事件可以用图 6-9 描述。

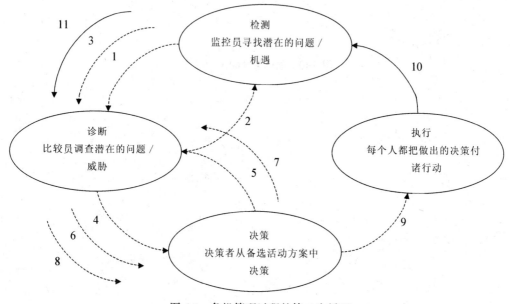

图 6-9　危机管理过程的第二次循环

　　第二个循环过程是第一个循环过程低效率的直接结果。承包人检测到这种延误已经有一段时间了，但就像第一循环中那样，对顾问工程师的不信任感使他们拖延通知发出的时间。另一个与第一循环相似的特点是建筑师用防御性的、不愿意接受问题的态度来进行接下来的诊断过程。这使得挫折感增加，最终导致危机过程的第二次升级。这又导致了一次新的诊断过程，在这个过程中，所有的问题都被那些既得利益集团考虑到他们的解决方案中了。

　　最后，各种观点汇集起来，承包人的索赔被批准了，工程的完工日期也被延伸了。这一系列事件可以用图 6-10 描述。

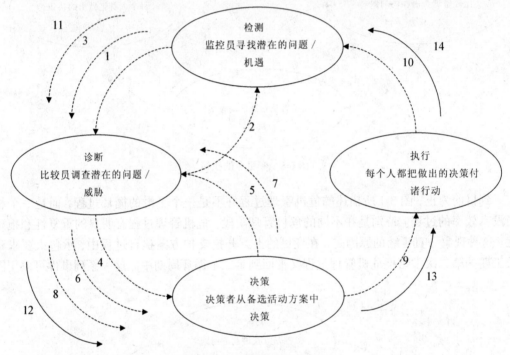

图 6-10　危机管理的执行过程

第七章

案例研究 II

工　程

这个工程是一个有关博物馆的建设工程。承包商将该工程看作是对他们进入这个地区建筑市场具有重要战略意义的工程。

危　机

当工程即将开始时，一项将一个供 8 人乘坐的电梯纳入原设计文件的决定带来了突然的危机。该决定的起因是有人抱怨原计划内没有考虑到为残疾人提供便利的设施。该决定对设计和计划有很大的影响，并且，因为决定得比较晚，留给工程队的执行时间就非常有限。

危机管理过程叙述

保证工程继续进行

由于建筑师没有参与原设计过程，这种危机对他来说困难和挫折尤为明显。他不完全熟悉设计文件，而且对必须来替别人改正错误感到有些忿忿不满。再说，当问题被明确提出来时，他已经着手给主承包商发招标文件了，而这些文件则必须根据可能要增加的电梯快速加以变更。当他和当地政府协商，拟采用其它方法来解决残疾人的进出问题没有被批准时，他决定在工程量清单中加入一笔暂定金，用来支付这套 8 人电梯的费用。在一个周内，委托人就正式批准了这笔费用，但电梯是否纳入原设计文件的批复却被搁置了起来，必须等来年的财政预算明确以后才能决定。

做出决定

5 个月以后，委托人联系到建筑师并确认电梯应纳入原设计文件中。主承包商已经准备上场了，但建筑物的重新设计工作还没有任何进展。现在建筑师面临的最大的问题就是大量的重新设计工作，时间的限制以及尽快的确定电梯分包商。

1 周以内，建筑师给 4 个电梯分包商发了招标文件，在开工前的会议上，建筑师向得标的主承包商宣布了纳入 8 人电梯的计划。最初的震惊和消遣之后，未来的现场经理要求发放设计图纸。建筑师指出，修正后的图纸暂时还没有，他将尽最大可能提供。建筑师对设计信息缺乏的解释是"纳入电梯的计划取决于预算限额，在这种压力下，哪怕仅仅只有万分之一的可能会给工程带来伤害，你都不能催促设计工作的进度。"

现场经理回忆到，"第二周我就上场了，但我不敢开始做任何事情。我就是不知道到底发生了什么事情……后来我们才发现，建筑师得知要纳入电梯计划已经有一段时间了。如果他直接告诉我们，我们可能会好好地检查这个计划。"虽然纳入电梯计划对承包商来说是个意外，对机电工程师来(M&E)说却不是。他是原设计组的一员，并且曾经提醒过可能需要考虑一部电梯："他们就是不理会我提的问题，于是我想'它是你的问题，而不是我的问题'，当然他们得到恶报了，不是吗？它是我的问题。迫于时间的压力，而且他们也知道，再怎么他们也不会参与到施工过程中去，于是他们便放过了这个问题。"

电梯的位置决定了

开工前会议的后一天，电梯在建筑物中的位置就被确定了下来。

现场开工

现场的基础施工已经开始了，现场经理与驻地工程师就信息匮乏问题，特别是电梯基坑位置问题进行了数次正式的讨论，驻地工程师将这些问题传达给了建筑师并解释到"围绕现场上的这些问题，现场经理面对着一大堆麻烦"。

提供的图纸中指出了电梯基坑的位置

在电梯基坑位置得到同意的一个月后，有关电梯基坑尺寸和位置的信息就以传真方式发给了承包商。电梯位于建筑物的中间位置，因为从工地进出电梯口只有一条通道，已完工的地基部分就必须回填，以便开挖工作者能通过它到达电梯基坑位置。这个信息一直被扣留着以防电梯位置有所变更，并且因为建筑师喜欢发放一个完整的信息包而不是零散的"信息条"，建筑师认为："我想在我愿意开始的时候再开始，在信息不完整时，我不会发放图纸，这样做的目的是为了防止以后会发生更多的变更。"然而，驻地工程师和现场经理对建筑师这种极为正规化的、缺乏灵活性的发放信息的做法感到极为恼火，并指出这样做给工程带来了不必要的损害，他们说："建筑师喜欢照本宣科，这在某些方面是好的，但当你需要信息时，就会引起很多麻烦，因为我们必须保证工地的正常运转。"

电梯分包商确定了

建筑师收到了电梯分包商们送来的标书，并且和报价最低的分包商就合同问题进行谈判。

信息持续匮乏

现场经理继续表示出对现场工作进度的关注和对修正后图纸的迫切需要。

电梯基坑部分的结构工程图纸发放

在现场经理和驻地工程师一再的要求下，发放了修正后的电梯基坑位置和邻近部分基础的结构工程图纸。建筑师继续和未来的电梯分包商协商，但分包协议中有关违约罚金条款出现了问题。这耽误了分包商正式的指定，也使得主承包商和分包商之间再没有任何接触。

第二次危机

最终，解决了合同问题以后，未来的电梯分包商参观了工地并注意到所挖的基坑根本无法放置招标文件中定义的电梯。因为电梯分包商没有一种标准的、能和基本完成的、所开挖的基坑相配的电梯，这使得形势更加恶化。同一天，工程师和驻地工程师对电梯基坑的深度表示关注，因为它对周围部分的基础有影响。

接下来的讨论使得重新设计工作得以继续进行，建筑师在选择电梯分包商以前就不准确地估计了一下电梯的尺寸。所有的顾问设计工程师都以此为基础对他们的设计文件进行了修改，现在，包括承包商在内，他们又都面临着一个大量的"重新再重新"工作，来适应电梯分包商所使用电梯的设计和规范。

为此专门召开了一次紧急会议，会上大家对这个问题表示普遍的关注。然而，对建筑师的困境，人们也表示出一定程度的敏感和同情，幽默在缓解人们之间紧张关系方面扮演了很重要的角色。利用这种局势，主承包商表现出了合作和容忍，建议使用另外一个临时的现场组织方案以缓解建筑师的压力："我们没想要额外支付，我们只想拿到图纸然后开始施工。我们和您一样想完成一个成功的工程，所以我们尽我们最大的努力来提供帮助。工程正常运行，现场经理有能力重新组织现场工作以便减少工期延误对我们来说至关重要。我们没有延误工期是因为我们不想延误，如果狠心一些，我们就会带来真正的麻烦。"这种灵活的做法和良好的意愿深深的感动了建筑师："很久以来，这是我遇到的最好的承包商了，无论在工地还是在办公室你所接触到的都是一些快乐的人们。我刚有过一次不愉快的工作经历，他们重树了我对承包商的信心。"

定制一台电梯

在另一次紧急召开的会议上，建筑师、现场经理和电梯分包商决定考虑使用一台定制的电梯。建筑师和分包商协商了一个在原始暂定金范围之内的电梯价格，这就意味着原来的预算限额并没有被突破。

正式指定电梯分包商

在没有正式指定以前，电梯分包商所做的所有工作都只是建立在一个良好的愿望上。正式指定电梯分包商以后，建筑师指示主承包商和分包商就细节问题进行讨论。同时，应承包商的要求，建筑师承诺将发出"变更令"将电梯的费用包括进去。现场经理再一次强调他们急需新定制的电梯说明书和电梯基坑设计图。

新定制的电梯基坑设计图发出

建筑师将电梯分包商的电梯说明书、设计图和合同条件都发给了主承包商。同样的东西也发给了机电工程师，并要求他们紧急修改机电设计图纸。机电工程师回忆起了他当时的恼火："他似乎没有认识到他一张图纸的变更会导致我们十张图纸的变更。"

更进一步的信息匮乏

在下一个月的现场会议上，承包商对变更令和机电图纸没有发出表示关注。在一种容忍和充满幽默感的环境里，承包商重申了这件事情的紧迫性。在紧接着的 3 周内，现场经理，承包人的计量师，建筑师和驻地工程师之间就尚未完成但现场却迫切需要的机电图纸进行了无数次电话和会议交流。最终，机电工程师将修改后的图纸交给了建筑师，在同一天，建筑师就将图纸发给了承包人。承包人的计量师继续表示对未颁布的变更令的关注，一个月后，建筑师终于颁布了它。"如果我们能早点得到变更令，我们心里也就踏实了，但这是建筑师喜欢的工作方式。"

行为阶段

对这个突然危机的反应历时大约 9 个月，耗费了大量的资源，时间和精力，危机所导致的正式会议 33 次，电话联系 27 次，来往信件 61 封。还有多次非正式会议没有计算。

和第六章所描述的危机的不同之处在于这个危机的行为没有明显的可辨认的阶段性。在整个过程中，主要问题是信息的管理而不是纠纷的处理，主要的压力都落在了建筑师的肩上。实际上，现场发生的所有的事情都能证明建筑师没能按要求提供所需的信息。他用一种"反应模式"来操纵信息，即：间歇式的大量的提供信息而不是连续不断的提供信息，而且他时常"追赶"信息的需求而不是领着它走。这其中大部分原因是委托人拖延对电梯计划的批准，使得建筑师忽视了位于招标和施工之间的重新设计的时间要求。这一次机会的错失，使得危机更加复杂化，因为施工过程不断地被信息匮乏所困扰。这给承包商造成了相当程度的不确定性，受挫感和组织上的不便利性，并且也考验了工程中人们之间的相互关系。

承包商的现场经理是该工程的救星，对建筑师经常性提供信息的延误，他的补偿方法是不断地要求信息供给。虽然建筑师很少应承包商的要求立即提供信息，但他却有足够的敏感度及时地提供信息以防具有伤害性的紧张关系的积累。

尽管存在信息供给方面的问题，但却有一种普遍存在的解决危机的承诺，随着危机的发展，受影响的人们之间出现了一种互相支持，互相谅解的氛围。这一点在电梯基坑的尺寸差异被发现后体现的最为明显，这个问题本来可以产生一场潜在的爆炸性的氛围，然而，这种亚危机非但没有破坏反而加强了人们之间的关系，因为人们用这个机会来证明对彼此之间以及对工程最后成功所做的承诺。几乎可以肯定，承包商决心要给这个新的、可能有利可赚的委托人留一个好印象的做法是他在危机中很少利用机会谋利和发生冲突的主要原因。再者，参与工程的很多人员都已经接近退休年龄，有过这方面的经验，能够有意识的控制情绪，保持平静和理智，冷静地处理危机，而不是制造恐慌、反复无常的环境。

在这个危机过程中，信息流通主要被两个集团控制着，见图 7-1。

从图 7-1 可以看出，最强大的集团是由现场经理，建筑师和驻地工程师组成的。在这个集团内，驻地工程师在信息沟通中起着一种重要的桥梁作用，在建筑师和现场经理之间又起着一种"缓冲器"的作用。这把在这种紧张的、具有潜在的爆炸性的危机的环境里冲突发生的可能性降到了最低。

虽然建筑师，驻地工程师和现场经理在工作中密切合作，但建筑师还是居于信息流通的中心位置，这就意味着没有竞争性的信息源和理解危机特征时很高的连贯性。令人遗憾的是，建筑师作为信息流通集中点的问题之一就是其他人都依赖于他，这使得危机管理过程极易受他既得利益和他处理加诸于他身上的极端压力的能力的影响。虽然没有事实能证明建筑师利用操纵信息的便利为自己谋利益，但事实却的确能证明建筑师对加诸于他身上的信息需求越来越无力应付。他处理这种信息过载的方法就是采用不断疏远的，正式的和不灵活的管理模式，这只能把问题更加复杂化，并引起更大的压力。结果给承包商造成了相当程度的不确定性和受挫折感。在这种压力转为冲突之前，承包商起了重要的缓和作用，对于建筑师不能及时提供信息，承包商的做法就是不断地向他催促、索取信息，当他没有能力处理时，承包商就对现场进行了重新组织。

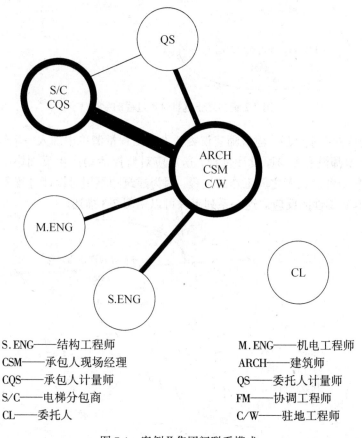

S. ENG——结构工程师   M. ENG——机电工程师
CSM——承包人现场经理   ARCH——建筑师
CQS——承包人计量师   QS——委托人计量师
S/C——电梯分包商   FM——协调工程师
CL——委托人   C/W——驻地工程师

图 7-1 案例Ⅱ集团间联系模式

结 论

结论部分采用图 3-1 的危机管理模式，来讨论本案例过程中危机管理的效率。

这个危机起源于设计阶段的一个问题，这个问题由于时间压力及设计和施工阶段人员的变动而被忽视。人员的变动使得施工阶段的设计队伍对潜在的问题反应不敏感，这意味着电梯遗漏问题被再次较晚地检查出来，并不是组织对环境认真监控的结果而是环境对组织监控的结果。当问题被检查出来以后，作为比较员的建筑师负责就这个问题对委托人最终目标造成的威胁程度进行估计。因为委托人最关注的是费用问题，所以建筑师的第一个反应就是去劝说当地政府，认为电梯不是必需的，想以此来试图避免这个问题的发生。实际上，他们试图把危机管理过程返回到原来的监控模式上。这一系列事件可以用图 7-2 描述。

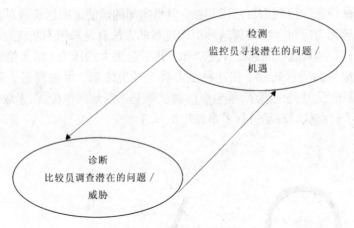

图 7-2 最初终止危机管理过程的尝试

认识到问题的严重性后，建筑师建议委托人给工程量清单中加入一笔暂定金。令人啼笑皆非的是，建筑师没有参与原设计过程，这本应对监控活动产生反面影响，现在反过来却可能加速比较员和决策者之间工作的进程，因为建筑师不用对设计过程中的任何失误负责，也就不会有防御性的反应。这一系列事件可以用图 7-3 描述。

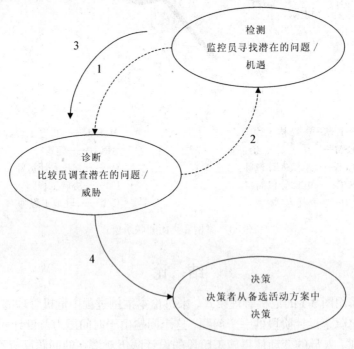

图 7-3 决策者的参与

作为决策者的委托人听取了建筑师的建议并迅速给工程量清单里加入了一笔暂定金。然而，这只是一个临时性的决定，委托人在最终决定是否安装电梯时耽误了太多的时间。委托人是否应该对这种延误负责任还有待商讨，但建筑师作为总顾问，却因没能让委托人意识到做一个快速而果断的决策的重要性而庆幸，是应该对这种延误负责的，建筑师的这种庆幸心理可能是被大量的重新设计工作所激发，他希望委托人的决策是否定的，这样问题就会自然而然的消失。无论原因如何，决策上的这种延误是后来信息供不应求的危机的真正根源。这是一个执行过程中的问题，建筑师从来也没能从这个问题中恢复过来，也正是这个问题迫使他更加频繁地采用"反应模式"的管理方法。执行过程中的这个问题可以用图 7-4 来描述。

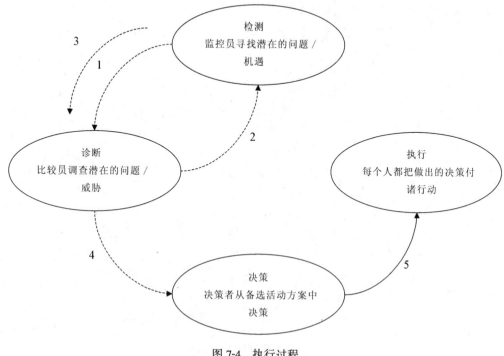

图 7-4　执行过程

当不断的信息需求压力压到建筑师肩上时，问题就像"滚雪球"一样的不断复杂化，促使建筑师匆忙中决定了电梯基坑的尺寸，这导致了施工中的电梯基坑尺寸偏小，把危机管理过程又推向第二次循环。在问题的诊断过程中，工程队很幸运，因为电梯分包商可以以和标准电梯相同的价格提供一个定制的电梯。从这种意义上说，这种亚危机没有给委托人的目标造成进一步的威胁，而且，作为决策者的委托人没有再第二次卷入危机中。所以工作的重点又返回到了修正后决策的执行过程中。这一系列事件可以用图 7-5 描述。

在第二次循环的执行过程中，建筑师仍然应对紧张的局面和承包商因不喜欢不确定性而体验到的挫折感负责。这使得他不适当地把非常规的事态当成常规的来处理，表现在没能使"正式"的信息生产过程去适应危机过程中极端的信息需求。主要问题是建筑师不断地坚持信息发放以前，信息包内的信息应该是完整无缺的，这就意味着信息是间断性的一批一批提供的，而不是像承包人所希望的那样连续提供的。建筑师也没能认识到承包商的信息优先权，表现在没能及时给承包商提供维持工地正常运转所急需的重要信息。

尽管存在以上问题，危机并没有引起工期的延误，费用超支也没有超出暂定金的范围。这些成果应归功于那些能认识并有效利用危机有利一面的人们。特别是承包人把危机看成是他们实现对工程承诺的一个机会，这表现在他们面对信息供不应求的不利条件时，没有要求索赔，而表现出了极大的忍耐性。几乎可以肯定，如果承包商愿意，他完全可以利用这个机会进行索赔。承包商也认识到他对信息提供也负有集体责任，这表现在他不断地向建筑师提出信息需求而不是仅仅依赖于建筑师所提供的信息。通过这种方式，承包商在弥补建筑师的不足方面扮演了一个很重要的角色，从而有助于提高工程队伍的内聚力，培养一种对问题的集体责任感。实际上，这个危机过程管理的有效性基本上应归功于对潜在的威胁和破坏性所提供的机会的充分利用。

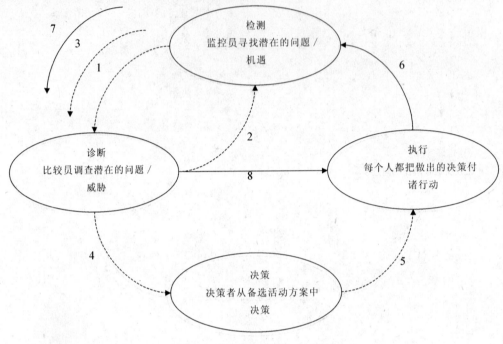

图 7-5　危机管理的第二次循环

第八章

案例研究 Ⅲ

工　程

这个工程是新建一个投资数百万英镑的半导体工厂。

危　机

邻近工地的一系列事件导致了一个突然性的危机，该邻近工地的区域由现存的已有12年历史的挡土墙抬高并支撑着。工厂的建设要求用新墙来替换旧的挡土墙。该新墙的设计以工地附近学校的荷载为基础。然而，设计该部分的工程师并不知道，学校也计划扩建一个分部，而且非常巧合的是，该分部的建设和挡土墙的替换同时开始。

当负责邻近学校分部工程的建筑师对现存的支撑工地的挡土墙附近基础开挖的不稳定性表示关注时，危机开始了。他坚持在对挡土墙的稳定性调查清楚之前，必须停工。

危机管理过程叙述

调查结果

调查的要求激起了一场紧张的信息交流，包括几次由工程内外利益相关者参加的现场会议。例如，政府安全卫生检查员和建筑管理官员未经通报就考察了工地，附近工地的建筑师，现场经理和工程师都被召集起来召开了会议。而且，附近学校的校长和部门领导被提醒注意孩子们的安全问题，对当地其他居民也都做了同样的提醒。调查结果发现，工程师由于不知道附近学校新建分部，对新墙的设计考虑不足。因此，必须进行重新设计。因为工地上几乎所有与新工厂建设有关的活动都依赖于挡土墙的完成，这就使得重新设计给施工带来了极大的冲击。

关闭工地

关闭工地的计划已经和委托人讨论过了，但在关闭之前，出于安全的考虑，必须对现存的挡土墙进行加固。对于地面稳定性问题，咨询了一位地质学家以后，立刻召开了现场会议来检查开挖工作。讨论了几种备选的开挖支护方案以后，决定必须建立监控系统，而且邻近学校的现存挡土墙后的所有工作都必须保持在5m宽的"隔离带"之外。在第二次和委托人举行的会议上，决定在工地上组建"骨干人员"，对开挖工作进行监控，禁止公众接近开挖地带，并承担一些不依赖于挡土墙设计的次要工作。也要求承包商作好准备，一接到通知马上开始工作。

重新设计工作开始

停工的决定使得设计工作进入高潮，设计工作从排水系统开始，以便承包商能尽快的重新开始工作。就像一位建筑师回忆时所说的那样，"只要醒着，我们都在做排水系统的重新设计工作，基本上把以前所做的工作又重新做了一遍。"

修改后的排水系统被拒绝

最后，修改后的排水系统设计文件递交到当地政府建筑管理部门进行审批，结果因为不符合当地建筑法规的要求而被拒绝。在披露这个亚危机所产生的压力时，建筑师回忆到，"每个人都受到了折磨，但最不幸的是工程师，你可以想象，每个人都站在周围等着，委托人的计量师用降低费用来烦扰他，现场经理需要信息，我们的领导要求工地重新开工。"同时，日益关注工程的委托人不经通报就考察了现场，并和现场经理讨论了工程进度问题。

修改后的排水系统被批准

最终，修改后的排水系统获得了批准，重新开工令也下达了。然而现场经理回忆到，"是的，他们给我们发放了排水系统详图，但大部分位于当时还没有施工，甚至还没有设计的挡土墙之后。换句话说，我没法使用它。"实际上，在下一次工地现场会上，现场经理警告如果不迅速提供挡土墙的详图，他将"马上停工"。

提供了修改后的挡土墙设计详图，但图纸不全面

工程师亲自给现场经理发放了大部分修正后的挡土墙详图。然而，经检查，现场经理发现，缺少混凝土配合比和钢筋的详图。工程师口头上给项目经理确定了这些缺少的信息。

新挡土墙施工中的后勤问题

新挡土墙的地基开挖工作开始了，施工中遇到一大片软地基，工程师口头发出指示，挖去软土，然后用混凝土回填。工程师不断下发信息不太全面的施工图纸，现场经理不断请求建筑师对有关现存的高架电线和电话线的重新架设问题做出决策，以便施工器械能在开挖区内安全操作。在现场会议上，现场经理对信息的匮乏现象表现出日渐增长的焦虑不安。

工程师图纸中出现新问题

工程师不断地下发信息不全的挡土墙图纸，考察现场并口头改正现场经理发现的问题。例如，有一次，工程师口头发出指令明确挡土墙墙面的抹光问题，增加基础内混凝土的用量以补偿工地基准面和图纸基准面的差别。工程师发现的另一个问题是挡土墙后预埋管数量不足，工程师又发出一条口头指令增加预埋管数量。

现场经理越来越有受挫感："这个时候我基本上是在没有任何信息的情况下施工的，工程师就是没有办法对付;他已经完全力所不能及了,我不得不根据我的经验在现场临时做决定。我们有这么多经验,他们真是很幸运;试想一下如果工程师的错误没被发现…….工程师受到了很大的压力……我们认为正是这些压力最终把他送进了医院。"

承包商对他们工作遭到的破坏提出索赔

承包商的计量师联络委托人的计量师讨论损害赔偿的问题。经过进一步的调查,委托人的计量师发现"无论是建筑师还是工程师都不知道他们在工地上所说的话有什么影响。他们做出变更就完事了,再也不去考虑变更后的影响。我坚持以后的变更令都要以书面形式发出。"他认为自己是故意被人排除在外的,因为他会限制工程师和建筑师凭冲动发变更令的权力。

在接下来的现场会议上,工程师口头上所发出的变更指令很少得到同意,也就没有什么损害赔偿问题了。现场经理有些情绪化的回忆到,"我们不能同意他们所做出的大部分决定,委托人的计量师开始说有些变更令根本就没有发出。但我在日志里详细记录了每一次变更,所以,我只用坐下来,在他们面前把这些记录一条一条地读出来就行了。我们认为总共有 55 项没有支付。"

承包商递交了工期和损失的索赔报告

承包商的计量师联络委托人的计量师警告现场条件继续恶化并提出了正式的工期和费用索赔。委托人的计量师所做出的反应是"所有的变更令都已通过常规的现场估价定出了价格,而且所有的支付都要以正式的书面变更令为依据"。有人直截了当的对承包商说"没那么多钱可赚了",这样,承包商和顾问工程师之间尖锐对立的氛围形成了。

对工程师所发放的图纸和计划中的缺陷人们继续表示关注。

一个突然的安全风险

一场大雨使得项目经理关注起现存挡土墙的安全问题,现在挡土墙的一部分还仍然保存着。现场经理对这个问题所做出的反应是禁止人们到那个区域去,经过几次紧急的现场会议后,又请回了地质学家对挡土墙的稳定性问题提出建议。后来做出决定,为了使开挖工作不再损害到旧挡土墙,将新挡土墙的位置向前移动。

更多的重新设计工作

将新挡土墙的位置向前移动就意味着部分新建筑物的重新布局,排水系统的第二次重新设计和工期的继续延误。而且,当新的图纸下发后,现场经理发现部分挡土墙内缺少钢筋。联系不到工程师,为了防止工期的进一步延误,驻地工程师和项目经理之间通过协商做出了决定:增加钢筋数量,钢筋在现场加工。现场经理不断的在后来工程师下发的图纸中找到不符合之处并自己解决了这些问题;在现场安排了一次有工程师参加的会议,但工程师没有露面。日志中现场经理是这样评论的"我们等到很晚,但工程师还是没来。工程师度假去了。我希望他已经做好了信息方面的安排!"现场经理回忆到"我对工程师表示抱歉,但我必须使现场运转,即使我给他施加了压力,我比他受到的压力更大。到这时候,他确实无能为力了,他的身体也非常不好。"

承包商重新提起索赔

承包商重新提起索赔，但当天就被回绝，理由是：里面都是些无法证实的索赔，而且因承包商没有积极工作，对工期延误也负有责任。现场举行了数次会议来解决不断出现的图纸上的不符合性问题。

试图解决有纠纷的索赔问题

委托人要求建筑师提供最新的施工动态，并不止一次出其不意地考察了工地。下一次现场会议是在尖锐对立的氛围中举行的，委托人的计量师重申了他拒绝索赔的原因，现场经理暂且以他个人的身份承认自己在工程中缺乏积极性。作为对这种说法的反应，他坚持要把他的日志一条一条的读出来，并要求建筑师和工程师立即对它们进行确认。其中大多数都被确认了，委托人的计量师感到非常吃惊，问他们为什么没有把这些变更通知他。现场经理回忆到，"我知道我这样做会使建筑师和工程师感到不舒服，但假如我不刺激他们，他们就只会沉默地坐在那儿。他们不想'自己掉进去'对吗？"

作为反应，委托人的计量师认为没有证据能证明这些工作曾经被做过，这促使现场经理愤怒地质问他们是否认为他是"一个撒谎者"。委托人的计量师拿出一些挡土墙排水系统的照片，争辩说没有证据能证明承包商索赔的材料已经安装到挡土墙上了。现场经理进行了反驳，会议没有什么实质性的进展。

试图解决有纠纷的索赔问题

会议继续在工地上举行，解决图纸上的不符问题，并讨论承包商的索赔。一个关键的会议持续了 5 个小时，会上对承包商的 55 个索赔项逐一进行了讨论。会上公开谴责了委托人的计量师非专业性的行为，这些谴责是由于委托人的计量师对承包人的计量师所提的不断的索赔会对将来的合同带来损害的建议而激发的。像前一次一样，会议没有什么实质性的进展。

纠纷的终止

将来合同会受到损害的建议刺激承包商使纠纷升级。这表现在委托人和承包商的总经理之间直接的接触，结果使得索赔完全而且立即得到了批准。

行为阶段

这个突然的危机历时大约 10 个月，耗费了大量的资源、时间和精力，危机所导致的正式会议 58 次，电话联系 67 次，来往信件 32 封，还有多次非正式会议没有计算。接下来的部分讨论危机过程中出现的主要的行为阶段。

第一阶段

危机开始时的特点是完全忽略了财务方面的问题，因为从进度上来说，为了保证工程能幸存，必须优先解决技术和组织上的问题。这对确保本阶段是一个有很强的前进动力的阶段也起了一定的作用。实际上，这一点在人们的信息流通模式上也有所体现，它的特点是只有一个起主导作用的集团，信息的有效交流穿过了传统的顾问工程师和承包商之间的界面，在解决问题上人们之间体现出了一种集体责任意识。这些情况可用图 8-1 阐明。

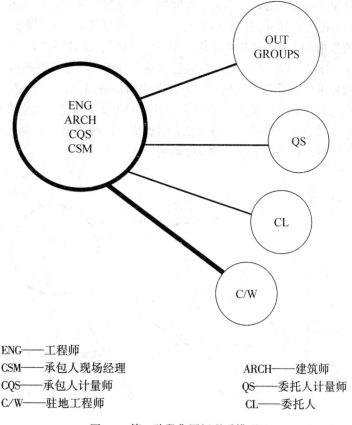

ENG——工程师
CSM——承包人现场经理
CQS——承包人计量师
C/W——驻地工程师

ARCH——建筑师
QS——委托人计量师
CL——委托人

图 8-1　第一阶段集团间联系模型

从人们之间信息流通的集中度来看，建筑师和现场经理是最主要的信息发放者，这表明他们在推动该阶段向前发展中起着主导作用。委托人的计量师位于相对边缘的位置上，这表明在危机的初始阶段，处理财务问题的优先权较低。人们能够直接交流，这表明有一个紧凑的信息流通结构模式，从而保证信息能够快速而又不失真地在人们之间流通。这使得人们普遍对问题有一个共同的理解。建筑师和现场经理常常是人们接触到的第一个人，在信息流通网络内占据着信息守门员的位置。然而，在他们对信息流通进行控制时，人们之间备选的信息流通路径能防止他们独断专行。这就意味着信息流通不易受少数人态度和观点的影响，这在人们尽可能地采用防御性的态度和有大量的信息不断产生的危机初期是一个潜在的问题。这个阶段信息流通模式上另一个明显的特点是信息网内人们之间较高的等同性，这表明，每一个受危机影响的人对危机都有一个共同的理解。

第二阶段

第二阶段开始于工地上重新开工之时，是对日渐增大的来自委托人和承包商的压力作出的反应。然而，很快就可以看出，重新开工的决策做出的有点为时过早，它低估了承包商对信息的需求，没能提供工程正常进展所需的信息。因此，和第一阶段比起来，这一阶段前进的动力大大降低，现场经理的受挫感不断增大。主要问题与提供给承包商的图纸中的信息遗漏和错误有关，这就意味着每次信息的输入都连带着不确定性的输入。这反过来又产生了对信息更进一步的需求，这把工程师置于越来越无法逃脱的不断循环的不确定性和压力之下。他不得不追赶着信息的需求而不是领导着它走，为了缓解他采用"反应模式"进行管理工作所带来的压力，他越来越依赖于现场经理发现问题并确定解决这些问题所需要的信息。从这个意义上说，现场经理在信息供给上扮演着一个重要的角色。

讨论的地位和第一阶段基本相同，口头指令作为提供信息的方法被越来越多的采用。这是工程师和建筑师在解决现场不断失控状态下的问题及重新建立他们对信息供给的主导地位时所采用的主要方法。和第一阶段相比，信息沟通综合水平在大幅度的下降，这也是这些积累问题的反应。这些情况可用图8-2阐明。

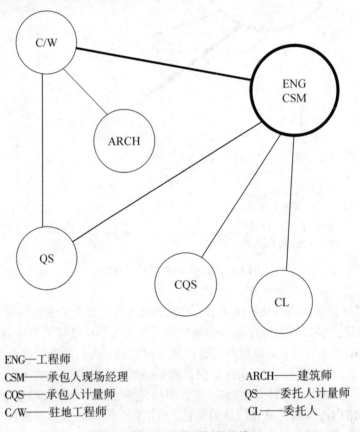

ENG—工程师
CSM——承包人现场经理　　　　　　　　ARCH——建筑师
CQS——承包人计量师　　　　　　　　　　QS——委托人计量师
C/W——驻地工程师　　　　　　　　　　　CL——委托人

图8-2　第二阶段集团间联系模型

和总体参与水平较高的危机的第一阶段相比，由工程师和项目经理组成的唯一占主导地位的集团的存在使信息流通的集中度大幅度提高。这种模式主要是由项目经理促成的，因工程师越来越无力应付施加于他身上的压力，面对这种情况，项目经理变得越来越趋于自己供给自己信息。实际上，在这一阶段的行为过程中，工程师越来越依赖于项目经理在现场发现问题的能力，然后口头做出一些变更令，特别是涉及设计的各个方面的变更令。

从信息守门员的角度来看，项目经理日渐变成重要的信息流通渠道，这使得整个危机管理过程易受他既得利益和个人能力的影响。然而，项目经理是一个有经验，有能力且相当合作的人，所以这种信息流通模式产生了一个正面的影响。相反的，工程师和建筑师在承包人和委托人的计量师之间守门员的位置却带来了消极的影响，因为他们利用这个权力在不通知委托人计量师的情况下做出即时的、非正式的决策，毫无疑问，委托人的计量师会限制他们的这种行为。这种做法带来了一个消极的影响，表现在将委托人计量师从整个过程中隔离了出去，这给第三阶段和最后阶段的行为带来很大的麻烦。

第三阶段

承包商索赔的提出开始了第三个行为过程，一个对财务问题关注力度大幅度提高的阶段，直到这时，财务问题基本上还是完全被忽略的。为了维持工地的正常进展，必须解决技术和组织上的问题，然而解决财务问题上的困难表明，他们的这种忽略，导致了人们对费用超支带来的问题持极为不同的观点。结果，与第二阶段相比，前进的动力进一步减小，危机管理过程也更加情绪化。

委托人的计量师为他被排除在做现场的变更的决策之外而表现出极端的情绪化和强烈的受挫感。因为这使他和相对充分掌握信息的承包人相比，在谈判中处于极为不利的地位。他的反应是采取防御性的措施，避免协商，这又导致了一种不断情绪化和尖锐对立的环境的产生，最终迫使承包商的总经理参与危机过程而使纠纷升级。

图 8-3 阐述了这个阶段各个集团之间的结构模式。例如，在财务问题上，很明显委托人的计量师和承包人的计量师相互之间的信息流通相对不频繁。而且，和第二阶段相比，承包商和顾问工程师之间的分裂现象更加严重。最后，和前些阶段相比，建筑师和委托人的计量师之间的合作更加密切，因为后者想确定第二阶段中，把他排除在外所做的那些非正式的设计变更。实际上，他是试图收集信息以便使他和承包人的计量师之间的信息差异等同化，因为这种差异使他在谈判中处于极为不利的地位。

结　论

结论部分采用图 3-1 的危机管理模式，来讨论本案例过程中危机管理的效率。

这个危机起源于邻近工地的学校扩建分部的决定，这个决定对新挡土墙的设计造成影响。早期的警告信号没被发觉，因为危机直到双方都开工以后才被检测出来。虽然不能指望设计挡土墙的工程师能够知道邻近工地上学校分部的平行施工计划，但工程一旦开始了，它对新挡土墙设计的影响就应该很明显了。看起来，组织的监控活动做得还有些欠缺。

虽然组织对潜在的问题不敏感，但问题一旦测出来，在诊断过程中对它的影响进行评估时，却表现出了极高的有效性和合作性，最后做出决定，工地进展和重新设计工作平行进行。危机的严重性意味着只有委托人才有权做这样的决策，而且这个决策很快就做了出来。这个决策的执行工作也立即开始了。这一系列事件用图 8-4 描述。

在这个决策的执行过程中，现场经理反馈回来的信息中又检测出了新的问题；因为信息供不应求，工期继续拖延。这又把危机管理推向到一个完整的以评估新问题，并做出适当的反应为开始的第二次循环中。在这一次循环中提出了暂停施工的建议，以便设计的进度能赶上现场施工的要求。再一次批准这个建议的决策又只能由委托人做出，该建议及时得到了批准。执行这个决策就意味着工地停工，以便设计进度能赶在施工进度之前。这一系列事件用图 8-5 描述。

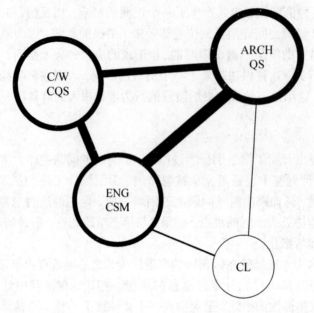

ENG——工程师
CSM——承包人现场经理　　　　　　　ARCH——建筑师
CQS——承包人计量师　　　　　　　　QS——委托人计量师
C/W——驻地工程师　　　　　　　　　CL——委托人

图 8-3　第三阶段集团间联系模型

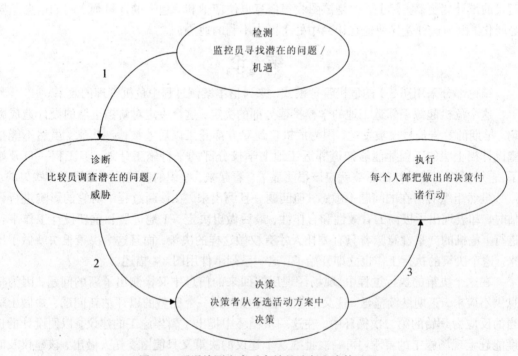

图 8-4　延误检测出来后高效的诊断和决策过程

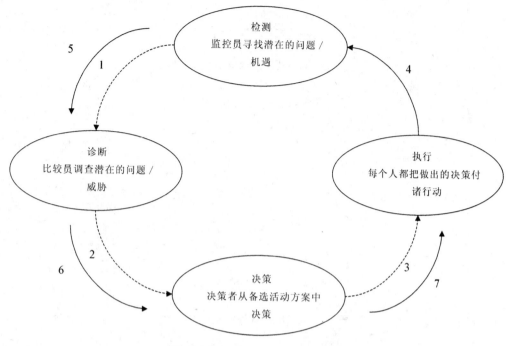

图 8-5　危机管理的另一个循环过程

　　在第二个循环的设计监控过程中，人们对这个过程需要多长时间的看法不一致。从委托人和现场经理那儿反馈回来的信息可以看出，对现场不断的工期延误，他们表现出日益增长的挫折感。

　　因此，他们施加了相当大的压力催促重新开工，最终，重新开工的决策做出了，这把危机管理的过程又推向了第三次循环。这一系列事件用图 8-6 描述。

　　在重新开工的决策做出时，对信息的供给情况进行了评估。几乎同时，从现场经理那儿反馈回来的信息表明，信息又处于供不应求的状态了。在停工的过程中，设计组过早的屈服于重新开工的压力，没能为施工的继续进行存储足够的信息。再一次，信息又处于供不应求的状态了，设计文件往往不能像人们期望的那样是一个预先的计划文件，而成了历史文件。施加于建筑师和工程师身上的压力使他们犯了个大错误，后来对这个错误的改正使得设计队伍陷于压力，紧张和错误的不断循环中难以解脱。

　　为了重新建立对工程的控制权，建筑师和工程师被迫更加频繁的采用"非正规的、反应模式"的管理方法，在现场即时发出变更指令。虽然这提高了信息的供给速度，却也造成了组织上的脱节。特别是，委托人的计量师被从危机管理中分离开来，不知道已经发出的变更令。一些事实证明建筑师和工程师故意筛去了应该送给委托人的计量师的有关变更的信息，因为他会限制使得他们能得以幸存的在现场发布变更令的权力。实际上，不同的利益集团之间为保护不同的项目目标也产生了冲突（费用——委托人的计量师，时间——建筑师和工程师），这阻碍了有些集团在工地上对问题的检测。特别是，把委托人的计量师从现场经理所反馈的有关现场问题的信息里隔离出来，使得危机管理在财务上完全失控。然而，现场经理最后还是绕过建筑师和工程师直接向委托人的计量师反应了工地上存在的问题，这就把危机管理过程推向以财务问题为重点的第四个循环。这一系列事件用图 8-7 描述。

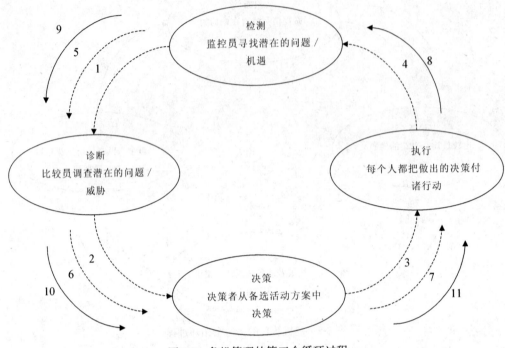

图 8-6　危机管理的第三个循环过程

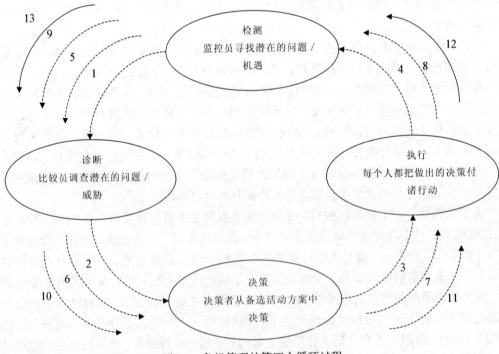

图 8-7　危机管理的第四个循环过程

在诊断过程中委托人的计量师和承包人的计量师之间进行了一场尖锐的争执。这是建筑师和工程师在发布现场变更令时把委托人的计量师排除在外的直接结果。在协商中的这种不利处境迫使他采取防御性的管理模式。实际上，委托人的计量师从来都没能收集到能和承包人相提并论的信息，双方使用的策略也就更加具有防御性，直到纠纷发展到必须让承包人的总经理来参与的程度。这一系列事件用图 8-8 描述。

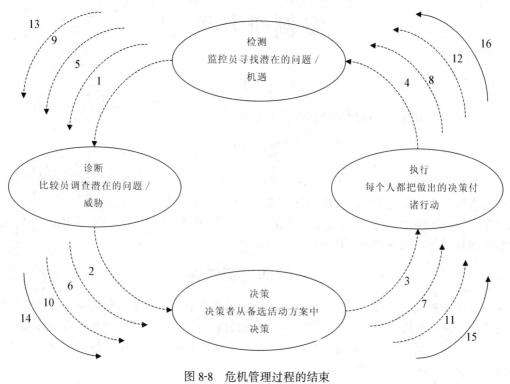

图 8-8　危机管理过程的结束

第九章

案例研究 Ⅳ

工 程

这个工程是围绕一个球场而建的综合办公楼。

危 机

当工程进行到一半时,当地一个黏土铺面材料制造商(X 公司)向委托人抱怨说当地的生产商没按工程的规范生产。尽管工程顺利的进行着,技术规范却被更改了,来适应 X 公司所生产的黏土铺面材料。然而,很快就出现了质量控制问题,引起了严重的工期延误,承包商和建筑师之间为经济责任开始了一场纠纷。

危机管理过程叙述

在变更工程的技术规范时,发现承包人工程量清单中的报价项目和建筑师原始指定的项目不同。建筑师认为他原来指定的是黏土铺面材料,后来技术规范的变更就只涉及到生产厂商的变更。然而,工程量清单却指定了混凝土铺面材料,这意味着如果由混凝土变更到黏土,承包人就应该得到额外的支付。

工程队伍内部的分裂现象不断发展

这种分裂现象起源于规范执行体系,它允许建筑师提名三个厂商让投标人从中挑选,然而建筑师却把问题搞混了,因为他指定的三个厂商中一个专门生产黏土产品,一个专门生产混凝土产品,另一个破产了。承包商选择了报价最低的厂商,赢得了该标。

委托人的计量师感觉受到了建筑师的谴责,"建筑师暗示,我们因错误的解释了规范而不知所措,他坚持规范内将黏土只作为一个选择项……最开始建筑师想采用黏土,因为在他的上一个工作中,用黏土做铺面材料看起来效果很好。但预算中却没有那么多资金,建筑师就只能把黏土作为选择项,希望承包商能选择黏土。换句话说,建筑师是想用混凝土的价格来做黏土铺面。"

努力降低黏土和混凝土的差价

承包商使用黏土超过使用混凝土的费用索赔主要由两部分组成:铺设黏土所需额外时间的费用(由于黏土的尺寸变化比混凝土大)及材料差价。为了验证这个问题,建筑师请现场经理用黏土制作一些试件板来测定它的允许偏差。他同时也要求 X 公司做出反应。X 公司指出,黏土铺面材料和混凝土铺面材料的允许偏差相同,所以应该没有额外的铺设费用。同时他们对黏土材料打了折扣,使黏土的价格和混凝土的价格相等。

做出决策

现场检测了试件板以后，建筑师决定采用黏土作为铺面材料。由于决策过程已经被调查过程耽误过一段时间了，所以决策做出后很快就开工了。承包商正式请求就技术规范的变更发变更令，建筑师拒绝了，他指出，厂商提供的折扣足以补偿额外的铺设时间和材料差价费用。承包商不同意这个观点，认为厂商的折扣价不足以弥补材料的差价。建筑师要求提出书面的解释。

现场出现问题

最终发出了弥补黏土对混凝土差价的变更令。然而，由于铺设的黏土材料在尺寸和色泽上有很大的可变性，使得估计的超支费用远远不足。这些意想不倒的变化在试件板上没能反应出来，因为试件板的尺寸相对太小了一些。建筑师决定继续铺设。

承包商请求返回到使用混凝土做铺面材料

除了铺设问题，承包商还面临着供应问题，导致了工期的继续延误。越来越有受挫感的承包商正式请求返回到使用混凝土铺设的方案上。

承包商表达了正式的索赔意向

X 公司被邀参加了正式的讨论铺设问题的现场会议。厂商承诺提供精选的黏土铺面材料，如果问题还继续发生，他们将自己铺设。问题继续存在着，当 X 公司自己的队伍也无法解决时，承包商写信给建筑师表达他们对工期继续延误的忧虑，并表明他们要求延长工期的索赔意向。他们再一次强烈地要求建筑师返回到使用混凝土铺设的方案上。建筑师没有采纳这个建议。

决定做出，返回到使用混凝土做铺面材料的方案上

最终，铺设问题变得如此严重以至于驻地工程师不得不召开现场会检查这个问题："我看见事情变得如此之糟，必须有个人做出决策了！建筑师不想这么做，因为他不想把自己卷入这个问题中。同样的道理，承包商也不想这么做。"在这次会议上，大家一致认为黏土铺面材料的质量不能让人满意，并做出决定返回到使用混凝土铺面材料的方案上。承包商被指令选择一些混凝土铺面材料制作试件板。最终，建筑师决定使用一种看起来和黏土比较相似的彩色混凝土作为铺面材料。

承包人正式提出索赔

承包人拆掉已经铺设好的黏土铺面材料，换上彩色混凝土铺面材料。承包商为自己已经完成的与原使用黏土作为铺面材料的变更令有关的工作提出索赔，同时要求对有关从黏土铺面材料变为混凝土铺面材料发出一道变更令，指出彩色混凝土比原工程量清单中指定并标价的无色混凝土价格要高。

索赔的讨论

经过一段时间的沉默，建筑师征求委托人的计量师的意见，委托人的计量师同意批准索赔。然而，建筑师正式拒绝了承包商的索赔要求和发出另一道变更令的要求，建筑师认为原规范执行体系规定承包人应该负起选择厂商的责任，既然是厂商引起的问题，它应该属于承包商的风险。他还认为，由于承包商没能按时把运货计划提交给厂商，对供应问题应该负有责任。最后，他认为返回到使用混凝土铺面材料，特别是彩色混凝土铺面材料是承包商的选择，建筑师只不过是批准了这个建议而已。

这引起了一场激烈的争论，承包商认为他们被引导选择了 X 公司，并且如果没有原始的采用黏土铺面材料的变更令，也就不会有这些问题了。

协商失败

建筑师和承包商都考虑要起诉厂商。同时，委托人的计量师与承包人的计量师对索赔问题进行了正式讨论，他们在前一个工程中建立了良好的关系，委托人的计量师仍对承包人的计量师存有一些同情心。尽管经过折衷考虑，问题的解决方案有了一些进展，但委托人的计量师回忆道："后来我不得不停止与承包人的计量师讨论此事，因为我有一种感觉，建筑师认为我对承包商产生了同情心，毕竟我还是应该忠于委托人的。"这使承包商的计量师进一步受挫，他回忆道，"我们得不到建筑师的任何同情，但至少你可以和委托人的计量师理智地讨论一下这个问题吧。"

纠纷解决

建筑师对委托人的计量师的忠心产生了怀疑，自己承担起与承包人的计量师进行交涉的任务。在委托人的计量师与承包人的计量师之间达成的非正规的解决问题的方案的基础上，建筑师同意在异常酷热的气候条件下，可以考虑铺面材料的费用及时间的延长问题。一个月内协议成交了，因为异常酷热的气候条件，建筑师批准了承包商的工期索赔和根据原工程量清单内单价计算的 1/3 的原始费用索赔。建筑师还发布了一条有关从黏土转为混凝土铺面材料的变更令，但同时也发布了一道书面说明，指出这仅仅是对承包商决策的确认，不会再有额外费用的支付。

行为阶段

这个渐进的危机历时大约 6 个月，耗费了大量的资源，时间和精力，危机所导致的正式会议 25 次，电话联系 22 次，来往信件 39 封。还有多次非正式会议没有计算。接下来的部分讨论危机过程中出现的主要的行为阶段。

第一阶段

这个阶段开始于人们调查从混凝土到黏土铺面材料的可行性问题之时，这个阶段的特点是公开的讨论和强大的前进动力。然而，变更令刚一颁布，现场就开始出现了铺设问题，承包商和建筑师之间因有关财务问题产生了纠纷，这表明变更令发布以前，任何人都没有认真考虑过组织和财务问题。其结果是前进动力的丧失和人们信息交流中出现的明显的受挫感、忧虑感和威胁感。建筑师在做从黏土铺面材料转回到混凝土铺面材料决定时的拖延更加剧了这种现状。这一阶段各集团间的结构模式见图9-1。

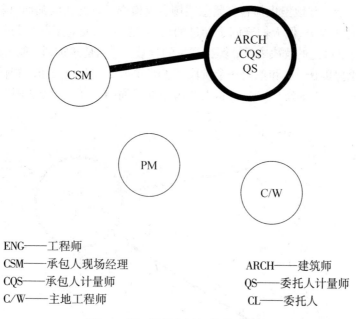

ENG——工程师
CSM——承包人现场经理
CQS——承包人计量师
C/W——主地工程师

ARCH——建筑师
QS——委托人计量师
CL——委托人

图 9-1　第一阶段集团间的联系模型

从图 9-1 可以看出，初始阶段只有一个由建筑师，承包人的计量员和委托人的计量师组成的集团，其中最强有力的成员是承包人的计量师和委托人的计量师。计量师频繁的参与表明在决策的初始阶段已经将财务问题作为重点。相反的，现场经理相对的被隔离开表明对组织问题重视程度不够，这最终造成了工期的延误和费用的增加。

从人们在信息流通中的集中度来看，建筑师是主要的信息源，他驱动着过程的进展。这反应在他竭力想使用黏土而不是混凝土作为铺面材料，他独断专行的管理模式以及他不愿意折衷的态度上。然而，委托人的计量师收集到了大多数信息，而且很明显承包人很愿意和他接触。此外，因为建筑师采用把自己从祸害工地的铺面材料问题中解脱开来的策略，委托人的计量师和承包商一样不断地被推向边缘位置。因此，虽然建筑师竭力想维持他的控制权，却因为他使得委托人的计量师对承包商的接受力不断增强反而削弱了这种控制权。另外，他迫使委托人的计量师和承包人的计量师不得不进行私下交往，使他失去了参与他们非正式协商的机会。

从信息守门员的角度来看，虽然建筑师试图想控制信息流，却没能在这方面处于主导地位。他之所以没能做到这一点是因为委托人的计量师将自己置于备选的、承包商的计量师喜闻乐见的信息流通路径上。虽然委托人的计量师没有多少决策的权力，他在缓解工程队之间紧张关系方面却起了举足轻重的作用。委托人的计量师的做法也使他成为建筑师和承包商之间的一座重要的桥梁，缩小了他们之间的信息差异，避免了误解和危机的进一步升级。

第二阶段

第二阶段开始于驻地工程师召开紧急现场会议检查日益恶化的铺面材料问题之时。虽然会议持续的时间很短，但人们充满了前进的动力，更愿意面对不断增长的现场上的组织问题，调查和讨论可能的解决方案，解决意见的分歧。特别是建筑师，他表现得更加果断，更愿意为问题承担责任，这和他前一个阶段把主要精力用在开脱问题的责任上形成明显的对比。因此，一个更注重公开讨论和非正式沟通的局面出现了。图 9-2 阐明了这个阶段的这种特点。

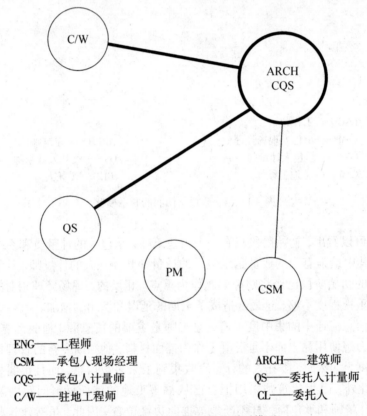

ENG——工程师
CSM——承包人现场经理   ARCH——建筑师
CQS——承包人计量师   QS——委托人计量师
C/W——驻地工程师   CL——委托人

图 9-2 第二阶段集团间的联系模型

在这个阶段，建筑师和承包人的计量师组成了唯一的一个集团，委托人的计量师也被联系着，但只作为一个信息接收者。这表明面对驻地工程师的干预，建筑师突然想重新获得危机管理过程的控制权。在这个阶段中，建筑师在承包商面前扮演着协调员的角色——迄今为止这个角色一直由委托人的计量师非正式的承担着。

从集中度的角度说来，建筑师和承包人的计量师在信息的发放和收集方面都占据着主导地位。这体现在这个阶段高度的合作性和穿过承包商、顾问工程师组织界面良好的信息沟通上。

这个短暂却又充满积极性的行为阶段的结束点正好是放弃黏土铺面，采用混凝土铺面的决策做出之时。

第三阶段

这个阶段的特点是更强调前两阶段没有完全解决的财务和组织问题。然而，这个阶段的大部分时间里对于风险的分配模式存在着相当大的分歧，这种分歧使得危机管理相对于第一、第二阶段来说，前进的动量大大减少了。只有当委托人的计量师非正式的介入，和承包人讨论索赔问题时，以及当建筑师重新获得控制权达成了那个协议时，组织才重新获得了前进的动力。在这个阶段最后时期集团的结构模式如图9-3所示。

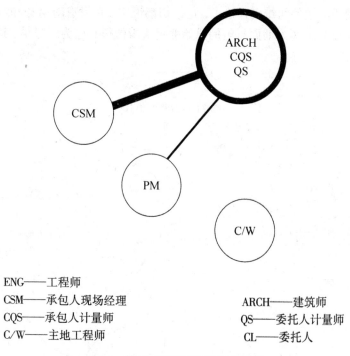

ENG——工程师
CSM——承包人现场经理
CQS——承包人计量师
C/W——主地工程师

ARCH——建筑师
QS——委托人计量师
CL——委托人

图 9-3　第三阶段集团间的联系模型

图9-3中集团的结构模式和第一阶段的相似，由建筑师，承包人的计量师，和委托人的计量师组成，其中力量最弱的成员是建筑师。

和第一阶段中一样，建筑师拒绝同意承包商的索赔，从他在第二阶段扮演的强有力的领导角色中撤离出来，回到像第一阶段那样扮演一个疏远的角色。虽然和第二阶段相比，建筑师周围的联系网更加紧密，但和建筑师之间的绝大多数联系都是起阻碍作用的阻力。从这个意义上说，虽然建筑师在空间上和其他人邻近，但从心里来说却更远。

像集团间联系模式一样，集中度的模式也和第一阶段类似，建筑师试图通过控制信息源及占据信息守门员的位置来维持他在控制过程中的主导地位，但却由于委托人的计量师充当了承包人备选的信息沟通渠道而没能如愿。像第一阶段一样，这种沟通基本上是非正式的，但它使得委托人的计量师驱散了潜在的挫折，使人们对承包人的要求有了一个更好的理解。最终，使得建筑师能和承包商妥协，为最终解决纠纷打下了基础。

结 论

结论部分采用图 3-1 的危机管理模式,来讨论本案例过程中危机管理的效率。

促使危机加速的 X 公司的来信是环境监控工程的结果,而不是工程监控环境的结果。处理来信的责任落在了既作为比较员又作为决策者的建筑师身上,他必须评估是否值得对这封信做出反应,如果是,会带来什么样的变化。采用黏土作为铺面材料的决策做出了,但执行过程中的问题紧接着就出现了,从现场反馈回来的信息表明,工期在不断的延误。紧接着,关于费用问题的纠纷也开始了,这一切都说明,在没有对财务和组织问题进行充分的调查以前,以黏土作为铺面材料的原始变更决策做得有些为时过早。这一系列事件可用图 9-4 来描述。

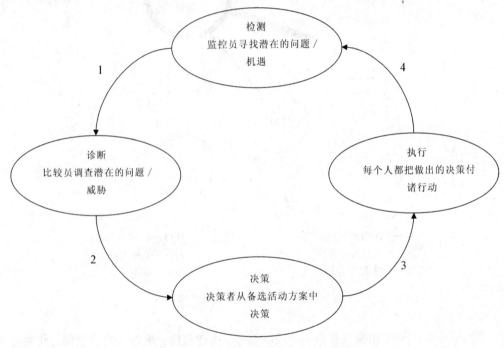

图 9-4　危机管理的第一个循环过程

建筑师拖延对从现场反馈回来的有关铺面材料引起的问题做出反应,希望这个问题能在工地阶层得以解决。而且,从建筑师的观点看来,这些问题都属于承包商的风险,任何干涉都会把他牵连进去。另一方面,承包商认为这是建筑师的责任,所以继续在现场使用低档的铺面材料。这种责任的混淆及害怕承认错误的心理导致了工期的进一步拖延和费用的更大损失,使得双方更不愿意面对这个问题。后来,驻地工程师干预了,迫使建筑师面对问题,做出拆除已经铺设的黏土铺面材料,换上彩色混凝土铺面材料的决策。这就把危机管理推向了第二次循环,决策的执行过程很顺利。见图 9-5。

现场上的铺设问题解决了以后,人们的注意力又转移到未解决的由第一次循环过程中的僵局所导致的工期延误和费用超支的责任归属问题。这个问题因为承包商的索赔而被排在了榜首,这使得危机管理过程又进入到第三个循环中。这一循环的诊断阶段因为建筑师和承包商对第一循环中出现的铺面问题责任归属持截然不同的观点而被拖延,而且出现了对立局面。实际上，只有当作为建筑师和承包人之间重要桥梁的委托人的计量师经过非正式的努力以后，诊断阶段的协议才得以达成。这使得沟通过程能够继续进行而且防止了纠纷的进一步升级。这一系列事件见图9-6。

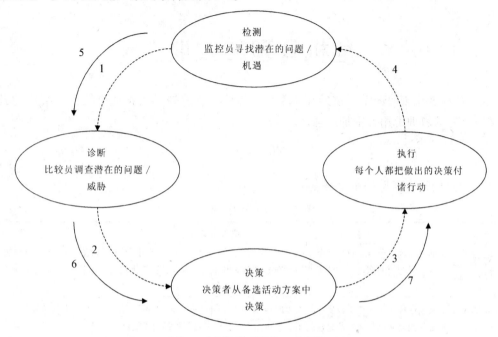

图9-5 危机管理的第二个循坏过程

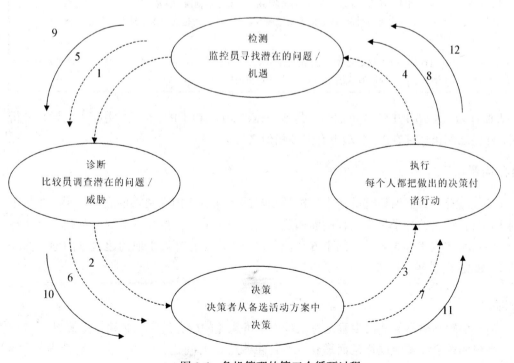

图9-6 危机管理的第三个循环过程

第十章

危机管理的教训

这一章通过比较前面学习过的几个案例，总结出有效处理工程危机的一些实用的教训。文中所有的教训都用方框加以强调。

简　介

所研究过的每个案例的主要特点都列于表 10-1 中。

表 10-1　案例的特点

案例	危机描述
1.(第六章) 土方开挖支护	渐进性危机——工程量清单中有关土方支护的差异导致了额外费用的索赔和尖锐的纠纷。对解决这个问题上的拖延又导致了相当可观的费用支出和工期拖延，并严重损害了工程中各方之间的关系
2.(第七章) 电梯	突发性危机——对增设新电梯决策的拖延导致了信息管理中的问题，使得工程队之间关系紧张。这些问题又反过来对信息流通系统造成损害，引起现场严重的组织问题
3.(第八章) 挡土墙	突发性危机——人们发现新的挡土墙设计不妥。工地被关闭了，很快又重新开工了。这引起信息管理中的问题和压力，导致了现场严重的费用超支和工期延误。因为建筑师不同意承包商的索赔，引起两者之间尖锐的纠纷。决策的延误导致了进一步的费用超支和工期延误，并使各参与方之间关系破裂
4.(第九章) 黏土铺面	渐进性危机——规范突然变更，决定使用黏土铺面材料，这导致了现场上的组织问题和有关的责任纠纷，给工程各参与方之间的关系带来严重的损害

表面看来，表 10-1 中的各个危机都是独一无二、互不相干的，然而，更深入的调查分析表明，他们之间虽然存在差别，却也有很多相似之处。

内在的问题

基本上说来，我们所研究的四个危机都是合同前期阶段内在错误的直接结果。在每个案例中，潜在危机的种子早在工程的前期阶段就已埋了下来且被接下来的一系列活动所掩盖，直到后来才诸如娱乐中心的土方开挖支护及工厂工程邻近工地的建筑师的抱怨这些问题所"触发"而暴露了出来。

> **教训：**
> * **当一切顺利时不要沾沾自喜。**对工程中不可避免的内在的问题必须保持警惕。
> * **简单问题会随着时间拖延而恶化。**不要隐藏潜在的问题，存在它会自动消失的侥幸心理，不要给"上一级"的人们"推卸责任"。

教训：

* **在整个工程的生命期中保持队伍的稳定性。**这能防止潜在问题随着时间的推移而被忽视。
* **如果你是新手，调查研究工程的历史。**这会使你发现过去存在的被后来一系列活动所掩盖的潜在的问题。

渐进性和突发性危机

有的时候，危机的触发事件出现在早期，这使得工程队可以采取预防措施。案例Ⅰ、Ⅳ就是这种情况的例子，但是人们没有利用这个机会，而且在他们做出反应的过程中又产生出他们自己的渐进性危机。另一些时候，触发事件出现在危机的晚期，是一个强有力的突发性的危机，案例Ⅱ、Ⅲ就是这种情况的例子。

突发性危机的主要问题都围绕在信息管理以及和它有关的压力和紧张上。相反的，渐进性危机的主要问题却与拖延、犹豫不决和各种冲突管理所导致的危机升级有关。当你仔细考虑每种类型危机的信息流通方式时，就会发现更进一步的区别。例如，在突发性危机过程中，早期的决策主要集中在技术和组织问题上，从本质上说这些决策是具有建设性的。这就是说，突发性危机使人们放下自身的利益而首先以组织的安危为重。与财务责任有关的问题都趋向于被推迟到危机的晚期。然而，当人们最终关注财务问题时，这种推延使得人们之间利益的分歧变得更加明显和强烈，常常导致非常激烈的冲突。

相反的，渐进性危机却注重解决财务责任的归属问题，这一点在危机的早期尤为明显。人们也关注技术和组织问题，但重视度非常低而且往往被推迟到危机的晚期。和突发性危机相反，渐进性危机给人们时间去考虑他们的不同利益，采取复杂的策略迫使资源的重新分配朝着有利于自己的方向发展。导致决策的拖延，冲突过程的延长及相关者相当长时间的不确定性和受挫感。

教训：

* **渐进性危机和突发性危机是两种截然不同的危机，要求不同的处理方法。**管理者的管理策略应随之而变。
* **突发性危机带来压力，紧张和信息管理的问题。**应急计划可以为初始的危机震撼后的重新定位提供时间，也可以帮助人们处理潮涌而来的信息。管理者应保证在危机的早期阶段不要忽略财务责任问题，因为面对工程的存亡问题，人们往往有一种把注意力集中在技术和组织问题上的倾向。
* **渐进性危机因其没有紧急性而导致拖延。**管理者应警惕不同的利益集团有时间拟定不同的策略来维护自身的利益，这些策略是潜在纠纷的源泉，而且非常危险的是它很容易将人们的注意力从主要问题上引开，这些问题可能是技术上或组织上的，却往往不是财务上的，若被忽视，会不断地积累起来。

危机过程中的信息管理

第五章把一个富有效率的危机管理者比作社会建筑师，他能深刻理解塑造项目成员间的信息流通模式的力量及它们对危机管理结果的影响。在这里我们来详细讨论这一点。

自私

第三章指出，人们有正式的或非正式的保护项目特定目标的责任。一个人对危机管理的参与程度往往取决于他或她所保护的目标受威胁的程度。然而，在我们所研究的案例中，有关这种责任和危机管理参与程度之间的关系的例证并不明显。一般来说，弱者被排除到过程之外而强者占统治地位。这常常使被压抑的一方有相当程度的受挫感和怨恨感。

> **教训：**
> * **意识到人们的不同利益及为这种利益服务的信息流通模式。**监控那些可能给工程造成伤害的信息流通模式。
> * **评估危机对目标系统造成的影响，确保适当的专家恰如其分地参与。**例如，如果工程费用受到最大的威胁，就应该保证负责预算控制的人员处于强有力的控制地位。
> * **危机的处理决策可能需要对不同集团的目标进行权衡，这给本来可以很好地在一块工作的人们之间带来了冲突。**管理者应该集中力量做这些紧张界面的管理工作，因为它们是潜在的纠纷和低效率的源泉。

危机管理的方式

在危机管理过程中，危机管理者的管理方式对人们之间的信息流通模式有很大的影响。为了重新建立控制地位，作为一种防御机制，人们常常变得独断专行。其结果几乎毫无例外的都是失去控制。

> **教训：**
> * **危机管理应该是独立、公平和开放的。**包括危机管理者在内的大多数工程成员都有自己对某种特定结果的既得利益。因此由第三方或外部顾问来进行危机管理可能是一种比较好的方式。

预料不到的亚危机

预料不到的亚危机常加剧原始的危机，且对人们的信息流通模式有很大的影响。这些亚危机是由于没能有效地处理好危机中潜在的紧张关系而产生的，从这个意义上说，他们都具有自生性。就像产生它们的原始危机一样，它们早期的征兆没能被检测到，具有潜在的破坏性。然而，它们常常也会带来积极的影响，提高人们之间的凝聚力，因为它给了人们一个共同的关注点，使他们有机会重新调整相互之间的关系。

> **教训：**
> * **对预料不到的亚危机应有个思想准备。**由原始危机所导致的亚危机可能是渐进性的也可能是突发性的。
> * **有些时候人们可能故意刺激一些亚危机以提高集团之间的凝聚力。**这就像用爆破来灭火一样，目的是鼓励人们的斗志。

人们之间的相互关系

在每个危机过程中，人们之间的相互关系对人们之间的信息流通模式也有很大的影响。人们之间的这种相互关系似乎是由以前工程的经验，对职业集团传统的看法，与生俱来的传统的一定集团之间相互的猜疑以及工程整个生命期中的经验所决定的。

> **教训：**
>
> * **在危机的压力下，人们之间的相互关系表露得一览无遗，任何潜在的紧张关系都会被加剧和暴露出来。** 理想地说，工程应该雇佣那些在过去工程中已经建立了良好关系的人们。如果做不到这一点，雇佣一些以前没有什么关系的人们。最后，时常监控人们之间的相互关系，寻找新的紧张点，因为这些紧张点能表明危机过程中那些地方最容易出现问题。

同僚间的压力

在许多危机中，同僚间的压力对人们之间信息流通的模式有很大的影响。具有相同利益的人们趋于组成暂时的联盟，这种联盟内部会产生强大的压力使其成员之间相互忠诚，遵守既定的行为模式和组织规则。这种强迫性行为的目的是压制那些可能让组织受到谴责的潜在问题，或在更高一级的决策者面前掩藏这一问题。

> **教训：**
>
> * **警惕集团间的恃强欺弱。** 在危机过程中，有些利益集团的力量特别强大，迫使决策在信息不完备或不符合工程利益的情况下通过。
> * **不要指望人们会把潜在的问题反应出来。** 工程内部的共同利益可以导致人们的防护性行为，特别是当某个人正好有过失时。那些不到现场去，想仅仅依靠那些有良好愿望顾问工程师向他或她汇报工程中存在的问题的项目经理最易受到伤害。为了防止潜在问题的不断恶化，项目经理必须深入危机之中，相信并接近那些通风报信者或告发者。

危机过程作为一个社会关系变更过程

前面章节的讨论中指出工程危机促使组织内部社会关系的调整。这种关系的调整过程是人们为了取得那些能使资源重新分配朝着有利于自己利益的方向发展的信息而不断斗争的结果。在这种斗争中，人们为了自己的利益不断努力地塑造自己和他人的社会关系模式，而他们的利益却往往和委托人的利益不一致。为了达到这个目的，人们可能会组成他们的利益集团来增强自己的力量。最终出现的信息流通模式取决于个人或利益集团能否把自己期望的信息流通结构模式强加给他人。

> **教训:**
> * **危机会带来社会混乱。**危机过程中，人们"常规的"忠诚和忠心改变了，这就不可避免地形成了暂时的联盟。这种联盟非正式性的特征使得他们很难被觉察或检测出来。它们最明显的表现就是对某人的判断或领导产生了一种持久的信任感和信心。

强加的解决方案是愚蠢的

　　虽然有些人或利益集团可能试图通过控制信息流通结构模式来为自己的利益服务，例如，排斥那些对他们带来威胁的人们，但我们所研究的几个事例却表明他们试图操纵的人们的利益和权力基本上决定着他们能否成功。有些人对被控制的状态表现出积极的响应，因为这符合他们的利益，另一些人却强烈的反对。这种支持或反对的状态一直持续着，直到他们的信息流通结构模式能为双方的利益服务或者一方能把自己期望的信息流通结构模式强加给另一方。然而，这强加上去的平衡不会比一个美丽的幻想好多少，因为受到压抑的人会越来越有紧张感和受挫折感。从长远的观点说来，这种紧张感能被压抑的时间是有限的。通过利益共享能很快的达到平衡而且平衡状态持续的时间会很长，因为人们自愿的选择了这种解决方式。

> **教训:**
> * **强加上去的解决方案不是持久的解决方案。**在危机过程中，人们自然而然的倾向于强加一个解决方案。虽然短期内它可能凑效，但这种解决方案只是暂时的，它会产生潜在的紧张状态，这种紧张状态会对后来的危机管理带来损害或者最终以亚危机的形式表现出来。最终，当涉及到很多利益集团时，只有那种让每个利益集团都有一种所有者的感觉的解决方案才能得以幸存，在达成这个决策过程中所耗费的额外时间都是值得的。
> * **通过风险共担，鼓励人们求同存异，放下偏见可以使人们的利益一致起来。**不像传统的那样寻找折衷的解决方案，而是鼓励人们共同努力寻找一种能符合每个人利益的解决方案。
> * **管理者在危机过程中必须注意权力的制衡。**他们必须深刻的了解危机，把自己看成是一个独立的，可靠的和公平的公断员。

富有效率的信息流通模式

　　这一节我们讨论不同类型的信息流通模式的发展及其效率。在危机过程中，管理人员可以用这些知识来预测、理解从而达到有效控制信息流的目的。

小集团

　　前些章节中，我们讨论了危机过程中出现的集团现象，指出这些集团趋于围绕人们的共同利益而产生。然而，集团赖以产生的共同利益是变化着的，集团成员也不总是我们所认为的那些建筑工程的传统利益集团。这些集团是有益的，因为他们打破了信息流通的障碍。然而，令人遗憾的是，相对说来，这种集团比较少，因为它的形成需要有相当的远见和漠视传统的职业间陈规的勇气。

大多数集团产生的原因是人们想增强他们在谈判中的力量，控制信息流或为保护个人利益而隐藏问题。当过失会归咎到某个人时，最容易发生这种现象。另一方面，集团也可能因为利他主义的原因而产生，比如想要分享信息或想帮忙解决问题时，就会出现这种情况。在风险共担的环境中，以及人们能认识到他们之间相互的依赖性时，这种集团模式最易产生。

令人遗憾的是，导致集团产生的消极因素往往大于积极因素，这常常使信息流集中在少数人之间，组织结构不连续及信息流通过程的中断。当然也有一些例外，当集团的活动被严密地监控着以保证它产生积极的效果，并且给人们提供和这些集团沟通的机会时，这种集团就不会带来问题了。实际上，管理者可以通过简化组织，减少界面来实现对集团有效的控制。

> **教训：**
> * **危机具有产生不可预料的且常常是令人吃惊的忠诚心的潜力。** 必须小心，忠诚心往往是不可预见的，它产生的原因可能是暂时的、隐藏的。
> * **管理者应该为有积极性的集团的产生创造条件。** 这可以通过鼓励组成职业间队伍，鼓励人们不要互相谴责以及强调人们之间的相互依赖性而做到。
> * **管理者应该警惕消极集团的形成并解散它们。** 消极的集团可以通过它隐藏的特征，它们对外界的怀疑和排挤而被辨别出来。这种集团中常包括那些害怕在危机中受到谴责的人们。

集中度

在我们所研究的几个案例中，在很多情形下，人们都试图占据信息流通网络的中心位置。他们这样做的原因和方法是多种多样的。

重新获得控制权

有些人占据信息流通中心位置的主要原因是他们想获得控制权，他们常常通过控制信息的供给和（或）需求来达到这个目的。获得控制权的另一个途径是占据信息流通中守门员的位置，因为这使得他们能够按照他们的利益对信息进行筛选和控制。

避免受到谴责

与危机紧密相关会使人产生一种会被牵连而受到谴责的惧怕感。防止这种现象的一种方法是减少与陷入危机中的人们的直接接触，以中间人的身份出现，这样他就可以被看成是一个建议者，而不会被卷入问题之中。

避免偏见

在危机过程中，许多既得利益集团都处于存亡攸关的时刻，当处于信息守门员位置的人们试图阻止信息在某些人之间流通时，就可能出现信息的封锁和变形。人们克服这个问题的一种方法就是寻找这种潜在的带有偏见的信息源周围的备选路径。

获得力量

　　危机过程中出现的集团利益的不同，使得人们对什么是危机以及谁应该对危机负责有不同的解释。这常常导致协商的过程，在这个过程中，信息是重要的力量源泉。基于对这一点的充分理解，有些人试图使他们的信息流通网络独一无二且不为人所知；另一方面，对手却常常试图渗入他的信息网络，找出能使对方据理而争的基本原因并最终破坏它。

什么样的信息流通模式最有效?

　　从信息流通的有效性来说，那种在信息提供方面有较高的集中度，而在信息接受方面有较低的集中度的信息流通模式最富有效率，这就是说，从一个受限制的信息源发送出广泛分布的信息流是最富有效率的信息流通模式。这能保证一个具有强有力的领导和最小的误解的信息流通模式的形成，因为人们都是在基本上相似的信息基础上进行工作的。这种"浓缩型"的信息流通模式还有一个优点就是危机过程中所涉及到的人们能不通过可能带有偏见的中间人而直接进行沟通。在这种浓缩型的信息网络中，人们被紧密的联系在一起，相互之间彼此接近。这就为危机管理提供了灵活性，能保证问题、观点和解决问题的方法广为流通而又变形较小。

　　以一个人为中心其他人都紧紧围绕在他周围的信息流通模式似乎是最高效的流通模式，因为这能保证流通过程具有高度的连续性。这种模式的另一个优点就是它把能提供信息备选路径的守门员出现的可能性降到了最低。守门员的危险在于他把信息集中在有限的渠道，增大了信息过载和信息瓶颈现象的可能性。它也给那些为了自己利益而操纵信息的人提供了机会。但信息守门员的作用也不总是消极的，这取决于占据这个位置的人的性格特征。当他独断专行，有消极心理且无力应付对他的信息需求时，他就会起消极的破坏作用；当他有经验，有能力且有良知时，就会有积极的作用。

　　最后，信息流通网络中人们之间高级别的相似性（等同性）能够缩小信息差异，使人们在相同的信息基础上进行合作。相反的，当信息流通网络中人们之间相似性（等同性）较低时，由于人们会被拉向不同的方向而使组织变得不连贯。

教训:

* **危机过程中信息流通模式对危机管理的效率有很大的影响。**管理者应该尽可能建立这样的流通模式:系统内包括尽可能少的消极集团和尽可能多的积极集团，限制性的信息源和广泛分布的信息供给路径，高密度（信息流通中的直接性），紧密围绕在一个人周围的流通模式，较少的信息守门员位置，个人之间在信息流通网络中有较高级别的等同性。

* **因为信息流通模式决定着人们的力量基础，它就成了人们试图控制的目标。**这使得信息流通过程中可能出现信息的筛选，变形和对某些流通方向的限制，从而降低了危机管理的有效性。一般来讲，人们倾向于占据信息流通的中心位置并使自己的流通模式有别于他人。管理者应该确保有正确动机的人们处于信息流通的中心位置，人们之间的信息流通网络能组成一个完整的体系。

> **教训：**
> * **一个警告**：虽然有效的信息流通结构模式能保证信息流通过程的清晰化和公开化，但却不能确保危机管理的成功。因为这还取决于网络所传输的信息的质量。而信息的质量又基本上取决于网络内成员的动机和能力。如果人们决心要搞些破坏或没有能力处理危机带来的压力，那设计再完美的信息系统也都无能为力了。从这个意义上讲，受危机影响的人们之间积极的相互关系，人们的动机和品质是决定危机管理效率的基础。

危机中的行为

　　任何危机都需要投入在工程一开始时没料到的额外的精力，时间和资源。然而，这些额外投入的使用效果却是变化多端的，每个危机过程都被一些转变点分成具有不同的行为和前进动力的独特的阶段。

渐进性和突发性危机中的行为特征

　　我们研究过的案例中有突发性危机，也有渐进性危机。若把二者进行比较，就会出现一些有趣的模式。例如，和突发性危机相反，渐进性危机的早期阶段的特征和人们预想的正好相反，组织内出现分裂，工作中带有情绪并存在问题。这种区别的原因可能是在突发性危机的震撼过后，人们不得不暂时放下自己的利益而首先为项目的生存而努力；而在渐进性危机过程中，人们有时间追求自己的利益，重要的被忽略了的问题会逐渐积累起来导致第二个较突然的亚危机，迫使人们把他们不同的利益搁置一边。

> **教训：**
> * **非常令人吃惊的是人们在渐进性危机中的行为比在突发性危机中的行为更具有不确定性和危险性**。突发性危机使人产生一种紧迫感，并产生了早期前进的动力，如果妥善管理，这种动力还能继续。这一点可以通过确定，加强和支持危机早期取得的成功和出现的建设性的工作关系来实现。相反的，渐进性危机很少给人们带来紧迫感，使他们有时间来维护自己的利益。管理者必须警惕那些隐藏着的代表着渐进性危机早期信号的紧张关系。一种克服作为渐进性危机特征的分裂性和缺乏危机感的方法就是人为地制造一个突发性危机，如果管理妥善，人为的突发性危机中出现的积极性可以用来驱散促使它产生的渐进性危机中的差别性。

危机中人们行为的不可预测性

　　危机中人们的行为具有不可预测性。例如，在土方开挖支护危机（案例Ⅰ）中，第一阶段人们行为的特点是缺乏前进的动力、犹豫不决、不确定性、正式性、不灵活性、防御性和冲突的不断升级。进入第二阶段后人们行为的特点转变为具有前进的动力、相互的敏感性、公开的信息流通、试图解决问题的倾向、集体责任感以及较低的不确定性和情绪性。危机的第三个循环又返回到缺乏前进动力、不确定性、混淆性和带有很大的情绪性的阶段。到了最后一阶段，人们的行为特点又返回到充满前进的动力、合作性、果断性、协商性、折衷性、集体责任感和低情绪性的阶段。铺面材料危机(案例Ⅳ)中人们的行为模式和上述的情形基本相同,但在挡土墙危机(案例Ⅲ)中,人们的行为模式却正好相反。开始阶段的特征是充满了前进的动力、人们普遍有解决问题的愿望、公开的讨论、集体责任感和相对较低的情绪。然后,就进入第二阶段,基本上没有前进的动力、不确定性和不果断性大大增强,不愿意提供信息,越来越强的受挫感和忧虑感。最后,进入到一个更加消极的阶段、没有前进的动力、没有灵活性、充满挫折感和情绪性。和其他任何案例完全不同的是电梯危机(案例Ⅱ),在这个危机中,一直维持着前进的动力,人们的行为也没有明显的阶段性。

> **教训:**
> * **建筑工程危机过程中,不存在具有通用性的行为模式。**应该防止千篇一律的危机管理方式。对于工程中出现的危机没有现成的、固定的解决方案,危机过程中人们行为的不确定性要求危机管理过程要更理智、更周全、更具有反应性,而这种能力基于对人们为什么要按一定方式行事的动机的深刻理解。

预测人们行为的变化

如果危机管理过程是在一种时进时退的循环中进行的,危机管理者面对的挑战就是及时抓住前进的动力并保持住它。这需要掌握如何引导人们积极的行为,对行为变化原因的理解和对行为变化早期信号的敏感性等多方面的知识。

引起危机过程转变的主要事件

危机过程的转变点都与一些诸如令人意外的索赔的提出,高层领导或委托人的突然介入等主要事件同时发生。虽然引起"危机过程转变的主要事件"的特征变化多端,它们却都是由危机过程的参与者有意或无意间引起的。因此,这种主要事件看起来是突然而至的,但事件到来之前却有无数的前兆。例如,在我们所研究的一个案例中,承包人的区域监督员的突然介入引起人们危机过程中行为的变化,但在这之前,组织内不断增长的紧张关系是可以检测出来的,其表现就是承包人不断的警告和工期延误的威胁。在每个重要的引起危机过程变化的事件来临之前,都有一些类似的警告信号出现。

尽管人们行为变化前存在警告信号,人们对它却不敏感,这有时是有意的,有时却是无意的。例如,在许多案例中,人们故意不理会对手明显的受挫感和他们发出的纠纷升级的信号。然而,也有一些例子表明,有些时候人们(常常是高级决策人)会被那些有过失而又不想受到谴责的人从警告信号中隔离开来。最令人烦恼的是随着时间的推移,这种不敏感性和抗拒变化的力量会日益增大,因为不断积累的损失使得如果接受变化,受到的消极影响会更大。在这同时,要求变化的一方促进变化的动力也越来越大。这就使得抵抗变化的阻力越来越大,如此等等,直到工程队伍陷入一种不敏感,尖锐对立和冲突不断升级的循环中。这就是说,当工程一旦进入一种消极的行为阶段,情况会加速恶化,变得越来越难以停止。

让人感到更加烦恼的是对变化的不敏感性不仅是消极阶段的问题,而且也是积极阶段的问题。例如,在许多案例中,进步的喜悦和人们之间关系的不断增进使人们看不到工程内部存在的紧张关系。因此和消极阶段那种自我加强型的、强有力的行为相反,积极阶段人们的行为更脆弱，更易受到伤害。

虽然行为的不稳定性似乎是不可避免的，有一个危机(案例 II)却具有独特性，在整个危机过程中没有行为的转变点。在这个危机过程中，建筑师对承包商的需求及情绪的敏感及反应性意味着他总是及时地提供信息以避免危机的升级。同样的，承包商决心要完成一个成功的工程就意味着他不会利用建筑师的不幸来谋私利，而且愿意表现出解决危机的灵活性。从效果上来说，承包商在培养人们之间的敏感性和相互信任感中起了一种重要的补偿作用，从长远来说，加强了危机管理过程的稳定性。

教训：

* **如果一切正常，那你有可能忽略了某些事情。**
* **最有效的危机管理过程就是人们行为最稳定的过程。** 在危机过程中行为的不稳定性不是不可避免的。人们面对的挑战是能够鼓励并保持一种积极的思想。为了能做到这一点，最有效的方法就是鼓励人们之间对别人的需求保持敏感性，公开的信息流通以及处理危机时的集体责任感。
* **对危机过程中的早期干预再强调也不过分。** 消极性具有自我循环发展的潜力，随着时间的推移，越来越难以从中解脱。
* **危机具有内在的防御机制，因为它能为危机升级的早期信号产生不敏感性创造条件。**
* **危机管理者可以通过对人们之间相互关系变化的信号保持高度警惕而使人们的行为稳定化。**
* **试着将危机看成是一种提高团队间凝聚力的一个机遇而不是破坏它的威胁。** 最重要的是，鼓励他人也以同样的观点来看待它。

危机过程中对人们行为的解释

为了控制人们的行为，理解行为产生的原因是非常重要的。危机过程中人们的行为似乎是被许多因素激发的。

陈规

从我们所研究过的案例中可以看出，工程中人们对其他职业集团都有一种大体上由他们的经验所形成的预先的成见。这些成见影响人们对危机反应的初期行为，特别是在工程的早期阶段。例如，在一个危机中，顾问工程师和承包商之间的紧张关系的根源在于前一个工程中他们之间激烈的纠纷；在另一个危机中，建筑师对承包商的早期行为部分地决定于前一个工程中建筑师和承包商之间"不愉快的经验"。虽然我们可以料想成见对人们行为的影响在危机的早期阶段可能最为强烈，然而，所研究过的案例却表明他们具有持久性，连续性和抗变化性。

> **教训：**
> * 虽然表面上看起来工程中人们间的关系可能是平静的、和睦的，然而工程队伍内部可能隐藏着紧张的关系。危机过程中产生的对资源高度的需求，不明确性和压力为这些危机表现出来和不断发展创造了理想的条件。
> * 成见是危险的，因为它具有武断性，过分的简单性和消极性的特点。如果集团内成员之间已经有过积极性的相互经验，且在一个工程或几个工程间一直在一起工作，成见对这种集团的影响是最小的。成功能为进一步的成功打下基础，熟悉能减少无知，而无知正是成见的基础。

财务责任

人们危机过程中的行为也受财务责任不确定性程度的影响。不确定性主要是由含糊不清的合同文件所导致的，这些文件常常最易被那些应该对危机负有责任的人所利用。合同责任高度的不确定性使得潜在的受损方试图从他们的利益出发重新定义事件，从而产生了更大的不确定性并延长了危机管理过程。相反的，在财务状况确定的环境中，人们行为的特点是公开的讨论、清晰性和具有前进的动力。

> **教训：**
> * 尽可能地均摊工程风险。如果工程风险被均匀分摊了，财务责任就变成无关紧要的了，人们的注意力就会转移到如何减少总的损失而不是如何转移损失。
> * 如果风险不能被均匀分摊，风险的分配方式应该清楚明白且被大家所理解。那种认为合同能使风险分配清楚明白且能提高大家对它的理解的想法只不过是一个幻想。通过简化合同，减少合同数量并坚持凡私下参与合同的人都应该来讨论它，能够保证风险分配最为清楚明白。

害怕

不进行风险共担使得人们把注意力集中在他们的差别点上而不是共同点上；产生一种充满惧怕、反指责和谴责的氛围；并且在最需要加强人们之间的相互交流时，关闭了信息流通的渠道。然而，在我们所研究的一个案例中，工程队通过努力，把力量集中在使危机造成的额外费用最小化上而不是集中在由谁来负责支付它的问题上，从而克服了合同中内在的分裂现象，其结果是危机所造成的费用增加小到了根本不值得一争的地步。

> **教训：**
> * 应该把注意力放在如何使费用最小化上，而不是争论由谁来支付它上。
> * 把注意力放在人们的相同点和相互依赖性上而不要放在不同点和独立性上。
> * 避免形成对危机产生那种反指责的反应。进行客观性的调查，防止只把精力放在追究责任上，把注意力放在寻找解决方案上而不是追究原因上，创造一种合作性的而不是惩罚性的环境。

组织的策略

人们的行为也受雇佣他的组织所采用的策略的影响。例如，在我们所研究的一个案例中，承包商鼓励进行索赔，这似乎对他的雇员的行为也造成了影响。在同样一个工程中，顾问工程师防御性的反应可能就是受委托人严格的预算费用控制策略的影响。相反的，在危机解决的非常成功的案例中，承包商无视组织的策略，以一种尽可能合作的态度给委托人留下了一个良好的印象。这种策略所鼓励的容忍和适应对危机的有效解决有很大的作用。

> **教训：**
>
> * **当组建一个工程队伍时，像注意一个人的个性和品质一样，要关注这个公司的文化。**留心那些行为放肆的、自私的组织，其中也包括委托人。
> * **在监控工程的目标系统和给予一定的灵活性以避免冲突发生这两者之间很难维持一种平衡。**缺乏灵活性导致交涉过程中的防御性和僵化性，这最终导致冲突的升级。目标系统的灵活性不是公开宣布目标的容许变化范围，因为这会使人们不尽最大努力去实现它。目标系统的灵活性是指做好在不超出应急费用允许范围内完成工作的准备，从这一点说，允许组织预留风险准备金是必不可少的。

工程危机管理中的两大讽刺

危机内在的防御机制使人们的行为和有效处理它所要求的行为正好相反。特别有讽刺意味的是，当集体责任心和团队精神特别重要时，冲突往往最容易出现；当高效的信息流通系统特别重要时，具有高效的信息流通系统的可能却非常小。

讽刺 1 号：当集体责任心和团队精神特别重要时，它似乎不可能实现

为了解释这种讽刺，我们返回到风险的分配问题上，以及危机的处理过程需要强大的额外资源注入的趋势上。

实际上，个别风险分配的主要问题是伴随危机而来的不可避免的，在资源重新分配上明显的赢家和输家的出现，这使得解决危机所需的集体责任感大为降低。当各个利益集团求助于正式的合同来明晰各自的责任，查找合同中的误解及解释的差异性时，问题就出现了。如果没有危机，这些差别性可能也就无关紧要，但危机时它却会造成一个不确定性的氛围，把人们的注意力从解决危机这个重要问题上引开。合同条款上的二意性给那些试图利用非正式谈判策略迫使资源重分配朝着有利于他们的方向发展的利益集团提供了机会。从这个意义上说，正式的合同只部分决定了危机过程中人们的责任的划分模式，各利益集团的策略和交涉能力也是重要的决定因素。

策略的失误和无意的升级

前些章节阐明了当危机和个别的风险分配方式相结合时，怎样通过暴露出人们之间那些本来可以继续隐藏下去的利益的冲突而导致工程队内部人们之间相互关系的巨大变化。危机过程中出现的任何异议都可能由于工程参与方的微薄利润以及危机所产生的高的风险

而演变成很激烈的争执。总的说来，这些条件使工程各参与方之间利益的冲突不断扩大，使得他们对盈利的机会更为敏感，而对潜在损失的抗拒力更强。在这种情形下，各参与方都准备好采用不同的交涉策略迫使资源的重新分配朝着有利于他们的方向发展。例如，在我们所研究的一个案例中，当承包人要求额外费用的索赔时，顾问工程师的反应是做出粗鲁笨拙的反击，称他们是在吓唬人，并想借此测试他们进行索赔的决心。也有许多例子说明，各参与方试图利用合同条款中的模棱两可性及危机本身的特征和起因来谋求自己的利益。这种策略被广泛使用的原因可能与危机升级的风险较小有关。然而，另一个被经常采用的危机升级的风险较大的策略是不理会对方的要求，这种策略常常产生警告和威胁并最终导致人为的危机升级。实际上，在我们所研究的案例中，除了一个例外，利益相关者所采用的各种策略的组合最终都产生了一个使危机升级的效果。假定没有任何一个利益集团刻意要制造一个全方位的大的冲突——也确实没有反面的例证——那么我们所观察的交涉过程都可以看成是决策的失误。

> **教训：**
> * **危机管理者必须进行管理**。这一点在危机过程中尤为重要，因为如果没有干涉，危机就有一种自然升级的趋势。
> * **危机使得工程队内部的弱点、误解和分裂更加明显和强化**。当集体责任心和团队精神特别重要时，冲突却最容易出现。
> * **当危机对资源方面有很大的影响，且参与各方的利润额都较小时，他们就越有保护自己利益的热情，冲突也就越容易由此而产生**。
> * **如果一方刻意要逃避责任，合同对受害方所能提供的保护是有限的**。无论合同上怎么讲，参与方可运用不合法的非正式的力量迫使资源的重分配朝着有利于他们的方向发展。在危机过程中，利益集团精明的策略比合同条款更能决定资源的重分配方案。
> * **当利益集团滥用它的非法权力时，力量较弱的一方可能是对的，却会遭遇极大的损失**。这会导致恶意，受挫感和潜在的冲突。应该努力保证一种公平的交涉过程。
> * **由于不同利益集团不正确的策略，使危机管理过程冲突偶然升级的可能性很大**。警惕潜在的各种危险策略的组合。

危险策略的组合

　　危机管理者应意识到并警惕能导致纠纷突然升级的各种策略的组合。通过了解这种策略产生的动机，危机管理者就能理解纠纷，预测它的历程，并拟定出纠纷升级风险低的、可行的解决方案。为了能鉴别出潜在的危险的策略的组合，分析我们所研究的每个案例的策略模式是非常有益的。见图 10-1 ~ 图 10-4。交涉准则参考表 5-1。

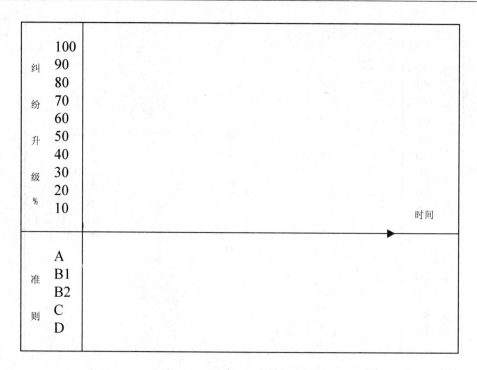

图 10-1　案例 I 过程中所使用的策略模式和纠纷升级的对比

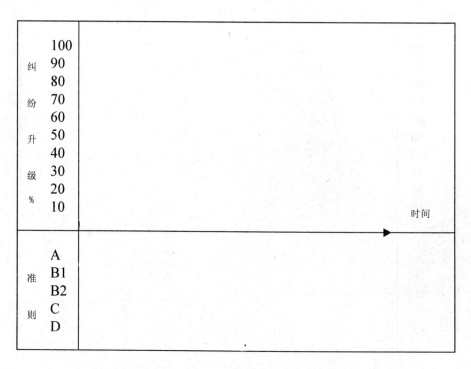

图 10-2　案例 II 过程中所使用的策略模式和纠纷升级的对比

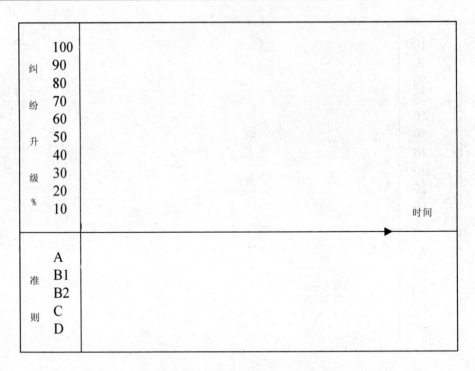

图 10-3 案例Ⅲ过程中所使用的策略模式和纠纷升级的对比

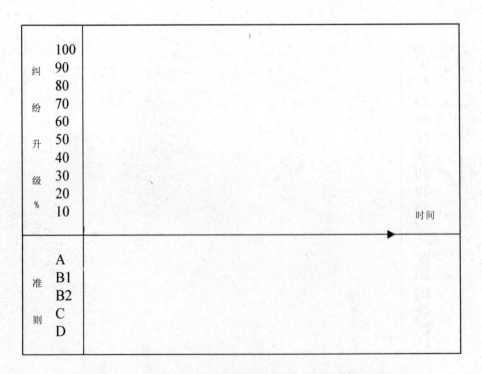

图 10-4 案例Ⅳ过程中所使用的策略模式和纠纷升级的对比

从这种策略模式的分析中可以看出，对立的利益集团趋于遵循平行的路径。这就是说，一方采用侵略性的策略，会导致另一方做出同样的反应，最终使得纠纷升级。这潜在的一前一后的纠纷升级模式似乎与项目内集团之间公平的相互均衡的权力有关。虽然合同赋予的合法权力可以使一方压制另一方的申辩，工程中各参与方也常常有能力且准备着要使用相当一部分非法的权力。为了防止纠纷升级，其中一方就必须打破这种模式，表现出和解、折衷和合作的意愿。这样一种承诺也常常会得到对手相同的反应。然而，采用和解的交涉准则的动机必须是坦诚的且能为对手所领悟到的。如果做不到这一点，就不能使问题得到缓解。

> **教训：**
> * **合同不能解决危机，人却可以。**合同不能代替好的管理方式。
> * **对手间高效的信息流通对避免纠纷的突然升级至关重要。**许多纠纷的起源都是相互之间非常简单的误解。
> * **强迫性的解决方案从长远来说不能解决纠纷，那种在折衷基础上达成的方案也不能。**折衷的结果不会带来最优的解决方案，也不能充分解决根本的分歧和紧张。强迫和折衷只是给了人们一种幻想的解决方案。
> * **合作是彻底解决危机所产生的紧张状态的唯一的方法。**因为它寻找有利于各个利益集团的最优的解决方案。然而，这个过程是很耗时间的，而且需要人们要有勇气放弃以前的观点，发挥创造力构想新的方案。

讽刺 2 号：当高效的信息流通系统特别重要时，这种可能却非常小。

良好的信息流通对高效的危机管理至关重要，因为信息是危机所产生的不确定性的良药。令人遗憾的是，当高效的信息流通系统特别重要时，危机所造成的环境使得这种可能性非常小。

信息是力量的源泉

在我们所研究的案例的危机中，在各利益集团的冲突被扩大的情况下，信息的价值日益增长。因为它代表着协商过程中重要的力量源泉，因此，它被严密地保护着。实际上，有相似利益的人们常常结合起来形成集团，为了能实现他们共同的利益，常有扣留信息内部分享的倾向。这样的集团会发展起一种神秘感，并强迫它的成员把集团的利益置于自己的利益之上。

大量的信息

危机过程中信息量的剧增和决策者责任的缩小耦合起来构成影响信息流通系统效率的另一个障碍。这个问题在突发性危机中尤为突出，因为组织结构中的"热点"处产生信息的瓶颈和信息的过载现象。使得信息的需求超前于信息的供给。占据这些位置的人们无法应付这些问题时就会采用一种不断增强的反应式的管理模式。一些人试图坚持那种正式的、标准的管理步骤，而另一些人更多的采用不正式的管理方式。然而，这两种极端的方法都会使得他们想要解决的问题更加复杂化。拘泥形式使得信息供给速度减慢，使人产生挫折感，而不拘形式又会导致信息流通过程的中断和产生误解。

> **教训：**
> * **因为危机过程中，人们之间的利益冲突加剧，使得人们有一种扣留信息的自然倾向**。危机过程中通过强调人们的共同利益，以及当信息供给和需求是唯一重要的议事日程时，定时召开"信息会议"能鼓励人们之间高效的信息流通。通过这种职业间会议产生和更新信息计划，阐明信息间的相互依赖性并负责信息的供给。
> * **信息的质量和数量一样重要**。减缓让人出错的时间的压力，雇佣称职的人们。
> * **突发性危机中会出现"热点"**。鉴别出处于"热点"位置的人们并给予支持。这些人在信息流通系统中占有至关重要的位置，讽刺的是他们也正是最易受压力影响的人们。
> * **用常规的、正式的方式处理危机和用完全非正式的方式对危机做出反应都是不合适的**。重点应放在灵活性和监控性的均衡上。令人遗憾的是，能做出这么良好的平衡的反应的可能非常小。相反的，工程参与各方常常采用极端正规或极端不正规的行为方式，使得工程陷入不良的信息流通，紧张、忧虑和压力的下滑循环之中难以解脱。

危机管理的动态性

作为对本章的总结，我们返回图 3 – 1 描述的危机管理模式中，研究每个案例中由于检测、诊断、决策及执行过程的无效率性而导致的危机管理过程中的惰性问题。

检　测

我们所研究的案例给出了多个对潜在危机的早期信号不敏感的例证。这种不敏感性可由以下原因造成：人员不称职，工程过程中队伍的变动，事件潜伏期，防御性以及害怕受到谴责等。实际上，人们对潜在问题是如此的视而不见，以至于环境对工程中问题的敏感度都比施工队伍对问题的敏感度要高。这更突出了把工程的所有利益相关方都包括到危机管理过程中的重要性。

除了在检测问题方面的无效率性外，在检测和诊断过程的过渡阶段也存在着问题。这就是说，潜在的问题常常被扣留住，不让决策者知道——这有时是故意的，其原因是利益的冲突以及监控员和比较员之间缺乏信任感。

诊　断

在危机管理的所有过程中，诊断过程中的问题最多。在这儿，危机的财务责任要明确起来，潜在的输家和赢家都要为他们的利益而斗争。在许多情况下，那些具有合同权力的人们为了保护它们的利益，防止潜在问题在高一级的决策者前暴露，控制并操纵着诊断阶段。

决策和执行

在决策执行阶段也存在无效率性，其基本原因是，在危机的压力下，人们倾向于匆忙中在信息不全面或不正确的情况下做出决策。在突发性危机中，人们以财务问题为代价，把精力集中在组织问题上；而在渐进性危机中，正好相反。结果，在突发性危机的执行阶段，财务问题出现了，而在渐进性危机的执行阶段，组织问题就出现了。

学习和恢复

危机过程中，人们之间的相互关系发生了相当大的变化，大多数情况下，朝着坏的方向而不是好的方向。然而，似乎没有什么事实能证明人们会关注危机后的学习和恢复过程。即使在很成功的危机管理后，人们也习惯于将明智的做法藏于身后，掩盖危机中工程队内部出现的冲突。

危机管理过程的重复性

令人感到似非而可能的是，虽然危机管理的无效性给危机管理过程带来了惰性，却又把危机管理过程推向了不断的循环过程中。例如，土方开挖支护和电梯危机经过了两个循环，粘土铺面危机经过了三个循环，而挡土墙危机经过了四个循环。在每一个案例中，每一个循环都是必要的，因为无效率性在人们中间产生压力，使他们感到自己的要求没被满足。每一个循环过程都是一个被没得到满足和受压抑的集团用来缓解压力的机制。压力越大，为了缓解它所需的循环次数就越多。例如，在一个危机中，建筑师拒绝同意承包商的额外费用索赔导致现场的延误，而这种延误又导致了工期的索赔，这就开始了危机管理的另外一个循环过程。危机管理过程将不断的循环进行着，直到达到平衡点，在这平衡点上，与以前没能满足的要求相关的、潜在的所有的压力都消失了。

> **教训：**
> * **无论谁将承担风险，激励人们去监控和交流潜在的问题。**这包括所有的利益相关者(工程内部和外部)。不要忽略外部利益相关者的意见。
> * **为了迅速的解决潜在问题，阐明人们之间的共同利益及相互依赖性。**
> * **在整个工程的生命期内，保证工程队伍的连续性。**
> * **警惕工程中当人们的注意力集中在别处时，危机的潜伏期。**
> * **鼓励和促进快速的、果断的、清晰的信息流通模式。**
> * **避免做出匆忙的、欠考虑的决策，保证所做出的决策是基于技术，组织和财务等各个方面的综合考虑。**在危机的早期阶段人们倾向于变得慌乱起来。一开始就把事情作好比到后来再来改正它效率要高得多。
> * **确保每一个利益相关者都能感觉到他们的利益公平的体现在了危机管理过程中。**没有解决的利益冲突会把危机推向下一个循环。最有效的危机管理过程只进行一次循环。
> * **注意危机过后的学习和恢复工作。**执行情况总结是危机管理的一个重要方面，它包括发现并弥补受损害的关系，进行独立的危机后管理过程。

结 论

这一章对前面讨论的四个案例的相似之点和不同之处进行了总结。其目的在于能识别出一些重要的有实用性的教训，来帮助管理者解决工程中的危机。讨论中强调了危机计划的重要性以及危机管理过程中自满情绪的危害性。所有的危机似乎都有一种内在的防御机制，使得危机管理工作更加困难。特别是，他们都有把本来隐藏的压力表现出来，给信息流通和人们之间的关系带来损害，使得人们的行为富有自私性和操纵性，能产生更进一步的问题并能不断累积自己破坏性的动力。虽然我们这一章所强调的这些教训对问题的缓解会有一些作用，但其主要目的却是帮助管理者们得出这个最重要的教训：如果进行妥善的管理，危机可以为我们所利用。

第十一章

结论——创建乐观性的组织

毫无疑问,危机给管理者带来了危险,但同时也带给他们独一无二的改进提高的机遇。这一章我们总结那些能充分利用这些潜在的生产力的组织的特征。这些总结中既包括文化性因素也包括实用性的因素。实用性因素是当项目管理者面对危机时,以指导的形式出现的;而文化性因素就带有更大的普遍性和支持性。本章开始时首先集中在对文化性问题的讨论上,因为没有积极的文化,任何实用性的观点都不会有什么实际意义。

乐观主义或者悲观主义——一种刻板的选择

本书开始时充满着一种乐观主义的意味。结束时使人们认识到,通过把不确定性和复杂性看成是一种威胁或者是一种机遇,管理者可以控制他们的命运。虽然这种刻板的陈述似乎有点太简单化,但这并不意味着管理者可以忽略危机所带来的不可否认的威胁。它指出,管理者可以以积极或消极的思想来对待危机,前者和后者的区别在于前者把精力集中在危机所赋予的机遇上,相信它可以为自己所利用。建筑行业的许多管理实践都是被悲观主义的缓解而不是最优化的原则所引导的。我们所研究的案例表明,工程一旦开始,传统的合同,组织的惯例和文化使人们陷入一种预定的、标准的行为模式中,很少有对这种模式进行改进的激励。他们还创造了一种惩罚性的充满怀疑,恐惧和不信任感的环境,抑制了那种充满革新性,勇气有无私性的乐观性组织文化所需要的公开性和自由性。在我们所研究的案例中,最大的成功似乎是属于那些准备和传统的组织模式作斗争的人们。

乐观性的组织机构

整本书中都一直在强调支持乐观性组织机构的一些原则。下面我们对这个问题进行讨论。

乐观的人们

乐观性组织机构的特点在于它有决心也有能力把危机看成是一种提高工作能力的机遇,并且有决心充分利用这个机遇。这就需要有积极的思想方式,而这只能通过雇佣那些充满了乐观,勇气和活力的人们才能达到。然而,工程中的任何一个人都受雇于某一组织,且在一定程度上受组织的控制,如果组织级别的关系不具备积极性,那么个人的乐观性很快就会消失。对管理者来说,鼓励那些受雇于缺乏动力甚至充满怨恨感的领导者的人们乐观起来是一个很大的挑战。从这个意义上说,能否创造一个乐观的环境依赖于建筑业能否从传统的雇佣制度、合同和组织结构中转变过来。这些惯例是从一种相对稳定但充满对立的环境里逐渐发展起来的,这种模式使得如果某处出现了问题,很容易使某个人受到谴责。因此,支持这种模式的原则就是集中性、统一性、等级制、部门划分、惯例及僵化性。然而今天这种机会主义的环境里,这些原则都已经过时了,因为它会导致悲观主义者的恶性循环,压抑人们赖以抓住未来机遇的个性、革新性、创造力和勇气。将来建筑业的运行将依赖于一种新的乐观主义的模式,这种模式基于一种和传统的原则相反的充满了灵活性、开放性、平等性、依赖性、集体责任感、信任感、利益和风险共享性以及相互的理解性等基础之上。通过这种转变,可以把建筑业的劳动力从那种充满恐惧感的限制潜在的生产力的环境中解放出来。

高效的信息流通

很明显,光有好的人们并不能保证工程的成功。好的人们需要有高效的信息流通系统来支持,以促进行业所需要的人们之间相互的信任感和开放性的形成。信息匮乏是危机过程中产生分裂和不信任感的主要原因,一个设计精良的信息流通系统,应该能够防止瓶颈现象的出现,均匀快速的传播信息,且能使信息被操纵的可能降到最低。

在建筑业,除了文化和组织会对信息流通系统构成障碍以外,日益增长的精简高效的趋势也成为信息流通系统的一大障碍。建筑业必须警惕这种趋势,因为它去掉了信息流通系统的可靠性所要求的、必要的多余部分。而且,建筑业必须改变它约束性的合同惯例,使得人们能合法的放弃那些正式的,在危机中给人们带来约束的,降低生产率的做法。

准 备

乐观主义在很大程度上依赖于组织对未来可能发生的问题的一种预测的能力。能预测未来的组织就能充分利用机遇。值得重申的是,世界上最成功的组织是那些愿意花费时间拟定最优的、能从深层次反应他们过去和未来脆弱怀的危机计划的组织。然而,面对组织的脆弱性决不意味着仅仅理解它所面临的风险,必须理解它应付危机的能力,这就意味着危机计划过程不但包括实现组织力量的过程,也包括克服组织弱点的过程。这使得组织能够把它的力量最大化,弱点最不化。

乐观性组织的另一个特点是,它并不是盲目的乐观。乐观性组织的计划中充满了现实主义的观点,他们明白未来的计划不可能做的很准确。因此,他们时刻警惕着风险和机遇的不断变化,并相应地对他们的计划进行调整。

学 习

乐观主义的意识建立在一种通过总结过去的教训,可以改进以后工作的信念上。但这是痛苦的,因为新的知识和经验往往是从以前的危机中总结出教训。这种乐观的组织有一种自我批评的机制,来回顾和分析过去对危机所做的反应,并推行变更,保证根除未来的弱点。相反的,悲观性组织喜欢把过去藏在身后,这可能会使他们不能充分利用可能是使令人不愉快的、但却非常有价值的教训。

保证早期的干预

危机趋向于引起分裂和冲突,进而迅速破坏组织内存在的任何乐观主义的意识。因为这个原因,乐观主义很重要的一方面就是早期的干预,这依赖于能否迅速地辨别出早期存在的问题隐患并能把它遏制在萌芽状态。这可以通过消除恐惧感,共担风险,给人们灌输一种无论问题大小,都有义务去关注的意识而做到。实际上,乐观性组织是一个充满自信的,团结的,具有自我支持能力的实体,它对所有的潜在的问题都保持敏感。

创造一个支持性的、稳定的环境

　　组织能否具有乐观性的思想,依赖于组织精神上的健康和它的成员的健康。他们需要一种富有效率的、有控制性的、有激励性的、有积极性和对新观点的支持性的工作环境。机会主义的组织提供了一种具有敏感性、谨慎性和回报性的环境,这种环境能使不确定性最小化,防止隔离状态,并能使受挫感最小化。这种环境可以通过最大可能的保持队伍的连续性,减少工程队伍之间的界面数量,以及减少决策中的不果断性和不必要的变更创造出来。

创造一个合作的环境

　　一些伴随着危机的冲突使人们把注意力集中在他们的不同点上而不是相同点上。我们已经看到了,如果人们能从被认为是建筑业解决纠纷最为有效的、折衷的解决问题的方法中摆脱出来,冲突会被解决得多么具有积极性。以时间和费用压力为特点的建筑工程驱使人们采用折衷的解决问题的方法,讽刺的是,这种方法很少能真正缓解这种压力。相反的,合作的精神却提供了充分利用人们的创新精神,为互利互惠的思想大下了基础,从而能制定出对每一个人来说都是有利的解决方案。

乐观主义的实用观点

　　一个注重创造乐观性文化氛围的管理者,就为他进行有效的危机管理打下了深厚的基础。这是一种化危机为机遇的管理模式,本书提供了一些实用的指导,以帮助达到这个目的。在这些实用的观点进行总结之前,很有必要指出,本书并没提供任何现成的解决问题的方案。因为没有什么东西可以代替对导致每一次危机的一系列独特的事件进行周全的分析,做出敏感的、反应性的处理这样一个过程。但是,从总体上来说,却可以使危机朝着有利于你的方向发展。

* 　不要忽视它。
* 　不要拖延。
* 　不要依赖合同,把它当成是管理方法的替代品。
* 　对形势的严重性进行广泛的交流,使每个人都知道危机的存在。
* 　如果缺乏紧迫感,灌输这种意识。
* 　给危机以优先权,且为它筹备资源。
* 　对不同的危机,采用不同的处理方法。
* 　执行通用的危机管理计划,以取得一些时间。
* 　委托一个能迅速对危机做出反应的独立的危机管理者,或许局外人士最适合这个角色。
* 　尽可能快的对危机做出一个定义。鉴别并将所有的利益相关者包括在内,因为不同的人会有不同的观点。
* 　组建危机管理小组。成员包括必要的专家,高层次的管理者以及能对解决方案做出贡献的主要利益相关者。
* 　公开危机管理小组每个成员的身份,明确他们的权力和责任。
* 　放松的过程。不要预先指定危机管理小组的运行规则,让人们充分发挥自己的管理风

格。

* 定义危机管理目标系统。拟定改进提高的目标。
* 期望有一个结果。监控方案的进行情况。
* 准备在目标系统之间进行均衡。
* 通过强调危机积极性的一方面,把危机看成是一个机遇的挑战。
* 考虑每一个利益相关者。独立性在危机管理中至关重要。
* 定义了危机以后,如果有详细的方案,就执行该方案,方案可能并不完美,应根据详细的反应情况做出调整。
* 明确表达对危机管理小组以外的利益相关的关注。
* 保证随时向任何人——包括系统内部的和系统外部的——通报危机的现状。
* 不要推测责任的划分和谴责的归属问题。往前看,去解决问题。
* 集中精力使费用最小化而不要去关注谁将去支付它。
* 鼓励公开的信息流通的个人工集团模式。信息能消除潜在的误解和冲突。均匀而至的信息比大批量涌来的信息要好。
* 警惕能控制信息流通的个人或集团。他们可能会利用这个便利条件来为自己的利益服务。
* 鼓励集体责任心。每一个人的未来都是连在一起的。
* 把注意力放在人们之间的相互关系上,而不要放在某一个人身上。
* 不要使危机人性化。
* 避免将过失归咎于某一个个人或组织。要看将来不要看过去。
* 不要谈及输赢。每一个人都应坚信自己能赢。
* 鉴别出那些把自己看成是输家和赢家的人。因为他们是压力和潜在的冲突的源泉。
* 注意潜在的输家,因为他们是决策方案主要的抵抗力源泉。
* 监控输家和赢家之间使用的策略。鼓励合作,并对相互关系恶化的信号保持警惕。警惕有侵略性的、自私的组织,包括委托人在内。
* 查找并制止工程队伍成员之间的寺强欺弱现象。
* 不到万不得已,不要使用强制性的解决方案。
* 避免采用现成的解决方案。草率的解决方案只能带来问题。
* 留心卫星式的问题,它可能变成新危机,危机又会产生更多的危机。
* 不要忽视组织其他方面的活动。
* 定期对进度进行交流。把注意力放在积极的方面,而不要放在消极的方面。
* 鼓励创造性和激进主义。危机属于极端事件,常常需要极端的处理方案。
* 保持平静。恐慌只能加剧危机。
* 鉴别压力会由此发展的"热点"。给予占据"热点"位置的人们以支持。
* 必要时提供咨询和医疗服务。表现出你的关怀。
* 危机过后,进行积极的反馈,总结经验,对目标系统进行重新评估,重新把注意力放在组织上,弥补受到损害的相互关系,敏感地进行调查管理工作,获得到能使组织不断前进的更多的知识。这样你将会变得更富有经验。

结 论

这本书以积极的评论的作为结束语。虽然它始于企业持续不断的与不确定性做斗争的环境里，却结束于洞察企业如何将看似充满敌意的环境转变成能为管理者所利用的有利条件。这种认识为我们如何以积极的态度对待危机提供了实用性的指导。它还提供了更多支持这种努力所需的文化环境。如何创造这种乐观的文化氛围是对工程管理者提出的一个令人兴奋的挑战。

CRISIS
MANAGEMENT
IN CONSTRUCTION
PROJECTS

MARTIN LOOSEMORE, PH.D.

American Society of Civil Engineers
1801 Alexander Bell Drive
Reston, Virginia 20191-4400

*Abstract:*This book focuses on preventing crises and, if that's not possible, turning them to advantage. It draws lessons from a range of industries, concluding that the secret of effective crisis management is balancing prevention with control. Unfortunately, crises have built-in defense mechanisms that cause people to act in ways that makes this difficult.The book also gives advice as to how to overcome the built-in defense mechanics that cause people to act in way that may impede effective crisis management.

Library of Congress Cataloging-in-Publication Data

Loosemore, Martin.
  Crisis management in construction projects/Martin Loosemore.
     p. cm.
Includes bibliographical references and index.
 ISBN 0-7844-0491-7
1. Building—Safety measures. 2. Emergency management. I. Title.

  TH443 .L75 2000
  690'.068'4—dc21

                                                              00-064569

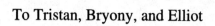

To Tristan, Bryony, and Elliot

TABLE OF CONTENTS

ACKNOWLEDGMENTS

Thank you, Heather, for your unending patience and support. Thanks also to my three children, without whom this book would have been much easier but far less worthwhile!

There are many other people I need to thank such as my parents, John and Anita, who have taught me so much and, the colleagues who have helped shape my ideas. In particular, I would like to thank Peter Hibberd, Will Hughes, Trevor Francis, Denny McGeorge, Goran Runeson, Melissa Teo and Derek Walker for their friendship, criticism, and support.

Finally, thank you to my colleagues at The University of New South Wales, for providing a supportive environment in which to write this book. It is a pleasure to work in a faculty that is so conducive to research.

PREFACE

Political, economic, and social instability; depleted natural resources; increasing global competition; and rapid technological advances are making business increasingly unpredictable. Unexpected problems are the norm rather than the exception and high-profile engineering disasters such as the Hyatt Regency Hotel Walkway collapse in Kansas City in 1981 are merely the tip of the iceberg. Risk theory suggests that for every reported crisis,the multipliers in terms of unreported incidents are enormous. For example, Smith (1996) indicates that for every fatality in the airline industry there are 10 major accidents, 30 minor accidents, and 600 near misses. This book draws an important distinction between the day-to-day problems that constantly punctuate the lives of managers and the occasional crises. The challenges of managing crises demand special attention because they hyper-extend organizational systems and personnel, posing managers with an extraordinary array of complex problems that can rapidly escalate into full-blown disasters. This book is about preventing this from happening.

One of the unique aspects of this book is its *preventative* and *reactive* focus. This contrasts with traditional construction management texts that have been dominated by prevention strategies rather than strategies for dealing with crises when they occur. While prevention is better than cure, it is increasingly unlikely that managers can create a crisis-free environment. This requires that organizations have reactive capabilities to deal with the unexpected.

Another unique feature of this book is its focus on *people*. This, too, is in contrast to traditional construction management texts, which are essentially scientific in their approach, being characterized by a plethora of bar charts, networks, and cash-flow graphs. While these texts emphasize measurement, control, and universal prescription as a means of reducing uncertainty, this book emphasizes thoughtfulness, flexibility, and the accommodation of uncertainty. This alternative approach to construction project management is important because there has been precious little research into the human aspects of construction project management. As Butterfield (1975) argues, "no field of thought can be properly laid out by men who are merely measuring with a ruler" (page 1).

Who is this book written for?

Crises have no respect for professional boundaries, which makes this book relevant to *all* who manage construction projects. While it has a construction flavor, it draws lessons from a wide range of industries and therefore, should also be of wider interest.

Although this book is primarily designed for practitioners, it challenges the traditional assumption that theory and practice are incompatible. Watson (1994) has shown how practicing managers intuitively develop, update, and draw on complex theoretical ideas in their day-to-day lives. Although they may not be formal management theories, managers are essentially "practical-theorists" and the most effective of them recognize the value of theories as conceptual frameworks to guide their actions. For this reason, this book marries an applied orientation with elements of strategic and basic research.

Distinctive text features

Experience is important when dealing with crises, but getting that experience is difficult and painful. The best substitute is to relay the experiences of others through case studies of past crisis management efforts. But, there are very few detailed accounts of crisis management in a construction context. To redress this deficiency, this book analyzes four actual construction crises. These case studies provide an excellent vehicle for readers to relive other peoples' experiences and the insights they provide are almost boundless. In particular, they help to develop an understanding of *how* and *why* people behaved as they did during a real-life crisis, thereby enabling judgments to be made about the influence of certain behaviors on crisis management outcomes.

In an educational sense, the case studies also provide interesting and amusing teaching material for analysis and discussion. The managerial issues covered include problem solving, decision making, leadership, communication, risk management, disaster management, health and safety, conflict and change management, organizational design, and teamwork.

Martin Loosemore, Ph.D., M.ASCE, MCIOB
Associate Professor
University of New South Wales
Sydney, Australia

Chapter 1

Introduction

This chapter challenges the anti-conflict value-system that causes most people to see crises as threats rather than opportunities. It demonstrates how well managed crises can strengthen projects rather than destroy them.

OUR ANTI-CONFLICT VALUES

To dedicate an entire book to crisis management may seem negative and defeatist. This is understandable in the context of modern business trends such as total quality management, partnering, and business process re-engineering. Such trends are increasingly evident within the construction industry and teach managers that prevention is better than cure, that crises are a sign of managerial failure and that any form of disharmony or conflict is wasteful and damaging.

The origin of these anti-conflict values lies in the institutions that indoctrinate us during our most impressionable and formative years. For example, at home we are often taught that our parents "know best," that we should "not answer back," and that we "should be seen and not heard." Church doctrines tell us that happiness is found in togetherness, harmony, peace, and tranquillity. At school, teachers have the right answers and are not to be challenged. Furthermore, traditional approaches to teaching tend to suppress any creativity and critical inquiry that children might possess, teaching them that the secret of success is giving the answers that coincide with what the teacher believes to be true. Indeed, as we mature, the institutional pressures to conform do not subside. For example, entry into a profession normally requires passing demanding examinations and subscribing to strict codes of professional practice. This system is designed to maintain and perpetuate the traditional roles that each profession has carved out for itself, which serve to distinguish its members from other professions and to define their status in society.

Many of the most vivid examples of institutions constraining the way we think can be found throughout the development of modern science where the church in particular, held back advances in understanding. For example, in the ecclesiastical universities of the middle ages, the belief was that it was necessary to separate the pursuit of truth from mankind's day-to-day cares and that the church was the high protecting power of all intellect, discovery, knowledge, science and speculation. While it is a fallacy that the church regularly punished and tortured those who criticized its doctrines, scientists, most of whom were monks, were expected to refrain from directly and explicitly challenging its authority. For example, although letters show that the church encouraged Copernicus to publish his theory that the sun rather than the earth was at the center of the universe, there is also evidence that he delayed its publication for 30 years because he was tortured by the inevitable criticism it would bring from his peers (Koestler 1975). Indeed, in 1633, when Galileo published research that supported Copernicus' earlier theories, he was forced to retract his findings before a Catholic church tribunal. Incredibly, the charges against him were only recently annulled by the Pope.

While we have come a long way since the middle ages, modern institutions still govern our lives and it is not surprising that two of mankind's most profound advances in knowledge, the theory of relativity and the theory of evolution, occurred largely outside their influence. It is interesting to note that both Einstein and Darwin were amateurs who were not strongly affiliated to any particular university or church. This strong sense of individualism is also recognizable in many of the most influential political thinkers of our time. For example, Margaret Thatcher is noted for saying that "there is no such thing as society" and Aleksandr Helzen, who developed the concept of Glasnost which was later adopted by Mikhail Gorbachev, lived in exile for most of his life and rejected any form of collective action that might have compromised his beliefs. It would seem that disharmony is not as undesirable as we are taught and that creativity often comes from those who challenge the powerful anti-conflict values which pervade society and shape our behaviour.

NECESSITY—THE MOTHER OF INVENTION

The anti-conflict values that are increasingly propounded in mainstream management and in construction management are worrying since they create organizations that are driven by strategies of mitigation rather than optimization. Such organizations are incapable of achieving their full potential. While this book may initially appear negative, its aim is to challenge this pessimistic mind-set by developing a framework for an optimistic organization. In contrast to pessimistic organizations, optimistic organizations are driven by values that see crises as potential opportunities rather than threats, which, if well-managed, can enhance rather than threaten their effectiveness.

The case for optimism is perhaps most vividly illustrated in our history books, which are littered with examples of people demonstrating their greatest capacity for ingenuity in the face, midst, or aftermath of crises. Epidemics, in particular, have provided fertile ground for innovation. For example, the Black Death prompted quarantine regulations, Small Pox led to vaccinations, and Cholera was the impetus for the first public health authorities. Major disasters have also stimulated our creative capacities. For example, the great fire of London in 1666 gave architects like Christopher Wren and Nicholas Hawksmoor the chance to build many beautiful cathedrals such as St Paul's and also provided Britain with its first building regulations. Similarly, the Great Fire of Chicago in 1870 provided architects and engineers with the chance to construct the world's first steel-frame skyscrapers. Indeed, Chicago is still renowned for its innovative and exciting architecture.

In modern times, the most prominent stimulant to invention has been two world wars, the second of which led to the development of radar, DDT, Penicillin, jet-propelled aircraft, the United Nations, the World Bank, and the International Monetary Fund. More recently, the cold war gave us nuclear power and the space race, out of which came the first communications satellites and manned space craft.

The field of management has also generated many innovations in the face of adversity. For example, the deprivation, exploitation, and social unrest during the early industrial revolution prompted pioneers like Charles Babbage and Robert Owen to experiment with more paternalistic and socially responsible management practices (Sheldrake 1996). This spurned new ideas such as participatory management, work-groups, the first profit-sharing schemes, and educational and welfare facilities for employees. More recently, the origins of many contemporary management trends that we encounter in construction texts can be traced back to problematic times. For example, value engineering was developed in World War II to cope with severe material shortages that forced manufacturers to identify unnecessary costs in production and to experiment with alternative raw materials. To people's surprise, the results were often cheaper and better quality products (Miles 1967). Total quality management (TQM) can claim the same origin. The momentum for TQM grew out of the economic devastation of Japan during World War II. According to Tsurumi (1982) the destruction imposed on Japan was responsible for the enthusiasm with which the principles of TQM were embraced, coupled with a certain degree of luck in terms of their suitability to Japan's traditional cultural values. As Demming has pointed out in reference to America's continued failure to grasp TQM: "you have to be in a crisis before you pay attention."

Coincidentally, it was Japan's increasing competitive advantage over the Americans during the 1970s and 1980s that gave birth to the modern concept of benchmarking by the Rank Xerox Corporation. When Rank Xerox was challenged by Japanese competitors who could sell copiers for less than U.S. manufacturing costs, they dismantled the Japanese products and used the components as models for their own standards of production (Camp 1989). Later, General Motors and Ford did the same with Japanese gear boxes which were far smoother than theirs, discovering that the tolerances that their competitors were working toward were far smaller than those set by American industry. These principles have now been extended to all areas of business activity in most of the world's leading organizations.

UNLEARNING THE PAST—THE FUTURE'S CHALLENGE

If crises provide the arena for mankind's greatest steps forward, then the future for managers is exciting. In 1971, Alvin Toffler's *Future Shock* portrayed an increasingly chaotic, volatile, and crisis-prone business environment, largely brought about by demographic changes, resource depletion, globalization, technological advances, and world-wide political and economic reform. Indeed, his predictions proved far too conservative and while our predecessors dealt with tried-and-tested technologies in an evolutionary fashion, modern construction managers are faced with an ever-faster flow of new and largely untested technologies, with less time to understand their performance and compatibilities. This increased technical complexity has led to increased organizational complexity, reflected in more specialists with different needs and elaborate interdependencies which are often difficult to understand. To compound these problems, an increasing awareness that the construction industry is a major threat to the health and welfare of its employees, to the general public and to the environment, is leading to increased levels of external regulation. While one can cite past projects as evidence that such pressures have always been present, closer inspection reveals that construction managers have never had to grapple with such a wide variety of pressures, needs, and regulatory constraints. For example, while, in 1931, the program for the 102-story Empire State Building was only 14 months, the technology was relatively well tried and tested, construction regulations were far more lax than they are today, and safety was of secondary concern (Theodore 1975).

Thus, it would seem that the managerial challenge of the future is one of complexity and change rather than shear scale, as it was in the past. As Kanter (1983) noted, there is more competition, more activities to manage and importantly, more limited resources to achieve and fail with. There are also new opportunities, but their exploitation will demand a change toward more thoughtful, flexible, responsive, and human-centered managerial styles. This is because, in an increasingly uncertain and competitive environment, rigid systems become restrictive and counter-productive and an organization's ability to harness the creative capacities of its human resources becomes the basis of its vitality and success (Pascale 1991). The challenge of the future is to use people more effectively to discover better ways of exploiting the exciting opportunities that will arise.

Unfortunately, meeting this challenge has proved difficult in the construction industry because, like many other industries, management continues to be underpinned by the scientific values Frederick Taylor advocated in the early 20th Century (Blockley 1996). As Bea (1994) found in his investigation of marine structure failures, this has meant that most engineers are still very uncomfortable with two things: uncertainty and people. It is a disability that has become an increasing concern within engineering recently and a growing number of engineers are recognizing that their profession's continued prosperity will depend on expanding its focus from "one that deals solely with objects to one that deals equally proficiently with people" (Johns 1999). It is argued that this will better equip engineers to maximize the potential value of an increasingly diverse workforce, ultimately improving the reliability of their buildings and structures.

RECOGNIZING A CRISIS WHEN YOU SEE ONE

One certainty in a world increasingly saturated with complexity and uncertainty is that the future will be punctuated by sudden, unexpected, and potent events that will require a rapid response. These relatively intense events are called crises and while they are less frequent than the day-to-day problems that constantly punctuate the lives of managers, most can expect to have to deal with at least one during their career. The way in which managers deal with such events can mean the difference between corporate life or death and in a construction project setting, minds automatically turn to vivid incidents such as fires, bankruptcy, serious disputes, serious accidents, collapses, strikes, and natural phenomenon such as floods. However, the variety of crises that can arise on construction projects is enormous and in a recent American survey, engineers ranked them in descending order of frequency as: construction delays, design errors; cost over-runs, management successions; local opposition to project; employee raided by competitor; third-party lawsuit; disgruntled employee; merger or acquisition and accidents (Reid 1999).

Whatever its precise nature, a crisis is generally accepted to be a low probability, unexpected, high-impact event that is not covered by contingency plans (Booth 1993). Crises represent an immediate and serious threat to high priority goals, placing managers under extreme time pressure to find a non-routine solution. They also have widespread financial, political, cultural and social implications, the consequences of which are likely to be subject to extensive public, media, and/or government scrutiny (Pearson and Clare 1998). Not surprisingly, these extreme characteristics tend to highlight unknown strengths and divisions within organizations, hyper-extending relationships, testing people to the limit, and producing stress and anxiety among organizational stakeholders. In this sense, crises pose managers with very different challenges to their routine day-to-day problems.

DISTINGUISHING BETWEEN DISASTERS AND CRISES

As we have established, crises are complex and unforgiving phenomena that drag high-level decisionmakers into uncharted waters, revealing weaknesses and strengths that would otherwise not be apparent. Most organizations struggle with the complexity and magnitude of the challenges posed by such events, and in contrast to day-to-day problems, the consequences of mismanagement can be "disastrous." This distinction between a disaster and a crisis is important and can cause confusion because the terms are often used synonymously. Essentially, a disaster is the consequence of a mishandled crisis and this book is about managing crises to prevent disasters from happening.

A CRISIS-PRONE CONSTRUCTION PROCESS

The potential for crises during the life of a construction project is enormous. This is due in part, to the increasing technical and organizational complexity that is affecting all industries, but also to the construction industry's peculiar culture and managerial practices.

Cultural problems

The professions

A good point at which to begin a discussion of the construction industry's most significant problems is by referring to the institutionalized divisions that have developed between the occupational groups that contribute to it. To fully understand the nature and significance of these divisions, one must go back to the 19th century, when the process of industrialization fostered the development of the professions and a hierarchical structure of social superiority with the architect and engineer at its pinnacle (Hindle and Muller 1996). The development of specialized professions led to the emergence of distinct occupational sub-cultures defined by unique beliefs, values, attitudes, languages, rituals, codes of conduct, codes of dress, expectations, norms, and practices. This emergence has not only damaged communications within construction projects, but has provided the foundations for the development of strong occupational stereotypes that have become deeply rooted into the modern construction industry's social fabric, influencing the way in which people behave toward each other. For example, Loosemore and Chin Chin (2000) found contractors were most often associated with negative stereotypes by other occupational groups while engineers were most favorably perceived, being characterized as proficient, systematic, confident, and composed. Managers have trouble eroding such deeply ingrained perceptions, particularly within the relatively short duration of construction projects. However, the most effective way is through procurement systems such as Design and Construct, which challenge traditional power balances, facilitate more participation, and require people to work together in multi-disciplinary teams.

Design management

Many construction problems arise from unresolved conflicts in design; therefore, better design management could contribute significantly to reducing the crisis-proneness of construction projects. For example, Bea's (1994) survey of engineering failures found that a majority had their origins before and during design, but that 98 percent were not detected until construction and operational phases. Indeed, there are numerous examples throughout history of disasters that have originated in poor design management. Perhaps the oldest documented example is the Quebec Bridge disaster in 1907. The bridge was to be the longest in the world with a span of 1,800 feet. However, disaster struck when, during construction, the structure collapsed, killing 82 construction workers. The Royal Commission of Inquiry's report, published in 1908, found that time and cost pressures had forced designers to compromise the designs and to "fast-track" construction on site with unfinished drawings that were only approximations of the final design. It was also found that during construction, designers had noticed two cantilever arms supporting 4,000 tons more than they were designed to support. Unfortunately, the problem was ignored so the imminent deadline for opening the bridge could be met.

In June 1995 a lack of design management was also a major contributory factor in the collapse of a shopping mall in South Korea that killed 501 people and injured 900. Investigations revealed that many illegal design changes were made, that designers were taking bribes and that they had not adequately monitored contractors on site. The majority of the design team, including the client and local government officials, were imprisoned for gross negligence. In response, many countries are now instigating legislation to make design teams more accountable for the long-term consequences of their actions. Nevertheless, legislation is no substitute for good management and with this kind of evidence, it is surprising that the construction industry has taken so long to focus on the problem of design management (Gray et al 1994). There is little doubt that the effective management of the design process can make a significant contribution to reducing a project's crisis-proneness.

Market problems

In contrast to the cultural problems described above, a harder economic position argues that the primary reason for the construction industry's crisis-proneness is its tendency to outgrow its market. Although one would expect industries and markets to naturally align themselves over time, construction companies have become survival experts from generations of exposure to stop-go government policies. The industry seldom has enough time to adapt before the next boom or bust reverses the trend again. This means the industry's size is invariably out of synchronization with its market and is generally larger. In such an environment, where too many companies are "chasing" too few jobs, the market forces margins and contingency allowances down and tempts companies to take risks that they cannot manage. This not only results in under-resourced projects but it creates conditions in which unscrupulous companies thrive. This confrontational environment encourages mediocrity, reducing the behavior of the industry to that of its lowest common denominator.

In the above environment, the clients' role is critical in that they determine the nature of the construction market. Unfortunately, apart from the most enlightened clients, which are relatively few in number, the majority have succumbed to the temptations of low price and have thereby perpetuated the problem. A good illustration of the dangers of this traditional cost-driven mentality, particularly on high-risk projects, was the 26 million pounds over-run on the 99 million pound Cardiff Millennium Stadium project, which was constructed to host the Rugby Union World Cup in Wales in October 1999. Many factors contributed to the cost escalations on this project, to the acrimonious disputes and to the serious delays that disastrously, could have forced a change of venue. However, a significant contributor was the guaranteed maximum-price contract that was signed with the main-contractor while the designs were still developing. The frequency of such problems in the construction industry has led to calls for more intelligent selection systems for contractors and consultants that consider a wider range of criteria than price alone (Hatush and Skitmore 1997). Furthermore, there has been wider advocacy of negotiated contracts and partnering arrangements that reduce the emphasis on price in the selection process (Latham 1994). Unfortunately, much of the industry has been slow to embrace these ideas and price remains the primary selection criteria for constructing project teams.

Man-made problems

Contracts

The cultural and economic conditions described above have nurtured the culture of conflict and mistrust that one associates with the construction industry. This is most vividly reflected in its voluminous, complex, and legalistic contracts which are underpinned by the following assumptions: that people's actions can be accurately controlled by those who have the legitimate authority of a contract behind them; that there is one best way to manage; that people cannot be trusted to do what is correct; that people prefer to be told what to do and that contract drafters know best. Much of the destructive conflict within construction projects emanates from the inappropriateness of this coercive contractual system. An emerging school of thought asserts that projects are better managed through a culture of mutual trust and collective responsibility. The underlying belief is that most conflicts are accidental and arise from misunderstandings between project members, and that such a culture can be created by simplifying the language and structure of contracts, making them less penal, more flexible, and more equitable. The Engineering and Construction Contract (1995) produced by the Institution of Civil Engineers in the UK, is based on these principles, although its effectiveness depends on eliminating the traditional divisive culture that traditional construction contracts have perpetuated. This has often proved difficult or has not been fully appreciated by managers, and the consequence has been a number of high-profile disputes.

Sub-contracting

The majority of disputes in the construction industry occur between principal contractors and sub-contractors. In fact, numerous studies have discovered a direct relationship between the incidence of sub-contracting and the performance of a project (NEDO 1983; Kumaraswamy 1996). Sub-contracting came about in response to increasing technological complexity and demands for faster construction times, but it also produced fragmentation, instability, short-termism, reduced customer orientation, legal complexities, unfair practices, and problems of communication, motivation and quality control.

The potential for disaster that can arise from sub-contractor management problems was well-illustrated in 1981 when two suspended walkways collapsed in the Kansas City Hyatt Regency Hotel, killing 113 residents and seriously injuring 186. Subsequent investigations by the National Bureau of Standards concluded that the collapse had been caused by undetected changes made by the steel fabricator to the original designs in order to make them more build-able (NBS 1982). This resulted in a serious reduction in load-bearing capacity to such an extent that the walkways could only just support their own weight, let alone any additional loads imposed by people.

Production problems

Uncertainty

Buildings vary infinitely in their scope and complexity and are produced in a relatively uncontrollable environment when compared to the products of many other industries. For example, how many managers in other industries have to take account of the breeding habits of bald eagles? This might seem ridiculous, but contractors involved in the construction of the U.S. highway through Snake Canyon in Wyoming had to stop work for six months because the site became a critical habitat for these birds. This meant that contractors had to work throughout the winter months which, in turn, necessitated special construction methods for sub-zero temperatures. While this particular event was predictable through the involvement of environmentalists, many natural events are not and it is not surprising that problems arise in construction projects.

People

Although attempts have been made to industrialize the construction process, the production of many engineering structures and in particular buildings is still essentially a craft-based, small-batch, out-of-doors process which, compared to most manufacturing processes, involves relatively little repetition, routine, or mechanization from one product to the next. In this sense, the construction industry is essentially a human one, and the process of managing construction, highly vulnerable to the unpredictability of peoples' idiosyncrasies. The vulnerability of construction projects to human error has been illustrated in numerous engineering disasters. For instance, we have already mentioned the collapse of the Quebec bridge in 1907, which the Royal Commissioners attributed to errors in judgment by the engineers who managed the project. Human error was also the underlying cause of other bridge collapses such as the over-ambitiously designed Tacoma Narrows suspension bridge in 1940; the Silver Bridge in Ohio in 1967, which killed 46 motorists; and the West Gate Bridge in Melbourne, Australia in 1970. In the West Gate Bridge disaster, the collapse was caused by engineers removing bolts to correct a misalignment at mid-span without appreciating the structural implications. Indeed, in a study of 604 construction failures in the United States between 1975 and 1986, Eldukair and Ayyub (1991) found that the majority were caused by insufficient knowledge, ignorance, carelessness, and negligence on the part of the engineer and contractor. Interestingly, while many of the contributory mistakes were technical in nature, 40 percent were managerial, relating to errors in work responsibilities and communications.

Project organization

The project organizations used to procure engineering structures and buildings have been referred to as "temporary multi-organizations" because they have defined start and finish dates and comprise people who are representatives of independent specialist organizations of a consultancy and contracting nature (Cherns and Bryant 1984). They are also highly transient in membership since the activities and specialists involved in the construction of a building vary over time. Furthermore, due to a traditional obsession with competition as a mechanism for selecting team members, it is common for teams to change entirely between different projects. These characteristics ensure that construction project organizations are made up of a constantly changing labor force that has loyalties to a wide range of interest groups. They also ensure that steep learning curves punctuate the continuously changing landscape of interpersonal relationships, particularly in the early phases of a construction project when the nature of the end product is often ill-defined or even unknown. The potential problems that can arise from these organizational characteristics were vividly illustrated in the Summerland leisure center fire disaster on August 2, 1973 in the United Kingdom that killed 50 people. According to Turner and Pigeon (1997), "a small architectural firm was undertaking its first large commission, designing a new kind of building, that posed new kinds of fire risks, and that was built with new kinds of construction materials. In addition, the conditions under which it was anticipated that the building would operate were changed significantly during the design process"(p. 46). This led to a catalogue of human errors, poor communications, misunderstandings, conflict and ignorance on the part of project members, all exacerbated by the time pressures under which the team was working.

MANAGERS AS A SOURCE OF CRISIS-PRONENESS

Despite having characteristics that would appear to be receptive to an open, flexible, people-orientated style of management, considerable evidence suggests that the managerial mind-set that predominates in the construction industry remains fundamentally scientific in nature. This is best reflected in the construction management literature, which indicates an increasing intoxication with popular business fads from mainstream management such as TQM, benchmarking, supply-chain management, and value-engineering.

Two recent buzzwords that have captured the imagination of managers in the construction industry are Business Process Re-engineering (BPR) and Lean Construction, which epitomize the increasingly radical approach to *"transforming"* organizations. While techniques such as BPR and Lean Production were designed to overcome the social problems associated with mass production by empowering workers to determine their own destinies, evidence indicates that their ruthless focus on productivity, process improvement, and efficiency, creates de-humanizing, under-resourced organizations that are more vulnerable to crises (Richardson 1996; Green 1998; Carmichael 1999). While re-engineering exercises need not involve down-sizing, in practice, they often do, and as Hall et al (1993) argue, they are often used as managerial facades to legitimize streamlining plans and to ask people to do more for less while paying token gesture to the introduction of meaningful change. The evidence to support this argument is compelling. For example, Xerox, one of the world's greatest advocates of re-engineering, spent $700 million over three years to shed 10,000 staff members. Furthermore, the Fortune 500 industrial companies in the United States "sweated off" 3.2 million jobs during the 1980s and four privatized companies in the United Kingdom (British Telecom, British Gas, British Airways, and Yorkshire Electricity) have recently re-engineered their operations to increase their collective turnover by 24 percent while reducing their workforce by 33 percent. This is worrying because one need look no further than the Westgate bridge collapse in Australia, the Ronan Point tower collapse in the United Kingdom, and the Challenger space disaster in America for examples of disasters that were contributed to by an element of stress from over-working. Indeed, not only does leanness increase crisis-proneness but it also reduces crisis-responsiveness by stripping away the spare capacity that organizations rely on, to respond to unexpected resourcing demands.

In addition to smaller and more pressurized workforces, new business trends have also produced a relentless shift toward more flexible employment practices.

Today, most organizations have fewer core employees than they did five years ago, and they rely on a workforce of corporate mercenaries who coldly drift from job to job with little sense of loyalty to anyone but themselves and with the prime objective of securing the greatest monetary return for their efforts (Loosemore 1999). This has created an environment of fear and selfishness that may well be contributing to the relatively high level of workplace accidents, discrimination, racism, and industrial relations disputes that characterise construction industries around the world.

HIGH-RELIABILITY ORGANIZATIONS

It seems ironic that the construction industry is attempting to create inflexible construction organizations precisely when the business environment is demanding more flexibility. According to Sagan (1993), a key feature of all "high-reliability" (low-crisis) organizations is redundancy and duplication. He illustrated this by referring to a number of situations where organizations have learnt to deal effectively with high risk environments. For example, U.S. aircraft carrier operations stress the critical importance of having both technical redundancy (backup computers, antennas, etc.) and personnel redundancy (spare people and overlap of responsibilities) in their systems. Overlapping responsibilities may seem inefficient in modern business terms, but on an aircraft carrier, it can be the difference between life and death by ensuring that potential problems that one person misses are detected by another. The same principles are used to manage nuclear power stations where independent outside power sources and several coolant loops, are incorporated into system designs, should existing provisions fail. Finally, Sagan illustrates that redundancy is also a feature of our body's immune system, which is why we can survive if certain body parts are severely damaged. For example, if one kidney is removed, the other can compensate. If our spleen is removed, our bone marrow takes over the job of producing red blood cells. These examples, illustrate that redundancy is essential to survival in a world full of potential risks.

THE ART OF CRISIS MANAGEMENT

While modern management innovations appear to help managers keep pace with a rapidly changing world, they have the opposite effect by reducing organizational flexibility, creativity and responsiveness. It would seem that the scientific school of management, masquerading as contemporary management trends, has little to offer the modern-day construction manager. Today's business world demands a different mind-set which sees management as an art rather than a calculated science, as it traditionally has been. This means less emphasis on controlling uncertainty via formal rules, prescriptive procedures, inflexible hierarchical structures, specialization, top-down information systems, close supervision, monetary rewards, and threats of punishment. Instead, uncertainty needs to be seen as opportunity rather than a threat, to be accommodated rather than suppressed. This is best achieved through flexible structures underpinned by a culture of openness, sensitivity, collective responsibility and trust. Today, people's idiosyncrasies and creativity are a vital organizational resource which harnessed, makes the difference between excellence and mediocrity and ultimately, success and failure.

CONCLUSION

Crises pose special managerial problems compared to day-to-day problems and the evidence presented in this chapter indicates that they will become an increasingly common aspect of managerial life. Unfortunately, traditional managerial values have diverted attention away from the need to build resilience into organizations to deal with the unexpected. To prepare better for crises, managers need to develop a mind-set that perceives them in a more positive way and that is more receptive to thoughtful, open, flexible, trusting and employee-centered management styles. Not only will this reduce the chance of catastrophic failure, it will release the untapped creative potential and energies that are yet to be exploited by traditional managerial practices.

However, while the employee-centered style of management appears more attractive, ethical, and appropriate for the future, this depends on the context in which a manager is operating. If the development of management thought has taught us nothing else, it is that *there is no one best way to manage in all circumstances*. Rather, the most appropriate approach to management depends on the nature of the task, the nature of the production technology, the instability of the environment, and the nature of the people being managed. In essence, a task-centered style is more suited to the performance of routine, uncreative and repetitive tasks undertaken in a stable, highly mechanized production environment by people with little desire for autonomy. In contrast, the employee-centered approach is more suitable for the performance of creative, non-routine tasks undertaken in a non-mechanized and unpredictable production environment by people who value autonomy. So, while there is strong justification for softening the scientific stance that dominates construction management practices, the most important determinant of success is being sensitive to context and responding accordingly. Unfortunately, those in charge of high-risk projects who need to make the greatest shift in mind-set are least likely to do so, because people in dangerous situations tend to seek safety in the familiar. In construction, that means numbers, rules, and procedures. This is one of the dilemmas of construction crisis management.

Chapter 2

Planning for Crises

Planning is the foundation of effective crisis management. This chapter discusses the various types of crises that can arise within construction and engineering projects and considers the appropriate response in each case.

INTRODUCTION

Preparation is essential in dealing effectively with a crisis, and the best-prepared organizations are those that have taken time to understand the different types of crises they may face. These organizations compile a crisis portfolio, prioritize it, and make considered decisions about those crises for which they should plan. However, they also constantly re-appraise the types of crises they are likely to encounter and if they fall outside existing categories, develop new strategies to deal with them. As Mitroff and Pearson (1993) found, a common cause of catastrophic failure in organizations is the temptation to focus only upon crises that are common to a particular industry or organization.

TYPES OF CONSTRUCTION CRISES

Several models of construction risks have been developed. A good example is Perry and Hayes' model (1985), which is reproduced in Table 2-1. While such models are useful in understanding risk exposure, they provide little insight into different types of construction crises and, in particular, into their managerial consequences. The focus is primarily upon causes. Consequently, there is currently little understanding of how to respond to different types of crises when they arise. However, mainstream crisis management research has developed crisis typologies that are based on both causes and consequences, and these are far more useful from a practical perspective.

MAJOR CRISIS CATEGORIES

Crisis management research has developed five broad categories of crises that are differentiated by their causes and consequences, namely: *technical; natural; political; social; and organizational. Technical crises* are defined by their human origins and their potential to cause major damage to human health and the environment. Outside construction, examples include the 1982 gas leak at the Union Carbide plant in Bhopal in India, which claimed 3,500 lives and caused

Table 2-1 A typical construction risk model (Source: Perry and Hayes 1985).

Category	Example
Physical	Loss or damage by fire, earthquake, flood, accident landslip.
Environmental	Ecological damage, pollution, waste treatment, public inquiry.
Design	New technology, innovative applications, reliability, safety. Detail, precision and appropriateness of specifications. Likelihood of change. Interaction of design with method of construction.
Logistics	Loss or damage in the transportation of materials and equipment. Availability of specialized resources – expertise, designers, contractors, suppliers, plant, scarce construction skills, materials. Access and communications. Organizational interfaces.
Financial	Availability of funds, adequacy of insurance. Adequacy of cash flow. Losses due to default of contractors, suppliers. Exchange rate fluctuations, inflation. Taxation.
Legal	Liability for acts of others, direct liabilities. Local law, legal differences between home country and home countries of suppliers, contractors, designers.
Political	Political risks in countries of owners and suppliers, contractors – war, revolution.
Construction	Feasibility of construction methods, safety. Industrial relations. Extent of change. Climate. Quality and availability of management and supervision.
Operational	Fluctuations in market demand for product or service. Maintenance needs. Fitness for purpose. Safety of operation.

more than 10,000 injuries (Shrivastava 1992). An example in the construction industry is the tower crane collapse which occurred on a London building site in May 2000. This killed three workers and could have injured many more, including passing pedestrians and motorists (Akilade 2000). Also included in this category would be the walkway collapse in the Kansas City Hyatt Regency Hotel (NBS 1982) and the West Gate Bridge collapse in Melbourne Australia (Bignell 1977). *Natural crises* have the same human consequences but differ fundamentally in that they are not man-made. Examples include the earthquakes which devastated Turkey in 1999 and the violent hail storm which hit Sydney, Australia in the same year, inflicting approximately $1.4 billion of damage to property (Clennell 1999). In contrast, *political crises* have their origins in political systems, wars, and public sector reform. For example, George (1991) analyzed a range of international conflicts including the Cuban Missile Crisis, the Arab-Israeli war, and the Gulf war, isolating the conditions that could precipitate an accidental war between the United States and the Soviet Union. In construction, a good example would be the costly and embarrassing seven year dispute over the UK's most expensive cladding contract at Portcullis House in London. This ended in 1999 when a curtain walling contractor successfully sued the House of Commons for selecting a more expensive bid at tender stage. Another example would be the public inquiry which threatened to delay the start of the new Wembley Stadium project in the UK. This arose out of a refusal by local government planners to recommend the scheme unless the developer made a 30 million pound contribution to a local development fund. *Social* crises relate to events such as the Rodney King riots in Los Angeles (Quarantelli 1993) and environmental protests such as those which caused considerable damage and delays on UK road projects in the early 1990s. Finally, there are *organizational* crises, which relate to high-profile corporate crises such as the Bearing's Bank scandal and Intel's Pentium chip flaw (Gonzalez and Pratt 1995; Sfiligoj 1997). In construction, a good example would be the public confidence crisis which Laing suffered as a result of its disastrous Millennium Stadium project in the UK. Also included in this category are labor relations crises like those which plagued the Jubilee Line extension in London, the first phase of which was delivered fourteen months late and more than 1.5 billion pounds over budget.

SPECIFIC CRISIS CATEGORIES

At a practical level, the broad categories identified above are of limited use because there is no indication whether, for example, technical crises demand a different response to organizational or natural crises. In a practical sense, more valuable typologies have been presented

Creeping, sudden, and periodic crises

Jarman and Kouzmin (1990) have distinguished between *creeping, periodic,* and *sudden* crises. These crises differ in their timing: a sudden crisis presents itself as one catastrophic event; a creeping crisis develops over time through a series of mutually reinforcing events that collectively escalate into a full-blown crisis. One example of a *sudden crisis* that has been all too common in the construction industry is the fatality of a worker. For example, while the European construction sector typically employs fewer than 10 percent of the working population, it accounts for more than 30 percent of all industrial workplace fatalities. In the year 1996-1997 alone, there were 90 fatalities on U.K. construction sites and non-fatal accidents were recorded at a rate of 15 per day (Anderson 1998). Indeed, in 2000, five years after the introduction of the European CDM regulations, fatalities were still at 70 per year and the number of major incidents had risen by 73 percent (Knutt 2000).

An example of a *creeping crisis* is continued sexual or racial harassment over a prolonged period of time that eventually results in a legal suit. In countries such as Singapore and Australia where the cultural diversity of the construction workforce is particularly great, discrimination has always been a serious problem which is badly managed (O'Rourke 1998). In the UK, similar problems exist, especially with increasing numbers of Eastern European immigrants entering the construction industry (Cavill 1999). Indeed, in the United States, equal opportunities suits have become so common that the Fortune 500 industrial companies spend over 2 percent of payroll on sexual harassment suits alone.

To broaden this typology, Booth (1993) has also pointed to the existence of an intermediate type of crisis that he has termed *periodic crises*. These occur at regular intervals but with varying predicability. Events that could cause periodic crises are annual budget cuts, changes in management, changes in government, etc. Booth also argues that organizations tend to respond to sudden, creeping, and periodic crises in different ways. For example, in response to a creeping crisis, organizations tend to increase their reliance on tried and tested procedures, rationalize it away or even ignore it. In contrast, periodic crises stimulate routinized responses manifested in rigid contingency plans that are constructed by internal bargaining processes between competing interest groups. Finally, sudden crises tend to produce a defensive response, particularly if no contingency plans were in place. After the initial shock wears off, which takes some time, a siege strategy can develop in which the organization becomes fragmented into its component interest groups. Booth's analysis is useful to managers in formulating an appropriate response because it allows them the foresight to put checks in place to mitigate potentially damaging behavior.

Perceptual and bizarre crises

Many crises are influenced by public perceptions, and these perceptions are, to a large extent, shaped by the mass media. Therefore, much hinges on the degree of understanding or, more often, the lack of understanding between industry and the media. Irvine (1997) produced a categorization system of "perceptual" and "bizarre" crises that relates to the role of the media in their creation. To Irvine, a perceptual crisis is a relatively insignificant problem that has been blown out of proportion by adverse media coverage. A bizarre crisis is one that has been fabricated by the media. Public scrutiny is becoming an increasingly important aspect of construction project management, particularly in landmark projects of national significance or in projects that have a major environmental impact. The issue of public relations is discussed in more detail later in this book but, to illustrate its importance, one can point to a whole range of construction projects in the United Kingdom that are perceived to be disasters as a result of what has been reported in the press. These include the new Royal Opera House, Channel Tunnel, Heathrow Terminal 5 (in its third year of public inquiry), the British Library, and the Channel Tunnel rail link project which, to the surprise of many, hasn't even started yet! Public relations are critical in such projects, because adverse media coverage can have an enormous impact on the morale and ultimately, the performance of project teams, resulting in a self-fulfilling prophecy for a hungry media. Perhaps, the greatest illustration of this is the Jubilee Line extension in London, which was a political instrument from the beginning, being announced at three Conservative Party Conferences. But then, as Gay (1998) states "it is a trophy project, so don't expect sympathy or the facts. Just keep your head down and dream of getting back to the simple life of simple contracts that simply make a modest profit, far from the public eye" (p. 29).

Triggering mechanisms

Benson (1988) categorized crises by their *trigger events* and Egelhoff and Senn (1992) indicated that these events could occur within an organization's *relevant* or *remote* environments. The difference between relevant and remote environments revolves around the directness of impact that events within them have on an organization. In essence, an organization's relevant environment comprises those influences that directly impinge upon an organization and represents a filter for events in the remote environment. Factors within the remote environment are divorced from the day-to-day activities of an organization and only influence it through elements in the relevant environment. For managers, this distinction is important because potentially problematic events within the remote environment are more difficult to detect and their impact is relatively indirect, creeping, and difficult to predict. An example would be the property crisis that developed in the late 1980s as a result of the stock market collapse. Over night this influenced the policies of financial institutions and reduced the viability of many projects, causing them to be shelved. In contrast, crises evolving in an organization's relevant environment are more easy to detect and relatively sudden in impact. A good example of a crisis arising from an organization's relevant environment is an industrial dispute revolving around pay or working conditions such as that which occurred in 1998 on the Jubilee Line underground extension in London, resulting in a strike by all 600 electricians on the project (Glackin and Barrie 1998).

Chains of events

Another useful way of distinguishing between different types of crises is to consider the chain of events that cause them. This strategy has been used for some time in safety science, based on the assumption that all accidents are precipitated by a chain of events traceable to its origins. Maps of such chains, which are often called "fault trees," may provide the basis for a greater understanding of crisis development and crisis management. To this end, one might argue that all crises are precipitated by a chain of events that can vary in three ways: *length, complexity,* and *conspicuousness.* Length refers to the number of events in a chain, complexity refers to the diversity of interdependencies between these events, and conspicuousness refers to their prominence and ease of detection. An example of a crisis with a long, complex, and inconspicuous chain would be a serious accident on a construction site that originates in the design phase by the incorporation of a dangerous detail or specification. The link between such an event and the eventual accident is so indirect and obscured by so many subsequent design decisions that it is likely to remain hidden until it manifests itself on site. However, the greatest challenges to managers are posed by crises that have short, inconspicuous, and complex causal chains because they have widespread implications, are difficult to detect, attack at a number of organizational levels, occur suddenly, and thus provide little opportunity for intervention. Furthermore, the complexity of causality is likely to create difficulties in constructing a response and to provide different interest groups with an opportunity to construct differing definitions of the crisis. In this respect, such crises have relatively high potential for conflict. In contrast, long, conspicuous and simple chains result in creeping crises, which are more obvious in definition, effect and present numerous opportunities for intervention and less potential for conflict.

CONCLUSION

Current frameworks of construction risk do not provide managers with knowledge of how to respond to different types of crises. This chapter has reviewed a number of classification systems from outside construction that might be useful in developing appropriate responses to crises. Different types of crises demand different responses and after identifing their organization's risks, managers can use this knowledge to plan appropriate strategies in advance. However, the typologies reviewed in this chapter provide only basic insights into appropriate responses to different types of construction crises and more research is needed in this area. Furthermore, by pigeonholing crises, typologies tend to oversimplify the complexity and uniqueness of every crisis. Standardized responses to crises may provide a useful initial response, but managers will need a detailed understanding of crisis dynamics if they are to deal with them effectively in the long-term. The following chapter considers this issue in more detail.

Chapter 3

The Dynamics of Crisis Management

This chapter divides crisis management into seven distinct phases: *detection*, *diagnosis*, *decisionmaking*, *implementation*, *feedback, recovery,* and *learning.* Each of these phases must be managed effectively if the crisis management process is to be successful. Unfortunately, during a crisis, people tend to behave in ways that make this difficult. The reasons for this destructive behavior are discussed.

INTRODUCTION

The purpose of any crisis management system is to maintain an alignment between organizational goals and performance by identifying and reacting to events that might cause major deviations. This system, which focuses on extreme risks, should be a specialized component of an overall risk management system, and its importance to an organization depends on several factors, the most obvious being the level of risk faced. However, all organizations are vulnerable to crises, no matter what the level of risk faced, and it is imperative that they should make some provisions for them.

DETECTION—THE FIRST PHASE OF CRISIS MANAGEMENT

The ability to react swiftly to any crisis depends on its early detection and this is achieved by monitoring potential risks to gather intelligence.

What is a risk?

Risk is exposure to the possibility of financial loss or gain, physical injury, damage, or delay as a consequence of the uncertainty associated with pursuing a particular course of action (Cooper and Chapman 1987). This definition is more useful than most because it emphasizes the opportunistic aspects of risk as well as its threatening aspects. Unfortunately, many definitions over-emphasize the latter, associating risk with exposure to peril or danger—thereby perpetuating people's anti-conflict values. Cooper and Chapman's definition is also useful because it draws a crucial distinction between uncertainty and risk. The distinction is that an uncertain event only becomes a risk for an organization when it has accepted the resourcing responsibility for loss or gain as a consequence of its occurrence. This is important because it indicates that the responsibility for good risk management practices lies in the hands of those that take, as well as those that transfer, risks. Good practice means not giving risks to parties who cannot control them, who do not have resources to bear them, and who have not been given the opportunity to provide a price for them (Abrahamson 1984). This mutual responsibility is under-emphasized in construction management literature and could be one of the reasons ineffective risk management practices continue to be a problem for the construction industry.

The breadth of risk in construction projects

The treatment of construction risks has been extensive in volume but narrow in scope. The main problem of the treatment is its focus, which is almost entirely upon *legal risks* imposed by legislation, common law, and the service and employment contracts that bind parties together. However, Gablentz (1972) also identifies those of a *moral* and *political* nature, indicating that an organization's risks are wider than its contractual responsibilities. Each of these types of responsibilities is discernible within construction project organizations. Moral responsibilities are imposed by the codes of conduct of professional institutions and society at large and political responsibilities are imposed by the culture of the construction industry and the organizational structure of individual projects. Morris (1998) provides a good example of this by describing the case of a developer who engaged an architect to design the shell-and-core of a shopping center. Contractually, the architect was not required to attend site during the construction period, saving the developer substantial fees. However, the architect was contractually required to supervise the fit-out, which the company had also been employed to design for the future tenant under a separate contract. In July 1993, fire destroyed the shopping center. Investigations revealed that construction defects had contributed to the spread of the fire. During court proceedings, it was held that there were no defects in the design that contributed to the fire but that the architect owed a general duty of care to the developer, beyond those in the contract, to report problems observed in construction of the shell-and-core while supervising the fit-out.

Another reason construction project participants have risks that are wider than their immediate contractual responsibilities is their interdependency. This was vividly illustrated in the Ramsgate disaster in the United Kingdom where a walkway collapsed, killing six people and seriously injuring seven. In this project, the client had relied entirely on a Design and Construct contract and, in accordance with it, did not interfere with the works. However, as a result of the accident, both contractor and client were convicted of a criminal offense, the former to the value of 1 million pounds, and the latter to the value of 400,000 pounds. This illustrates that despite the contract, the fortunes of construction project participants are inextricably linked and that it is folly to consider one's risks in isolation. The example also illustrates that organizations participating in construction projects are exposed to both voluntary and involuntary risks. This distinction has been neglected in the construction risk management literature, despite considerable evidence to suggest that due to unfair and unclear risk distribution practices, incompetence, ignorance, and time pressures, it is misunderstandings about involuntary risks that are the primary cause of conflict in the construction industry (Barnes 1991; Uff 1995). The problem with involuntary risks is that by definition, responsible parties may be unaware of them or reluctant to accept them.

Internal and external risks

Essentially, all risks exist either outside or inside an organization. This means that to be fully efficient, an organization needs both external and internal monitors.

External risk

Those who have external monitoring responsibilities for client risks should operate at the project boundary and "scan" the project environment for potential problems. Chapter Two discussed "remote" and "relevant" environments, leading to the conclusion that some risks are less obvious than others and less rapid in their impact. It follows, then, that to completely cover project risks, external monitors should have remote, relevant, long-term, and short-term dimensions to their activities. The importance of having a remote dimension to external monitoring activities is particularly acute in high-profile public sector projects where political maneuvering can have a significant impact on decisions at project level. Consider, for example, the Channel Tunnel Rail Link in the United Kingdom, which required a bill through parliament and the negotiation of Britain's largest planning application in history, which had to consider the opinions of approximately 258 pressure groups that were against the scheme. As Gay (1998) stated, "it did not need a project manager so much as a project resuscitator...." (p. 29). Similarly, Hemsley (1998) highlighted the importance of having a long-term dimension to external monitoring activities. He pointed to the problems that many companies suffered in the United Kingdom in the early 1990s as a result of not predicting the deepest recession in memory. To the majority of companies in the construction industry, the recession was a complete surprise and consequently, "all sorts of people found themselves in situations where their workload was reliant on a few market sectors, all of which were falling apart at the seams" (p. 33).

Internal risk

In contrast to external risks, internal risks tend to be far more "relevant," short-term, and largely the result of the industry's organizational, contractual, and employment practices manifesting themselves in the form of poor project performance. It is for this reason that internal monitoring activities focus on performance feedback that travels through management information systems (MIS), running vertically through an organization's structure.

Most organizations have an array of MISs, each specializing in information that specifically relates to one of the organization's range of goals. Most construction projects have five principal MISs that deal with cost, time, quality, scope, and functional information (Oberlender 1993). Each should be managed by a specialist with the necessary skills to interpret that information in a meaningful way. For example, in the United Kingdom, once site work begins, the quantity surveyor is primarily responsible for the cost MIS, the architect or engineer for the functional, scope, and quality MISs; the head contractor is responsible for the time MIS once work commences on site. Regardless of the professions that head them, the relative prominence of each specialist MIS should be a reflection of a client's goal priorities and the interdependency between construction project goals means that there should be cross fertilization of feedback between them. That is, the parties mentioned above should be constantly communicating and notifying each other of potential problems they discover. This is essential, because most crises have an impact across a wide spectrum of project goals. For example, the recent discovery of Aboriginal burial remains during a major engineering project in Melbourne, Australia, demanded foundation and design changes that affected its duration, costs, scope, function, and quality. For a complete response, it is critical that such events are fully communicated throughout an organization.

Monitoring problems

Unfortunately, while potential problems must be detected and communicated rapidly, monitors may be insensitive to the risks they are responsible for. If a potential crisis is not detected, it cannot be managed and managers must understand the reasons why this can happen.

A lack of focus

The most common reason organizations suffer a crisis is that no one realized the organization was vulnerable to it. This is best illustrated by moving outside construction to the Bearings Bank crisis where officials warned of possible calamity should Leesson's independent trading unit continue its current activities. Even after an internal audit in 1994 repeated these official misgivings, Bearings Bank sanctioned Leesson's double-role as chief trader and internal auditor, which enabled him to conduct his crippling activities unabated. Sheaffer et al (1998) discovered that the primary cause of this disastrous oversight was the confused state of the bank's boundary spanning activities and internal conflicts between different departments that had muddled lines of responsibility and accountability for the reporting of potentially damaging events. The huge time pressures under which people worked and the ability of Leesson to legitimately override the controls that were in place exacerbated this state of confusion, which resulted in risk not being monitored in some areas. Similar problems exist within construction projects where performance feedback is often deficient because of time pressures, conflicting interests, and arbitrary and unclear risk distribution within contracts.

An ignorance of risk management practices

Potential problems often go undetected in the construction and engineering industries because of the widespread ignorance of risk management techniques (Smith 1999). Risk management is crucial because it is about foreseeing potential pitfalls and identifying methods to avoid them and to deal with them in advance. The infinite variability of construction projects often makes this difficult. For example, on a recent wharf renovation project in Sydney, Australia, the highly unusual risk of workers contracting Hepatitis B from syringes washed into Sydney harbor was anticipated and minimized by establishing a regime of regular medical check-ups and hepatitis B injections for all construction workers.

Another problem is the perception that risk management is a construction phase process. Recent research in the US indicates that only 16 percent of designers consider worker safety, that 29 percent occasionally do so, that 45 percent never do so and that 10 percent might do so in the future (Gambatese 2000). This is despite considerable evidence that many project risks arise during design and can be identified and eliminated there. For example, engineers on the controversial residential building behind the Sydney Opera House, nicknamed "The Toaster", designed temporary steel lugs into the structure to receive safety barriers during construction. These were burnt off when the operation was complete. Other design measures to improve safety could include beam sizes that allow adequate headroom for workers, the specification of non-hazardous materials, component standardization to streamline the construction process and prefabrication to reduce material handling and storage on site.

Design generated risks are particularly likely when there are new or unusual materials, new or complex design guidelines and considerable cost and time pressures. An example of a project that included many of these elements was the Thames Barrier project in London which was constructed to avoid a repeat of the disastrous flood of 1953 that killed 300 people and flooded 64,750 hectares of farm land, 24,000 houses, 200 industrial premises, 320 kilometers of railway, 12 gasworks, and two electric power stations. Clearly, the potential environmental impact of such a project was huge, but the risk to construction activity was minimized by a sensitive design and by considerable efforts to involve the local community and environmentalists in the design process (Morris and Hough 1987). However, this project also illustrates the dangers of not adequately considering risks early enough in large engineering projects. While the barrier was undoubtedly a technical and environmental success, it must be classed as a failure from a project management perspective. The final cost of 440 million pounds was four times the original budget (although inflation was not allowed for) and the project took seven and one-half years to complete—almost twice as long as planned.

The reasons for failure were largely related to a lack of attention to identifying management risks associated with the project's implementation, which was in total contrast to the exhaustive investigations of technical risks in determining the project's viability. For example, there was little understanding of the effect that river level changes and river traffic would have upon the project program. Furthermore, the impact of deep-seated political tensions between local and central government, which affected the client's willingness to manage the project and exacerbated the already fraught industrial relations situation, were underestimated. Given the project's location and era, labor militancy was inevitable and more effort should have been made early on to secure a binding and comprehensive site agreement on pay and conditions.

In addition to analyzing risks early in a project's life, it also important to remember that the design process is influenced by a large number of people and that it never stops. This means that managers must be constantly vigilant to the influence of design changes on project risks. This was beautifully illustrated in the shipping industry in 1990 when Mitsubishi heavy industries had to recall its new generation of crude carriers because a large number of cracks were found in their cargo tanks. In subsequent investigations, it was found that, because the ship had been designed without consulting the builder, the ship construction yard unilaterally changed the design by, among other things, reducing the weight of the steel, thereby lowering construction cost, and reducing the time for construction. In addition to more continuous control, this financial disaster could have been avoided by involving all project stakeholders in the design process.

Competition between project goals

In addition to the problem of poorly focused monitoring, there are substantial difficulties in the cross-fertilization of feedback between different MISs on many construction projects. Baxendale (1991) found this to be a particular problem between MISs responsible for the supply of time and cost information because solving a cost problem often meant creating a time problem and vice-versa. As a consequence, problems detected in one system would not be communicated to the other, a deficiency that prevented a balanced and comprehensive crisis response.

The potential problems that can arise from competition among interdependent parts of an organization's control system was vividly illustrated on the 99 million pound Cardiff Millennium Stadium project that was being constructed to host the Rugby Union World Cup in Wales in 1999. According to Sir Martin Laing, the contractor's chairman, one of the reasons for the 26 million pounds loss suffered on that project was "a local baron" philosophy in their civil engineering division and a lack of management controls (Barlow 1999). One way of overcoming this problem is to share project risks, as was the case on London's Millennium Dome project, in which consultants equally shared responsibility for budget and time overruns. As David Trench, the site and structures director for the project, commented, this provided more rapid feedback, which gave one an instinct for when things were going wrong (Knutt 1998).

Changing project teams

Project managers face special problems in monitoring project risks because of their reliance upon the diligence of project teams, which are constantly changing. The dangers of changing team members within and between projects was vividly illustrated in 1991 when, during a ballast test operation, the Sleipner A oil platform sank 200 meters to the bottom of a fiord outside Stavanger, Norway. Accident investigators found that a contributory cause of this $1 billion accident was a loss of corporate memory associated with a complete replacement of the team who had been involved in similar platform projects where the problem had become well-established and simple solutions had been developed (Bea 1994).

A lack of loyalty

A further problem for project managers is the varied and often conflicting interests that characterize construction projects. This means that those monitoring client risks may not always have a client's interests in mind. To overcome this problem, construction contracts normally require project participants to monitor a range of specified client risks and react in a prescribed manner if they arise. There is little point quoting individual contract clauses here, but it is worth noting the obvious efforts being made in the Engineering and Construction Contract (ECC 1995) to overcome these potential problems. For example, the ECC gives consultants far broader monitoring responsibilities than they normally have, producing a far more integrated and wide ranging monitoring system. Furthermore, there is a requirement for "early warnings" if parties recognize the potential for a future problem. Such clauses are common in American construction contracts but not so in UK contracts, where clauses can often be construed to imply that only "actual" problems need reporting, providing a legitimate foundation for delayed notification and the escalation of simple problems into fully-blown crises. While early-warning requirements may be difficult to enforce, the American courts have recently demonstrated their willingness to do so. For example, in A.H.A. General Contracting Corporation v City of Houston, Court of Appeals of Texas, July 23 1998 (CE/02/M), a New York City Housing Authority awarded two construction projects worth a total of $4.7 million to A.H.A. Contracting with a requirement to warn of potential problems in a timely manner in order to receive the right to payment for extra work. However, A.H.A. waited until the end of the project to present claims for an extra $906,000 and the authority refused to pay anything other than minor extras. The Court of Appeals held that A.H.A.'s failure to notify of the problems in a timely manner prevented the owner from taking early steps to mitigate damages and precluded them from seeking recovery.

Cost and time pressures

It may be economically irrational or indeed impossible, due to limited resources, to monitor every potential risk an organization faces. For this reason, people tend to make "trade-offs" between the costs and benefits of doing so. For example, when the costs of sensitivity are considered too high, a conservative "lets think it over" predisposition develops, which results in warnings of crises lagging behind their occurrence.

This tension between diligence and costs burdens a project manager with heavy moral and economic dilemmas in establishing acceptable parameters for compromise. The moral dimension is particularly acute when considering safety issues because a price has to be placed on a person's health. The recent electricians dispute on the new extension to London's underground Jubilee Line was a good illustration of how the moral dimension can be forgotten under extreme time and cost pressures and how trade-off decisions in areas such as safety can be highly sensitive. While an array of problems led to this acrimonious dispute, electricians insisted that the main problem was managers' willingness to put workers at risk in order to increase productivity (Glackin and Barrie 1998). Glackin and Barrie documented a range of frightening safety lapses such as operatives working on a live 22kV transformer with aluminum ladders, an electrician being ordered to work on a live 415V panel before proper permits had been issued to isolate the power, operatives not receiving safety inductions and an operative having his finger amputated after losing his grip on a drill when another operative tripped over the power lead.

Defensiveness

Because monitors invariably generate information that threatens the status quo, organizations tend to develop norms that castigate such people (Argyris 1984). Furthermore, people are often required to provide higher standards of evidence than those who provide information that supports existing expectations and hypotheses. This is particularly so when intelligence information requires policymakers to do things they prefer not to do or that they are not prepared to deal with. The potential dangers of this defensiveness have been vividly illustrated in many disasters such as the Hillsborough football stadium disaster in the United Kingdom and the Challenger space shuttle disaster in the United States. In each case, chief decisionmakers, under pressure from external constituencies, filtered-out and ultimately ignored the advance signs of impending disaster (Jarman and Kouzmin 1990; Richardson 1993). For example, in the Challenger disaster, several aborted launches had led to ridicule from the press. This embarrassed policymakers and team leaders. On the night before the launch, engineers warned that the predicted temperature at the time of launch would be below the safety limit for the fuel tank seals. However, evidence indicates that engineers were pressured by their teammates to re-analyze their calculations about the fuel tank seals and subject them to stricter tests than would normally be required. This caused the engineers to question their original calculations, to place a greater degree of faith in the secondary seals than was normal, and to agree to the launch.

Superiority

Turner and Pigeon (1997) indicate that defensiveness can be a particular problem when the information that challenges existing mind-sets originates from sources outside an organization. For example, their analysis of the Aberfan coal slip disaster in South Wales in 1966, which killed 144 people, indicates that a sense of organizational exclusivity can lead to a sense of superiority over non-members. In Aberfan, the local council members foresaw the problem but were labeled as "cranks" and repeatedly "fobbed-off" with ambiguous and misleading statements such as "we are constantly checking these tips." As Turner and Pigeon (1997) argue, there was an "attitude that those in the organization knew better than outsiders about the hazards of the situation with which they were dealing" (p. 49).

In large construction projects, with annual turnovers that exceed many companies, defensiveness to outsiders can be a particular problem. The pressures, cohesion, loyalties, focus, and momentum that can develop on such projects can become so intense that they effectively seal themselves off from the outside world, considering outsiders as an unnecessary distraction and even covering up problems that may expose internal weaknesses to them. However, as Turner and Pigeon's example illustrates, the occasional involvement of outsiders, who are unfamiliar with a project is often the most effective means of detecting potential problems. Their exclusion only increases a project's crisis-proneness.

Shut down

Research in "killology," a new branch of behavioral science concerned with the psychology of killing in human combat, has shown that during a crisis, people tend to shut down all senses apart from the one that is most needed to survive under the circumstances (Bullock 1999). To illustrate this, Bullock cites an example of a playground shooting in the United States where two boys gunned down 15 teachers and students. In de-briefing sessions after the shooting, those directly affected recalled how their sense of sight and hearing had shut down according to their situation. After being initially stunned by the first shots, many people's eyes became their main sense—they began to see everything but heard almost nothing, just distant popping noises at the very most. In contrast, those that were actually shot seemed to go physically blind but hear everything that was going on in the finest detail.

The importance of this research for managers is that during a crisis, some monitoring systems may be shut down, leaving the organization vulnerable to further crises. This means that monitoring problems can arise because of crises elsewhere in an organization and that one of the challenges of crisis management is to prevent tunnel vision by maintaining vigilance to the early warning signs of further crises.

Timing

Monitoring problems may also arise because not all crises are equally visible. As Chapter One pointed out, some crises may be acute, sudden, and self-evident, while others may be creeping, emergent, and ambiguous. For example, some instances of poor monitoring may be related to the incremental manner in which creeping crises develop because this would make their early warning signs less easily detectable. This was the case in the Occidental Piper Alpha disaster on July 6, 1988. The long chain of events that led to the eventual fire were initiated by a simple unfinished maintenance job in the gas compression module (DOE 1990). A more bizarre example is McDonald's hot coffee crisis in which a customer was awarded $2.9 million in damages for third degree burns sustained from spilling a cup of coffee (Gonzalez and Pratt 1995). McDonald's records showed that prior to this highly public court case that subsequently led to numerous of copy-cat cases around the world, there had been 700 previous complaints about coffee burns.

Sudden crises may also be difficult to detect because managers tend to become flooded with a sea of contradictory information from which it is difficult to draw any sensible meaning. People have a limited capacity to handle information and are forced to "selectively perceive" incoming signals. Unfortunately, the natural tendency is for people to do so in a way that confirms their existing expectations and that suits their personal needs. Inevitably, the result is a self-fulfilling prophecy and the filtering-out of any early warning signs of pending crises (Comfort 1993).

Invincibility

Pascale (1991) highlighted the self-destructing nature of the world's largest and most successful companies. According to Pascale, "nothing fails like success" because a history of successes tends to induce a sense of invincibility and a "it can't happen to us" attitude that blinds organization members to potential problems. Furthermore, the growth that often accompanies success tends to confuse monitoring responsibilities and spurn bureaucratic systems that are slow in responding to potential problems that are detected. Indeed, this "back-lash" effect from past successes has been posed as one factor that contributed to the Challenger space shuttle disaster where the "can do" culture of NASA down-played the early warning signals of impending problems (Pearson et al 1997).

Mistrust, fear, and not speaking up

Chapter One identified the sources of mistrust and fear in construction projects. Ryan and Oestreich (1998) found that the most dangerous side-effect of such an environment is a hesitation to "speak up" for fear of punishment that creates a situation in which working relationships become clouded in *undiscussables*. These are secrets that everyone knows but which are only talked about privately. The danger is that the longer they remain undiscussed, the harder it becomes to talk about them and the more damage is done. Interestingly, Ryan and Oestreich found that certain types of problems were particularly likely to become undiscussables. These are summarized in Table 3-1.

Table 3-1 Undiscussable problems in organizations.

Category	Percentage of response
Management performance	49
Coworker performance	10
Compensation and benefits	6
Equal employment opportunities	6
Change	4
Personnel systems other than pay	4
Individual feelings	2
Performance feedback to respondent	2
Bad news	2
Conflicts	2
Personal problems	2
Suggestions for improvement	2
Others	9

The implications of creating an environment where people are afraid to speak up can be enormous. Ryan and Oestreich provide a good example of a financial crises in a small Midwestern software company that was a result of this phenomenon. Employees frequently described the CEO of this company as a tyrant. He created an environment of fear by bullying employees, publicly criticizing them, setting arbitrary deadlines without consultation, expecting unreasonable hours from everyone, and deliberately pitting people against each other. The negative climate resulted in the release of a faulty software package that cost the company $6 million, its reputation and customer base, and several key employees. Ironically, one employee had detected the fault earlier and voiced her concerns during a meeting. Her reward was her dismissal and a humiliating dressing-down in front of other employees. As one employee revealed, "The program was a disaster. The software wouldn't do what we said it would do. There was no ownership, no pride in the product. People were not asked for their input. More energy and time was spent covering your butt than on the quality of the program."

Shell Oil Company is a good example of an organization that has recognized that cultures of blame are unlikely to produce efficient or just outcomes. They have developed a management program designed to generate a corporate safety culture with no-blame practices. Interestingly, the accident record of Shell's tanker fleet, expressed in terms of frequency of injuries, has fallen dramatically since its introduction in the late 1970s (Horlick-Jones 1996).

The visibility of early warning signals

The visibility of early warning signals is another factor that is likely to determine the sensitivity of people to them. Essentially, the visibility of early warning signals is determined by their intensity, duration, and subtlety. Intensity refers to the strength of a signal; duration refers to the time over which it is detectable; and subtlety refers to its complexity and blatancy in terms of the degree of investigation required to detect it. Potential crises that emit low intensity, short duration, and subtle signals such as those originating in design, would be more difficult to detect than those that emit high intensity, long duration, and blatant signals such as those physically apparent in construction. The problem with mistakes made during design is that the high degree of reciprocal interdependency among design team members ensures that they are rapidly buried in and obscured by a labyrinth of subsequent and interdependent activities. In this sense, construction project managers must be particularly diligent to potential risks during the design phase of a project where monitoring traditionally has been lacking.

DIAGNOSIS—THE SECOND PHASE OF CRISIS MANAGEMENT

After detecting a potential problem, an organization should investigate it further to arrive at a diagnosis that will indicate an appropriate response. In control systems terminology the person responsible for this function is called the "comparator," and since the role demands specialist knowledge, such people should be professionally qualified specialists such as structural engineers, architects, quantity surveyors, cost engineers, or site managers. While the roles of monitor and comparator are distinct, ideally, the same person should perform them, because those who have collected specialist information are likely to be in the best position to assess its significance, highlight potential problems, and thereby ensure a rapid and appropriate response. By separating monitors and comparators, potential communication problems are introduced that can distort or slow down a crisis response.

Diagnostic problems

The diagnostic process is essentially one of data collection, and any problems encountered in the monitoring phase also affect the diagnosis process. However, some special problems are peculiar to the process of diagnosis.

Unclear goals

To make judgments about the potential impact of a problem upon project goals, comparators must have a clear idea of the standard of performance required in their particular specialist area of expertise. Unfortunately, as Kelly et al (1992) point out, even the most competent consultants can experience difficulties in identifying clear performance standards because of client inexperience, difficulties in identifying a client body, internal politics within client organizations, exclusion from early strategic reviews of client business processes, poor communication, and insufficient time for briefing. Further problems can be caused by continual changes in goals throughout the life of a project. Indeed, this was a problem that afflicted the new British Library in London, which exceeded its original budget by 400 percent and which provided spaces for only 12 million of the originally planned 25 million books.

Here, changes in requirements were largely the result of changes in government policies and structural changes within government departments responsible for monitoring the project (Spring 1998). As the architect stated, "If you really want to devise an insane way of developing a building, you would go about it the way that the politicians have done. When Mrs. Thatcher came, it was constantly stop-go, stop-go, which was infinitely more expensive. They pulled the building up by the roots every 18 months, chopped a bit off, and put it back in the ground to grow." Comments from others involved in the project support this portrait of constant change: "They kept changing responsible departments, and every time the department changed so did the personnel"; "You can't run a long-term project on Treasury allocations that change each year and can't be passed onto the following year. This meant it had to be run on a cost reimbursable basis, so the consultants and contractors had no financial incentive to contain costs."

Indeed, these problems would seem to be common to many landmark public projects such as the $284 million flood control project in Las Vegas, which began in 1995 and will not be finished until 2007, six years later than originally planned (Feature 1999). This project, which is meant to protect Las Vegas from devastating floods has become something of a juggling act for engineers who must constantly chase federal funds and be ready to work whenever money becomes available.

Defensive routines

Further problems can arise in the diagnosis process because of "defensive routines"—behavior designed to prevent individuals or organizations from experiencing embarrassment or loss. This is particularly likely during a crisis because of the severity of potential ramifications and is even more certain if there is an element of personal blame associated with it (Argyris 1990). According to Sinclair and Haines (1993), uncertainty over patterns of responsibility for crises also causes this behavior because it is easier to justify ignoring a problem by passing it onto someone else. This is highly relevant to construction projects because many construction contracts are ambiguously drafted and there is a widespread inability to interpret them correctly.

Typical defensive behavior involves bypassing problems or covering them up by crafting messages that contain inconsistencies and discourage debate. Leavitt and Bahrami (1988) use the term "repression" to refer to this process of denying an unwelcome reality, and argue that it is a survival mechanism in the face of extreme change or threat. Unfortunately, this process creates an "organizational shadow," a darker side that haunts an organization until the repressed problems grow to the point where they have to be dealt with. This phenomena and its potentially disastrous consequences was vividly illustrated by Intel in 1994, who after discovering a flaw in its Pentium chip, declined to issue a recall or notify its customers. In a classic illustration of defensive behavior, Intel down played and trivialized the problem by arguing "no chip is ever perfect" (Gonzalez and Pratt 1995). Indeed, the company kept marketing the chip until IBM refused to use it in their computers and the value of its shares plummeted, causing a financial crisis within the company.

The research that led to the discovery of defensive routines was conducted in situations where the interests of those affected by a problem were similar. Consequently, the defensive behavior reported was largely uniform and widespread. However, people's behavior within a construction project is likely to be quite different because wide ranging and often conflicting interests will ensure that some party's interests will be served by covering up the problem, while others' will be served by its wider communication and even its exaggeration. This results in a wide range of tactics being employed by crisis stakeholders to force circumstances in their favor—one of the reasons construction crisis management is so challenging.

DECISION MAKING—THE THIRD PHASE OF CRISIS MANAGEMENT

If the diagnosis process indicates that the performance implications of a detected problem fall within acceptable tolerances, the crisis management process terminates at that point. However, if a comparator perceives an unacceptable threat, the process progresses to the next stage, which involves formulating an appropriate response. This is the responsibility of a person who has the authority to make the necessary decision to bring actual performance levels back into line with project goals. A decision can only be made by one person, even though it may be with the advice of many.

Decisionmaking problems

Problems of monitoring and diagnosis influence the efficiency of the decisionmaking process but numerous problems are also peculiar to the process.

Conflicting advice

Essentially, the decisionmaker's task is to choose from a range of alternative courses of action. These decisions may be self-generated, but are more likely to take the form of recommendations from specialist comparators who are more qualified to make such judgments. The challenge arises from the magnitude and complexity of crises, which means that they inevitably affect a whole range of project goals. This creates the need to synthesize potentially conflicting advice from a wide range of comparators—a process that demands a great deal of experience, sensitivity, political prowess, and a good understanding of the client's goal priorities. For example, in resolving a budgetary crisis in a construction project where costs are of the highest priority, an expensive design detail which adds to a building's appearance and to which the architect is attached, may have to be sacrificed to bring the project back within budget.

A further challenge for decisionmakers arises from resource constraints because decisions that exceed them will not receive corporate support from senior executives.

For example, there is little point approaching a client for extra money if their budget is fixed. While all clients have resource constraints, they may be particularly inflexible and acute in government funded projects in which issues of public accountability usually ensure that any increase in funding or extension of time will have to be audited before a decision is made. In the event of a crisis, there may not be enough time to wait for this process, and difficult trade-offs with more flexible and less conspicuous goals may need to be made. Perhaps the most famous example of an organization making trade-offs between different objectives is the Ford Pinto case (Haroon 1999). During the 1960s, the demand for sub-compacts was rising and the Pinto was to be the first in a new generation of lightweight, low-cost cars. The specifications were uncompromising and inflexible and the car was not to weigh an ounce over 2,000 pounds nor cost a cent over $2,000. To maximize sales, it was also to be in the showrooms faster than any other car in Ford's history. However, during design and production, tests revealed that in crashes over 25 miles-per-hour, the gas tank would rupture and cause fuel to spill onto the road. At 40 miles-per-hour, the doors of the car would jam shut and trap its occupants inside. However, production continued, Ford deciding to ignore the problem, calculating that the cost of compensating the estimated 360 deaths and serious burns per year would be about one-third the costs of recalling sold cars, stopping production, and redesigning the gas tank.

Centralized decisionmaking authority

Decisionmakers exists at all organizational levels and it is the significance of a threat that partly determines the level of decisionmaking invoked. Since crises are events of significant magnitude, they would normally command the attention of higher-level decisionmakers such as the project manager and occasionally the client. However, the level of decisionmaking invoked is also likely to depend on the degree to which decisionmaking authority is decentralized. A decentralized structure facilitates lower-level decisionmaking. This issue, of hierarchical location, is an important consideration in crisis management because the closer the decisionmaker to a threat, the faster the response, as the need for communication between organizational levels decreases. Highly centralized structures are notoriously slow to adapt to change. This often results in poor decisions that are based on the distorted and restricted judgments of one individual. The fastest response to a threat would arise when a monitor, comparator, and decisionmaker were the same person but; in the extremes of a crisis, senior people will want to be involved and it is highly probable that getting a decision will mean a tedious, frustrating, and potentially damaging journey through the organizational hierarchy.

The dangers of having a highly centralized management structure was illustrated by DeMichiel et al's (1982) analysis of accidents in the coal industry where it was found that low-accident mines allowed supervisors more freedom to make decisions and miners to suggest improvements that were genuinely considered and often implemented. Numerous corporate disasters over the years have illustrated this danger when an autocratic chief executive who controlled decisionmaking dominated companies. For example, the collapse of the Brent Walker empire in the 1980s was partly attributed to a single decision that the overwhelmingly persuasive Chairman, George Walker, made in buying the William Hill chain of betting shops for 689 million pounds. As Weyer (1994) points out, if there is one reliable indicator that a company will eventually head into trouble, it's having a charismatic, high-profile executive chairman who resists advice. No doubt, the same is true for construction projects.

Dealing with external constituencies

One characteristic of a crisis is that it affects high-level decisionmakers. However, the implications of the most high-profile crises are likely to burst through the top of an organization and implicate external stakeholders such as financiers, insurers, users, public pressure groups, unions, government departments, and others affected in the project such as sub-contractors and suppliers. At the very least, these external constituencies will need to be considered, informed of proposed solutions, and in extreme circumstances, handed the entire responsibility to deal with a crisis. For example, in the case of a site fatality, subsequent investigations by the health and safety inspectorate or union officials may deem that a site be closed until certain improvements are made. Similarly, in the case of bankruptcy, legally appointed company administrators, liquidators, or accountants may temporarily take responsibility for managing a project.

Dealing with the rights of external constituencies can be a complex, delicate, and highly political process with significant potential to exacerbate a crisis and delay response. Consequently, responsibilities for integrating these stakeholders into the decisionmaking process must be clearly defined in advance. The potential consequences of not considering the rights of external stakeholders were vividly illustrated in the Rugby Union World Cup Millennium Stadium project in Wales. During construction, poor relationships between the Welsh Rugby Union and its neighbor, Cardiff Rugby Football Club, led the latter to refuse permission for tower cranes to swing over its air space and for raked structural masts to over-sail its ground. This led to a very late redesign of the masts that supported the stadium roof and to the recalculation of loads on the entire structure.

Outside construction, a good example of the problems that external constituencies can bring was illustrated in the TWA flight 800 disaster, which killed 230 people. Subsequent analyses of this disaster have highlighted the problems experienced by crisis managers in deciding how best to deal with the crisis while considering the rights of distraught families, an eager press, an emotional public, and external emergency services (Fennelle 1996).

In the construction industry, the integration of external constituencies is likely to become a more prominent issue in the future. One likely source of increased intervention is the growing Green movement whose members have identified the construction industry as a major contributor to waste. For example, 25 percent of

America's solid waste is generated from construction activity and much of this waste, which can seriously damage the environment, can be either eliminated or recycled (Mincks 1996). Indeed, in high-profile road building projects around Europe, the civil engineering industry has already begun to experience the potential power of the environmental movement, facing considerable delays to programs and damaging publicity to the companies undertaking them. As new housing estates spring up around this infrastructure, a knock-on effect to the house-building sector is inevitable. Indeed, even those involved in the redevelopment of inner-city sites will be affected because, in addition to having to comply with increasingly stringent waste management requirements, the repopulation of many inner-city areas will demand greater respect for the quality of life of those who reside there. For example, in a recent 55-story commercial development in the center of Sydney, Australia, local residents had to be integrated into the management structure of the project and consulted about an extension of working hours needed to recover accumulating delays. Sydney is trying to repopulate its central business district and the power of the local residents was such that they were able to insist on a $250,000 bond that would be unconditionally sacrificed if the project generated any noise outside certain hours.

Irrationality

A decisionmaker's task is to make a decision and Brecher (1977) argues that the decisionmaker can follow a number of alternative routes. For example, when a decisionmaker has experienced a similar problem in the past, he or she tends to follow the cognitive routines that were developed for that situation. In other words, a decisionmaker will make an *automatic* decision by relying on a predetermined response. In contrast, when a problem is unusual, non-routine, and not anticipated in people's cognitive routines, they tend to follow an *analytical* process, assessing the costs and benefits of various alternatives. Finally, when a problem is unique, complex, surrounded by uncertainty, and difficult to measure in terms of its costs and benefits, Brecher advocates a purely *cognitive* model in which a person would make an intuitive decision based on gut-feelings.

Unfortunately, during the pressures and stresses of a crisis, decisionmakers are unlikely to follow the rational paths laid out within Brecher's framework. For example, Knight and McDaniel (1979) found that during a crisis, people tend to follow an inappropriate decisionmaking path by "process-following" in a situation that demands a non-routine, analytical response. People move into an automatic mode during a crisis for many reasons. For example, Knight and McDaniel suggest that the non-routine information a crisis generates is not easy to classify, involving lengthy and costly searches before it is understood. There simply may not be the time to do this information gathering during a crisis, particularly if attention has not been given to crisis management systems that can supply people with appropriate information at the appropriate time. Other researchers have shown that during a crisis, the ability to make an automatic decision may be an important survival mechanism (Bullock 1999). For example, studies of soldiers' physiology while under fire show that heartbeats can rise to 300 beats a minute, which causes a loss in complex motor skills, peripheral vision and hearing. For this reason, the army, in training people to kill, attempts to develop a conditioned reflex in which soldiers can move into automatic pilot and respond to combat in a predetermined way. In extreme crises, organizations need similar capabilities.

Reluctance to alter performance standards

A decision, whether it is *automatic*, *analytical*, or *intuitive*, should realign organizational performance and planned goals. With this goal, a decisionmaker may legitimately decide to *do nothing* if, for example, there is a possibility of the deviation correcting itself in time. However, in most instances, something will have to change, and logically, this can either be planned goals or existing performance levels. One other alternative is to attempt to reverse the force that is causing the deviation. For example, if a problem is being caused by a local government planner refusing to countenance a design change, it might be solved by reasoning or bargaining with him or appealing to an ombudsman.

Argyris (1984) argued that decisionmakers tend to shy away from the goal-changing option because "group-norms" can develop that castigate challenges to organizational objectives. One could imagine that such pressures would be strong in high-profile, landmark projects such as the Sydney Olympic Stadium or London's Millennium Dome where the consequences of altering budgets and programs would be subject to immense media criticism and scrutiny. For example, we can return to the Millennium Stadium in Wales that was being constructed for the start of the Rugby Union World Cup in October 1999. The Rugby World Cup draws the third highest TV audience of any regular sporting event in the world and the pride of a whole nation rested upon the successful completion of this project. Consequently, when the intense media scrutiny that constantly surrounded this project revealed it might not be completed on time, the contractor, John Laing PLC, was subjected to fierce public pressure. The potential humiliation to the Welsh nation of having to host the World Cup elsewhere was too unbearable to contemplate and the chairman, Sir Martin Laing, was forced to publicly reassure the Welsh public that "we are jolly well going to finish the damn thing" (Barlow 1999).

While the pressures to alter performance rather than goals may be high on major public projects, it may be the opposite on the majority of construction projects. Hermann (1963) argued that under the pressures of a crisis, standards that once appeared reasonable tend to appear unattainable and are likely to be relaxed because of the alleviating effect this produces. Indeed, numerous clients such as the British Property Federation (1983) have often complained that project managers too quickly advised them to lower their sights instead of demanding greater efforts to increase the project team's performance to stay on target.

IMPLEMENTATION—THE FOURTH PHASE OF CRISIS MANAGEMENT

By definition, crises have widespread *social, technical,* and *monetary* implications and any decision is likely to require a significant change in these aspects of an organization. *Technical* implications relate to modifications in the physical routines of the project; *social* implications relate to the way in which project members must alter their established patterns of relationships; and *monetary* implications relate to the extra resources required to implement those changes. In a highly interdependent organization like a construction project, such changes are brought about through a network of communications that originates from a decisionmaker and spreads throughout the organizational structure. For example, in a recent construction project in Melbourne, Australia, the unexpected discovery of Aboriginal burial remains required a design change in a building's super-structure which, in turn, affected structural engineers, designers, services engineers, contractors, sub-contractors, suppliers, and external interest groups such as the media, archaeologists, and Aboriginal interest groups.

Implementation problems

Problems implementing decisions are likely to arise for a number of reasons.

Poor communication

If implementation takes place through a network of communications between project members, then any communication problems will reduce the effectiveness of the crisis management process. We have already discussed the potential for communications to be damaged during a sudden crisis because of information overload and people's natural tendency to panic, become irrational, and shut down certain senses. However, aside from these natural phenomena, the nature of the construction industry can also contribute to communication breakdowns during a crisis. Communication difficulties have long been recognized to arise from historical divisions between construction professions; fragmentation of the process due to sub-contracting practices; sequential procurement systems that separate construction phases such as design and construction and conflicts of interests due to tendering and contractual practices. These problems create underlying tensions in all construction projects and it is during the pressures of a crisis that they are likely to be exacerbated and to surface by damaging the effectiveness of interactions among individuals.

Resistance to change

By definition, implementation involves technical, monetary, and social change, to which there is likely to be a natural level of resistance. People resist because all change requires the abandonment of past efforts and considerable rework. Furthermore, when risks are not shared, as is normally the case in construction contracts, change will inevitably create both winners and losers. Although winners are likely to support such change, Machiavelli reminds us that they are likely to provide only lukewarm support for change efforts, compared to the vigorous defense of the status-quo from potential losers.

External constituencies

The problems of integrating external constituencies into the crisis management process were considered in relation to the decisionmaking phase and they are mirrored during implementation. Indeed, here they can be more acute because the implementation process is likely to be more lengthy and widespread in its implications for organizational members, than the decisionmaking process. This was vividly demonstrated during the Zeebrugge ferry disaster in 1987 when emergency plans did not adequately account for the mass influx of the media who jammed communications lines to the extent that shore and sea-based rescue teams could not communicate with each other (Wagenaar 1996). A further unexpected problem was traffic chaos in the port area caused by an inquisitive public and the many emergency services needed at the scene.

In the temporary environment of construction projects, the integration of external constituencies is particularly difficult because there is little time to build a long-term working relationship with them. This is why it is unusual to find on a construction project, the kind of on-going relationship that most companies have with the emergency services such as the fire brigade. For example, mock fire drills are relatively rare on many construction projects, even though the risks of fire may be considerably higher at times. Another factor that causes difficulties in integrating external agencies into crisis management activities is the transient nature of construction project workforces. For example, imagine the difficulties of integrating into the crisis management process, sub-contractors who will soon be completing their work and moving to another project being funded by a different client and being organized by another contractor.

FEEDBACK—THE FIFTH PHASE OF CRISIS MANAGEMENT

Throughout the implementation phase, knowledge of results is critical to ensure that planned and actual performance are realigned. This information is known as "feedback" and it is acquired by internal monitoring of the organization to collect performance data. Performance feedback should be continuously assessed in relation to project goals and if necessary, further adjustments made until planned performance is in line with actual performance. This may take some time and in this respect the crisis-management process is likely to be a cyclical one that should continue until the organization is back on its feet.

Unfortunately, in the reality of a construction project, getting performance feedback can be a problem, due to factors related to monitoring, such as poor communication, conflicts of interests, time pressures, and difficulties identifying and measuring project goals. Acquiring feedback from those who stand to lose from a change is likely to be particularly problematic and an important aspect of crisis management must be the identification of potential losers. Even better, would be the creation of a risk-sharing structure that ensures such conflicts of interest do not exist in the first place.

RECOVERY—THE PENULTIMATE PHASE OF CRISIS MANAGEMENT

Depending on how well the crisis was handled, the aftermath may present significant psychological and physical damage that must be rectified and come to terms with. The initial emphasis during this phase should be on *recovery,* which involves returning an organization to "normal" as soon as possible. Recovery demands time and sensitivity since there may be internal and external investigations to handle and damaged relationships to repair. Furthermore, much of the psychological damage is not likely to surface immediately since people, traumatized by events, may bury unpleasant memories in their sub-conscious. In relieving these post-crisis traumas, the main problem for crisis managers arises from people's natural desire to look forward and from their reluctance to recall uncomfortable events. However, this issue must be fully addressed, not only for ethical reasons but because latent psychological disturbances may re-emerge at some point in the future and play a part in inducing further crises. As Bullock (1999) points out, the basic principle that underlies psychology is that people are only as sick as their secrets and that full recovery from a crisis depends on sharing them with others. The same is true for an organization.

LEARNING—THE FINAL PHASE OF CRISIS MANAGEMENT

Managers must not see the return to normality as the end of the crisis management process. As Gonzalez and Pratt (1995) point out, crises present profound *learning* opportunities by revealing important improvements for application to future crises. Furthermore, they can reveal weaknesses in an organization that would otherwise not be evident. In this sense, they can contribute to improved effectiveness through the *unlearning* of crisis causing behaviors and procedures that may be ingrained within an organization.

In many ways, learning and unlearning are arguably the most important phases of crisis management because much of the knowledge we use today to construct, manufacture, and operate engineering and built facilities has been acquired from analyses of past mistakes. For example, Carper (1989) points to the Gothic period of cathedral construction in Europe when repeated failures of spire towers such as that of the cathedral at Beauvais in France led to questions that extended the frontiers of builders' technical knowledge. In a more recent example, Pritzker (1989) cites a fire in a new hotel under construction in New York that led to changes in building codes and standards that now afford better fire protection to employees during construction.

Unfortunately, the time-pressured, temporary, transitionary, fragmented, and divided nature of construction project organizations does not encourage the far-sighted attitudes that inspire people to learn and unlearn. Evidence of this can be found in the emerging literature about facilities management that shows little evidence of the construction industry evaluating the effectiveness of its final product, let alone individual crises that occur during its production (Barrett 1995). Despite these potential problems, a desire to learn, however difficult and painful, is the key to preventing repeated mistakes and improving performance. This brings us to the role of the forensic manager—the person charged with investigating an incident to establish its lessons.

The process of forensic management

In addition to internal investigations to learn from an incident, a project may be involuntarily subjected to external forensic investigations with legal ramifications due to mandatory government investigations or claims for compensation by an injured party. Whatever the source of and motive for an investigation, everyone on a project is affected and it is useful to briefly consider what the process involves and how it is best managed to produce positive results.

Although every forensic investigation is different, they all involve data collection and analysis. Usually, an investigator works back from the time of an incident to its origin. The first step is to identify what may have changed between the time of the incident and the start of the investigation (Hendry 1989). For example, in the investigation of a fire, rescue services may have disturbed the scene by cutting fallen beams to release trapped workers. The second step is to determine and map the exact sequence of events that led to the incident by using techniques such as fault-tree analysis. For example, if a chemical spill on a construction site caused toxic fumes and, as a result, made workers sick, where was where was the initial point of discharge? How were the chemicals released? How much chemical was discharged? Where did the chemical flow? How was the chemical contained? What emergency procedures were in place? Were safety procedures followed? The final phase of analysis is the evaluation of pre-existing conditions that set the accident in motion. For example, was a vital piece of equipment missing? Was there adequate training for employees? Were employees "larking around"?

Forensic investigation data is usually collected via interviews, observation, surveys, photography, and document inspection. Often, inspections of documents and interviews with key personnel may need to be repeated. In this sense, full access to the site, to its personnel, and to its documentary records must be afforded to the investigation team if the process is to be effective. The process may also involve laboratory work to test materials or even a full simulation or reconstruction of events surrounding an incident. Either of these options could mean temporary closure of the site.

Clearly, the approach to data collection depends on the nature of the event being investigated. For example, structural failures such as the collapse of the Kansas City Hyatt walkway in 1981 may require significant testing of structural members. In contrast, during a recent tax avoidance crisis on a $400 project in Sydney, Australia, the focus of investigations was wholly upon people. Subsequent investigations by tax officials resulted in all of the sub-contractor's employees being interviewed and served with demands for $30,000 tax bills, which caused major disruption to morale on site and to the physical progress of the work. Further investigations by union officials and by managers from the principal contractor eventually resolved the problem, but not without considerable disruption.

Clearly, investigations need to be managed sensitively to avoid severe disruption, in a physical and psychological sense, to a project. One way to do this is to ensure that everyone knows what the investigative process will involve and if necessary, is given support to get them through it. Psychological support is particularly important if the process may involve recalling very unpleasant memories or revealing evidence that may implicate working colleagues.

The forensic team

Since most crises will have a variety of technical, physical, procedural, and human causes, the forensic manager would normally coordinate a team of people who have the necessary range of skills to investigate these dimensions. This may include such divergent professionals as management consultants, psychologists, police, fire investigators, engineers of all types, union officials, lawyers, traffic accident investigators, accountants, manufacturers, surveyors, and pure scientists. One of the dangers of forensic investigation is the tendency for various interest groups to direct its focus. This is because most investigations take place within highly political environments and may have important financial implications for people and organizations in terms of legal actions and insurance payouts. Parties with considerable financial clout can be particularly persuasive in such situations, as can individuals who are personally injured by an incident and who need some form of compensation to help rebuild their life. However, an investigator must not be swayed by personal feelings, sympathies, and external pressures because the impartiality of the process and people's trust in it is essential for it to have any value. For example, Hendry (1989) describes an accident in which commercial pressure, personal sympathies, and distorted data from injured parties could have easily interfered with the investigative process. In this accident, someone who was leaning against a tower crane when it touched an overhead cable suffered a severe electrical injury. The success of the injured party's insurance claim depended on his proving that the cab was badly manufactured in terms of the visibility it afforded to the cab driver, and that the cab driver and crane director on the ground were not negligent. However, after inspecting excellent site photos of the accident, examining the crane, and talking to those involved, the investigation concluded that there was no contributory deficiency on the part of the crane manufacturer.

To ensure impartiality in the investigation process and widespread acceptance of its results, it is often best to appoint an "outsider" who has the respect of all parties to manage such investigations. Expert representatives of all potential stakeholders who may be implicated in blame should also be included. Such a complex team of divergent skills and interests clearly needs skilful management, and this task is made easier if the forensic manager is competent, is able to make difficult decisions, is able to offer a timely opinion, and is able to perform an objective analysis of the various pieces of, often conflicting information, which he or she will receive. Furthermore, it would help if members of the team are not only experts in their field, but that they have prior experience of such investigations, enjoy field work, are trustworthy and ethical, are determined, are able to deal with ambiguity and frustration, are good communicators, and have interminable patience. There is no substitute for these attributes since no amount of expertise in an area will prepare an investigator for the physical and mental chaos that surround the scene of most crises.

The forensic report

Clearly, the whole process of conducting a rigorous investigation takes considerable time and money and it should be started as soon as possible after the event, as evidence is often destroyed during rescue or clean up operations. Furthermore, sabotage by guilty parties may result in the destruction of important documents; important witnesses may leave a project; and the memory of potential witnesses may fade. The end result of the process is a report that should identify the causes of an accident rather than to allocate blame. However, investigators are often asked to highlight illegal or improper activity or to produce a damage evaluation. Furthermore, it is inevitable that some forensic reports do implicate people in blame and consequently, it is useful if the forensic manager has some knowledge of legal processes. While implications of blame may be unavoidable, the investigative process must not degenerate into a "witch-hunt" for a scapegoat, which is a common reaction to the powerful psychological shock of a crisis (Horlick-Jones 1996). Although the identification and punishment of wrongdoers has some potential to prevent recurrence, blaming others can easily backfire and detract attention from the important lessons to be learned from a disaster. This is what occurred in the Exxon Valdez oil spill when, during the post-crisis phase, Exxon sought to avoid blame by focusing their energies upon discrediting the coast guard rather than seeking to learn from the disaster. Not only did this prevent Exxon from learning many important lessons, it led to further public relations problems that merely exacerbated the costs of the original crisis. Blamism also occurred in the aftermath of the Purley rail crash on March 4, 1989 in London, where 5 passengers were killed and 88 were seriously injured (Horlick-Jones 1996). After this disaster, government investigations blamed one of the drivers of the train. As a result, he was prosecuted for manslaughter and received an 18- month jail term. The report and courts dismissed behavioral research that showed that the repetitive tasks involved in monitoring warning signals can produce a mind-set in which a person could believe that he or she had performed a task when, in fact, that was not the case. The decision caused an outcry with rail unions threatening strike action and claiming that there was one law for managers and another for workers.

While the best forensic reports stick objectively to the facts, sometimes it is simply impossible to determine the causes of a crisis. In such circumstances a report should not indulge itself in speculations because the forensic manager is responsible for protecting the professional reputation of all parties under investigation at all times. While many forensic teams carry out their work under the specter of legal action, few reach court apart from those that involve injury or loss of life. For this reason, reports should be written more constructively, as a basis for constructive negotiation between potential stakeholders implicated in a crisis. In this sense, such reports, if undertaken with the cooperation of all parties can be a useful method of third-party dispute resolution.

CONCLUSION

This chapter has identified the phases of the crisis management process that must be managed efficiently for a reaction to be successful. These phases are detection, diagnosis, decisionmaking, implementation, recovery, and learning, and their interrelationships are illustrated in Figure 3-1. This model isolates a series of distinct but interrelated phases of activity, each of which must be performed effectively if the overall crisis management process is to be effective. The model also identifies the roles of monitoring, diagnosing, and decisionmaking, which people play in the crisis management process. These functions can be performed by separate people or combined under the responsibility of one person, and it is likely that the efficiency of crisis management would, in part, be determined by the extent to which these responsibilities are separated. Any problems in the performance of these functions would likely lead to inefficiencies in crisis management. Indeed, crises seem to have an unfortunate tendency to create conditions that would be conducive to problems, which suggests that inefficiencies would be probable rather than possible.

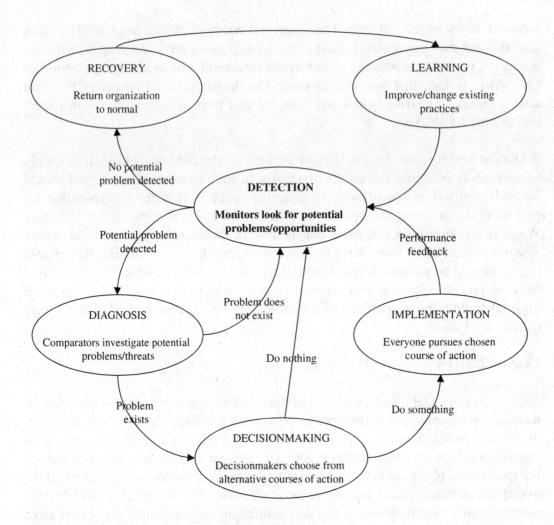

Figure 3-1 A model of crisis management.

Chapter 4

Emergency Planning in Construction Projects

Many of the problems discussed in the previous chapter can be attributed to a lack of preparation. Planning is the "bedrock" of effective crisis management because it helps avoid the damaging chaos that characterizes the early stages of a crisis.

INTRODUCTION

The importance of a well-conceived crisis management plan cannot be overstated. This has been illustrated many times, such as in the Occidental Piper Alpha disaster where appropriate operating manuals on how to interrupt a potentially catastrophic sequence of events were almost totally lacking (Bea 1994).

Unfortunately, all too often, organizations think they are prepared for crises because they have reviewed insurance policies, implemented back-up computer systems, and installed sprinkler systems. The fact is, the average insurance pay-out only covers one-eighth of the financial costs of an insured event and insurance policies cannot compensate for the indirect costs of a crisis arising from damaged employee morale and tarnished customer relations. To illustrate this, we return to the much-maligned Ford Pinto and Ford's calculated decision to rely on insurance pay-outs to cover the costs of potential legal suits. This proved a disastrously misguided decision because Ford had to recall 1.5 million cars and pay out compensation claims that were more than three times what was anticipated. Furthermore, they became the first American corporation to be indicted on criminal homicide charges and in 1980, almost 10 years after the car's production, Ford's reputation for safety was so bad that it ceased production of the model (Haroon 1999).

EMERGENCY PLANNING

The subject of emergency planning is receiving considerable attention in the crisis management literature, although many companies are reluctant to undertake the process (Mitroff and Pearson 1993). Indeed, in the construction industry, Teo (1998) found that corporate philosophies do not support crisis management and that any emergency planning is restricted to safety issues. Planning for other types of crises is almost non-existent and when it is present, is undertaken in an insular, informal and haphazard manner and supported by little strategic guidance and resources. One might expect this in an industry where over 90 percent of firms employ fewer than 10 people. However, Teo's research focussed on the world's largest contractors involved in the world's most complex projects and it would be reasonable to have expected some consideration of emergency planning.

Not surprisingly, the most crisis-prepared companies in the world are those operating within relatively high-risk industries such as shipping nuclear power, chemical processing, airport management, and oil. For example, Shell Oil uses crisis planning as part of their long-range strategic planning process and find that it often leads to many unexpected and indirect benefits such as new ideas that produce more innovative ways of doing business. Shell also finds that crisis planning highlights interdependencies and weaknesses that may otherwise go unnoticed and can bring people closer together by forcing them to act out and think through extreme scenarios. The emergency services have also invested a considerable amount of time researching and advising upon such plans and the construction industry could benefit from their collective experience. This is particularly true for companies involved in high-risk projects of national and international significance that are subject to public scrutiny, have a relatively high potential for large numbers of causalities, and have the scope to involve many external agencies.

THE AIMS OF AN EMERGENCY PLAN

Emergency plans should be constructed prior to a project's commencement and cover major risks in all stages of a construction project from inception to operation. Emergency plans are designed to mitigate the potential damage exacted by crises by enabling the most rapid response. They can do this because they are constructed outside the pressures normally responsible for the destructive behaviors which tend to develop during a crisis and magnify its impact. Having a preconceived plan that can be automatically implemented takes away some of the initial pressure and shock associated with the early phases of a crisis. This creates a valuable "breathing-space" within which people can calmly investigate the problem and agree on an appropriate response. The importance of a good start in crisis management cannot be over-stated. During a crisis, every second counts and the first few hours are particularly critical. This is especially true if external constituencies are involved because initial impressions play a disproportionately large role in shaping their judgments of competence and blame. If initial impressions are bad then an organization will be judged guilty until proven innocent and in many instances this can intensify a crisis and accelerate its escalation. This was demonstrated when John Laing PLC issued a profit warning as a result of its severe losses on the Rugby World Cup Millennium Stadium in Wales. As Sir Martin Laing stated, (Barlow 1999) "As soon as we issued the profit warning it was obvious that everyone in the construction press was going to be interested…. But there are a few twists that could have been put on it that are a little more positive than those that came out" (p. 24).

PREPARING AN EMERGENCY PLAN

Many organizations in high-risk industries have a permanent disaster committee that is responsible for championing the need for crisis management, identifying current preparedness and vulnerabilities, devising disaster plans, and coordinating people during a crisis (Kutner 1996). The membership of such committees is an important factor in determining their ability to do this, and they should consist of senior managers, managers from all functional departments, and external professionals who have experience of crisis management, public relations, the law, and physical and mental health issues. In particular, commitment from the top of an organization is essential if the activities of a disaster committee are to be taken seriously and if they are to have a chance of success. The various aspects of these activities are discussed below.

Conducting crisis audits and creating crisis portfolios

A crisis audit assesses an organization's crisis capabilities and identifies the inherent risk factors in its environment, internal activities, technology, infrastructure, and culture that need to be addressed to improve its crisis preparedness (Mitroff and Pearson 1993). The first stage in this process should be to develop a working definition of a crisis from the organization's viewpoint and to then identify and rank, in probability and consequence terms, the *types* of crises the organization is vulnerable to. This involves learning from past events, looking into the future and exploring unusual combinations of events that may seem unlikely, but could combine to produce a serious crisis. Ranking allows appropriate judgments to be made about the relative costs and benefits of constructing a crisis management plan in each case because planning for every possible crisis is not economically rational.

The importance and difficulty of exploring an organization's crisis vulnerabilities was well illustrated in the debilitating crisis that the Australian insurance company, Manchester Unity, suffered in 1993 (Forman 1993). This crisis originated from routine maintenance on its headquarters that caused a fire and, in turn, destroyed the power supply for the whole building. Since insurance companies are almost completely computer reliant, the lifeblood of the business was cut off in seconds. While Manchester Unity had embarked on emergency planning, its plans dealt only with extremes such as bomb scares and serious fires. No one had thought what might happen if the building was still standing and functional without any of the modern means of communication that were central to its business. Consequently, maintaining business operations were difficult and eventually a decision was made to set up a temporary communications center in a local hotel and to transfer head-office staff to suburban branches. Although the crisis was handled well, there is little doubt that it could have been handled better if these events had been anticipated and if simple measures such as manual typewriters and filing systems had been available as a back-up system.

Establishing monitoring systems and standard operating procedures

One aspect of the disaster committee's job is to establish monitoring systems to detect potential crises. The disaster committee should also develop standard procedures that define precisely *who* should be involved in a crisis response, *what* they should be doing, *when* they should be doing it, and *how* they should be doing it. These procedures, in effect, establish a pre-defined emergency communication network that needs to be followed during a crisis' early but critical phases, when people are disorientated by events. The intention is to "buy" the organization some time to come to terms with events, to allow people to re-orientate themselves, and to ensure that appropriate resources are mobilized quickly and that they are commensurate with a crisis' scale. To do this, the procedures should be achievable, simple, flexible, and understandable by all internal and external stakeholders. For example, in Australia and Singapore, construction sites have many migrant workers and this may require the production of manuals in a range of different languages.

In most crisis-prepared organizations, emergency procedures are set out in clear and easy-to-follow manuals with which everyone is familiar. Normally, such procedures consist of a number of tiers, the first being instigated during the very first hours following a crisis when there is little information available about it. This lack of information demands that these initial procedures should be as standardized as possible, covering broad families of crises. For example, many types of crises may require an evacuation of the site and others may have common health implications that demand first-aid treatment. Grouping crises into specific categories enables emergency procedures to be simplified, ensures a more rapid response, and thereby minimizes the chances of the incident escalating. However, the effectiveness of such generic procedures is limited, since different types of crises quickly demand different responses. Consequently, when the type of crisis has been identified but a detailed response not yet formulated, a second and more detailed tier of procedures should be initiated. For example, fire authorities often employ a graduated response, ranking accidents as Category 1,2,3, or 4 depending on their seriousness. A range of emergency plans is then formulated to match the weight of each category in terms of the people, time, and resources involved (Davis 1995). Once again, such procedures are only designed as a temporary response to alleviate pressures upon the project team and eventually, to buy time for the development of a strategy that is specifically tailored to the unique demands of the crisis at hand. An over-reliance on standard procedures will almost certainly lead to an ineffective crisis response.

Creating a command center

During a crisis, information is constantly being generated from a multitude of sources and it is critical that it is supplied "live" to the correct place, at the correct time, and in an understandable format (Davis 1995). In this sense, a key aspect of a disaster committee's job during a crisis is to identify a clear command center that represents a single point of responsibility for decisionmaking and information management. Such centres are a critical coordination mechanism that helps facilitate a unified crisis management effort since one of the greatest problems that can emerge during a crisis is the tendency for people to act independently. For example, in the case of a fire emergency, the command centre should have the sole responsibility to contact emergency services and to coordinate individual supervisors who are charged with clearing certain areas of the site. In the case of an economic crisis such as the bankruptcy of a major sub-contractor, the command center should be responsible for reorganizing work and re-employing another sub-contractor. In addition to being of practical importance during a crisis, command centers also play an important symbolic role. Nicodemus (1997) provides an example of a company that faced a crisis and named their command center "the war room," where they declared war on the problem.

Security

Security is another important issue for a disaster committee to consider since interference from unwanted elements can exacerbate a crisis or, at the very least, interfere with its management. This involves identifying external constituencies who feel that they have a stake in a crisis' outcome but who cannot contribute to its solution. Those involved in crisis management efforts should be insulated from these disruptive elements so they can develop a strong focus on the problem.

In some situations, it is also important that the site of a crisis is physically cut-off from these elements, particularly when it continues to represent a danger to the public. In such situations, evacuation procedures may need implementing and it is essential that they are clearly communicated to everyone on a project and reinforced by regular training and mock-drills. For example, public address systems, sirens and horns can be used to notify people of an incident if they are placed at strategic locations so everyone can hear them. Whatever signal is used, it must be as simple and as unequivocal as possible. Responsibilities for using them must be clear, as should appropriate back up if, as Murphy's Law dictates, key people are away on the day of an incident or if essential equipment malfunctions. An important part of evacuation is the clear labelling of exit routes from all parts of the site. In particular, people should know that mechanical hoists cannot not be used in an evacuation and that all potentially dangerous machinery in the vicinity of escape routes must be switched off. Since a construction site is a constantly changing physical environment, the positions of notices and their maintenance needs constant monitoring. Furthermore, all evacuation routes should follow the shortest possible route to checkpoints where role-calls can be taken in safety. They should also be wide enough to facilitate an orderly evacuation of the building. On inner-city sites, this may be the street and the hazards to the public, to traffic, and to site workers must be assessed in association with public services such as the police.

The potential danger of not having adequately thought out evacuation plans and well-marked evacuation routes was demonstrated in the Beverly Hills Supper Club fire in May 1977 which killed 164 people. The official investigation report reveals that the club had no evacuation plan and that employees were not schooled or drilled in the duties they were to perform in the case of fire. Furthermore, means of egress were not marked and the escape route itself was too narrow to take the number of people who were in the building at that particular point in time (Best 1977).

Developing a culture of collective responsibility

The need to insulate a disaster response team from unwanted elements does not mean it should be allowed to become introverted. Consideration also needs to be given to the reorganization of non-crisis management activities so the remainder of an organization can function as normally as possible. Crises inevitably drain a considerable amount of energy from other functional areas within an organization, demanding special efforts from the people who operate there. Clearly, without a considerable degree of peripheral goodwill and a sense of collective responsibility, the impact of a crisis can spread to other parts of an organization. Such goodwill cannot be expected if it did not exist before a crisis, and in this sense, the crisis management process needs to be continuous.

One way of developing a culture of collective responsibility is to communicate everyone's interdependency during a crisis and to clarify and, ideally, share project risks as much as possible. Most crises demand an injection of extra resources into a project and if the disaster committee does not identify their source in advance, then a crisis will stimulate negotiations and potential conflicts that will delay a response.

Decisions concerning risk distribution are particularly relevant to economic crises, and earlier we provided evidence to suggest that they have been a major cause of conflict within construction projects. We also identified a series of principles to guide risk decisionmaking. These principles apply at all points along the contractual chain and to consultants, as well as contractors. It is also important to realize that the client's initial risk management practices are inevitably transferred along the contractual chain. For example, if a contractor is employed under a high-risk contract and has not been given the opportunity to price for those risks, then it is likely that they will attempt to transfer those risks along the chain by using back-to-back contracts and similar employment practices with their sub-contractors. Indeed, sub-contractors may do the same and so on, until all project risks have been dissipated to the end of the contractual chain. Unfortunately, it is here that the most vulnerable, crisis-prone organizations exist, and when problems begin to occur that demand extra resources, the end result of this risk-cascade is inevitably a backlash of conflict up the contractual chain as parties deny any responsibility for them.

Public relations

Public relations are an essential aspect of crisis management since most types of crises have implications beyond an organization's boundaries. In essence, the three "publics" that need to be involved in a crisis are employees not directly affected by it, external and quasi-external interest groups and the general public. We have already discussed the first two publics and it would be foolish to ignore the third. As Aspery (1993) argues, "crisis communications built on well-established relationships with key audiences stand a better chance of protecting, even enhancing your reputation during difficult times. A company which decides to start communicating during a crisis will have little credibility" (p. 18).

Unfortunately, construction companies tend to attach little importance to the building of sound relationships with the media, seeing it as a non value-adding activity and perceiving most journalists as dangerous, untrustworthy, and irresponsible (Moodely and Preece 1996). This rejection of the media tends to be particularly strong during a crisis when organizations look inward and consciously hide from the public, seeing them as an unnecessary distraction to rescue efforts. However, this is precisely the time when it is most dangerous to ignore the media, since in the aftermath of a crisis, the public has a tendency to embark on a process of ritual damnation. This is particularly true of high-profile, publicly financed projects in which people may feel a greater right to recrimination as a result of having paid their taxes to finance it. As Horlick-Jones (1996) notes, "Since the abolition of capital punishment, the British public has turned to those in charge during lurid disasters to satisfy its lust for retribution. Find someone to blame, cries the mob, and off runs Whitehall to offer up someone for lynching" (p. 61). Indeed, throughout this book we have discussed numerous examples to illustrate how poor public relations have been the downfall of many organizations that have underestimated the power of the media in shaping public opinion of how a crisis is being handled. One of the best examples of this was the collapse of Gerald Ratner's jewelry empire in the United Kingdom in 1991, which was caused by his throw-away line during a speech to the Institute of Directors in London. Ratner bragged that he could sell a sherry decanter for 15 pounds even if it was "total crap." The next day, the press exposed his mocking insincerity toward the customers that had made Ratner his fortune, and overnight, they abandoned his shops (Weyer 1994).

The media

The construction industry is particularly vulnerable to poor media coverage because of its very negative public image. This was demonstrated in a 1997 national United Kingdom opinion poll, in which only the oil industry was viewed less favorably by teenagers (Building 1997). Furthermore, there is increasing scrutiny of the industry as a result of the ever-greater appreciation of its impact on the built and natural environment (Moodley and Preece 1996). This, coupled with growing sympathies with the environmental movement amongst the general population, has resulted in increasing numbers of confrontations with the public, particularly on road and housing projects. Notably, in many of these increasingly common and public confrontations, the media has portrayed construction companies in a heavy-handed and unsympathetic light and there is little doubt that the future viability of many projects will have been affected by this coverage. In this sense, media relations is an area of traditional neglect to which companies operating in the construction industry must turn their attention. Construction managers cannot rely upon the media to put their case and a continued reluctance to communicate with the media will almost certainly lead to negative reporting of the industry's activities. In contrast, open relationships with the press and more sensitivity to environmental issues will enable managers to better shape the public's attitudes and thereby obtain a more balanced presentation of the facts from the media during a crisis.

One way of ensuring open communication with the press during a crisis is to establish a 24-hour-a-day press office, which has the responsibility of providing factual and up-to-date information to the media and to employees. If managed well, such an office should be able to turn media inquiries into opportunities rather than problems by initiating, rather than reacting to, press, radio, and TV coverage. Public relations are best handled by one trained person who is named as an official spokesperson and who has skills in dealing with the media. TV interviews with untrained staff who appear uncaring, flustered, and unsure of the facts are damaging to the public's perception of competence whereas, a trained person with experience of such events can portray a positive image. The importance of identifying such a person was illustrated during the aftermath of the TWA flight 800 crash when the rush of distraught families, an eager press, and an interested public were left to the management of one chief ticket agent who, through no fault of his own, released inaccurate information which fuelled uncertainty, anxiety, and false speculation about the handling of the affair (Bobo 1997). This was a primary reason TWA was widely criticized afterward by public relations counsellors, crash victims' families, and the media for having an uncaring attitude.

Post-crisis management

After a crisis, a disaster committee should organize follow-up meetings so lessons can be learned and fed into subsequent crisis management efforts. Everyone affected by a crisis must be involved in this process. In addition to managing the learning process, the disaster committee should also turn its attention to the recovery. This can be a lengthy and sensitive process that is likely to be influenced by how well a crisis was managed. For example, it may involve delicate challenges such as conducting investigations into causes, mending damaged relationships, reorganizing the project program, settling on-going disputes and re-assessing project requirements. At the same time, attention must be given to the long-term consequences of a crisis such as rectifying damage to the environment, or dealing with government or legal investigations. Clearly, the less effectively a crisis is managed, the more arduous is the recovery process.

FORMULATING AN EMERGENCY PLAN FOR A CONSTRUCTION PROJECT

Formulating an effective emergency plan takes time and depends on advance planning and the involvement of those who will be affected within and outside an organization. This is often difficult in construction projects due to time and cost pressures, yet perhaps the greatest barrier to emergency planning is the transitionary nature of construction project teams. This requires crisis management plans to reflect the continuous changes in project personnel over time, which has a knock-on effect to training since every change in plan needs to be clearly communicated to those affected. This is best achieved through regular emergency management workshops for everyone and through induction meetings for every new person who enters a project, at whatever level. The complexities and, ultimately, time and costs involved in doing this are a major barrier to the development of emergency plans on construction projects. Despite these practical problems, the importance of planning cannot be overstated. Without a plan, a crisis is likely to stimulate an uncontrollable period of reactionary chaos, which would waste time, resources and energies and inevitably, lead to the deepening of a crisis.

CONCLUSION

While emergency planning can alleviate many of the potential problems that can arise during the crisis management process, it is appropriate to finish this chapter with a warning that managers should not over-rely on their crisis management plans. First, they require continuous maintenance and efforts to ensure that people remain familiar with them. Furthermore, emergency plans cannot cover all eventualities and can be misinterpreted, ignored, or deliberately distorted during a crisis. Ultimately, no matter how well-designed and heavily resourced emergency plans are, *people* are both the weakness and strength of an organization during a crisis. While some people will act selfishly, others will exhibit courage, ingenuity and commitment beyond the call of duty. There is no substitute for good people and responsive management during a crisis.

Chapter 5

Crisis Managers as Social Architects

A construction crisis stimulates a network of communications between internal and external stakeholders. This chapter explores these networks in more detail, arguing that the best crisis managers are social architects, designing, creating, and maintaining appropriate social relationships among project participants.

THE CONCEPT OF SOCIAL ARCHITECTURE

Bennis (1996) introduced the concept of social architecture to encapsulate the contemporary idea that organizations are self-organizing social systems comprising a multitude of interdependent, culturally diverse people with varied and changing interests. Cultural diversity, in an occupational and geographical sense, ensures that these people attribute unique meanings and interpretations to their world and respond differently and unpredictably to managerial actions (Tsoukas 1995). From this perspective, management is no longer seen as a mechanical, regulatory activity designed to control some objective and static scene, but as a social activity that involves coordinating purposeful individuals who are embedded in complex and constantly changing social networks. These networks tie discrepant parts of an organization into a coherent whole by providing channels through which information flows and new ideas are spread. In this sense, they are the central mechanism through which mangers must work to achieve integration, coordination, and cooperation. In practical terms, this view of organizations implies that managers should focus on relationships rather than on individuals and that they need to understand the dynamics and structures of these social relationships and how they influence an organization's ability to achieve its goals.

SOCIAL STRUCTURE AND CRISIS MANAGEMENT EFFICIENCY

The first evidence to support a link between the structure of people's relationships and crisis management efficiency was provided by the pioneering work of Bavelas (1950), Leavitt (1951) and Shaw (1954). They assembled small groups of people, requiring them to solve a simple problem that required the pooling of information. The members of each group were physically separated and only permitted to use predetermined communication channels, as illustrated in figure 5-1.

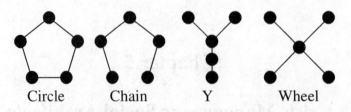

Figure 5-1 Leavitt's experimental patterns.

Through observations, interviews, and analysis of each group's communications, the researchers found that there were significant differences among the communication patterns in terms of their problem-solving efficiency. When problems were simple, organizational efficiency developed most rapidly in the chain followed by the Y, the wheel, and finally the circle. In terms of leadership, the circle was seen as active, leaderless, unorganized and erratic, yet enjoyed by its members. In contrast, the wheel was relatively inactive, well-organized, less erratic, and unsatisfying to its membership. The researchers used the concept of "centrality" to explain the results. Centrality is defined as "the degree to which information flow is centered around one or a few individuals in a communication network." Low-centrality organizations are characterized by no leader, high activity, slow problem-solving, but high satisfaction. However, the problem-solving efficiency of each network depended on the nature of the problem faced by a group. When the problem complexity increased, the relative efficiency of various patterns completely reversed; the circle became the fastest and the wheel the slowest. The central person in the wheel became overloaded with information and peripheral people were less willing to merely accept the solution offered by the central person.

Although Leavitt and Shaw conducted their experiments in an artificial environment where all the complications of real-life were stripped away, their findings suggest that crisis management efficiency would be influenced by management's ability to control the structure of people's communication patterns. Therefore, it is worth considering further the various dimensions of communication structure that are likely to be important in a crisis management setting.

Formal and informal communication structures

At the most basic level, communication structure can be categorized as formal or informal. Formal communications during a construction crisis are determined primarily by employment contracts that bind project participants together. These contracts set down prescriptive procedures designed to dictate the patterns of interaction of organizational members, thereby imposing an element of predictability in a situation where managerial control is naturally threatened. Such procedures are also designed to ensure a rapid response to crises by keeping information channels free from irrelevant information and by defining the boundaries of acceptable behavior. In this sense, it appears that construction contracts have a significant influence on the actions of project members during a crisis. However, Sagan (1991) argues that the influence of contractual rules and procedures diminishes during a crisis. His research indicates that standardized procedures are most helpful when the nature of the task is simple whereas, when task complexity and time-pressures increase, they become restrictive and counter-productive by removing people's autonomy. Furthermore, Bax et al (1998) indicate that during a crisis, a gap can open between what workers consider to be a legitimate and effective way of dealing with a situation and what formal procedures prescribe. This is particularly likely if workers have not helped formulate those rules. As Loosemore and Hughes (1998) found, the tendency in such situations would be for formal procedures to be bypassed and for people's patterns of communication to revolve around common interest groups and friendships.

The dangers of contracts as a means of control

Thus, the network of communications that emerges in response to a construction crisis has a significant informal element that could be dangerous if managers relied too much on contracts as a means of control. Contracts, however well drafted, are no substitute for good management. Rather, managers facing a construction crisis must ensure that formal procedures complement informal systems and recognize that a successful outcome may depend on their willingness to release people from potentially restrictive rules and procedures. This demands some courage, since there is a natural tendency to turn to contracts during a crisis in order to re-impose control. It also demands a certain degree of confidence and trust in fellow project members, which may not exist due to the organizational practices and historical divisions discussed in Chapter One. Indeed, under the traditional confrontational environment that pervades many construction projects, a sudden movement to a more flexible stance may be disastrous because it would be alien to the expectations of individuals who have developed behavior patterns ideally suited to an untrusting environment. The likely result is that people will see such a cultural change as an opportunity for exploitation rather than for increased cohesion. This is precisely why a number of projects using the more flexible Engineering and Construction Contract (1995) produced by the Institution of Civil Engineers in the United Kingdom have not been as successful as hoped.

Thus, it would seem that the voluminous, rigid, and prescriptive nature of traditional construction contracts is a necessary response to the untrusting and confrontational environment that pervades many construction projects. Ironically, such contracts perpetuate this environment, indicating that the construction industry is caught in a downward spiral of mistrust and control that is increasingly difficult to stop. This problem led Loosemore and Hughes (1998) to propose "the emergency option" as an intermediate step in making traditional contracts more flexible with a minimum risk of exploitation. In essence, the emergency option is a separate clause that can be legally incorporated into traditional construction contracts, enabling parties to mutually agree to opt-out of normal contractual procedures for a specified period in order to cope with a crisis. If one party abuses this trust, then there is a facility for any party to unilaterally return the project to a formal mode.

Groups, factions, and cliques

People are social animals, spending much of their time in formal and informal groups that have their own unique norms (expected standards of behavior), agendas, orientations, and cultures. Groups perform many important functions, particularly during a crisis, such as enabling people to solve tasks of much greater magnitude and complexity than they would be able to tackle alone. Groups also provide for people's social, identity, and belonging needs and can represent an important source of power in negotiations. An awareness of group formation is an important aspect of crisis management. However, Tichy et al (1979) argue that the roles people play within and between factions are also important to managers. For example, a "liaison" is an individual who is not a member of a faction but who links two or more factions, and a "bridge" is an individual who is a member of multiple factions. Liaisons and bridges perform important linkage functions in organizations and their removal destroys its connected unity. Their identification by a crisis manager is particularly important because they can be used to prevent communication breakdowns and to mediate among groups of opposing interests before misunderstanding and conflict emerge. A third inter-faction role that may be valuable during a crisis is the "isolate," who is not affiliated to any one faction in particular. Isolates may be crucial sources of independence that crisis managers can use to their advantage, but the danger is that in the heat of a crisis, powerful factions can dominate communications and divert attention away from them. Therefore, managers may need to make special efforts to integrate isolates into the crisis management process. Indeed, by increasing the power base of isolates or by focusing on them, crisis managers can minimize the potential for conflict arising from the competing interests of different groups.

The dangers of groups

While groups can perform many useful functions during a crisis, they can also be at their most dangerous. For example, Hornstein (1986) has expressed alarm at the in-roads being made by the social ethic that espouses groups, not individuals, as the prime source of creativity and that proclaims group membership, an experience akin to being in a family, as the ultimate need of an individual. In Hornstein's view, groups have a capacity for producing a special, perniciously subtle tyranny that can damage communications, slow down decisionmaking, produce compromise decisions, and suppress creativity and innovation. Marsh et al (1978) also noted the powerful influence a group can exert over its members. Their research into football hooliganism concluded that group norms can cause people to blindly exhibit almost tribal behavior that their personality and wider society would normally suppress. Janis (1988) refers to the tendency of groups to emphasize the importance of consensus and agreement as "groupthink." The potency of this effect depends on the attractiveness of a group to its members and the extent to which conformance enhances a group's power, aids its survival, benefits its members, simplifies its processes, and expresses its central identity and values. The potential danger of groupthink was vividly illustrated in the Challenger Space Shuttle disaster when, on the evening before the launch, engineers, with full knowledge that the expected temperature at the time of launch would be below safety levels, were pressured by peers to sanction the launch. It would seem that during a crisis, when effective communication, open-mindedness, creativity, and flexibility are most valuable, groups could be at their most dangerous.

Structural equivalence

Another aspect of social structure that is relevant during a crisis is peoples' structural equivalence. Two people in an organization are structurally equivalent if they have exactly the same pattern of contacts. At first it was thought that such people play the same role in an organization and were inter-changeable with one another. However, the concept of structural equivalence only considers similarities between people's "patterns" of interaction and ignores the nature of people within them. That is, people can be structurally equivalent by having the same patterns of connections with different people. Scott (1991) argues that this does not mean that they are playing the same social role and advocates the alternative concept of "regular equivalence."

Regular equivalence

Two people are regularly equivalent if they are connected to the same people in the same way. The level of regular equivalence in an organization is important to crisis managers because it is reasonable to assume that communication would be better and the crisis management process more efficient within highly equivalent groups. The members of such groups would have common neighbors, shorter communication routes, and higher levels of communication.

While highly equivalent groups seem desirable, they could be particularly susceptible to groupthink. Variety in social relationships is clearly important in generating the creativity needed to resolve a crisis. Therefore, it would seem that crisis managers have a "tight-rope" to walk in balancing the level of regular equivalence and independence they encourage.

Centrality

Organizational centrality is the degree to which information flows are centered on one or a few people. The concept of centrality is important to crisis managers because substantial evidence suggests it may be closely related to crisis management efficiency. Leavitt (1951) and Shaw (1954) found that the influence of centrality depended on the nature of the problem an organization faced—more complex, non-routine problems such as crises demanded less centralized structures to alleviate the potential for information overload. However, Mintzberg (1976) found that during a crisis, people tend to tighten control, the consequence of which is dysfunctional behavior. It is a paradox of crisis management that if inappropriately applied, centrally imposed order can lead to disorder where disorder would eventually lead to order.

Thus, the concept of centrality is important to crisis managers who must seek to control the degree to which their organization is centralized around particular individuals. This is best achieved with an understanding of the different types of centrality that exist. Freeman (1979) is credited with clarifying the literature in this area. He differentiated between the concepts of *degree centrality*, *closeness centrality* and *betweenness centrality*, each having sharply different implications for the management of crises.

Degree centrality

Degree centrality refers to people's roles as senders or receivers of information within an organization. A person with a relatively high sending role is a prominent *source* of information to others, is in the "thick of things," is a highly active member of the network and is a focal point for instruction and leadership. Such people sustain an organization by providing the information that is its "life-blood," and in this sense, an organization is highly dependent on them. This places them in a powerful position, particularly during a crisis when people's appetite for information naturally increases. In contrast, people with a relatively high receiving role are prominent *sinks* of information and are likely to play an important information storage or synthesizing role within an organization. They are especially important during a crisis because of the great volume and variety of information that is generated and that needs to be synthesized, converted, or condensed into a manageable, meaningful, and consistent format

Betweenness centrality

Betweenness centrality measures the extent to which a person lies between others in an organization and reflects the degree to which they play an information "gate keeping" role. People with high betweenness centrality are important because they have the capacity to manipulate or filter information flowing between people. In this sense, they have a great deal of power, acting as the valves within a network and occupying a critical position in maintaining free and open communication. Essentially, these people act as the glue that holds an organization's parts together, and weaknesses at these critical points can lead to disintegration.

Thus, an organization's betweenness centrality is an important measure of its vulnerability to people's integrity in not manipulating information to satisfy their own ends and to people's ability to manage the information passing through their hands. These vulnerabilities are naturally exacerbated during a crisis because high stakes cause people to pursue their interests with more tenacity and because organizations can become flooded with information at the same time as high stress levels reduce people's information handling capacities.

Closeness centrality

People have a high closeness centrality if they are positioned at short "distances" (measured by the number of intermediaries) from every other person in an organization. The closeness of a person to all others is a reflection of his or her independence since high closeness makes it difficult to act alone, without others knowing. Conversely, people with a high closeness centrality have the capacity to directly monitor and control others and to communicate their ideas more rapidly to a wide audience with minimal distortion. During the pressures of a crisis they represent a very important channel of communication for a manager.

CRISIS BEHAVIOR

In the midst of a crisis, managers must control people's patterns of communication because the patterns determine the ease with which information flows within an organization and thereby, the level of uncertainty, misunderstanding, and ultimately, conflict that arises. In this section, we explore the unfortunate tendency for crises to cause people to behave in ways that make this difficult. This behavior is largely a consequence of two forces: people's difficulties coping with the pressures and stresses of a crisis and their difficulties coping with the significant levels of change induced by a crisis.

Psychological pressure and stress

By definition, crises are potentially serious events that require inventive solutions under extreme pressures. This ensures that those affected feel a certain degree of tension and anxiety—conditions that induce both positive and negative behavior. For example, while some argue that such feelings produce a determination that is important to the efficient resolution of problems, others point to them increasing suspicion and reducing communication. The explanation for this contradiction lies in the distinction between pressure and stress. Robertson and Cooper (1983) argued that *pressure* is a force acting on an individual to perform in a particular way or to achieve a particular end result. It can be a source of some discomfort and anxiety but at the same time it can be exciting, challenging, and growth- producing. On the other hand *stress* has only negative outcomes for an individual because it arises from an inability to cope, which produces defensive and maladaptive behavior.

The impact of stress on crisis management outcomes

According to George (1991), stress is a "generic problem that poses severe threats to crisis management" (p. 559). The stress associated with a crisis arises from the dramatic challenge to previously held views, from the dislocation to social relations and from the physical challenges posed. Stress can also come from the psychological shock of a crisis, which can manifest itself immediately or in the form of post-trauma. An example of a crisis that could cause this type of shock is a workplace death. A co-worker's death on the job could devastate an organization's employees. However, the impact of stress is never uniform in its effect and those who were physically or emotionally close to the individual would be more likely to experience difficulties. Furthermore, during a crisis like this, only higher levels of management have the authority to deal with the enormity of decisions required. This means that the burden of pressure would fall upon their shoulders and it is the people occupying these positions of responsibility who are also in particular danger of suffering stress.

The behavior resulting from stress is precisely what is not needed during a crisis. Hermann (1963) pointed to a loss of attention to problem-solving, increased decisionmaking errors, greater rigidity in exploring alternative courses of action, panic, anxiety, and withdrawal. Stewart (1983) found that individual reactions to stress include agitation, reduced attention span, absenteeism, sickness, aggressive behavior, impulsive behavior, depression, lower tolerance of risk, and lower tolerance of other's opinions. T'Hart (1993) reported that stress also amplifies personal insecurities and feelings of vulnerability and may decrease the self-confidence and self-esteem of those affected. Finally, in extreme circumstances, stress can seriously impair psychological well-being and might even activate latent psychological vulnerabilities or borderline psychopathological tendencies (George 1991).

In this sense, managers must appreciate that the costs of a crisis are not all physical and that its psychological impact can paralyze an organization by traumatizing its employees. Indeed, Kutner (1996) points out that stress-related disabilities now account for 14 percent of worker's compensation claims and are twice as costly as the average physical injuries claim. Clearly, the location of "stress-points" within an organization is something to which crisis managers should give serious attention. To alleviate potentially problematic behavior it is critical that sufficient consideration is given to the personalities and capabilities of people occupying these points and that adequate support is provided for them. This process should be a continuous one that should extend beyond the solution of a crisis because the effects of stress are often delayed in their impact and the location of stress points is constantly changing.

Coping with change

Crises inevitably induce a significant amount of social, monetary, and physical change that most people find unsettling because it represents an abandonment of past efforts and a threat to the status quo. This often produces resistance to change that can take many forms, ranging along a continuum from passive disagreement to positive hostility. The level of resistance is likely to depend on the extent of change required, the extent to which people's interests are damaged, the power of those whose interests are damaged, and the manner in which change is introduced. Ansoff (1979) argues that while change may eventually result in resistance, its emergence might be delayed by the inherent seriousness of a crisis. For example, if a crisis is serious enough to threaten the very existence of an organization, the initial response may be to put differences of interest aside, to tackle the crisis and thereby ensure the organization's survival, which is in everyone's interests.

The growth of a conflict

While resistance may be the natural response to change, the conflicts of interests that exist within most organizations complicate people's behaviors. Changes that are a threat to one party will be an opportunity to another. While managers can empower these potential allies to champion the changes that need to be implemented, they also have to deal with the tensions created between potential beneficiaries and losers because it is within such tensions that conflict is born.

Conflict is a progressive phenomenon that gathers momentum as it escalates through the phases of simple disagreement, contention, dispute, limited warfare and all-out warfare, where parties are trying to destroy each other at all costs (Philips 1988). The natural tendency for crises to generate conflict has caused Snyder (1972) to describe a crisis as a transition zone between peace and war where the speed of transition depends on factors such as the gap between opposing parties, past and current relationships, attitudes toward compromise, and the way bargaining is managed. Since bargaining is the initial and informal means by which people attempt to resolve their differences, an understanding of bargaining processes should represent the foundation of a crisis management strategy. A better command of this process should reduce the possibility of escalation and the associated movement toward more formal, costly, public, and time-consuming methods of resolution such as arbitration and litigation (CME 1997). As Pinnell (1999) argues, conflict management skills are like an insurance policy against catastrophic loss, regardless of that project's complexity and size. This was well illustrated in two recent construction disputes that went wrong. One occurred during a simple $600,000 sewer contract in Arizona and resulted in the plaintiff being awarded $300,000 in damages and both parties having to pay $257,000 in costs. In another more complex case, the attorney's fees alone exceeded $5 million.

The bargaining process

The term "bargaining" implies a difference in interests, objectives, and expectations and is concerned with reaching accommodations between them. More precisely, bargaining is "a process whereby parties negotiate over the distribution of scarce resources, money, status or power" (Morley 1981, p. 113). In essence, the process involves a struggle between adversaries who attempt to move, step-by-step toward an agreement over resource redistributions that is in their own favor. In this struggle, which is like a game of chess or poker, people employ a range of tactics that, in a construction project, may be motivated by a complex web of interpersonal and inter-organizational forces. This is because negotiators belong to and represent the interests of distinct profit-making organizations that ensures that their attitudes and behavior is determined not only by their own values, but by those of their employers and of any informal interest-groups or temporary coalitions to which they are affiliated. Indeed, some employers may impose real restrictions on a negotiator's decisionmaking authority and autonomy at the bargaining table, making it difficult to resolve issues quickly.

Bargaining tactics

The essence of the bargaining process is the "tactics" or "moves" negotiators use to influence each other. Rogers (1991) argues that the tactics adopted by an individual depends on their "bargaining code"—their set of beliefs about an opponent that influence the way they interpret and respond to their messages. According to Rogers, the beliefs that are important in a bargaining setting are those relating to *an opponent's objectives,* to *dispute dynamics* (i.e., the manner in which war might erupt) and to *the optimal mixture of coercion, accommodation, and persuasion in a bargaining strategy.* On this basis, Rogers grouped bargaining codes into four broad categories: types A, B, C, and D. The characteristics are depicted in Table 5-1 and lead to the employment of certain tactics.

Tactical miscalculations and accidental escalations

Table 5-1 illustrates that during bargaining, negotiators make tactical choices guided by various beliefs. Unfortunately, under the pressures of a crisis, negotiators are often forced to make decisions with incomplete information and consequently there is a chance of tactical miscalculations that can precipitate an unintentional escalation of a dispute. Many vivid illustrations of this danger can be found in the area of international relations. For example, America's war with Japan in 1941 was precipitated by a U.S. oil embargo and inflexible demands for Japan to absolve claims to sovereignty in Asia. This forced the Japanese into a corner and gave them no alternative other than to initiate war by making a pre-emptive strike in Pearl Harbor. Other, more recent examples of conflicts precipitated by tactical miscalculations are the wars between South Korea and North Korea in the 1950s, the Falklands war in the 1980s, and the Gulf War in the 1990s. In each case, the aggressor served a *fait accompli* upon its opponent, failing to predict the nature and intensity of their response. The South Korea/North Korea war illustrates the difficulties in predicting an opponent's response, even with good intelligence gathering, since the U.S. unexpectedly reversed its earlier policy of non-intervention and quickly came to the assistance of South Korea.

As Dixon (1988) points out in his psychological analysis of military incompetence, the likelihood of tactical miscalculations becomes an increasing danger as a dispute escalates, which means that they tend to gather momentum, once initiated. This is because people's perceptions of each other become less rational and more guided by emotions. The most frightening illustration of the fragility of conflicts, when they escalate, occurred on October 25, 1962 when nuclear armed bombers sat on runways around America ready for war with the Soviet Union. Pilots had been told that there

Table 5-1 Bargaining codes and tactics (Adapted from Rogers 1991).

CODE	BELIEFS
A	**Adversary**: Seen as aggressive. **Dispute dynamics**: Only intentional war is possible. Little consideration needs to be given to the response of an adversary and its escalating impact. Any escalation is easily controllable. **Tactics**: Open use of aggression, *fait accompli*, or strong coercive action is the best way to resolve a dispute. Success in negotiations is best measured in military rather than diplomatic terms.
B	**Adversary**: Likely to employ offensive, rather than defensive tactics. **Dispute dynamics**: Control of a dispute is possible to a point where unintended escalation is possible. It is possible to understand the dynamics of escalation and thereby avoid the point where control is lost. Probabilities of escalation can be assigned to various tactics and strategies. **Tactics**: Incremental small-step escalations will be seen as timid and a sign of weakness and are likely to lead to an escalation. Failure to show resolve is the most common cause of war. **TYPE B-1** **Adversary**: Willing and able to take advantage of any signs of weakness. **Dispute dynamics**: Escalation is assumed to come from failure to communicate a determination to protect one's vital interests at any cost. **Tactics**: Coercive diplomacy (i.e. verbal threats of extreme actions and all-out war) and bluffing are the best means of dispute resolution. It is dangerous not to brandish the ultimate weapon. **TYPE B-11** **Adversary**: Seen as unpredictable. **Dispute dynamics**: Bluffing and threats are dangerous since they may inadvertently induce a counteractive aggressive response. **Tactics**: It is better to use limited force to avoid an all-out war rather than to use threats of all-out war.
C	**Adversary**: It is difficult to determine whether adversary is offensive or defensive. **Dispute dynamics**: Two images of escalation - failure to show resolve and spiralling responses to perceived provocations. Many unpredictable paths to escalation, difficult to avoid slippery slopes, brink cannot be recognised in advance. **Tactics**: Tactics must be cautious and context-driven rather than automatic. Only partial control of dispute is possible and threats or use of power are dangerous. Tread carefully, limited escalations and compromises preferred. Carrot and stick approach is best means of manipulating an adversary.
D	**Adversary**: Assume adversary operates in a defensive mode. **Dispute dynamics**: Control of disputes is very problematic if not impossible with even a modest emphasis upon coercion. Highly cautious approach in fear of triggering an uncontrollable escalation. **Tactics**: Accommodation and compromise is best means of resolution. Entire effort should be aimed at avoiding bargaining situations.

would be no practice drills during this tense crisis and when a sentry in one military base spotted someone climbing a fence, he suspected a soviet saboteur and sounded an alarm. The intruder was, in fact, a brown bear but in one base, the wrong alarm was sounded and pilots were sent running to their aircraft, fully believing that a nuclear war was beginning. Only when the base commander realized the mistake and drove onto the runway to prevent them taking off was the mission to bomb the Soviet Union aborted.

In addition to the problem of irrationality, which can fuel a dispute, there is the problem of increasing inflexibility. This occurs as people become progressively embedded in their own position as increasing investments of resources reduce their willingness to compromise. Under these conditions, winning at all costs becomes increasingly important and people become caught up in a self-perpetuating spiral of conflict that becomes increasingly difficult to break and that sucks in unjustifiable quantities of resources. This was vividly illustrated in the Vietnam War where military commanders were responsible for executing policies that cost the United States $300 billion. During this war, which achieved nothing in strategic terms, almost 2 million people died and the U.S. released 13 million tons of high explosives (more than six times the weight of bombs dropped in the whole of World War II).

The dynamics of conflict – the use of inducements not threats

In conflict resolution, parties attempt, by negotiation or other means, to force an adversary to come to the table, to make concessions, and to accept an agreement that meets their interests and needs. Third parties also influence the process by backing one party, mediating between them, or by manoeuvring to protect their own interests. This process of trying to influence an opponent normally relies on a series of threats and inducements. For example, in construction projects, a threat could be to withhold payments, an inducement to trade-off a settlement against other outstanding disputes. In most construction projects, the use of threats far outweighs the use of inducements, yet inducements are particularly effective if they meet the needs of an opponent and encourage reciprocations that can transform the landscape of a bargaining setting. An example of this occurred in 1977 when Egyptian president Anwar Sadat visited Jerusalem and made an unexpected concession in accepting Israel's position in the anticipation that they would reciprocate. This initiative was designed to transform a seemingly unresolvable conflict into a new constructive relationship that would enable the stalemate to be resolved by peaceful means. As Kelman (1997) points out, while an emphasis on positive inducements rather than negative threats is more risky in the short-term, it has the potential to be far more positive in the long-term. However, the effective use of positive inducements requires more than just offering an opponent the rewards and promises that are most readily available. Rather, it depends on the use of inducements that address an opponent's fundamental needs and fears and on their willingness to reciprocate.

Unfortunately, the high levels of understanding, altruism, and trust needed to initiate this process are lost rapidly as a conflict escalates and third party intervention is often required. A key aspect of this person's role is to facilitate mutual reassurance, which can be brought about by acknowledgments, symbolic gestures, and confidence-building measures that demonstrate mutual sensitivity. Such gestures need not cost any party a great deal. For example, it may be necessary for one party to simply acknowledge past mistakes or agree to meet. Such gestures have a powerful psychological impact in opening the way to negotiations, even though they may not be immediately transferable into concrete actions. This is because most conflicts are marked by a history of accusations and denials of another's experiences, authenticity and legitimacy. For example, at the beginning of Sadat's visit to Israel, Sadat offered a symbolic gesture that had a disproportionately large impact upon the Israeli negotiators: he offered to shake their hands. Previous officials' refusal to do so had come to symbolize Arab denial of Israel's legitimacy and the very humanity of its people. Thus, positive incentives, if they are genuine and well-thought through, have an advantage over threats as a means of conflict resolution because they provide the basis for the building of new, more positive relationships, which can become an incentive in their own right. Once this process has been initiated, parties will be inclined to live up to each other's expectations in order to maintain and extend the relationship. If the relationship blossoms, then adversaries will be able to approach their conflict as a shared dilemma and are more likely to reach an effective resolution.

Conflict as a positive force

The traditional view of conflict in the construction industry is as a disruptive force that should be avoided and eliminated at all costs. However, in Chapter One we saw that conflict is inevitable in organizations and that it can have positive implications if managed effectively. A well-managed conflict can force a more thorough investigation of a wider range of crisis solutions and can act as a useful release-valve for accumulating tensions that would otherwise remain concealed. In this sense, the potential for conflict during a crisis must not be seen as entirely destructive. However, Loosemore et al (1999) found that the skills and attitudes to manage conflict constructively do not yet exist within the construction industry. In this sense, the encouragement of conflict would seem premature. However, this is no justification for the current trend toward reducing construction conflict at all costs. This would incur significant opportunity-costs for the construction industry by reducing the possibility of benefits arising from the effective management of construction conflicts. In the long-term, a more intelligent and beneficial strategy would be to change people's attitudes to provide the foundations for constructive conflict management. The problem for the construction industry is not necessarily in the existence of conflict but in the way it is managed.

PHASES OF BEHAVIOUR DURING A CRISIS

The previous discussion highlighted the different types of behavior that might be expected during a crisis. However, it did not identify when, during the life of a crisis, certain types of behavior might evolve. For example, Cisin and Clarke (1962) proposed a three-stage model of *impact, reaction,* and *reconstruction.* During the period of *impact* people can do very little to deal with the crisis. Behavior is primarily aimed toward survival and unintelligent behavior can significantly contribute to a magnification of the possible losses to the individual and to the community as a whole. The *reaction* period is one of maximum disruption characterized by immense communication difficulties and deviant behavior. It is a phase of damage assessment, high anxiety, and confusion in which people behave irrationally and inappropriately. The main managerial problem is one of coordinating different individuals who tend to act individually and on their own definitions of the problem. Finally, the period of *reconstruction* is the beginning of the return to normality where the damage done is put right.

Fink et al (1971) produced a more detailed model that also showed patterns of behavior evolving in a predictable order. They argued that initially, crises have a disorienting effect that induces a sense of panic, disorganization, and chaos. Once this period of *shock* has subsided, people's minds turn to self-preservation and a period of *defensive retreat* where people seek to protect their own interests and to maintain the status quo. Furthermore, interpersonal relations become inwardly orientated as people turn to the protection of their interest groups. Unfortunately, this behavior deepens existing divisions and afraid of losing control, leaders tend to centralize decisionmaking power and information flow. However, this only divides an organization into factions and ritualizes communication to the extent that information is exchanged without any useful exchange of meaning. As it becomes increasingly apparent that the crisis cannot be resolved in this way, the process moves onto a phase of *acknowledgment,* self-examination, and interpersonal confrontation. During this stage, psychological stress and tension are high and there is the danger of communications degenerating into accusation and blame that can rapidly lead the organization back into the *defensive retreat* phase. However, eventually, in a need to solve the problem, individuals will resolve their differences and move to a more constructive orientation of *adaptation and change.* In extreme circumstances, this may require the involvement of a third party and the intention is to search for better ways of communicating which lead to genuine understanding and a meaningful sharing of information. As this occurs, leadership becomes more relaxed and there is a greater emphasis upon collective decisionmaking. Furthermore, people work more interdependently and let go of the dysfunctional behaviour that characterised the early phases of the crisis. Eventually, inter-group relations become coordinated and the organization once again begins to resemble a stable state.

Finally, Sipika and Smith (1993a) propose a three-phase model. The first phase is *the crisis of management* where the organization's culture serves to incubate the crisis until it becomes unsustainable and a trigger event propels the organization into the *operational phase* that is typified by convergence and the presence of high energy levels. Confusion reigns as the level of complexity in communication increases in an attempt to cope with the crisis. Eventually, the organization moves into the *legitimization phase* where a recovery strategy is developed.

The value of these models is not in the detailed behavior they describe but in the behavioural dynamics they depict. This illustrates that crisis management strategies need to be as dynamic as the behaviour they seek to control.

CONCLUSION

This chapter has discussed the ways in which people tend to behave during a crisis. The various principles that have been introduced will be used in the following chapters to analyze the management of four real-life construction crises. The data that form the basis of each case study was collected from diaries that were completed by project members before, during, and after each crisis, from observations of project meetings, from documentary inspection, and from retrospective interviews with project participants. They are both amusing and shocking and provide revealing insights into life on a typical construction project.

Before progressing, it is important to point out that the crises that form the basis of the following case studies occurred during one of the worst construction recessions in living memory. This undoubtedly affected people's behavior. Furthermore, the case studies do not describe the aftermath of construction disasters that made the headlines. The purpose of this book is to help managers avoid such disasters through a better understanding of crisis management skills. Instead, the case studies describe the development of four construction crises that posed a serious threat to the viability of their host projects. They are typical of the crises experienced on many construction projects at some time during their life, and although they did not make the headlines, there are responsible for the majority of the cost and time overruns in the construction industry.

Chapter 6

Case Study One

INTRODUCTION

The next four chapters will refer to professions that may be unfamiliar to some people. For example, the quantity surveyor (QS) creates and controls budgets at various project stages. On most projects a consultant QS represents the client's interests and a counterpart works for the main contractor. Traditionally, in the pre-contract phases of a project, the consultant QS produces a "bill of quantities" that itemizes operations involved in the construction of a building. This document is priced by tendering contractors and used as a basis for comparing their tenders. Once construction has commenced, it is then used to value construction work for payment purposes.

The clerk-of-works is another role that may be unfamiliar. This person has the responsibility to monitor site activities during construction and to report back to the architect on a regular basis. In essence, the clerk-of-works is the architect's eyes and ears on site, although with limited contractual power.

THE PROJECT

The project that represents the basis of this case study was a major extension to an existing leisure-centre on a difficult, constrained site that bordered a major road. The main contractor and all consultants had been employed on the basis of the lowest bid on a competitive tender, and coincidentally, had worked together on a recently completed project. During this project, relationships had become strained and the contractor had gained a reputation among the consultants for being "claims-conscious."

THE CRISIS

A creeping crisis began when, during basement excavations, the main contractor encountered an unexpected problem. In the contractor's opinion, permanent earthwork support was needed to construct the basement wall in this area adjacent to the road, but the bill of quantities had only enabled them to price for temporary earthwork support. The contractor contended that the QS should have made the provision in the bill of quantities for permanent earthwork support and that consequently, there was an entitlement to extra payment. The consultants disagreed. Polarized positions combined with the contractor's cessation of work on critical path activities led to an acrimonious dispute that lasted for approximately 10 months and eventually resulted in serious delays, costs, and the replacement of the contractor's entire site team.

AN ACCOUNT OF THE CRISIS MANAGEMENT PROCESS

A chronological account of the crisis follows. It is divided into separate periods of activity to highlight the dynamics of the crisis management process.

The contractor states an intention to claim extra payment

During a site meeting, the contractor's QS stated his intention to claim for extra payment to cover permanent earthwork support. He warned that work would stop in the affected area until the claim was sanctioned.

The contractor's justification for this tactic rested on his distrust of the architect. This distrust had also delayed notification of the bill of quantities discrepancy that had been apparent to the contractor for some time, but was withheld until the last minute to pressure the consultants into making a quick decision. The contractor's distrust of the consultants was mutual. The client's QS was suspicious of the contractor's motives in making a claim because of their very low tender, ambitious program; claims-conscious reputation; and a concern previously expressed by the contractor, that the consultants' excavation rates had been under-priced.

The consultants reject the contractor's claim

The contractor's claim for extra payment was formally rejected by the architect who simply stated that alternatives to the contractor's suggested permanent earthwork support system were available that would fit within the scope of the original bill of quantities description. Although the consultants' had not established alternative systems, the initial tactic was to make the "*bald*" statement that one existed. The aim was to send "*a clear message to the contractor that claims would not be tolerated*" and to "*test the contractor's resolve*" in pursuing the claim.

The consultants construct an opposing case

While waiting for the contractor's response, the client's QS and engineer constructed an argument to discredit the contractor's proposed earthwork support system. The client's QS admitted to "*guiding the engineer to look for alternatives because if there was an alternative, however expensive, then it was covered by the bill description.*" The contractor's site manager was aware of this tactic because the engineer, uncomfortable with being coerced into suggesting unreasonable solutions and being sympathetic with the contractor's case, had confided in him, "blowing the whistle" on his fellow consultants. This exposed divisions within the consultant's team and made the contractor's site manager pursue his claim with greater tenacity.

The client's project manager is alerted to the on-going dispute

The client's project manager was alerted to the claim by the contractor but was reassured by the consultants that it had been rejected.

The contractor formalizes the dispute

The contractor's site manager eventually wrote to the architect, complaining about the ongoing dispute, warning of accumulating delays, and threatening further action. This was a significant step in formalising the dispute, yet, the opportunity to discuss the problem in the next site meeting was not taken, the architect merely making a formal statement that "*alternative systems were being investigated by the engineer*". The architect's rationale for not discussing the dispute was that it was not an appropriate forum. The contractor's site manager offered a more cynical explanation that reflected deteriorating relationships: "*[the architect] did not particularly want it minuted and he didn't feel capable or want to talk about it. There was no point me pursuing it with him because if you are going to talk to someone then you have to do it in a fairly positive way.*" The contractor's site manager wrote to the architect again, reiterating his warnings of accumulating delays on site.

The contractor bypasses the architect

The contractor's site manager bypassed the architect by directly telephoning the engineer to discuss alternative earthwork support systems. The engineer suggested ground-freezing but both agreed it was unreasonable to classify this as a temporary earthwork support system as described in the original bill of quantities. Despite this, the contractor's claim was rejected once again in the next site meeting on the basis that ground-freezing was a viable alternative.

A second problem arises

The client became involved for the first time because heavy rain undermined a water main that had been exposed by the excavations and left unattended due to the on-going dispute. This required the diversion of the main and the temporary cutting-off of water supplies to the existing leisure center, which was still in use.

The dispute escalates

The sudden involvement of the contractor's regional surveyor escalated the dispute. This was a desperation tactic by the contractor's site manager who felt that "*relationships had become so poor that the problem could not be resolved at site level.*" The regional surveyor immediately telephoned the architect and client's project manager, threatening litigation. This prompted the consultants to verbally sanction the extra payment.

Payment is refused

The client's QS asked the client's project manager to formally sanction the extra expenditure, but he refused, requesting evidence that all alternative earthwork support systems had been considered. He was under the impression that the claim had been rejected and was surprised that there had been an on-going dispute. He was also annoyed at being excluded from preceding communications and was suspicious that his fellow consultant's had done this deliberately: "*I was informed that the claim had been rejected and as far as I was concerned, nothing had changed. It's a cynical view but I think there had been a lot of work going on behind the scenes to cover it up. We will often contra-charge consultant omissions against their fees.*"

The evidence provided by the client's QS was not satisfactory to the client's project manager and he requested a verbal explanation of events. This further delayed the sanctioning of the claim and frustrated the QS who felt that the architect was trying to distance himself from the problem.

Eventually, the client's project manager sanctioned the extra payment, although discussions still continued between the client's QS and engineer about the possibility of alternative earthwork support systems.

A third problem becomes evident

More severe rain caused the unsupported excavations to collapse, making un-viable, the contractor's newly sanctioned earthwork support system. After a period of relatively intense communication among all parties, the contractor proposed another new earthwork support system that cost less than that which was originally proposed. The rates for payment were amicably agreed upon, although the client's QS refused to permit the contractor the benefit of re-negotiating rates at a higher level than they had under-priced in their original tender.

The contractor serves a second claim for loss and expense and an extension of time

The contractor served a second claim for extension of time and loss and expense arising from the delays in sanctioning their first claim. This had been planned for some time, but had not been issued in fear of jeopardizing the original claim.

The architect ignores the claim

The architect's initial response to the contractor's second claim was to ignore it, which prompted the contractor's QS to re-serve it. Again, there was no formal response from the architect, apart from pronouncing its rejection during the next site meeting. There was no opportunity for discussion and no reasons were given. The architect explained that "*in my view the whole problem is resolved, they will go on and on restating their demands and won't get anywhere and so it will go on until completion of the project, to the final account and so on and so forth and ultimately they will go away.*" This meeting was made more tense when the client's project manager complained that the contractor's delay in making the claim made the monitoring of project progress difficult: "*Perhaps I am a bit cynical but I do feel that problems are kept quiet so that they can rumble on to give them something concrete.*" This complaint prompted a defensive response from the contractor's QS, who maintained that contractually they were not obliged to notify about potential problems, only actual ones.

The second claim is formally rejected

The architect formally refused the second claim but with no detailed explanation. After two months, the contractor's regional surveyor intervened again. This was prompted by the architect writing to the contractor's directors complaining about the "*unprofessional conduct*" of their project team. An acrimonious exchange occurred between the regional surveyor and architect.

A break in the stalemate

The contractor's site manager again wrote to the architect, demanding an explanation of the second claim's rejection. The architect conveyed the contents of the letter to the client's project manager who immediately contacted the contractor's site manager to promise action. Once again, the client's project manager had been unaware of the ongoing dispute, as had the client's QS, who discovered it in an unrelated conversation with the contractor's site manager. In two subsequent meetings, the second claim was discussed but progress was hindered by disagreements over the extent of delays.

The second intervention of the regional surveyor

The contractor's regional surveyor intervened again, writing to the client's project manager complaining about the ongoing claim. The client's project manager wrote to the client's QS expressing regret that the problem had been allowed to get this far. This prompted the consultants to meet and suggest a global settlement of all outstanding claims on the project. This was an exercise in damage-limitation designed to "*save some face and wipe the slate clean for the next phase of the project*". An increasingly concerned client pushed for a solution and the idea of the global settlement was presented at a meeting. This was met with an uncertain response because their regional surveyor, who now wanted control of the situation, had removed the decisionmaking authority of the contractor's team.

The crisis is resolved

Eventually, the client's QS and contractor's QS negotiated an acceptable formula for the valuation of the second claim and agreed on a global settlement of all outstanding claims. The second claim was formally accepted and sanctioned by the client and the contract completion date was extended.

PATTERNS OF BEHAVIOR

This creeping crisis lasted approximately 10 months and consumed a considerable amount of resources, time, and energy. In all, the crisis involved people in 29 formal meetings, 68 telephone calls, and 42 letters. There would also have been many more informal meetings that were not recorded.

The exact point at which the original earthwork support problem became a crisis is uncertain, but there is little doubt that it need not have become a crisis and that eventually, it did pose a serious threat to the viability of the project, not only in terms of delays and increased costs but also in damaged interpersonal relationships. Testimony to this was the contractor's eventual decision to replace much of their project team for the second phase of the project because relationships had deteriorated to the point where they could no longer work effectively with the consultants.

The following section discusses the main phases of behavior that emerged during this crisis and explains how and when the deterioration in relationships occurred.

Phase one

Early in the crisis there was little sense of forward momentum. Communications were characterized by a sense of opposition and confrontation. This emerged out of the contractor's determination to obtain what they saw as a valid contractual entitlement and the consultant's refusal to countenance it. This period was also highly tactical. The contractor stopped work in the area affected by the earthwork support problem and the consultants called the contractor's bluff. Tactics also played a role within the "loosely-coupled" consultant's team, as the architect appeared to distance himself from the problem and the client's QS pressured the engineer to generate alternative earthwork support systems to the contractor's. The contractor retorted with expressions of commitment to the claim and warnings of delays on site. In turn, the consultants responded with delaying tactics, and eventually, a second outright rejection of the contractor's claim. Collectively, this behavior led to a phase of increasing frustration, anxiety, and confrontation. This was evident in people's communication patterns, which were characterized by numerous factions with little intercommunication as is illustrated in Figure 6-1. In Figure 6-1, factions are circled with a line thickness equal to the average number of interactions between their members. This is indicative of their relative strength and cohesion. Lines connecting factions indicate communication routes; their thickness varies according to the frequency of communication. This is indicative of the strength of ties between factions.

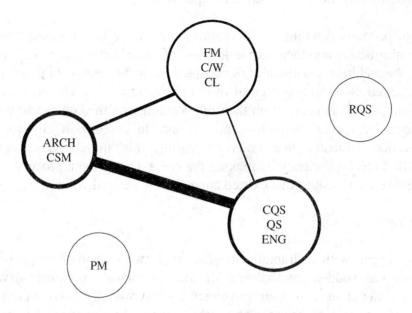

PM – Client's project manager   ENG - Engineer
CSM – Contractor's site manager   ARCH - Architect
CQS – Contractor's quantity surveyor   QS - Client's quantity surveyor
RQS – Contractor's regional surveyor   FM – Facilities manager
C/W - Clerk-of-works   CL - Client

Figure 6-1 Factional patterns during phase one.

Figure 6-1 shows three factions and two isolates. The relative isolation of the client's project manager indicates that he was excluded from negotiations surrounding the claim. His mistake was to rely on the architect as his only point of contact with the project team, thereby making himself vulnerable to the architect's vested interests, which were best served by not widely publicizing the problem. Most noticeably, the architect and client's QS were in separate factions, supporting the emerging picture of the architect's desire to distance himself from the problem. Despite their separation, they did have a healthy level of communication, although the architect primarily acted in a receiving capacity, relying on the client's QSs to coordinate a response. Indeed, the architect, being in the strongest faction with the contractor's site manager, appeared to use the client's QS's advice to perform an important bridging role between the consultants and contractor. This would have enabled him to maintain control of the situation but at the same time avoid direct implication in it. As a further point, the engineer was by far the weakest member of his faction, only having contact, in a receiving capacity, with the client's QS. This is evidence of the pressure being exerted upon him to generate alternative earthwork support solutions to that proposed by the contractor. However, his strong connection with the contractor's site manager in the architect's faction was also evidence of his sympathies with the contractor's case. This eventually led him to "leak" information, which equalized information differences between the contractor and consultants, thereby undermining the latter's bargaining position.

In terms of people's centrality to communications, there was no clear "source" or "sink" of information and therefore little sense of clear leadership during this phase. However, the architect and client's QS occupied the main gate-keeping positions and thereby, exerted considerable control over information flow. This made the crisis management process dependent on their relationship with the contractor, which was characterized by mutual suspicion and distrust. In essence, it appears that the communication structure that emerged during this initial phase contributed significantly to its inefficiency by making the crisis management process vulnerable to the negative relationships that existed among a few key individuals.

Phase two

Phase two began with a dramatic increase in forward momentum compared to phase one. The sudden involvement of the contractor's regional surveyor, an escalation of the crisis, a sudden movement toward more aggressive tactics, and a greater show of emotion brought about this change. In response, the consultant's policy of opposition and suppression in phase one was replaced by increased attention to resolving the problem. The level of opposition fell, parties were more concessionary, and there was a higher level of discussion about the contractor's claim. In essence, the regional surveyor's intervention induced a more productive and supportive phase where open discussion replaced the manipulative, coercive tactics that characterized most of phase one.

Collectively, these conditions led to a gradual decline in emotions, frustration and anxiety that was reflected in higher levels of more effective communication among project participants. This is illustrated in Figure 6-2 which shows the client's project manager in the strongest faction with the architect and client's QS. His increased involvement appears to have been a defensive response to the sudden escalation, brought about by the regional surveyor's (RQS) intervention. The engineer is now in a faction with the contractor's site manager and regional surveyor, his separation from the consultants reflecting a greater focus on resolving the problem rather than merely generating alternative earthwork support systems to the contractor's.

A further contrast to phase one was a higher level of direct contact among people and a higher level of equivalence in their personal communication networks. This indicated widespread access to similar information and a greater chance of mutual understanding of relative positions in negotiations. In phase one, conflicts of interest forced people to protect their information sources, thereby causing confusion, misunderstandings, frustration, and mistrust.

In addition to being more direct and open, communications were more centralized around specific individuals, indicating a more closely integrated and tightly knit team. By far the most central people were the contractor's site manager and the client's QS, indicating their leading role in resolving the dispute. In contrast, the architect had a relatively low centrality compared to phase one, confirming the architect's continuing desire to see the client's QS take responsibility for the problem. The information gate-keeping structure was similar to phase one but it did not adversely affect information flow because of more positive attitudes among the consultants and the contractor.

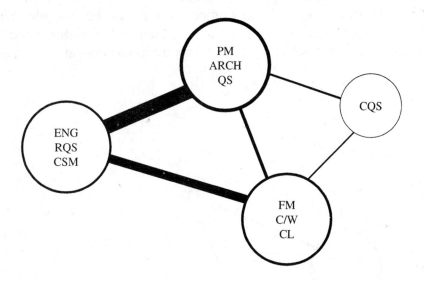

PM – Client's project manager   ENG - Engineer
CSM – Contractor's site manager   ARCH - Architect
CQS – Contractor's quantity surveyor   QS - Client's quantity surveyor
RQS – Contractor's regional surveyor   FM – Facilities manager
C/W - Clerk-of-works   CL - Client

Figure 6-2 Factional patterns during phase two.

Phase three

Phase three coincided with the contractor's second claim and was characterized by a dramatic reduction in forward momentum compared to phase two. This was largely a consequence of the architect's tactic of ignoring it, which prompted the contractor to respond with warnings of delay, threats, and eventually, an act of escalation that involved the second intervention of their regional surveyor.

This increased sense of division and confrontation was reflected in the dominance of two loosely coupled factions, one comprising the architect and contractor's site manager and the other comprising the facilities manager and clerk-of-works. This is illustrated in Figure 6-3, the latter faction being primarily concerned with the technical challenge of resolving the collapsed water main and the former with the contractor's second claim.

During this phase, information flow increasingly centered around the architect and the contractor's site manager, indicating that they were considerably more knowledgeable about the ongoing dispute than other project members. This widespread ignorance of the on-going dispute, beyond the architect and contractor's site manager, would have been exacerbated by the gate-keeping roles they played within the project's communication network. This gave them considerable control over information flow among people, making the crisis management process vulnerable to their poor relationship. In a reflection of phase one, it would seem that the communication structure that evolved among people during this phase would have played a considerable role in the lack of forward momentum and acrimony that characterized it.

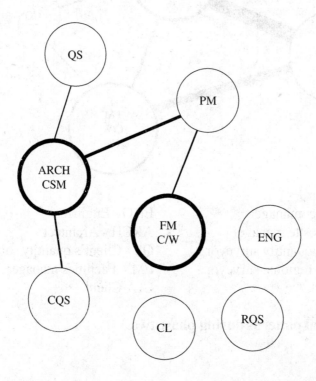

PM – Client's project manager   ENG - Engineer
CSM – Contractor's site manager   ARCH - Architect
CQS – Contractor's quantity surveyor   QS - Client's quantity surveyor
RQS – Contractor's regional surveyor   FM – Facilities manager
C/W - Clerk-of-works   CL - Client

Figure 6-3 Factional patterns during phase three.

Phase four

The final phase of behavior was characterized by a dramatic increase in forward momentum and an increasingly cooperative, compromising, and supportive atmosphere, compared to phase three. This was brought about by the second intervention of the contractor's regional surveyor, a tactic designed to resolve the stalemate surrounding the contractor's claim. There was also a greater focus upon problem resolution through open discussion and negotiation, which was reflected in calmer emotions, growing contentment and reduced rhetoric in communications. Patterns of communication were also less divided in that there was only one dominant faction, which consisted of the architect, client's QS, contractor's QS, and client's project manager. This is illustrated in Figure 6-4.

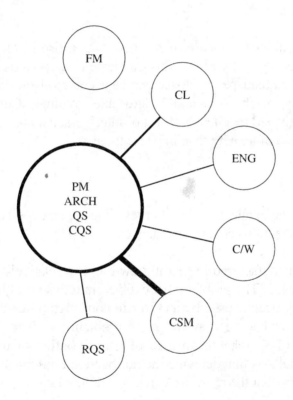

PM – Client's project manager   ENG - Engineer
CSM – Contractor's site manager   ARCH - Architect
CQS – Contractor's quantity surveyor QS - Client's quantity surveyor
RQS – Contractor's regional surveyor FM – Facilities manager
C/W - Clerk-of-works   CL - Client

Figure 6-4 Factional patterns during phase four.

Figure 6-4 indicates that one very tightly knit group who took control of the crisis, working closely to bring it to a conclusion, dominated the final phase of the crisis management process. While the contractor's site manager was excluded from this faction he was strongly connected to it.

The central players during this phase were the contractor's QS, client's project manager, architect, and client's QS. This reflects a breaking down of the contractor/consultant divide that had developed in phase three and an injection of consultant effort to get the problem resolved. In contrast to phase three, the architect played a far more dominant sending role, indicating that his policy of silence had ended and that he was driving the process toward a conclusion.

A particularly interesting development was the client's project manager's movement into a position of high "betweenness," which enabled him to exert greater control over the crisis management process. In essence, he presented himself as an alternative route for the contractor's communications thereby overcoming the dominating effect of the poor relationship between the contractor's site manager and architect in phase three.

Finally, in a further contrast to phase three, there was a rise in the equivalence of people's communication networks. This indicated a period of widespread communication that enabled people to construct a common understanding of the problem and thereby reach a mutually agreeable solution. Collectively, these communication patterns led to a healthy level of inter-personal communication and a far more positive period of activity than in phase three.

CONCLUSION

This conclusion uses the cyclical model of crisis management depicted in Figure 3-1 to discuss how effectively this crisis was managed.

This crisis was self-manufactured in that it grew out of a relatively simple problem that was poorly managed. The problem that evolved into this crisis had laid dormant for some time, having been caused by an error in constructing the bill of quantities. Although the contractor had been aware of the problem for some time, he delayed notification because of an inherent distrust of and a conflict of interests with the architect. The rationale was that delaying the notification until the last minute would increase the probability that the response would go in their favor.

Thus, early inefficiencies were not of monitoring, as superficially appears, but of poor communication among monitors and comparators caused by a conflict of interest. Once notified of the problem by the contractor, the consultants, acting as comparators, decided that the problem was the contractor's. Essentially, they attempted to terminate the crisis management process at the first opportunity, forcing the project team back into a monitoring mode. This series of events are illustrated in Figure 6-5.

This tactic was a protection mechanism, motivated by self-interest and designed to avoid the problem, call the contractor's bluff, test the contractor's resolve, and transfer the onus of proof back onto the contractor's shoulders. In essence, the consultants attempted to keep the problem contained within the confines of their own power base by acting as both comparator and decisionmaker. Indeed, by avoiding the need to invoke higher levels of decisionmaking authority, the consultants managed to conceal the problem from the client's project manager. To reinforce this tactic, they became inwardly oriented and imposed strong group-norms, particularly on the engineer, to construct a highly biased definition of the problem from their own perspective.

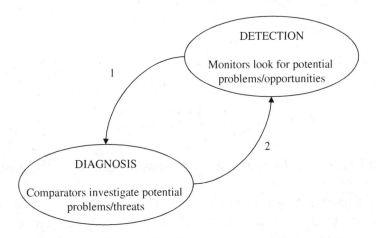

Figure 6-5 Initial attempt to terminate the crisis management process.

Faced with increasingly polarized positions, the contractor resorted to coercive power tactics by threatening the consultants with delays and an escalation of the dispute. Although this tactical escalation was successful in getting their claim recognized, the consultants made a decision that was outside their authority. While diffusing short-term tensions, long-term tensions were increased because the client's project manager, who had the necessary authority to act in a decisionmaker's capacity, refused to do so. Before sanctioning the consultant's decision, the client's project manager insisted on a reassessment of alternative earthwork support systems and in doing so, returned the crisis management process to a diagnosis stage, prolonging it and frustrating everyone concerned.

This series of events is illustrated in Figure 6-6 where the dotted lines record previous movements among the phases of the crisis management process.

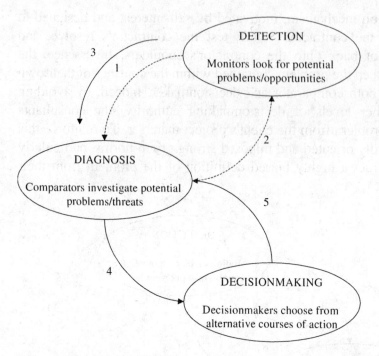

Figure 6-6 Returning the crisis management process to a diagnostic mode.

The client's project manager eventually sanctioned the claim but then, the earth bank to be supported by the disputed earthwork support system collapsed. This made the claim irrelevant and threw the crisis management process back into a diagnostic mode to resolve the new problem. This series of events is illustrated in Figure 6-7.

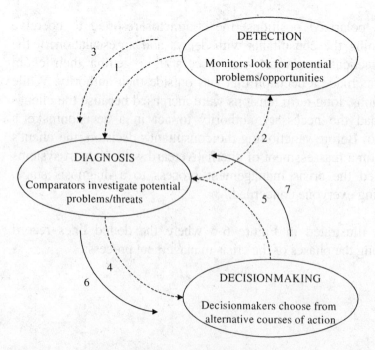

Figure 6-7 Returning the crisis management process to a diagnostic mode again.

Paradoxically, this sudden sub-crisis caused a temporary alignment of interests and increased cohesion within the project team because the contractor advocated a lower cost earthwork support system that was duly sanctioned by the consultants. This series of events is illustrated in Figure 6-8.

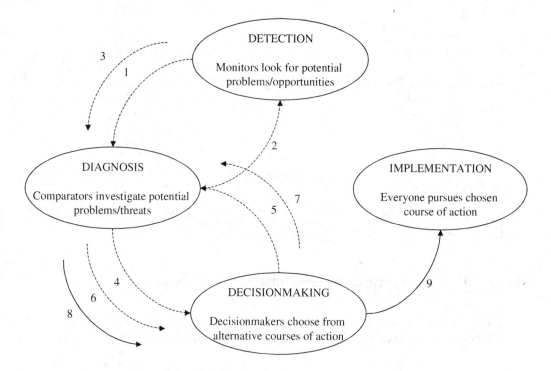

Figure 6-8 The issue and implementation of a new change-order.

Up to this point, the crisis management process as depicted in Figure 3-1 had not been a smooth cycle but one characterized by considerable inefficiency. In particular, the process appears to have been characterized by a considerable degree of repetition and procrastination in moving between the different phases of the crisis management process. Indeed, this continued because during implementation of the revised earthwork support system, the crisis management process was thrown into a second full cycle by the contractor's second claim for an extension of time. This is illustrated in Figure 6-9.

The need for a second cycle of the crisis management process was a direct consequence of delays caused by inefficiencies in the first cycle. The contractor had monitored these delays for some time, but in a reflection of the first cycle, mistrust of the consultants caused them to withhold their notification. Another similarity with the first cycle was that the subsequent diagnostic process was characterized by defensiveness on the part of the architect and a reluctance to recognize the problem. This led to a build-up of frustration and eventually a second escalation of the crisis. This initiated a new diagnostic process that involved a full consideration of the problem by all of those with vested interests in its solution.

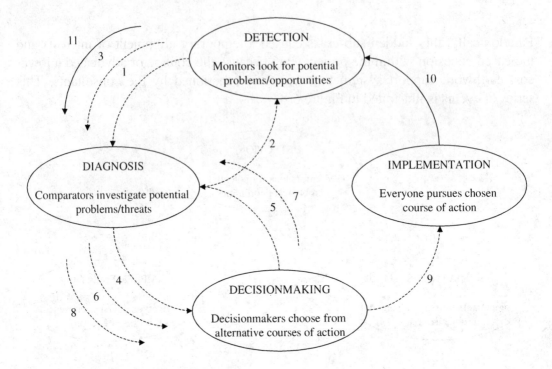

Figure 6-9 A second cycle of the crisis management process.

Eventually, after a convergence of views, the contractor's claim was granted and the project's completion date extended. These events are illustrated in Figure 6-10.

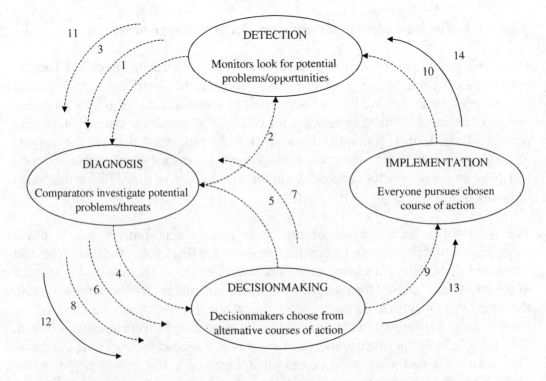

Figure 6-10 The completion of the crisis management process.

Chapter 7

Case Study Two

THE PROJECT

This project involved the construction of a new museum. The contractor considered this project of strategic importance in moving into a new geographical area and had no previous experience of working with any of the client's consultants.

THE CRISIS

A "sudden" crisis was caused by a decision to incorporate an eight-person elevator into the scheme, as construction was about to begin on site. This decision was prompted by complaints regarding the lack of provisions for disabled people in the scheme. The decision to include an eight-person elevator had significant design and programming implications, and because the discussion came late, gave the project team very little time to implement.

AN ACCOUNT OF THE CRISIS MANAGEMENT PROCESS

Keeping the project going

What made this crisis particularly difficult and frustrating for the architect was his lack of involvement in the original design process. He was not fully conversant with the designs and felt slightly resentful about rectifying someone else's mistakes. Furthermore, when the problem was highlighted, he was about to send out tender documents to main contractors. These had to be rapidly adjusted to incorporate the possibility of including an elevator in the scheme. To this end, after first failing to persuade local government inspectors to permit other means of access for the disabled, a decision was made to include a provisional sum of money in the bill to cover the cost of an eight-person elevator. The client formally authorized this provisional sum within a week but withheld the final decision about the elevator's inclusion until budgets were clarified for the next financial year.

A decision is made

After five months, the client contacted the architect to confirm the elevator's inclusion in the scheme. The main contractor was about to begin construction work on site but no progress had been made on redesigning the building. The main problem now facing the architect was the enormity of re-design work, the timeline for undertaking it and the need to get an elevator sub-contractor on board as quickly as possible.

Within a week, the architect had sent tender documents to four elevator sub-contractors and during the pre-construction meeting with the successful main contractor announced the inclusion of the elevator. After the initial shock and amusement had subsided, the prospective site manager requested the drawings. The architect pointed out that revised drawings were not yet available and that he would try to supply them as soon as possible. The architect's explanation for the lack of design information was that "*the inclusion of the lift was dependent on budget allowances and with the pressure we are under, you just can't progress with design if there is the slightest chance of it being wasted work.*"

The site manager recalled, "*I was starting on site the next week but I was afraid to start anything. It was just not knowing what was happening…we discovered later that the architect knew about the lift for some time. If we had been told straight away, we could have been looking at the program.*" While the elevator's inclusion was a surprise to the contractor, it was not a surprise to the mechanical and electrical (M&E) engineer. He had been a member of the original design team and had warned of the need for an elevator: "*They just ignored me, so I thought, 'it's your problem not mine.' Of course, it's come home to roost now hasn't it? It is my problem. They were just under time pressure and they knew that, in all probability, they would not be involved in construction and so they could just pass the problem up the line.*"

Location of elevator is decided

The day after the pre-construction meeting, the elevator's position in the building was agreed upon.

Work commences on site

As foundation work proceeded on site, the site manager had numerous informal discussions with the clerk of works about his growing concerns over the lack of information, particularly about the elevator pit position. The clerk of works conveyed these concerns to the architect and explained that, "*the site manager was having to go to a lot of trouble to work around the problem on site*".

Drawings are supplied indicating elevator pit position

One month after the elevator pit's position had been agreed upon, information about the pit size and position was faxed to the contractor. The elevator was to be positioned in the center of the building, and because there was only one point of access to and from the site, completed foundations had to be backfilled to allow excavators to track across them to get to the elevator pit location. This information had been withheld in fear of the elevator position changing and because the architect preferred to issue complete packages of information rather than *"drip-feeding"* it: *"I wanted to start as I meant to go on, by not issuing drawings until they were complete. That's all I needed was more changes."* However, both the clerk-of-works and site manager were becoming increasingly frustrated at the architect's formality and inflexibility in issuing information and pointed to the unnecessary disruption it was causing: *"[the architect] likes to do things by the book. Its good in some ways but when you need the information it causes lots of problems because we've got to keep going on site."*

The elevator sub-contractor is selected

The architect received tenders from elevator sub-contractors and entered into contractual negotiations with the lowest cost tenderer.

A continuing lack of information

The site manager continued to express his concerns about progress on site and his desperate need for revised drawings.

Structural engineering drawings provided for elevator pit area

Revised structural engineering drawings for the new elevator pit and adjacent foundations were supplied after continuous requests from the site manager and clerk-of-works. The architect continued to negotiate with the successful elevator sub-contractor but a problem arose over liquidated damages provisions in the sub-contract. This delayed formal nomination, preventing any contact between the main contractor and sub-contractor.

A second crisis

Eventually, after resolving contractual problems, the prospective elevator sub-contractor visited the site and noticed that the elevator pit excavations were too small to accommodate the elevator, which had been specified in their tender documents. The situation was made worse because the sub-contractor did not have a standard elevator to fit the pit that had been substantially completed. On the same day, the engineer and clerk-of-works became concerned about the depth of the elevator pit foundations, something that had implications for adjacent foundations.

It emerged in subsequent discussions that to enable re-design work to progress, the architect had made an inaccurate assumption about the elevator pit size before the elevator sub-contractor had been selected. All design consultants had worked on the basis of this inaccurate decision in re-designing their part of the building, and along with the contractor, now faced a huge amount of "re-re-work" to accommodate the elevator sub-contractor's standard elevator specifications and designs.

An urgent meeting was called, during which there was widespread concern about the problem. However, there was also a degree of sensitivity and sympathy for the architect's predicament and humor played a great part in diffusing interpersonal tensions. Rather than exploiting the situation, the contractor was supportive and accommodating in suggesting another temporary reorganization of the site to alleviate the immediate pressure on the architect: "*We didn't want extras, we just wanted to be able to pick up the drawings and build. We wanted a successful project as much as the architect, so we did anything we could to help. It is important to us that the project goes well and [the site manager] was able to reorganize things on site so that we only lost a few days. We didn't have a delay because we didn't want one, but if we were bloody minded we could have really made trouble.*" This flexibility and goodwill impressed the architect: "*this contractor is the best I have dealt with in a long time, all on site and in their office are exceptionally pleasant people to deal with. I had a bad experience on my last job and they have re-confirmed my faith in contractors.*"

Specifying a custom-made elevator

In another rapidly convened meeting, the architect, site manager and elevator sub-contractor decided to consider a custom-made elevator. The architect and sub-contractor negotiated a price that was within the original provisional sum, which meant that budget allowances were not exceeded.

Formal nomination of the elevator sub-contractor

The elevator sub-contractor had not yet been formally nominated and any involvement so far had been on the basis of goodwill. Upon formal nomination, the architect instructed the contractor to start discussing program details with the sub-contractor. Also, in response to contractor requests, the architect promised a formal "change order" to cover the costs of the elevator's inclusion. The site manager stressed his urgent need for a revised elevator specification and pit design for the new custom-made elevator.

New elevator pit designs are issued

The architect sent the elevator sub-contractor's specification, designs and contractual conditions to the contractor. The same were sent to the M&E engineer with an urgent request for amended M&E drawings. The M&E engineer recalled his annoyance: "*He doesn't seem to realize that when he changes one of his drawings we have to change ten of ours.*"

Further information shortages

During the next monthly site meeting the contractor expressed concern about the lack of change-order and M&E drawings. In a tolerant and good-humoured environment, the contractor was reassured of their imminent issue. The following three weeks were characterized by numerous telephone calls and meetings between the site manager, contractor's QS, architect, and clerk-of-works about the outstanding M&E drawings that were desperately needed on site. Eventually, the M&E engineer sent his revised drawings to the architect and they were issued the day they were received. The contractor's QS expressed continuing concerns about the lack of change-order; a month later, the architect issued it: *"It would have put our minds at rest if we could have had it earlier but this is just the way [the architect] likes to work."*

PHASES OF BEHAVIOR

The response to this sudden crisis lasted for approximately nine months and consumed a considerable amount of resources, time, and energy by involving people in 33 formal meetings, 27 telephone calls, and 61 letters. There would also have been many informal meetings that were not recorded.

In contrast to the crisis described in Chapter Six, there were no discernible phases of distinct behavior during this crisis. Throughout, the problem was one of information management rather than of handling a dispute, the pressure being focussed primarily on the architect's shoulders. Indeed, everything indicates that the architect failed to come to terms with the information demands placed on him. He operated in a reactive mode, supplying information in periodic surges rather than continuously, and he was always "chasing" the demand for information rather than leading it. This was largely a consequence of the client's procrastination in sanctioning the elevator, causing the architect to ignore the "time-window" for re-design, which occurred between tendering and construction. This missed opportunity made a complex problem a crisis by ensuring that construction activity was plagued by a lack of information. This caused a considerable degree of uncertainty, frustration, and organizational inconvenience for the contractor and tested interpersonal relationships on the project.

The project's savior was the contractor's site manager who compensated for the architect's periodic lapses of attention to information supply by increasing his persistence in requesting information. While the architect rarely responded immediately to the contractor's requests for information, he was sensitive enough to supply information in enough time to prevent any damaging accumulation of tension.

Despite these information supply problems, there was widespread commitment to resolving the crisis, and as the crisis continued, there emerged a sense of mutual support, sensitivity, and consideration among everyone affected. This was particularly evident when the pit-size discrepancy was discovered—a problem that created a potentially explosive atmosphere. However, this sub-crisis strengthened inter-personal relationships rather than damaged them because people used it as an opportunity to demonstrate their commitment to each other and to the project's success. There is little doubt that the contractor's determination to impress what was a new and potentially lucrative client was a major factor that contributed to the lack of exploitation and conflict throughout this crisis. Furthermore, the majority of people involved in this project were nearing retirement and took a very philosophical approach to the crisis, having seen it all before. This enabled them to place it in its proper perspective, and rather than panicking and creating a volatile atmosphere, they made a conscious attempt to suppress emotions, stay calm, and remain rational.

The communication patterns that emerged during this crisis were dominated by two main factions, as is illustrated in Figure 7-1.

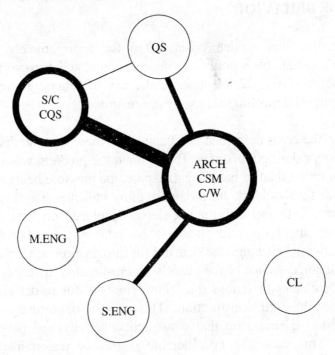

S.ENG – Structural engineer   M.ENG – M&E Engineer
CSM – Main contractor's site manager   ARCH - Architect
CQS – Main contractor's quantity surveyor   QS - Client's quantity surveyor
S/C – Elevator sub-contractor   C/W - Clerk-of-works
CL - Client

Figure 7-1 Faction structure during case study two.

Figure 7-1 indicates that the strongest faction was among the site manager, architect, and clerk-of-works. Within this faction, the clerk-of-works played an important bridging role by maintaining communications and creating a "buffer" between the architect and site manager. This minimized the chances of conflict in a stressful and potentially explosive environment.

Although the architect, clerk-of-works and site manager worked closely, the architect held the most central communications position, which meant that were was no competing source of information and a high degree of consistency in understanding the nature of the crisis. Unfortunately, one of the problems with the architect's high centrality was other's dependence on him, which made the crisis management process highly vulnerable to his vested interests and to his ability to deal with the extreme pressures on him. Although there was no evidence of the architect manipulating information to serve his own interests, evidence did indicate that the architect became increasingly unable to cope with the information demands on him. His survival mechanism in coping with this information overload was to adopt an increasingly distant, formal, and inflexible managerial style, which only compounded the lack of information that was causing the pressure. The result was a considerable degree of uncertainty and frustration for the contractor. Important in alleviating this pressure before it caused conflict was the site manager's compensating role in proactively seeking information from him and reorganizing work on site, when he was unable to cope.

CONCLUSION

This conclusion uses the cyclical model of crisis management depicted in Figure 3-1, to discuss how effectively this crisis was managed.

This crisis arose out of a design-stage problem that had been ignored due to time pressures and changes in project membership between design and construction stages. The personnel change also desensitized the construction-stage design team to the potential problem meaning that the re-detection of lifts omission came late, arising not out of the organization's diligent monitoring of its environment but vice-versa. Once the problem was detected, the architect, as the comparator, was responsible for determining the extent to which it threatened the client's goals. The client's main concern was to control costs and the architect's initial response was an attempt to avoid the problem by trying to persuade local government inspectors that an elevator was not required. In essence, he tried to return the crisis management process to a monitoring mode. This series of events is illustrated in Figure 7-2.

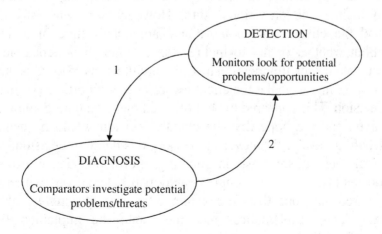

Figure 7-2 Initial attempt to terminate the crisis management process.

Recognizing the seriousness of the problem, the architect recommended that the client include a provisional sum in the bill of quantities. Ironically, while the detachment of the architect from the original design process may have adversely affected monitoring activities, it probably helped speed progress between comparator and decisionmaker because the architect was not implicated in any blame and therefore, was not defensive. These events are illustrated in Figure 7-3.

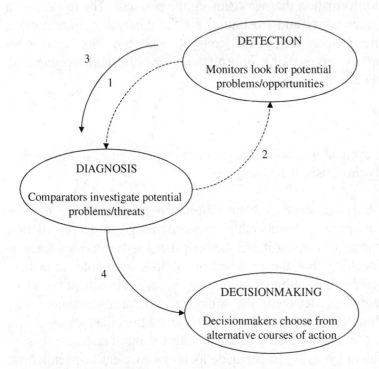

Figure 7-3 Involving the decisionmaker.

In acting as decisionmaker, the client took the advice of the architect and quickly decided to include the provisional sum. However, this was only a provisional decision and the client took an inordinate amount of time in making the final decision about whether or not to include the elevator. It is debatable whether the client was to blame for this delay, since the architect, as lead consultant, was also complacent in failing to make the client aware of the importance of making a quick and firm decision. This appeared to be motivated by the daunting amount of redesign work involved and the hope that the client's decision would be negative and the problem would go away. Whatever the reason, this delay in decisionmaking proved to be the real cause of the crisis in allowing information demand to run ahead of information supply. It was an implementation problem from which the architect never recovered, and one that forced him into an increasingly reactive mode of management. This problematical movement into the implementation phase is illustrated in Figure 7-4.

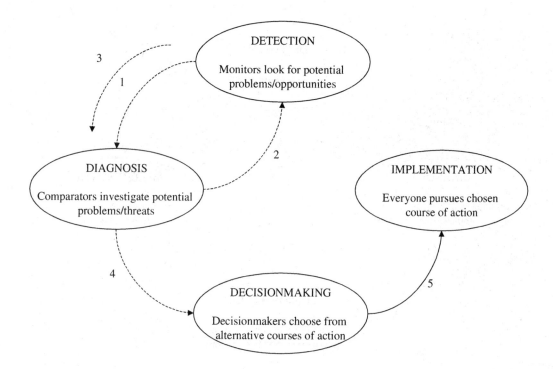

Figure 7-4 Implementation.

Problems began to "snowball" as the constant pressures to supply information caused the architect to make a hasty assumption about the size of the elevator pit. This led to an under-sized elevator pit being constructed, which launched the crisis management process into a second cycle. During the diagnostic process, the project team was lucky because the elevator sub-contractor was able to supply a custom-made elevator for the same cost as a standard elevator. In this sense, this sub-crisis did not pose a further threat to client goals and the client, as decisionmaker, was not involved for the second time. The emphasis then returned to the implementation of this revised decision. This series of events is illustrated in Figure 7-5.

During the second implementation process, the architect continued to contribute to the pressure of the situation and to the contractor's frustration through his dislike of uncertainty. This caused him to inappropriately treat a non-routine situation as routine, by not adapting his "normal" information production procedures to the extreme demands of this crisis. The main problem was that the architect continually insisted that information packages were fully complete before issuing them, which meant that information was supplied in surges rather than constantly, as preferred by the contractor. The architect also failed to recognize the contractor's information priorities by not giving special attention to particularly important items of information that were urgently needed to maintain progress on site.

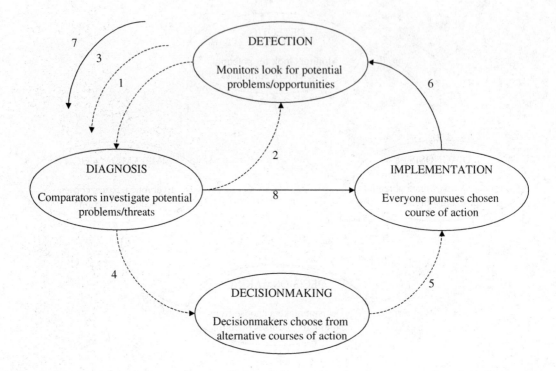

Figure 7-5 A second cycle of crisis management.

Despite the above problems, the crisis did not result in an extension of the project's completion date and the extra costs were contained within the monetary limits of the provisional sum. This considerable achievement was largely a consequence of individuals who recognized and capitalized on the opportunistic aspects of the crisis. In particular, the contractor treated it as an opportunity to demonstrate commitment to the project by exhibiting a willingness to tolerate the inconvenience of poor information supply without claiming compensation. There is little doubt that the contractor could have exploited the situation. The contractor also recognized its collective responsibility for information supply by constantly keeping the architect informed of information needs rather than merely relying on him to supply it. In this way the contractor played an important role in compensating for the architect's weaknesses and thereby helped to nurture a sense of cohesion within the project team and to generate a culture of mutual responsibility for the problem. In essence, the efficiency of this crisis management process is largely attributable to the exploitation, by all, of the opportunities presented by a potentially threatening and destructive situation.

Chapter 8

Case Study Three

THE PROJECT

This project was to build a new multi-million pound semi-conductor factory.

THE CRISIS

A "sudden" crisis arose as a result of a series of events on an adjacent site that was elevated and supported by an existing 120-year-old retaining wall. The construction of the new factory necessitated the replacement of the existing retaining wall with a new wall. The design of this new wall had been based on the loadings of an existing school that occupied the adjacent site. However, unknown to the engineer who had designed it, an extension to the school was planned and coincidentally, this extension started at the same time the retaining wall was being replaced.

The crisis began when the architect in charge of the adjacent school extension became concerned about the destabilizing effect of excavations near the base of the existing retaining wall that supported his site. He insisted that work stop until the wall's stability could be investigated.

AN ACCOUNT OF THE CRISIS MANAGEMENT PROCESS

The results of the investigation

This request initiated an intense period of communications that included several meetings on site with internal and external stakeholders in the project. For example, government health and safety inspectors and building control officers visited the site unannounced and meetings were held with the architect, site manager, and engineer from the adjacent site. Furthermore, the head master and board of governors of the school on the adjacent site had to be informed of the safety implications for children, as did others in the local community. The end result was the discovery that the engineer, unaware of the new extension to the adjacent school, had under-designed the new wall. Consequently, a new design was required. Since almost all site activities on the new factory depended on the retaining wall being completed, this had an enormous impact on construction work.

The site is shut down

The option of shutting down the site was discussed with the client, but before the shut down, the existing retaining wall had to be restabilized for safety reasons. A geologist was consulted regarding ground stability and a meeting was quickly convened on site to inspect the excavations. After the various options for supporting the excavations were discussed, it was decided that a monitoring system should be set up and that an *"exclusion zone"* of 5 meters be imposed on any work behind the existing retaining wall on the adjacent school site. In a second meeting with the client, a decision was made to keep a "skeleton-staff" on site to monitor the excavations, to keep the general public out, and to undertake minor works that did not depend on the retaining wall designs. The contractor was also asked to be ready to re-start the site at short notice.

Re-design commences

The decision to stop the site initiated a period of intense design activity, starting with the drainage system so the contractor could recommence site activities as soon as possible. As the architect recalled, *"We worked every waking hour to re-do the drainage layouts, which involved going right back to the beginning and starting again."*

The revised drainage system is rejected

The revised drainage drawings were eventually sent to the local government building control department for inspection but were rejected because they did not comply with local building regulations. In a revealing comment about the stress induced by this sub-crisis, the architect recalled, *"everyone suffered, but unfortunately it all took its toll on [the engineer]. You imagine it, everyone standing around waiting for you. The QS was on his back to keep costs down, [the site manager] for information, and our director to restart the site."* In the meantime, an increasingly concerned client visited the site unannounced to discuss progress with the site manager.

The revised drainage system is approved

Eventually, the revised drainage system was approved and a decision was made to restart the site. However the site manager recalled, *"they gave me the drainage details, yes, but most of it was behind the retaining wall which was not built at that time or even designed. In other words I couldn't use it."* Indeed, during the next site meeting the site manager warned that he would *"soon be on stop again"* if information about the retaining wall was not forthcoming.

The revised retaining wall details are supplied but are incomplete

The engineer issued, in person, to the site manager, the majority of the revised retaining wall details. However, upon inspection, the site manager discovered that information about concrete mixes and reinforcement details were missing. The engineer verbally gave the site manager the missing information.

Logistical problems in constructing the new retaining wall

Excavations for the new retaining wall began, but a large pocket of soft ground was encountered and the engineer issued a verbal instruction to excavate it and fill it with concrete. Engineer's drawings continued to be supplied with incomplete information and the site manager repeatedly requested a decision from the architect about the relocation of existing overhead electrical and telegraph cables so machines could operate safely in the excavation area. In site meetings, the site manager was becoming increasingly agitated with the constant lack of information.

New problems with the engineer's drawings

The engineer continued to deliver incomplete retaining wall drawings and to visit the site to verbally redress the deficiencies the site manager discovered. For example, on one occasion, the engineer issued a verbal instruction specifying the retaining wall's finish and increasing the volume of concrete in its foundations to compensate for differences in site datum compared to those shown on the drawings. Another problem that the site manager detected was related to insufficient pipe bedding behind the retaining wall. Once again, the engineer issued a verbal instruction to increase it.

The site manager became increasingly frustrated: "*At this time I was operating on site with virtually no information. The engineer just couldn't cope; he was totally out of his depth and I was having to make the decisions on site as we went along from my experience. They were lucky I've got so much experience; imagine if the engineer's mistakes hadn't been picked up.... [The engineer] was suffering a lot of stress.... Eventually we reckon it put him in hospital.*"

The contractor raises the issue of compensation for disruption to their work

The contractor's QS contacted the client's QS to discuss compensation for disruption. Upon further investigation, the client's QS discovered that "*neither [the architect] nor [the engineer] had any idea of what had been said on site. Both of them had just been making changes and had obviously not given a second thought to their implications. I insisted that any further instructions had to be issued in writing.*" He suspected that he had been deliberately excluded because he would have restricted the engineer's and architect's ability to make spontaneous changes.

In a subsequent site meeting, there was little agreement about the verbal changes that the engineer had made on site, and therefore, about any reimbursement for disruption. With some emotion, the site manager recalled, "*We didn't agree on a lot and [the client's QS] started to say that some of the instructions hadn't been issued at all. But I had recorded every single change in my diary so I just sat there and read them out, one by one, in front of them all. We reckoned that there were about 55 that hadn't been paid.*"

The contractor submits a claim for an extension of time and loss and expense

The contractor's QS contacted the client's QS to warn of the continuing site disruption and served a formal claim for extension of time and loss and expense. The response of the client's QS was that "*all instructions had already been valued through normal site valuations and that any payment had to be formally justified in writing.*" The contractor was bluntly informed that "*there was no more money in the pot*" and an increasingly acrimonious atmosphere developed between the contractor and consultants.

Concerns continued to be expressed about on-going deficiencies in the engineer's drawings and schedules.

A sudden safety risk

Heavy rain caused the site manager to become concerned about the safety of the existing retaining wall, parts of which were still remaining. In response, the site manager refused to put men in that area and after a number of urgent meetings on site, the geologist was called back to advise on its stability. A decision was made to move the new retaining walls forward so excavations would not undermine the old retaining wall further.

More re-design

Moving the new retaining walls forward meant re-positioning parts of the new building, a second redesign of the drainage system, and further delays on site. Furthermore, when the new drawings were issued, the site manager detected a lack of reinforcement in some parts of the retaining wall. Unable to contact the engineer, a decision was made on site between the clerk-of-works and site manager, to increase the amount of reinforcement in the wall and to cut and bend bars on site to prevent further delays. The site manager continued to detect discrepancies in subsequent engineer's drawings, and to resolve them; a meeting was arranged on site with the engineer. The engineer did not show up. The comment in the site manager's diary was "*Waited until late but [engineer] did not arrive. [Engineer] on holidays. I hope he has arranged the information!*" The site manager recalled that "*I felt sorry for [the engineer] but I had to keep the site going and even though I did pressure him I could have been a lot harder. By this time though, he just couldn't cope and his health was suffering.*"

The contractor re-serves the claim

The contractor re-served the claim but it was rejected the same day on the basis that it was full of unsubstantiated claims and that the contractor had contributed to delays by a lack of diligence. Numerous meetings were held on site to resolve continuing drawing discrepancies.

Trying to resolve the disputed claim

The client requested an update from the architect and unexpectedly visited the site on more than one occasion. The next site meeting was very acrimonious, the client's QS re-stating his reasons for rejecting the claim and the site manager, taking personally the accusation that he lacked diligence. In response, he insisted on reading out his diary entries one by one, asking the architect and engineer to confirm them immediately. Most instructions were confirmed, and with some consternation, the client's QS asked them why he had not been informed of these changes. The site manager recalled, "*I knew I would make [the architect] and [the engineer] feel uncomfortable but unless I prompted them they just sat there in silence. They weren't going to "drop themselves in it" were they?*"

In response, the client's QS suggested that there was no proof of the work having been done, causing the site manager to angrily ask them whether they were calling him "*a liar.*" The client's QS then produced some photographs of the retaining wall drainage and argued that there was no evidence to show that certain materials, included in the contractor's claim, had been installed. The site manager disputed this and the meeting ended with no tangible progress.

Trying to resolve the disputed claim

Meetings continued to be held on site to resolve drawing discrepancies and to discuss the contractor's claim. One critical meeting lasted five hours, during which each of the contractor's 55 "heads of claim" were discussed in turn. The meeting included open accusations of unprofessionalism directed at the client's QS. These accusations had been prompted by the client's QS's suggestion to the contractor's QS that continual pursuance of their claim could jeopardize future contracts. As on previous occasions, this meeting ended with little sense of movement in relative positions.

The end of the dispute

The suggestion that future contracts would be jeopardized stimulated the contractor to escalate the dispute. This involved direct contact between the client and the contractor's managing director and resulted in the immediate and full granting of the claim.

PATTERNS OF BEHAVIOR

This "sudden" crisis lasted approximately 10 months and consumed a considerable amount of resources, time, and energy by involving people in 58 formal meetings, 67 telephone conversations, and 32 letters. There would also have been numerous informal meetings that were not recorded. The following section describes the main phases of behavior that emerged during this crisis.

Phase one

The start of this crisis was characterized by a complete neglect of financial issues because solving technical and organizational problems took priority in ensuring the immediate survival of the project in terms of physical progress on site. This may have had a role to play in ensuring that it was a predominantly positive phase with a strong sense of forward momentum. Indeed, this was also reflected in people's communication patterns, which were characterized by only one dominant faction and illustrates effective communication across the traditional consultant-contractor divide and a sense of collective responsibility for dealing with the problem. This is illustrated in Figure 8-1.

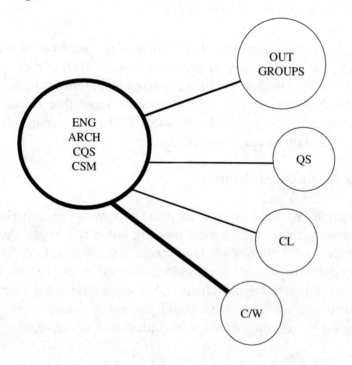

ENG – Engineer   ARCH - Architect
CSM – Main contractor's site manager   QS - Client's quantity surveyor
CQS – Main contractor's quantity surveyor   CL - Client
C/W – Clerk-of-works

Figure 8-1 Factional structure for phase one.

In terms of people's centrality to information flow, the architect and site manager were the greatest senders of information, which indicated the leading role they played in driving this phase forward. The client's QS occupied a relatively peripheral position, indicating the low priority afforded to financial issues during this initial period of activity. People were also able to communicate directly with each other, indicating a tightly knit communication structure where ideas were transferred rapidly with minimal distortion. This resulted in a widespread mutual understanding of the problem. The architect and site manager were most commonly the first point of contact for people and occupied the main gate-keeping positions within the communication network. However, while they exercised control over information flows, alternative routes among people prevented them from dominating communications. This meant that communications were not vulnerable to the attitudes and perceptions of a few people—a potential problem in the early phases of a crisis when people are likely to be at their most defensive and when the largest amount of information is generated. A further positive characteristic of communication patterns during this phase was the high equivalence in people's personal communication networks, which indicated that there would have been a common understanding of the crisis between everyone affected.

Phase two

Phase two started with the recommencement of work on site in response to growing pressure from the client and contractor. However, it quickly became apparent that the decision to restart had been premature and based on an underestimation of the contractor's information needs and an insufficient reservoir of information to fuel continued progress on site. Consequently, this phase was characterized by a reduction in forward momentum relative to phase one and by the site manager's growing sense of frustration. The main problem was related to omissions and errors in the designs supplied to the contractor, which meant that each injection of information brought with it an equivalent injection of uncertainty. This, in turn, generated a further demand for information, which drew the engineer into a spiralling cycle of uncertainty and pressure from which he found it increasingly difficult to escape. He had to chase the demand for information rather than lead it and to alleviate the pressures associated with this reactive style of management, he increasingly relied on the site manager to detect problems and identify the information needed to deal with them. In this sense, the site manager played a crucial role in supplying information.

While levels of discussion remained similar to phase one, the use of informal, verbal instructions increased substantially as a means for supplying information. This was the main mechanism used by the engineer and architect in attempting to cope with an increasingly out-of-control situation on site and to re-establish their command over information supply. These accumulating problems were reflected in the dramatic reduction in overall levels of communication compared to phase one. This is illustrated in Figure 8-2.

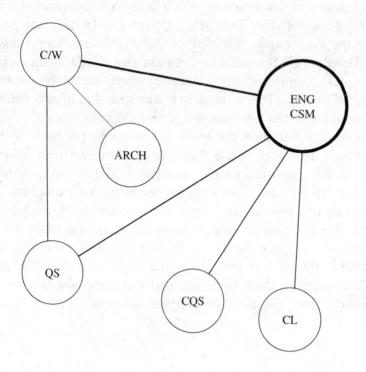

ENG – Engineer   ARCH - Architect
CSM – Main contractor's site manager   QS - Client's quantity surveyor
CQS – Main contractor's quantity surveyor   CL - Client
C/W – Clerk-of-works

Figure 8-2 Factional structure in phase two.

The existence of only one dominant faction between the engineer and the site manager indicates a dramatic focusing of communications compared to phase one, where there was a higher level of overall involvement in the crisis. This pattern was largely precipitated by the site manager who became increasingly proactive in generating his own information supply in the face of an engineer who seemed unable to cope with the pressures put on him. Indeed, during this phase of behavior, the engineer increasingly relied on the site manager's abilities to detect and notify problems on site, responding with numerous verbal instructions to change, ad-hoc, various aspects of the designs.

In terms of gate-keeping roles, the site manager became an important channel for information flow, which made the whole crisis management process vulnerable to his vested interests and personal abilities. However, the site manager was capable, experienced, and cooperative, and therefore this communication pattern had a positive influence. In contrast, the engineer's and architect's gate-keeping position between the contractor and the client's QS had a damaging effect because they used it to their own advantage to make spontaneous and informal decisions without the knowledge of the client's QS who would have undoubtedly constrained their actions. This behavior had a negative effect by isolating the client's QS from the process, which caused considerable problems in the third and final phase of behavior.

Phase three

The serving of the contractors claim initiated a third distinct phase of behavior—one that produced a dramatic focus on financial issues which, until that point, had been almost completely neglected. While a focus on technical and organizational issues had been necessary to maintain progress on site, difficulties in resolving financial issues indicated that their neglect had led to the development of very different perceptions about the costs of disruption. The consequence was an increase in emotions and a further reduction in forward momentum compared to phase two.

The client's QS became particularly frustrated and emotional about his exclusion from the design changes that had been made spontaneously on site. This placed him in a disadvantaged and vulnerable negotiating position with a relatively well-informed contractor. His response was to become defensive and avoid negotiations, which resulted in an increasingly emotional and acrimonious environment that eventually forced the contractor to escalate the dispute by involving the managing director.

This pattern of events is reflected in the factional structure that characterized this phase and that Figure 8-3 illustrates. For example, considering the focus upon financial issues, it is evident that the client's QS and contractor's QS communicated relatively infrequently. Furthermore, the divide between the contractor and the consultants seemed to strengthen compared to phase two. Finally, the architect and the client's QS worked more closely than in previous phases as the latter tried to identify the informal design changes that had been made during phase two, and from which he had been excluded. Essentially, this was an attempt to gather information that would equalize the information differences between himself and the contractor's QS, which were placing him in a disadvantaged negotiating position.

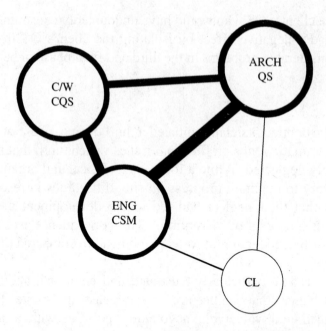

ENG – Engineer   ARCH - Architect
CSM – Main contractor's site manager   QS - Client's quantity surveyor
CQS – Main contractor's quantity surveyor   CL - Client
C/W – Clerk-of-works

Figure 8-3 Factional patterns in phase three.

CONCLUSION

This conclusion uses the cyclical model of crisis management depicted in Figure 3-1 to discuss how effectively this crisis was managed.

The origin of this crisis was the decision to extend a school building on an adjacent site, which, in turn, influenced the design of a new retaining wall. The early warning signs were missed because the crisis was not detected until some time after construction had commenced on both projects. While the engineer who designed the retaining wall could not have been expected to know of the parallel plans for an extension on an adjacent site, once its construction was started, its implications for the retaining wall's design should have been obvious. It would appear that the monitoring activities of this project organization were deficient.

Although the project organization was insensitive to the potential problem, once detected, the diagnostic process to evaluate its implications was characterized by a high level of efficiency and cooperation, resulting in a recommendation to maintain site progress in parallel with redesign. The seriousness of the crisis meant that only the client had the authority to make such a decision and this was quickly forthcoming. The implementation of this decision began immediately. This series of events is illustrated in Figure 8-4.

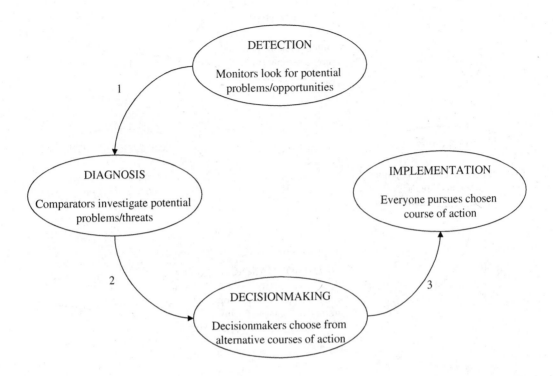

Figure 8-4 Efficient diagnosis and decisionmaking after delayed detection.

During the implementation of this decision, feedback from the site manager resulted in the detection of a further problem; delays were accumulating on site because information supply could not keep up with demand. This initiated a second full cycle of the crisis management process that began with an assessment of the new problem and the appropriate response. The process produced a recommendation to temporarily stop the site to enable design to progress to a point where it was possible to maintain construction activity on site. Once again the magnitude of this recommendation meant that it had to be referred to the client for a decision; the recommendation was duly sanctioned. The implementation of this decision meant that the site stopped, which allowed the design team to get ahead of the construction team. This series of events is illustrated in Figure 8-5.

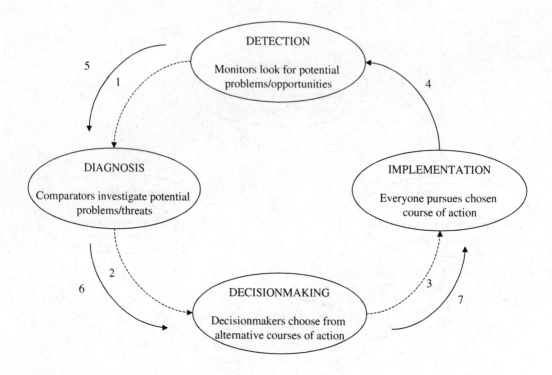

Figure 8-5 Another cycle of the crisis management process.

During the monitoring of this second period of design activity, it was determined that people had different perceptions of how long this process would take. Feedback from the client and site manager indicated increasing frustration with the delays that were accumulating on site.

As a result, they exerted considerable pressure to restart construction, which eventually resulted in a decision to do so, throwing the crisis management process into a third cycle of activity. This series of events is depicted in Figure 8-6.

The state of information supply was assessed when the decision was made to restart the site. Almost immediately, feedback from the site manager indicated that the demand for information was running ahead of its supply once again. During the stoppage, the design team had not built up a sufficient reservoir of information to support construction and they had succumbed too early to the pressures to re-start the site. Once again, information demand ran ahead of its supply and the designs increasingly became historical documents rather than the forward-planning documents they were meant to be. The pressures and stresses that this exerted on the architect and engineer led to fundamental errors and the further re-work associated with correcting them led the design team into a spiralling cycle of pressure, stress, and error from which it was increasingly difficult to escape.

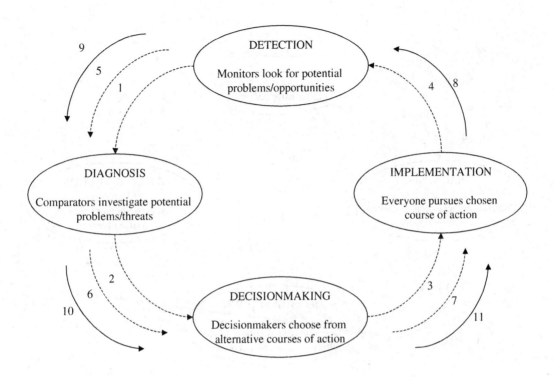

Figure 8-6 A third cycle of activity.

In an attempt to re-establish control, the engineer and architect were forced into an increasingly reactive and informal mode of management, issuing design changes spontaneously on site. While this speeded up information supply, it also created an increasingly disjointed organization. In particular, the client's QS became detached from the crisis management process and ignorant of the changes being made. Some evidence suggests that the architect and engineer deliberately filtered information to the client's QS about their design changes because he may have reduced their flexibility in issuing the verbal instructions that ensured their survival. In essence, the crisis seems to have created a conflict of interest between those responsible for the protection of different project goals (costs—the QS, and time—the architect and engineer) which prevented some parties from monitoring problems on site. In particular, the insulation of the client's QS from the site manager's feedback about continual problems on site resulted in a complete loss of financial control. However, the site manager eventually bypassed the engineer and architect to notify the client's QS of the problem, which initiated a fourth full cycle of the crisis management process which was specifically concerned with financial issues. The above series of events is depicted in Figure 8-7.

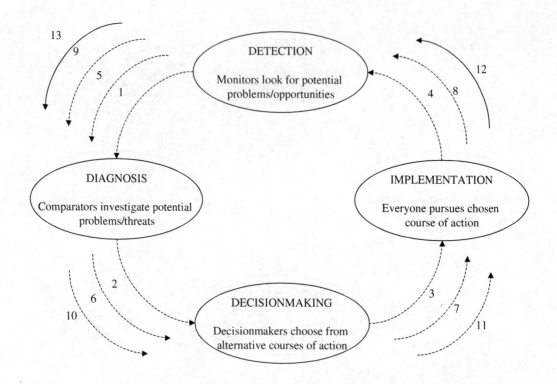

Figure 8-7 A fourth cycle of activity.

The diagnostic process was characterized by a series of acrimonious disputes between the client's QS and contractor's QS. These were a direct result of the client's QS's exclusion from the informal changes that had been made on site by the architect and engineer. This disadvantaged negotiating position forced him into a defensive mode of management. Indeed, the client's QS was never able to accumulate enough information to compete with the contractor and tactics became increasingly offensive on both sides until the dispute escalated to the point where it had to be resolved at managing director level. This is depicted in Figure 8-8.

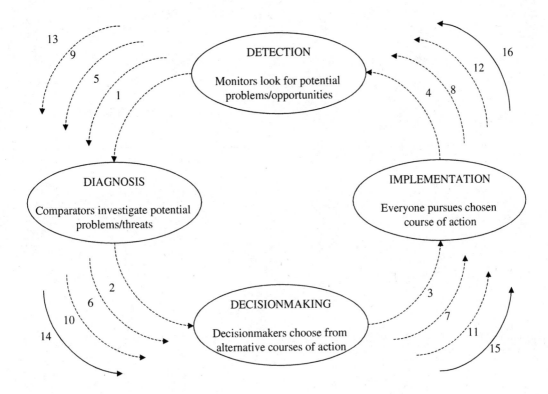

Figure 8-8 An end to the crisis.

Chapter 9

Case Study Four

THE PROJECT

This project involved the construction of a new office complex that was centered around a courtyard.

THE CRISIS

A creeping crisis began when half way through construction, a local brick paviour manufacturer of clay pavings (Company X) complained to the client that local producers did not feature in the project specifications. Although the project was well advanced, the specification was changed to incorporate Company X's clay paving. However, quality control problems quickly arose, causing serious delays and a dispute began between the contractor and architect over financial responsibility.

AN ACCOUNT OF THE CRISIS MANAGEMENT PROCESS

During the decision to change the project's specification, a discrepancy was discovered between what the contractor had priced in the bill of quantities and what the architect had originally specified. The architect argued that he had originally specified clay pavings and that the change of specification would merely involve a change of manufacturer. However, the bill of quantities had only specified concrete pavings, meaning that a change to clay would entitle the contractor to extra money.

A rift develops within the project team

This discrepancy arose from a performance specification system that allowed the architect to name three possible manufacturers from which tendering contractors could choose. However, the architect had confused matters by naming one company that only manufactured clay products, one that only produced concrete products, and one that was bankrupt. The contractor chose the cheapest option to win the bid.

The client's QS felt blamed by the architect, saying, *"The architect intimated that we were at fault for misinterpreting the specification which, he maintained, specified clay as a possible option.... The architect originally wanted clay because apparently it looked really good on his last job. But there wasn't any money in the budget so he put clay in, as an option, hoping that the contractor would go for clay. In other words he wanted clay for the price of concrete."*

Trying to reduce the extra costs of clay over concrete

The basis of the contractor's claim for extra money in using clay pavings over concrete pavings was the extra laying time (due to higher dimensional variability in clay products than in concrete products) and higher material prices. To test this argument, the architect asked the site manager to build some sample panels using the clay pavings to demonstrate the dimensional tolerance problems. He also asked Company X for their response. Company X indicated that the tolerances of clay pavings were the same as concrete and that there should be no extra laying costs. They also offered a discount that lowered their price to that of concrete.

A decision is made

After inspecting the sample panels on site, the architect opted for clay. Work quickly commenced on site because the decision had been delayed by the investigations. The contractor formally requested a change-order to cover this specification change but the architect refused, pointing to the discount offered by the manufacturer to cover the extra laying and material costs. The contractor disagreed that the discount was enough to cover the increased costs and the architect formally requested a written explanation.

Problems arise on site

A change-order was eventually issued to cover the extra costs of clay over concrete. However, the estimation of the extra costs quickly became inadequate as serious problems begin to arise on site due to high variability in paving sizes and colors. These unexpectedly wide variations had not emerged within the sample panel because of its relatively small area. The architect decided to continue with the laying.

The contractor requests a change back to concrete pavings

In addition to laying problems, the contractor began to experience supply problems and consequently, accumulating delays. The increasingly frustrated contractor formally requested a change back to concrete pavings.

The contractor communicates an intention to serve a formal claim

Company X was invited to a formal site meeting to discuss the laying problems on site. They offered to hand-pick the clay pavings, and if problems continued, to lay them themselves. Problems continued and after Company X's own team failed to cure them, the contractor wrote to the architect expressing concerns about the continuing delays and their intention to claim an extension of time.

Again, they strongly requested that the architect revert to concrete. The architect did not take the advice.

A decision is made to revert back to concrete

Eventually the laying problems became so bad that the clerk-of-works called a meeting on site to inspect the work: "*I could just see it getting worse and worse. Someone had to make a decision! The architect didn't want to because he did not want to implicate himself in the problem and the contractor didn't want to for the same reason.*" In this meeting, it was agreed that the quality of the clay pavings was unsatisfactory and a decision was made to revert back to concrete pavings. The contractor was asked to select some concrete pavings and to lay sample panels. Eventually, the architect decided on a colored concrete paviour that resembled clay.

The contractor formally serves a claim

The contractor lifted the clay pavings that had been laid and began replacing them with colored concrete pavings. The contractor also served a claim for the aborted work that was associated with the original decision to change to clay pavings. The contractor also requested another change-order to cover the latest change from clay to a colored concrete, pointing out that colored concrete cost more than the non-coloured concrete, which had originally been specified and priced by the contractor in the bill of quantities.

The claim is discussed

After a prolonged period of silence, the architect requested the client's QS's advice, which was to grant the claim. However, the architect formally rejected the contractor's claim and their request for another change-order, arguing that the original performance specification system made the contractor responsible for the choice of manufacturer. The architect argued that since the manufacturer caused the problems, it was a contractor's risk. He also maintained that the contractor caused the supply problems by being late in providing a delivery schedule to the manufacturer. Finally, he argued that the reversion back to concrete, particularly a colored concrete, had been the contractor's choice and that the architect had merely agreed with that recommendation.

This initiated a heated exchange where the contractor responded with the assertion that they had been guided to choose Company X and that without the original decision to convert to clay, there would have been no problems.

Negotiations break down

Both the architect and contractor considered suing the manufacturer. At the same time, the client's QS was informally discussing the claim with the contractor's QS, with whom he still had considerable sympathy and a good relationship from a previous project. Despite making some progress toward a compromise solution, the client's QS recalled "*In the end I had to stop talking to [the contractor's quantity surveyor] because I got the feeling that [the architect] suspected I had sympathies with the contractor and at the end of the day, my loyalties must be to the client.*" This further frustrated the contractor's QS, who recalled, "W*e just couldn't get any sense out of [the architect] but you could have a sensible conversation with [the client's quantity surveyor].*"

The dispute is resolved

The architect became suspicious of the client's QS's allegiance and took control of negotiations with the contractor's QS. Using the informal progress that had been made by the client's QS, the architect agreed to consider the increased costs for laying clay pavings and to give an extension of time, but only under the "head" of inclement weather. Within one month, a deal was struck and the contractor was given an extension of time for inclement weather and reimbursed approximately one-third of his original financial claim by using rates in the original bill of quantities. The architect also issued a change-order to revert back to colored concrete from clay, but added a written note that this was merely a confirmation of the contractor's decision. No extra costs were paid for this latter change.

PHASES OF BEHAVIOR

This creeping crisis lasted six months and consumed a considerable amount of resources, time, and energy by involving people in 25 formal meetings, 22 telephone calls, and 39 letters. There would also have been numerous informal meetings that were not recorded. The following section describes the main phases of behavior that emerged during this crisis.

Phase one

This phase started with open discussion and a strong sense of forward momentum as people investigated the feasibility of changing from concrete to clay pavings. However, soon after the decision to change to clay was made, laying problems began to emerge on site and a financial dispute developed between the contractor and architect, indicating that the decision to revert to clay was made before everyone had a complete understanding of organizational and financial issues. The result was a loss of forward momentum and a period when frustration, growing anxiety, and threats figured prominently in people's communications. The uncertainty of the architect's procrastinations in deciding to revert back to concrete contributed to further decline. The factional structure during this phase is illustrated in Figure 9-1.

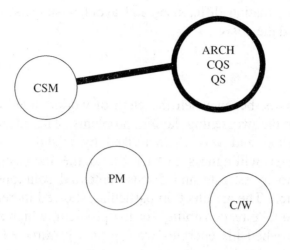

ENG – Engineer
CSM – Main contractor's site manager
CQS – Main contractor's quantity surveyor
C/W – Clerk-of-works

ARCH - Architect
QS - Client's quantity surveyor
CL - Client

Figure 9-1 Factional patterns in phase one.

Figure 9-1 illustrates that there was only one faction in this initial phase, and it consisted of the architect, contractor's QS, and client's QS, the strongest members being the two quantity surveyors. The heavy involvement of the quantity surveyors reflects the focus on financial issues in making the original decision. In contrast, the relative exclusion of the site manager reflects the lower importance attributed to the organizational issue, which eventually delayed the project and increased its cost.

In terms of people's centrality, the architect was the main source of information and drove the process forward. This reflected his enthusiasm for using clay rather than concrete pavings, his autocratic management style, and unwillingness to compromise. However, the client's QS received the most information and was clearly more popular as a point of contact for the contractor. Furthermore, like the contractor, the client's QS was being increasingly marginalized by the architect's policy of distancing himself from the laying problems that began to plague the site. Thus, while the architect was trying to maintain control by being dominant, he undermined his own position by increasing the client's QS's receptivity to the contractor. Furthermore, he drove the client's QS and contractor's QS "underground" and lost contact with their informal negotiations.

In terms of gate-keeping roles, there was no dominant person, although the architect tried to control information flow. His failure to do so was a result of the client's QS who presented himself as an alternative and much more pleasant communication route for the contractor's QS. Although he had little power to make decisions, his role was invaluable in diffusing tensions within the project team. The client's QS's actions also made him an important bridge between the architect and contractor, helping equalize information differences and avoid misunderstandings that could have further escalated the crisis.

Phase two

This phase of behavior began when the clerk-of-works called an urgent on-site meeting to inspect the worsening laying problems. The meeting lasted for a relatively short period and was characterized by a sudden surge in forward momentum, a greater willingness to face up to the increasing organizational problems on site, to investigate and discuss potential solutions, and to resolve differences of opinion. The architect, in particular, showed increased decisiveness and a willingness to take responsibility for the problem, which was in contrast to the previous phase when his energies were primarily directed toward avoiding responsibility. Consequently, a far greater emphasis on open discussion and informality emerged. This is reflected in the factional structure that emerged during this phase, and that is illustrated in Figure 9-2.

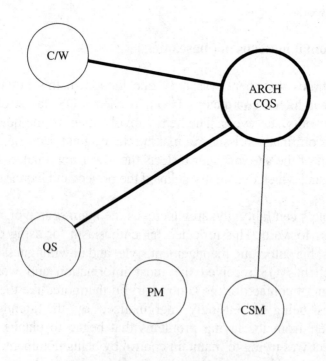

ENG – Engineer   ARCH - Architect
CSM – Main contractor's site manager QS - Client's quantity surveyor
CQS – Main contractor's quantity surveyor CL - Client
C/W – Clerk-of-works

Figure 9-2. Factional structure in phase two.

In this second phase, the architect and the contractor's QS formed the only faction, the client's QS was connected, but only in a receiving capacity. This reflects the sudden attempt of the architect to regain control of the process in response to the clerk-of-works' intervention. During this period, the architect assumed the role of negotiator with the contractor—a role that had hitherto been performed informally by the client's QS.

In terms of centrality, the architect and contractor's QS became dominant in both a sending and receiving capacity. This is more evidence of a new cooperative phase with a good level of communication across the contractor/consultant divide.

The end of this short-lived but positive phase of behavior coincided with the decision to abandon clay pavings and revert back to colored concrete.

Phase three

This phase was characterized by an emphasis on the financial and organizational issues that had not been fully resolved in the previous phases. However, during much of this phase there continued to be considerable disagreement over risk distribution patterns, which was responsible for a further reduction in forward momentum compared to phases one and two. A sense of forward momentum returned only when the client's QS informally intervened by discussing the claim with the contractor and when the architect assumed control to strike a deal. The factional structure that arose during this final phase is illustrated in Figure 9-3.

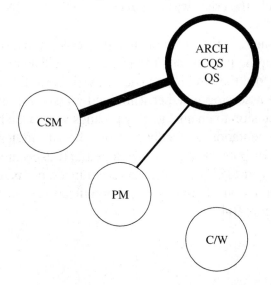

ENG – Engineer   ARCH - Architect
CSM – Main contractor's site manager   QS - Client's quantity surveyor
CQS – Main contractor's quantity surveyor   CL - Client
C/W – Clerk-of-works

Figure 9-3 Factional structure in phase three.

The factional pattern in Figure 9-3 is similar to that which arose in phase one and consists of one major faction comprising the architect, the contractor's QS, and the client's QS. The architect is the weakest member.

As in phase one, the architect refused to countenance the contractor's claim, withdrawing from the strong leadership role he played in phase two and returning to the distant role he played in phase one. Although structure was tightened around the architect compared to phase two, the majority of interactions with the architect were obstructive and prevented progress. In this sense, while the architect might have been physically close to others he was emotionally distant.

Like the factional patterns, the centrality patterns were also similar to phase one when the architect tried to maintain control by being a dominant source and gatekeeper of information supply but, in fact, lost control to the client's QS who became an alternative communication route for the contractor. Like phase one, such communications were largely informal, yet they enabled the client's QS to diffuse potential frustrations and to develop a good understanding of the contractor's needs. Ultimately, this resulted in important advances toward a compromise solution with the contractor that provided the basis for the final settlement of the dispute.

CONCLUSION

This conclusion uses the cyclical model of crisis management depicted in Figure 3-2 to discuss how effectively the crisis was managed.

The letter from Company X that precipitated this crisis arose as a result of the environment monitoring the project rather than vice versa. The responsibility to deal with the letter fell upon the architect who played both the comparator's and decisionmaker's role in assessing whether it merited a response and if so, what that change should be. A decision to change to clay pavings was made but problems soon developed in its implementation as feedback from the site indicated accumulating delays. Furthermore, a dispute over costs developed and it became evident that the original decision to convert to clay pavings had been made prematurely, on the basis of an insufficient examination of financial and organizational issues. This series of events is depicted in Figure 9-4.

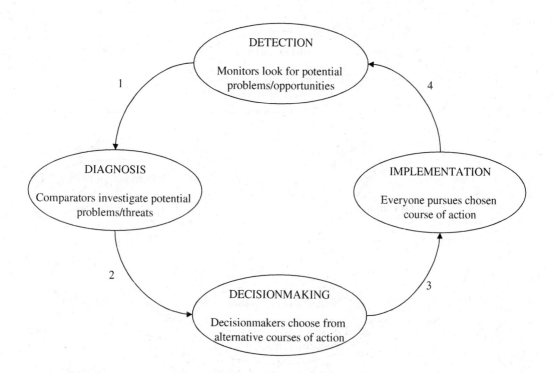

Figure 9-4 The first cycle of the crisis management process.

In responding to the feedback from site level about the laying problems, the architect procrastinated, hoping they would be resolved at site level. Furthermore, in the architect's opinion, these problems were the contractor's risk, and any intervention would implicate him. On the other hand the contractor considered it the architect's responsibility and continued laying the low-quality pavings on site. This confusion of responsibility and the fear of admitting fault, led to accumulating losses and delays that increased each party's reluctance to take the initiative to deal with the problem. Eventually, the clerk of works intervened, forcing the architect to face up to the problem and to decide to lift the clay pavings that had been laid and to replace them with a colored concrete paviour. The crisis management process was thrown into a second full cycle, the implementation of which went smoothly. This is illustrated in Figure 9-5.

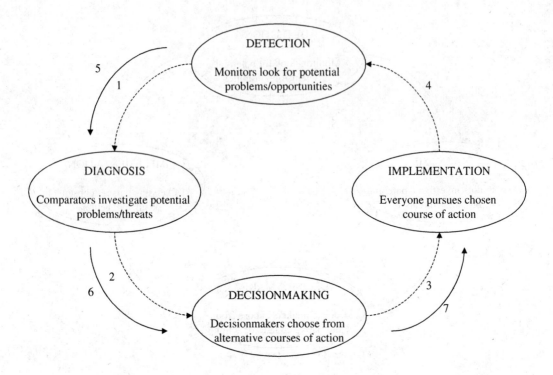

Figure 9-5 A second cycle of the crisis management process.

With the resolution of the laying problems on site, people turned their attention to the unresolved problem of responsibility for the delays and costs that had arisen as a result of the stalemate in the first cycle of the crisis management process. This issue was brought to a head by the serving of the contractor's claim, which forced the crisis management process into a third cycle of activity. The diagnosis phase of this third cycle was prolonged and confrontational because of the architect's and contractor's diametrically opposed views about who was responsible for the laying problems that had occurred on site in the first cycle. Indeed, agreement on a diagnosis of the problem was only reached because of the informal efforts of the client's QS, which played an important bridging role between the architect and contractor. This kept communications alive and prevented the dispute escalating further. This series of events is illustrated in Figure 9-6.

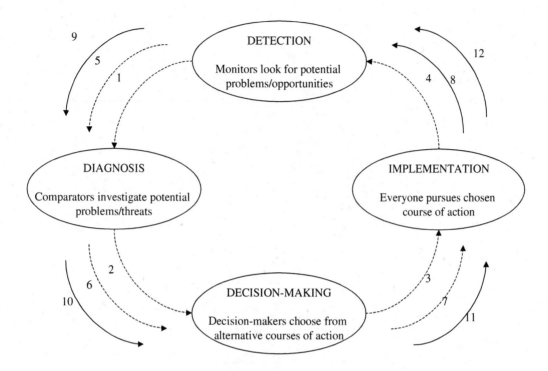

Figure 9-6 A third cycle of the crisis-management process.

Chapter 10

Lessons for Crisis Managers

This chapter compares the case studies to identify practical lessons for effectively dealing with construction crises. These lessons are highlighted in boxes throughout the text.

INTRODUCTION

The main characteristics of each case study are illustrated in Table 10-1.

Table 10-1 Case study characteristics.

Case study.	Description of crisis.
1. (Chapter 6) Earthwork support	**Creeping crisis** - A bill of quantities discrepancy relating to an earthwork support problem led to a claim for extra money and an acrimonious dispute. Procrastinations in settling it incurred considerable costs and delays and severely damaged project relationships.
2. (Chapter 7) Lift	**Sudden crisis** - Procrastinations in incorporating a new lift leads to information management problems which caused damaging stresses within the project team. These problems, in turn, damaged communications and caused significant organizational problems on site.
3. (Chapter 8) Retaining wall	**Sudden crisis** - It was discovered that a new retaining wall was under-designed. The site was shut-down but re-started too soon. This caused information management problems and stresses which caused serious delays and costs escalations on site. An acrimonious dispute also developed because of the consultants' refusal to grant the contractor's claim. Procrastinations led to the accumulation of further costs and delays and to the breakdown of project relationships.
4. (Chapter 9) Clay pavings	**Creeping crisis** - A rushed change in specification to clay pavings caused organizational problems on site and a dispute over responsibility which damaged project relationships.

A superficial inspection of Table 10-1 suggests that each crisis was unique. However, deeper investigation reveals important similarities and differences.

Built-in problems

At the most basic level, all four crises were the direct result of errors made during pre-contract stages. In each case, the seeds of potential crises were sown into the project from an early stage and were hidden by subsequent activities, only to be revealed by a "trigger event" such as the earthwork support problem in the leisure center project and the complaints of an architect from an adjacent site on the factory project.

> *Lessons:*
> - **Don't be complacent when things are going well.** *Be vigilant to the early warning signs of the inevitable problems built-into projects.*
> - **Simple problems grow over time.** *Don't suppress potential problems hoping they will go away, and don't "pass-the-buck" to people further "up-stream."*
> - **Keep project teams together for the life of a project.** *This will prevent potential problems being lost in time.*
> - **If you are new to a project, investigate its history.** *This will reveal potential problems that are hidden in the past and obscured by subsequent events.*

Creeping and sudden crises

Occasionally, trigger events occur early enough to allow the project team to prevent a crisis. This happened in case studies one and four, but the chance was not taken and the project teams manufactured their own creeping crises in the way they responded. On other occasions, the trigger event occurs late in a crisis' development and the result is a far more potent and sudden crisis, as illustrated in case studies two and three.

The main problem in the sudden crises revolved around information management and, in turn, the pressures and stresses associated with this. In contrast, the creeping crises were constantly plagued by problems relating to procrastination, indecision, escalation, and by the management of the resultant conflict. Further differences emerge when one considers communication throughout each type of crisis. For example, in the sudden crises, early efforts at resolution were primarily focused on technical and organization issues and were largely constructive in nature. That is, the suddenness of the crises appeared to make the immediate survival of the organization an initial priority over the pursuit of self-interest and forced people together. Problems relating to the settlement of financial responsibilities tended to be postponed and be attended to later in the crisis. However, when attention was eventually turned to financial issues, the delay appears to have allowed differences of interests to have become stronger and more clearly defined, resulting in particularly acrimonious conflicts.

In contrast, the creeping crises were primarily concerned with the resolution of financial responsibilities, particularly early on. Technical and organizational issues were a concern, but to a far lesser extent and typically postponed until later in the crises. In contrast to sudden crises, creeping crises gave people time to think about their differences and to formulate complex tactical strategies to force resource redistributions in their favor. This resulted in procrastination in making decisions, prolonged conflict episodes, and considerable periods of uncertainty and frustration for everyone involved.

Lessons:

- *Creeping and sudden crises present different managerial challenges.* *Managers must adapt their crisis management strategies accordingly.*
- *Sudden crises pose problems of pressure, stress and information management.* *An emergency plan can provide time for reorientation after the initial shock of a crisis. It also helps people cope with the rapid influx of information. Managers should ensure that financial responsibilities are not neglected in the early phases of a sudden crisis. There is a tendency to focus on technical and organisational problems to ensure the survival of the project.*
- *Creeping crises encourage procrastination by not appearing urgent.* *Managers should be vigilant to the tactical manipulations of interest groups which have time to formulate strategies to serve their financial interests. These tactics are a source of potential dispute and a dangerous distraction from the real problem, which may be technical or organizational rather than financial. If neglected, these problems will accumulate.*

MANAGING COMMUNICATIONS DURING A CRISIS

Chapter Five portrayed effective crisis managers as social architects who exhibit an intimate understanding of the forces that shape communication patterns among project members and of the impact that these have on crisis management outcomes. This is discussed in more detail here.

Selfishness

Chapter Three pointed to people's formal and informal responsibilities to protect specific project goals. A person's involvement in the management of a crisis should be determined by the extent to which the goals he or she protected were threatened. However, in the case studies, there was little evidence of this match between responsibility and crisis management involvement. The weak tended to be excluded from the process and the powerful dominated it. This caused a considerable degree of frustration and resentment for the suppressed.

Lessons:

- *Appreciate peoples' varied interests and the communication patterns that serve them.* *Monitor communication patterns that might damage the project.*
- *Assess a crisis' impact on project goals and ensure the appropriate specialists are involved to the appropriate extent.* *For example, if costs are primarily threatened, ensure the person responsible for budgetary control is in a position of power.*
- *The resolution of a crisis may demand trade-offs between different goals, bringing into conflict people who would otherwise work together.* *Managers should identify and focus energies on managing these tense interfaces since they are a source of potential disruption and inefficiency.*

The way the crisis was managed

The managerial style of the crisis manager appeared to have a significant influence on people's communication patterns during a crisis. People tend to become autocratic as a defence mechanism, often in an attempt to re-establish control. The outcome was, without exception, a loss of control.

Lesson:
- ***Crisis management needs to be independent, fair, and open.*** *Most project members including the crisis manager may have a vested interest in a particular outcome. It may be worthwhile considering third-party intervention or an external consultant to manage the process.*

Unexpected sub-crises

Unexpected sub-crises punctuated each crisis and significantly affected people's communication patterns. These sub-crises were the consequence of latent tensions from mismanaged crises and in this sense were all self-manufactured. Like the main crises they occurred within, their early warning signs were not detected and they had the potential to be destructive. However, they often had a positive influence, increasing the cohesion of the project team because they gave people a common focus and an opportunity to re-adjust their relationships.

Lessons:
- ***Expect the unexpected during a crisis.*** *Crises spurn sub-crises that can be creeping or sudden.*
- ***Occasionally it may be useful to stimulate a sub-crisis in order to increase group cohesion.*** *This is like using an explosion to extinguish a fire and takes considerable courage.*

Personal relationships

Personal relationships also shaped peoples' communications during each crisis. These relationships appeared to be determined by experiences on previous projects, stereotype views of occupational groups, in-built traditional suspicions among certain occupational groups, and by experiences during the life of a project.

Lessons:
- ***Under the pressures of a crisis, personal relationships are tested to the limit and any underlying tensions are exacerbated and exposed.*** *Ideally, construct project teams using people who have positive relationships from past projects. Where this is not possible, use people with no previous relationship. Finally, monitor interpersonal relationships continually for new tensions which will indicate where problems are likely to arise during a crisis.*

Peer pressure

In many of the crises, peer pressure played a considerable part in shaping peoples' communication patterns. People of common interests tended to group into temporary coalitions that developed strong internal pressures to be loyal to fellow members and to conform to established patterns of behavior and group norms. The intention of this coercive behavior was to suppress a potential problem that could implicate a group in blame or to hide it from the view of more senior decisionmakers.

Lessons:
- *Look out for corporate bullying. During a crisis, some interest groups can become excessively powerful, forcing through solutions which are inequitable or not in a project's interests.*
- *Don't rely on people to communicate potential problems. The common interests that develop within projects can lead to protective behavior, particularly if someone is at fault. The absentee project manager who relies on the goodwill of individual consultants to inform him or her of problems is most vulnerable. To prevent the incubation of potential problems, managers must be intimately involved in a crisis, trusted and accessible to potential informers or whistle-blowers.*

CRISES AS PERIODS OF SOCIAL CHANGE

The previous discussion indicates that construction crises activate a process of social adjustment within its host organization. This adjustment process is the product of a constantly developing struggle for information that will enable people to force resource redistributions in their favor. During this struggle, individuals attempt to mold the structure of their personal social network and those of others to suit their own interest—interests that may not necessarily coincide with the client's. To this end, individuals may form interest groups that increase their power base. The structure of the communication network that eventually emerges is determined by the relative success of each individual or interest group in imposing his or her desired structure on others.

Lesson:
- *A crisis causes social chaos. During a crisis, "normal" loyalties and allegiances change, and it pays to be sensitive to the inevitable formation of temporary coalitions/factions. Their informal nature makes them invisible to the eye and difficult to detect. They are best identified by engendering an enduring sense of trust and confidence in one's judgment and leadership.*

The folly of imposed solutions

While individuals or groups may attempt to manipulate communication structure to serve their interests by, for example, marginalizing those who represent a threat, the case studies showed that the interests and power of those they sought to manipulate largely determined their success. While some people responded positively to the manipulation because the direction suited their own interests, others resisted vehemently. This process of reinforcement and resistance continued until the interests of the interacting parties were mutually served by the structure of their communication network or, alternatively, when one party was able to forcibly impose a communication structure on another. However, these forced social equilibriums turned out to be little more than a pleasant illusion because, they resulted in increased tension and frustration for the person who was suppressed. In the long-term, there was a limited amount of time over which this tension could be contained. Equilibrium was most rapidly and lastingly achieved when those involved had shared interests because they voluntarily arrived at the same solution.

Lessons:
- *Imposed solutions are not lasting solutions. The natural temptation during a crisis is to forcibly impose a solution. Although they may appear to work in the short-term, such solutions are temporary and create covert, latent tensions that compromise subsequent crisis management efforts or eventually manifest themselves in the form of a sub-crises. Ultimately, when a multitude of interests are involved, lasting solutions only come through a process that gives all parties a sense of ownership over the eventual solution. The extra time this takes is a good investment.*
- *Peoples' interests can be aligned by sharing risks, by helping people focus on common interests rather than their differences, and by encouraging people to put their preconceived solutions aside. Rather than traditionally searching for compromise solutions, help people work together to search for the solutions that may suit everyone's interests.*
- *Managers must control the balance of power during a crisis. They should be knowledgeable about a crisis and portray themselves as arbiters who are a source of independence, reliability, and fairness.*

EFFICIENT COMMUNICATION PATTERNS

This section discusses the development and efficiency of various communication patterns. With this knowledge, managers can predict, interpret, and thereby control information flow more effectively during a crisis.

Factionalism
The emergence of factions was discussed in the previous section, as was their tendency to develop around those with common interests. However, the range of

common interests that seemed to underpin the development of factions was varied, and factional membership did not always mirror the traditional interest groups we associate with construction projects. Such factions were useful because they broke down barriers to communication. However, unfortunately they were relatively rare because their formation often demanded considerable insight and courage to ignore traditional occupational stereotypes.

Most factions emerged because people wanted to increase their power base in negotiations, to manipulate information flow, or to defend personal interests by hiding a problem. These types of factions tended to develop more easily in environments where blame could be attributed to someone. On the other hand, factions also emerged for altruistic reasons, such as wanting to share information and to help solve a problem. They tended to develop when risks were shared and when people recognized their mutual interdependency.

Unfortunately, the negative reasons why factions developed outweighed the positive, which caused them to have a damaging affect by focussing communications into intense pockets, fragmenting the organizational structure, and leading to an overall breakdown of communications. There were some exceptions to this rule, and it was evident that factions were not a problem if their activities were monitored to ensure they had positive outcomes and if opportunities were provided for people to communicate with them. Indeed, effectively controlled factions could be useful to managers by simplifying the organizational structure of a project into fewer component groups with fewer interfaces.

Lessons:
- *A crisis has the potential to generate unpredictable and often surprising allegiances. Be careful, allegiances are not always predictable and the reasons behind their formation can be temporary and obscure.*
- *Managers should create conditions that promote the development of positive factions. This is done by encouraging interdisciplinary teams, by sharing risks, by being non-recriminatory and by emphasizing people's interdependence.*
- *Managers should be vigilant to the formation of negative factions and disband them. Negative factions can be recognized by their secretive nature and by their suspicion of, and resistance to, outsiders. Negative factions often include people who are afraid of being blamed for a crisis.*

Centralization

In many instances within the case studies, people sought to occupy central positions within the communication networks. They did so for a variety of reasons and in a number of different ways.

Regaining control

Some people sought central positions to gain control. Often, they did this by attempting to dominate information supply and/or demand. Another tactic to gain control was to seek gate-keeping positions within the communication network that would permit them to filter and manipulate information to their own ends.

Avoiding blame

The high stakes associated with a crisis exacerbate the sense of fear about being implicated in blame. One way to avoid blame was to reduce one's directness of communications with those who were implicated in the problem. By working through intermediaries, a person could distance him or herself from a problem and be seen as merely acting on the advice of others.

Avoiding bias

Many vested interests are at stake during a crisis and information blockages and distortions can arise as people in gate-keeping positions attempt to block its transfer between certain people. One way in which people attempted to overcome this barrier was to find alternative routes around these potential sources of bias.

Gaining power

The differences of interests that emerge during a crisis produce different interpretations of what a crisis is about and who is responsible for it. This often led to a process of negotiation during which information was an important source of power. In full knowledge of this, some people sought to ensure that their information networks were unique and they cloaked them in secrecy. On the other hand, opponents sought to infiltrate these communication networks in an attempt to reveal the basis of their arguments and ultimately undermine their case.

What was the most efficient pattern of information flow?

In terms of efficiency, the best pattern was one that had a high level of centrality for information supply but a low level of centrality in information receipt—that is, where there was a widespread supply of information from a restricted source. This resulted in a strong sense of leadership and a minimum level of misunderstanding because everyone was operating on the basis of similar information. Advantage also seemed to arise from "denser" communication networks where everyone implicated in a crisis could communicate directly with each other without having to go through intermediaries who could be biased. In dense networks, people are tightly knit and close to each other. This provides flexibility, enabling problems, ideas, and solutions to spread rapidly with little distortion.

Particularly high levels of efficiency seemed to arise when the communication network was tightly knit around one person because this ensured a high degree of consistency in communications. Another advantage of high density was that it minimized the possibility of gatekeepers emerging by providing a variety of alternative routes through which information could flow. The danger of gatekeepers was that they focussed information through restricted channels and thereby increased the possibilities for information overload and bottlenecks. They also provided opportunities for people to manipulate information in their own favor. The influence of gatekeepers was not always negative, being determined by the personal characteristics of people occupying those key positions. When they were manipulative, negative, and unable to cope with the information demands on them, the effect was damaging; when they were experienced, capable, and conscientious, the effect was positive.

Finally, a high level of similarity (equivalence) between people's communication networks equalized information differences and ensured that everyone was working on the basis of the same information. In contrast, when the level of similarity was low, the organization became disjointed and characterized by people pulling in different directions.

Lessons:
- **The patterns of information flow during a crisis are an important determinant of crisis management efficiency.** *As far as possible, managers should build communication structures with few negative factions, many positive factions, a restricted source and widespread supply of information, a high level of density (directness in communications), a single point around which communications are tightly knit, few gate-keeping positions, and a high level of similarity in contacts at individual level.*
- **Since communication patterns determine people's power-base, they become the subject of considerable manipulation.** *This may cause information filtering, distortion, or restriction in certain directions, harming crisis management efforts. Generally, people seek positions of high centrality and try to differentiate their communication network from those of others. Managers should ensure that the people with the right motives are in the central positions and that people's communication networks are well-integrated.*
- **A warning:** *While an efficient communication structure can help ensure open and clear information flow, it cannot guarantee crisis management success. This is also determined by the quality of information that is transferred within it. This, in turn, is largely influenced by the motives and competencies of its members. No system, however well-designed, can compensate for the effects of people who are determined to sabotage or who are unable to cope with the pressures of a crisis. In this sense, attention to positive relationships and to the motives and personal qualities of people affected by a crisis represent the foundations of efficient crisis management.*

CRISIS BEHAVIOR

All of the crises demanded a major investment of energy, time, and resources beyond that envisaged at the start of a project. However, the efficiency with which this extra energy was expended varied, each crisis being punctuated by change points that separated distinct phases of behavior and forward momentum.

Behavior during creeping and sudden crises

The case studies included examples of creeping and sudden crises. When their behavioral characteristics are compared, some interesting patterns emerge. For example, in contrast to sudden crises, creeping crises are more emotionally charged, divisive, and problematic for managers during their early stages—precisely the opposite of what would be expected. The explanation may be that the shock of a sudden crisis forces people to temporarily abandon their differences in an attempt to secure the immediate survival of the project. During a creeping crisis, people have more time to selfishly pursue their own interests, resulting in neglect of important problems that gradually accumulate in proportion until a second, but sudden sub-crisis forces people to put their differences aside.

> *Lessons:*
> - *Surprisingly, people's behavior during a creeping crisis is more unstable and dangerous than during a sudden crisis. Sudden crises create a sense of urgency and early forward momentum that can continue, if managed effectively. This is achieved by identifying, reinforcing, and supporting early successes and the positive working relationships that emerge. In contrast, creeping crises create little sense of urgency, allowing people to pursue personal interests. Managers must be sensitive to the covert tensions that often represent the early warning signs of a creeping crisis. One way of overcoming the lack of urgency and division that often characterize creeping crises is to artificially generate a sudden crisis. If managed effectively, the positives that emerge can be used to diffuse the differences that were fuelling it.*

The unpredictability of crisis behavior

People's behavior during a crisis is unpredictable. For example, the earthwork support crisis (case study one) began with a phase of negative momentum, indecision, uncertainty, formality, rigidity, defensiveness, and escalating conflict. It proceeded to a second phase characterized by forward momentum, mutual sensitivity, open communication, attentiveness to the problem, collective responsibility, low uncertainty, and low emotions. The crisis then fell back into a third phase of negative momentum, uncertainty, confusion, and heightened emotions. Finally, it returned to a phase of forward momentum, cooperation, decisiveness, negotiation, compromise, collective responsibility, and low emotions.

While the paviour crisis (case study four) followed a similar pattern, the retaining wall crisis (case study three) induced an opposite pattern of behavior, beginning with a period of strong forward momentum, widespread commitment to resolving the problem, open discussion, collective responsibility, and relatively low emotions. It then proceeded to a phase of zero momentum, increasing uncertainty, indecisiveness, reduced attention to information supply, growing frustration, and anxiety. Finally, it moved into a deeper phase of negative momentum, inflexibility, confrontation, and heightened emotions. In complete contrast to any other crisis, the elevator crisis (case study two) was characterized by a consistent sense of forward momentum and no significant changes in behavior.

Lessons:
- *One cannot generalize about a common pattern of behavior emerging in response to a construction crisis. Beware of universal models of crisis management. There are no quick fix solutions to construction crises and the unpredictable patterns of behavior that emerge, demand a more intelligent, thoughtful, and responsive approach to crisis management founded on a clear understanding of what motivates people to behave in certain ways.*

Predicting changes in people's behavior

If the crisis management process is likely to move through self-perpetuating periods of forward and backward momentum, the crisis manager is challenged to get it into an accelerating mode and to keep it there. This requires knowledge of the conditions that induce positive behavior, an understanding of what causes behavioral changes, and sensitivity to the advance warning signs of change.

Major change events

Every change point in every crisis coincided with a major event such as the surprise serving of a claim or the sudden intervention of a senior manager or of the client. While the nature of the "change events" varied, they were all manufactured by those involved in the crisis management process—sometimes deliberately but at other times, unintentionally. Furthermore, while each of these change events seemed to be sudden, numerous signs of impending change preceded them. For instance, in one crisis, where the involvement of the contractor's regional surveyor induced a sudden change in behavior, there was a detectable and steady increase in tension before the event. This manifested itself in the contractor's constant warnings and threats of delay. Similar warning signs preceded all the major change events.

Despite the existence of early warning signs of behavioral change, people showed insensitivity to them, sometimes voluntarily and at other times, involuntarily. For example, in several cases, people deliberately ignored their opponents' obvious frustrations and their warnings that they were going to escalate a dispute. However, there were also instances when people (normally senior decisionmakers) were insulated from these warnings by those who stood to lose from exposure to blame. The most disturbing fact to emerge was that as time went by, insensitivity and resistance to change grew because accumulating losses magnified the negative implications of accepting change. At the same time, the parties who wanted change became increasingly forceful in pursuing it. This created further resistance to change, and so on, until the project team became drawn into a spiral of insensitivity, acrimony, and escalation. That is, when a project entered a negative phase of behavior, it deepened rapidly and became increasingly difficult to stop.

More disturbing was the evidence that insensitivity to change is as much a problem in positive periods as it is in negative periods. For example, in several instances, the euphoria of progress and of strengthened project relationships blinded people to the real tensions that existed within their projects. Thus, in contrast to negative phases of behavior, which are self-reinforcing and robust, positive phases are fragile and easily destroyed.

While behavioral instability seems inevitable, one crisis (case study two) was unique in its absence of behavioral change points. In this crisis, the architect's sensitivity and responsiveness to the contractor's needs and emotions meant that he would always take action to supply information in time to counteract any escalation of the crisis. Similarly, the contractor's site manager's determination to make the project a success meant he did not seek to exploit the architect's misfortunes and was willing to demonstrate flexibility in helping resolve the crisis. In effect, the contractor performed an important compensating function that helped nurture a relationship of mutual trust and sensitivity that in the long run, reinforced the stability of the crisis management process.

Lessons:
- *If everything is going well you have probably overlooked something.*
- *The most efficient crisis management processes are the most behaviorally stable. Behavioral instability is not inevitable during a crisis. The challenge is to encourage and then maintain positive thinking. The most effective way to do this is to encourage mutual sensitivity to the needs of others, open communication, and collective responsibility for dealing with crises.*
- *The importance of early intervention in crises cannot be over-stated. Negativity is self-perpetuating and over time, is increasingly difficult to break.*
- *Crises have in-built defense mechanisms because they create conditions that produce insensitivity to the advance warning signs of escalation.*
- *Crisis managers can stabilize behavior by being constantly vigilant to the signs of changing interpersonal relationships.*
- *Try to see crises as opportunities to increase team cohesion rather than as threats that can destroy it. Most important, encourage others to see it in the same way.*

Explaining behavior during a crisis

To control people's behavior, it is important to understand what causes it. People's behavior during a crisis appears to be motivated by a number of factors.

Stereotypes

The case studies indicate that people enter projects with pre-conceived stereotype images of other occupational groups that are largely shaped by their experiences. These stereotypes influenced people's initial behavior in response to a crisis, particularly early in a project's life cycle. For example, in one crisis, tensions between the consultants and contractor were rooted in an acrimonious dispute stemming from a previous project; in another crisis, the architect's early behavior toward the contractor was partly determined by a "bad experience" with a contractor on a previous project. While we would expect the behavioral influence of stereotypes to be at their strongest during the early phases of a project, the case studies indicate that they are persistent, enduring, and resistant to change.

> *Lessons:*
> - *Although project relationships may seem tranquil and amicable on the surface, there may be underlying tensions within the project team.* *The high resourcing demands, ambiguities, and pressures induced by a crisis create ideal conditions for these tensions to surface and grow.*
> - *Stereotypes are dangerous because by definition they are arbitrary, overly simplistic, and negative.* *Stereotypes have minimal influence in teams whose members have had positive experiences with each other and been kept together for the life of a project and between different projects. Success breeds success and familiarity erodes the ignorance that is the basis of stereotypes.*

Financial responsibility

People's behavior was also shaped by the degree of uncertainty surrounding financial responsibility for a crisis. Uncertainty primarily arose from ambiguities in contractual documentation that were exploited by those who were most likely to be held responsible for a crisis. High levels of uncertainty surrounding contractual responsibilities enabled potential "losers" to redefine events in their favor, creating further uncertainty and prolonging the crisis management process. In contrast, in an environment of financial certainty, people's behavior was characterized by open discussion, clarity, and a sense of forward momentum.

> **Lessons:**
> - ***Share project risks equally whenever possible***. *With equally shared risks, the issue of financial responsibility is irrelevant and the focus becomes the collective minimization of mutual losses rather than the transfer of them.*
> - ***When risks cannot be shared, patterns of risk distribution should be clarified and a mutual understanding of them developed***. *It is an illusion that using a standard contract automatically increases mutual understanding and clarity. Risks are best clarified by simplifying contracts, minimizing their number, and insisting that people who are privy to them, discuss them.*

Fear

Not sharing project risks caused people to focus on their differences rather than on their similarities; to create an atmosphere of fear, recrimination, and blame; and to shut down communication channels precisely at the time when increased communication was needed. However, in one case study, the project team managed to overcome built-in contractual divisions by focusing on ways to minimize the costs of a crisis rather than on resolving responsibilities to pay for it. The result was cost implications that were not significant enough to argue about.

> **Lessons:**
> - ***Focus on how to minimize costs rather than on who will pay for them.***
> - ***Focus on people's similarities and mutual interdependencies rather than on their differences and independencies.***
> - ***Avoid a recriminatory response to a crisis***. *Depersonalize investigations, refrain from allocating fault or blame, focus on solutions rather than causes, and create a supportive rather than penal environment.*

Organizational policies

People's behavior was also guided by the policies of their employing organizations. For example, in one case study, the contractor encouraged the pursuit of claims, which likely influenced the behavior of its employees. In the same project, the consultants' defensive response was probably guided by the client's strict policy on budgetary control. In contrast, in the most successfully resolved crisis, the contractor's overriding company policy was to be as cooperative as possible in order to make a favorable impression on a new client. The resultant tolerance and accommodation this policy encouraged within its workforce contributed toward the effective resolution of the crisis.

Lessons:
- *When constructing a project team, give as much attention to the cultures of the companies as to the personalities and attributes of individuals. Beware of aggressive, selfish organizations. This includes the client.*
- *It is difficult to maintain a balance, between controlling project goals and providing the flexibility required to avoid conflict. Inflexibility engenders defensiveness and rigidity in the bargaining process, which leads to escalation. Goal flexibility is not about publicizing acceptable tolerances on projects goals because this will induce a lack of diligence. Flexibility means being prepared to work within contingency allowances and in this respect, it is essential that organizations are permitted to price for their risks.*

THE TWO IRONIES OF CONSTRUCTION CRISIS MANAGEMENT

Crises have built-in defence mechanisms that cause people to behave in ways opposite of what is necessary for effective resolution. In particular, it is ironic that at a time when collective responsibility and teamwork are important, conflict is more likely, and at a time when effective communication is important, it is less likely.

Irony #1: When a sense of collective responsibility and teamwork are more important, they are less likely to materialize.

In explaining this irony, we return to the issue of risk distribution practices and the tendency for crises to demand a significant injection of extra resources into a project.

In essence, the main problem with separate risk distribution is the emergence of distinct winners and losers in the resource redistributions that inevitably follow a crisis. This generates a lack of collective responsibility for resolving the crisis. Problems arise as different parties turn to their formal contracts to clarify patterns of responsibility, only to discover differences in interpretation and misunderstandings. If it were not for the crisis, these differences would remain irrelevant, but their effect is to create an air of uncertainty and to detract attention from the resolution of a crisis. Contractual ambiguities also provide opportunities for parties to employ a range of informal bargaining tactics to force resource redistributions in their favor. In this sense, formal contracts only partially determine patterns of responsibility during a crisis; a party's tactical prowess and bargaining power are also strong determining factors.

Tactical miscalculations and unintentional escalations

The previous section illustrates how crises, when coupled with separate risk distribution, can lead to fundamental changes in the nature of interpersonal relationships within a project team by exposing conflicts of interests which would otherwise remain hidden. Any disagreements that emerged during a crisis were made more contentious by the low margins under which parties were employed and the high stakes that, by definition, each crisis created. Collectively, these conditions magnified any conflicts of interest between project participants, making them more sensitive to money-making opportunities and more resistant to potential losses. In this situation, parties were prepared to use a variety of bargaining tactics to force resource redistributions in their favor. For example, in one case study, where a contractor served a claim for extra monies, consultants responded by generating outlandish counter-arguments to call their bluff and test their resolve in pursuing it. There were also numerous examples of parties attempting to take advantage of any ambiguities they could find in contractual clauses or in the nature and causes of the crisis itself. The popularity of this tactic seemed related to its low risk of escalation. However, another common tactic with a higher risk of escalation was to ignore a counterpart. Such a tactic always produced warnings and threats and eventually, deliberate acts of escalation. Indeed, in all but one of the crises, the combination of tactics employed by the various stakeholders had an escalating effect. Assuming that no party wanted to deliberately precipitate a full-blown conflict—and there was no evidence to the contrary—the observed bargaining processes can be seen as a catalog of tactical errors.

Lessons:
- ***Crisis managers must manage****. This is particularly important during a crisis, when there is a natural tendency toward escalation if there is no intervention.*
- ***Crises highlight and exaggerate any weaknesses, misunderstandings, and divisions within a project team****. At a time when collective responsibility is more important, conflict is more likely.*
- ***The more serious a crisis in terms of resourcing implications, and the lower the margins of implicated organizations, the more passionately they will defend their interests and the more likely it is that conflict will occur.***
- ***Contracts afford little protection against parties who are determined to avoid responsibility****. Tactically, parties wield considerable illegitimate informal power to force resource redistributions in their favor, despite what the contract says. Party's tactical astuteness rather than contractual obligations are the main shaper of resource distributions during a crisis.*
- ***When parties abuse their illegitimate power, weaker parties, who may be in the right, suffer unduly****. This causes malevolence, frustration, and the potential for conflict. Try to ensure fairness in the bargaining process.*
- ***The process of crisis management is fraught with the danger of accidental escalation resulting from miscalculated tactics of differing interest groups****. Be vigilant to potentially dangerous tactical combinations.*

Dangerous tactical combinations

Managers should be aware of and vigilant to tactical combinations that can produce accidental escalations of disputes. With knowledge about the motives that drive such tactics, managers are better equipped to understand a dispute, to predict its course, and to identify workable solutions with a low risk of escalation. To identify potentially dangerous tactical combinations it is useful to analyze the tactical patterns that characterized each of the case studies. These are depicted in Figures 10-1, 10-2, 10-3 and 10-4. The bargaining codes refer to those depicted in Table 5-1.

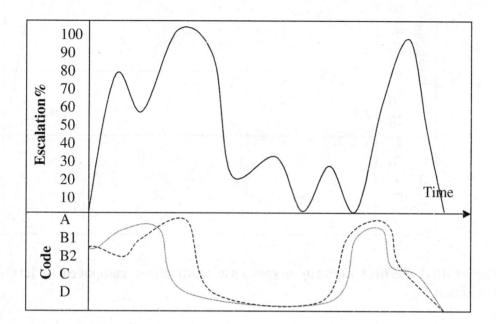

Figure 10-1 Tactical patterns across case study one compared to levels of escalation.

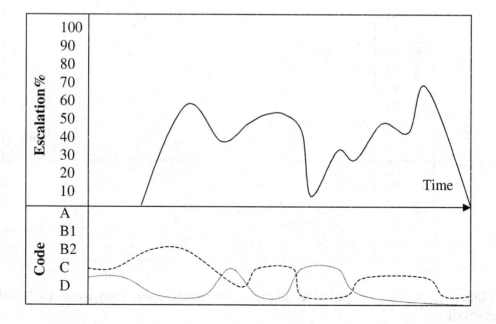

Figure 10-2 Tactical patterns across case study two compared to levels of escalation.

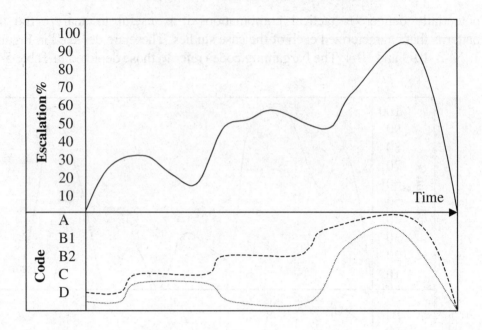

Figure 10-3 Tactical patterns across case study three compared to levels of escalation.

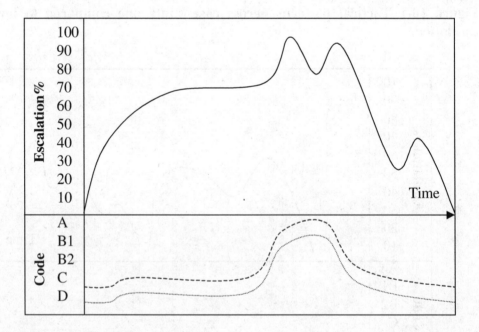

Figure 10-4 Tactical patterns across case study four compared to levels of escalation.

This analysis of the tactical patterns suggests that opposing parties tend to follow parallel routes. That is, one party's adoption of aggressive tactics is likely to eventually produce a similar response from an opponent, leading to an escalation of the situation. The potential for this tandem escalation seems to be related to the equitable balance of power that exists in construction projects. While the legitimate power that derives from contractual conditions may enable one party to forcibly suppress an opponent's case, parties to a construction project are also able to wield a considerable amount of illegitimate power, which most seem prepared to use. To prevent escalation, one party needs to break the mold and show a willingness for conciliation, compromise, and collaboration. Such a commitment is likely to induce a similar response from an opponent. However, a move to a conciliatory bargaining code must be genuine and be perceived as such by an opponent. If it is not, it will not alleviate the problem.

Lessons:

- **Contracts do not resolve crises. People do.** *Contracts are no substitute for good management.*
- **Effective communication between opposing parties is critical to avoid accidental escalations**. *Most disputes are based on simple misunderstandings.*
- **Coercive power tactics cannot bring about a successful long-term resolution of a dispute, nor can those based on compromises**. *By definition, compromises result in sub-optimal solutions and do not fully resolve underlying differences and tensions. Coercion and compromise merely create the illusion of a solution.*
- **Collaboration is the only way to fully resolve the tensions generated by a crisis.** *This is because it seeks optimal solutions that benefit all interest groups. However, this process is time-consuming and it demands courage to let go of preconceived ideas and creativity to generate imaginative alternatives.*

Irony #2: At a time when effective communication is important, it is less likely.

Good communication is essential to efficient crisis management because information is the antidote to the uncertainty that crises generate. Unfortunately, at a time when effective communication is of particular importance, crises tend to create conditions in which it is less likely to occur.

Information as a source of power

Under the exaggerated conflicts of interest that emerged during the case study crises, information became an increasingly valuable commodity. This was because it represented an important source of power in negotiations and, consequently, it was more closely guarded. Indeed, the inclination to withhold information was magnified by the tendency of people with similar interests to collect into groups to share information for their common good. Such groups developed a sense of secrecy and pressured their members to put the group's interests before their own.

The volume of information generated

Another barrier to effective communication was the shear volume of information generated during a crisis, coupled with a contraction of responsibility for decisionmaking. This was a particular problem in the sudden crises, when "hot points" emerged within the organizational structure, creating bottlenecks and information overload. This caused information demand to run ahead of its supply. Unable to cope, the people occupying those positions fell into an increasingly reactive style of management. Some people attempted to cope by insisting that formal and standardized procedures be adhered to while others coped by becoming increasingly informal. However, both coping strategies deepened the problems they were designed to resolve. Formality slowed down information supply and caused frustration, and informality lead to breakdowns in communications and misunderstandings.

Lessons:
- ***People naturally withhold information during a crisis because of exaggerated conflicts of interests***. *Encourage communication during a crisis by emphasizing common interests and by having regular "communication meetings" when information demand and supply is the only agenda item. Use these multi-disciplinary meetings to generate and update information plans and to clarify information interdependencies and responsibilities for information supply.*
- ***Information quality is as important as quantity***. *Alleviate the time pressures that cause people to make mistakes. Employ competent people.*
- ***"Hot points" emerge during a sudden crisis***. *Identify the people who might occupy these points and support them. These people have the most critical positions in relation to information flow but ironically they are the most vulnerable to the stresses that can damage it.*
- ***It is as inappropriate to deal with a crisis in a routine, formalized manner, as it is to respond in a completely informal manner***. *The emphasis should be on a balance of flexibility and control. Unfortunately, during a crisis, this type of finely balanced response is less likely. Instead, project participants exhibit extremes of formal or informal behavior that lead the project into a downward spiral of poor communication, tension, anxiety, and stress, which becomes increasingly difficult to break.*

THE DYNAMICS OF CRISIS MANAGEMENT

To conclude this chapter, we turn back to the model of crisis management presented in Figure 3-1 and to the numerous inefficiencies in detection, diagnosis, decisionmaking, and implementation that created inertia within the crisis management process in each case study.

Monitoring

The case studies provided numerous instances of insensitivity to the early warning signs of potential crises. This insensitivity was caused by ineptitude, changes in project teams during a project, the timing of events in dormant periods, defensiveness, and fear of blame. Indeed, the blindness to potential problems was so extreme in some cases that the project's environment was more sensitive to problems within the project than the project team themselves. This highlights the importance of including all stakeholders in the management of a project.

In addition to monitoring inefficiencies there were also problems in the transition between the phases of monitoring and diagnosis. That is, knowledge of potential problems was often withheld from decisionmakers—sometimes deliberately, due to conflicts of interests and a lack of trust between monitors and comparators.

Diagnosis

Of all the phases in the crisis management process, diagnosis emerged as the most problematic. It was here that the financial responsibility for a crisis was determined and that potential winners and losers fought to safeguard their interests. In many instances, those in positions of contractual power dominated the process of diagnosis and manipulated it to protect their interests by blocking the exposure of potential blame to higher-level decisionmakers.

Decision making and implementation

There were also inefficiencies in the decisionmaking phase of the crisis management process, largely because, under the pressures of a crisis, people tended to rush their decisions and base them on inadequate or inaccurate information. In sudden crises, the focus was on organizational issues at the expense of financial issues, while in creeping crises, the opposite was the case. Consequently, financial issues emerged as a problem during the implementation phases of sudden crises and organizational issues emerged as problematic during the implementation stages of creeping crises.

Learning and recovery

The landscape of interpersonal relationships changed considerably during a crisis—in most instances, for the worst rather than for the better. However, there was no evidence of any attention being given to the process of learning and recovery. Even in the most successfully resolved crisis, people's preference was to put the sager behind them and to "gloss-over" over the conflicts of interest that had emerged within the project teams.

Repeated cycles of the crisis management process

Paradoxically, while the managerial inefficiencies, introduced inertia into the crisis management process, the effect was to force it through repeated cycles. For example, the earthwork support and lift crises went through two cycles, the paviour crisis went through three cycles, and the retaining wall crisis went through four cycles. In each case, repeated cycles of the crisis management process were necessary because inefficiencies created tensions among people who felt that their needs had not been satisfied. Each subsequent cycle was the mechanism by which unsatisfied and oppressed parties attempted to alleviate this tension. The more tension, the more cycles were needed to alleviate it. For example, in one crisis, an architect's reluctance to countenance a contractor's claim for extra monies led to delays on site which, in turn, led to another claim for an extension of time, which initiated another cycle of the crisis management process. The crisis management process will continue to go through repeated cycles until a point of equilibrium is reached where all the latent tensions associated with previously unsatisfied needs are dissipated.

Lessons:
- *Provide incentives for people to monitor and communicate potential problems regardless of who bears their risk. This includes all stakeholders (external and internal to the project team). Do not ignore the opinions of external stakeholders.*
- *Clarify mutual interests and interdependencies in resolving potential problems rapidly.*
- *Keep project teams as consistent as possible for the duration of a project.*
- *Beware of dormant periods during a project when people's attentions are focused elsewhere.*
- *Encourage and facilitate rapid, firm, and clearly communicated decisions.*
- *Avoid rushed, ill-considered decisions, and ensure they are based on complete and balanced information relating to technical, financial, and organizational issues from a broad range of perspectives. People tend to panic during the early stages of a crisis and prioritize issues. It is more efficient to take time to get it right the first time than to spend time coping with the aftermath of a poor decision.*
- *Ensure that every stakeholder in a crisis feels his or her interests have been fairly represented in the crisis management process. Unresolved interests will initiate repeated cycles of the crisis management process. The most efficient crisis management processes move through one cycle only.*
- *Give attention to learning and recovery. De-briefing is an important aspect of crisis management. This involves discovering and attending to damaged relationships and initiating independently managed post-mortems on the crisis management process.*

CONCLUSION

This chapter draws similarities and contrasts among the case studies described in the four previous chapters. The goal was to identify important practical lessons to help managers resolve construction crises. The discussions highlight the importance of planning for crises and the dangers of complacency in managing them. All crises appear to have built-in defence mechanisms that create conditions that make their management more difficult. In particular, they all have the potential to bring otherwise hidden tensions to the surface, to damage communications and interpersonal relationships, to cause people to behave selfishly and manipulatively, to generate further problems, and to gather their own destructive momentum. While the lessons that have been highlighted in this chapter can help mitigate these problems, their main purpose is to help managers realize their most important lesson: that a crisis can be turned to advantage if it is managed effectively.

Chapter 11

Conclusion – Creating an Optimistic Organization

While crises undoubtedly hold dangers for managers, they also present unique opportunities for improvement. This chapter summarizes the organizational attributes that can unlock this productive potential. This summary has both cultural and pragmatic elements. The pragmatic element takes the form of guidance for managers who are faced with a crisis; the cultural element is more generic and supportive. The chapter begins by focusing on cultural issues because without a positive culture, nothing pragmatic is realistically achievable.

OPTIMISM OR PESSIMISM – A STARK CHOICE

This book began with a sense of optimism for the future. It ends with the realization that managers can control their destiny by seeing uncertainties and complexities as threats or as opportunities. While this stark statement seems simplistic, it does not mean that managers should ignore the undeniable threats that crises pose. It does illustrate that managers can approach crises with a positive or negative mind-set, the former being differentiated from the latter by a determination to turn them to advantage by focusing on their opportunities. Most managerial practices in the construction industry are pessimistically guided by the principle of mitigation rather than optimisation. The case studies have demonstrated that once a project commences, traditional contracts, organizational practices, and cultures, lock people into a set of predetermined performance standards with little incentive to improve on them. They also create a penal culture of suspicion, fear, and mistrust that stifles the openness and freedom which defines the innovative, courageous, and altruistic culture of an optimistic organization. In the case studies, the greatest success seemed to be enjoyed by those people who were prepared to fight the system.

THE OPTIMISTIC ORGANIZATION

The discussions throughout this book have highlighted the principles that underpin an optimistic organization. These are discussed below.

Optimistic people
The defining characteristic of optimistic organizations is their determination and ability to see opportunities for performance improvement and their courage to take advantage of these opportunities. This demands a positive mind-set that can

only be achieved by employing people with a sense of optimism, courage, energy, and determination. However, every individual on a project is employed by and to some extent controlled by an organization, and if relationships at the organizational level are not positive, then any sense of individual optimism can rapidly disappear. This is a problem for construction project managers who are often faced with the challenge of motivating individuals who are working for demotivated and even resentful directors. In this sense, generating optimism will depend on changing the construction industry's traditional employment practices, contracts and organizational structures. These practices developed within a relatively stable but highly confrontational environment and were designed to make it easy to blame someone when something went wrong. Consequently, the principles that underpinned them were centralization, uniformity, hierarchy, compartmentalization, prescription, and rigidity. However, in today's opportunistic environment, such principles are obsolete since their effect is to fuel a self-perpetuating cycle of pessimism that suppresses the individuality, innovation, creativity, and courage that allow organizations to take full advantage of the future. A more optimistic construction industry will depend on new models of operation based on the opposing principles of flexibility, openness, equality, interdependence, collective responsibility, trust, sharing, and understanding. Making this transition can liberate the industry's workforce from the atmosphere of fear that has limited its potential productivity.

Effective communication

Clearly, good people alone cannot guarantee success. Good people need the support of an effective communication system that facilitates the sense of trust and openness that the industry needs. Information shortages are the main cause of division and mistrust during a crisis, and a well-designed communication system should prevent bottlenecks, disperse information rapidly and evenly, and minimize the potential for manipulation.

In addition to the cultural and organizational barriers to communication in the construction industry, there is the growing obsession with efficiency and leanness. The industry must be wary of this trend, since it will eradicate the redundancy needed to make communication systems reliable. Furthermore, the industry must change its restrictive contractual practices to enable people to legitimately opt out of formal procedures if they are restrictive and counter-productive during a crisis.

Preparedness

A sense of optimism depends to a large extent on an organization's ability to look for things that can go wrong. Organizations that know the future are better equipped to exploit the opportunities it may hold. It is worth reiterating that the world's most successful organizations are those that take time to compile prioritized crisis plans that demonstrate an in-depth understanding of their past and future vulnerabilities. However, confronting your organization's vulnerabilities means more than merely understanding the risks it faces. It is also about understanding its crisis capabilities, which means that the process of crisis planning involves realizing your organization's strengths as well as its weaknesses. This allows an organization to plan to maximize its strengths and minimize its weaknesses.

Another important aspect of optimistic organizations is that they are not over-optimistic. Optimistic organizations have a sense of realism in their plans and appreciate that the future cannot be planned accurately. Consequently, they are vigilant to continually changing risks and opportunities and adapt their plans accordingly.

Learning

A sense of optimism is founded on the belief that one can improve things by learning from past mistakes. Although this is often painful, many of the most profound sources of new knowledge are in the lessons to be learned in the aftermath of a crisis. Thus optimistic organizations have self-critical procedures in place to retrospectively dissect their crisis responses and to implement changes that can eradicate any future weaknesses. In contrast, pessimistic organizations prefer to put the past behind them and in doing so, fail to exploit what might be uncomfortable but valuable memories.

Securing early intervention

Crises tend to cause division and conflict, and thereby rapidly destroy any sense of optimism that may exist in an organization. For this reason, an important aspect of opportunism is early intervention, which depends on identifying potential problems quickly and nipping them in the bud. This is best achieved by eliminating fear, sharing risks, and instilling a sense of duty to notify potential problems, however small they may be. In essence, optimistic organizations act as confident, unified, self-supporting entities that are sensitive to all potential problems.

Creating a supportive and stable environment

The ability to achieve an opportunistic mind-set depends on the mental well-being and health of an organization's members. They need to work in an environment that is effective, controlled, stimulating, positive, and supportive of new ideas. Opportunistic organizations provide a sensitive, caring, and rewarding environment that minimizes uncertainty, prevents isolation, and minimizes frustration. Such an environment is possible by keeping project teams consistent, by minimizing the number of interfaces within a project team, and by reducing indecision and unnecessary change.

Creating a collaborative environment

Some degree of conflict accompanies a crisis, focussing people's minds on their differences rather than on their similarities. We have seen how conflict can be resolved positively if people move away from the compromising approach that is perceived as the most positive method of dispute resolution in the construction industry. The time and budgetary pressures that characterize construction projects drive the tendency to compromise; ironically, the process rarely alleviates those pressures. In contrast, collaboration provides the basis for exploring innovative and mutually beneficial ideas and solutions that can improve life for everyone.

The Pragmatics of Optimism

Managers, who put in place the preconditions for an optimistic culture, have the foundations for effective crisis management. This is management that turns crises to advantage and this book has offered practical guidance to help achieve this. Before the points of good practice are summarized, it is important to appreciate that this book offers no quick-fix solution. There is no substitute for thoughtfulness, sensitivity and responsiveness in dealing with the unique chain of events which precipitate every crisis. However, in general, to turn a crisis to your advantage:

- Do not ignore it.
- Do not procrastinate.
- Do not rely on contracts as a substitute for good management.
- Communicate the gravity of the situation. Everyone must know there is a crisis.
- Instill a sense of urgency if it is absent.
- Give priority to the crisis and resource it.
- Treat every crisis differently.
- Implement generic crisis management plans to buy some time.
- Identify an independent crisis manager to lead the crisis response as soon as possible. This may need to be an outsider.
- Define the crisis as soon as possible. Identify and involve all stakeholders because each will have a different perspective.
- Create a crisis management team. Involve necessary specialists, high-level managers, and main stakeholders who can contribute to a solution.
- Communicate the identity of the crisis management team. Define their powers and responsibilities.
- Loosen procedures. Do not be prescriptive about the way the crisis management team operates. Let them find their *modus operandi*.
- Define crisis management goals. Set targets to improve performance.
- Expect and demand results. Monitor and measure progress toward a solution.
- Be prepared to trade-off project goals.

- Present the crisis as a challenging opportunity by emphasizing the positives that can emerge.
- Care for every stakeholder. Independence is critical in crisis management.
- Having defined the crisis, implement detailed plans if they exist. They will not be a perfect fit and a detailed response will need formulating.
- Indicate clear concern for stakeholders outside the crisis management team.
- Keep everyone—insiders and outsiders—informed at all times.
- Do not speculate about responsibility or blame. Move on and solve the problem.
- Focus on minimizing costs rather than on who will pay for them.
- Encourage open communications. Information eliminates potential misunderstandings and conflicts. Continuous information is better than bursts.
- Be sensitive to people or groups who are able to control information flow. They will do so to serve their own interests.
- Encourage collective responsibility. Everyone's future is connected.
- Focus on relationships rather than individuals.
- De-personalize a crisis.
- Avoid blaming individuals or organizations. Look to the future not to the past.
- Do not talk about losers and winners. Everyone must feel that they can win.
- Identify people who see themselves as potential winners and losers. These represent the sources of tension and potential conflict.
- Focus on potential losers since they are the primary source of resistance to solutions.
- Monitor tactics between potential winners and losers. Encourage collaboration and be vigilant to the signs of deteriorating relationships. Beware of aggressive, selfish organizations—including the client.
- Look for and stop corporate bullying between project members.
- Do not impose solutions, other than as a last resort.
- Avoid quick-fix solutions. Rushed solutions return as problems.
- Look out for satellite problems that could become new crises. Crises create more crises.
- Do not neglect other aspects of an organization's activities.
- Communicate progress regularly. Focus on positives, not negatives.
- Encourage creativity and radicalism. Crises are extreme events that often demand extreme solutions.
- Stay cool. The symptoms of panic fuel crises.
- Identify "hot points" where stress can develop. Support the people that occupy them.
- Provide counselling/medical support where necessary. Show you care.
- In the aftermath of a crisis, provide positive feedback, conduct post-mortems, learn lessons, re-evaluate goals, re-focus the organization, repair damaged relationships, manage investigations sensitively, and move forward with a greater knowledge of your organization. You'll be stronger for the experience.

CONCLUSION

This book ends on a positive note. While it began with an enduring image of an industry that is struggling to cope with uncertainty, it ends with some insight into how the industry's apparently hostile environment can be turned to a manager's advantage. This insight has provided practical guidance of how to cope with crises in a positive manner. It has also provided a more holistic view of the supporting culture needed to underpin such efforts. The task of creating this optimistic culture is one of the most exciting challenges construction managers face.

REFERENCES

Abrahamson, M. W. 1984. Risk management. *International Construction Law Review* 1(3): 241-64.

Anderson, N. 1998. Health and safety—addressing barriers to improved safety performance. *Construction Manager* November: 14-15.

Akilade, A. 2000. What now? *Building* 2 June: 18-20.

Ansoff, H. I . 1979. *Strategic management.* London: Macmillan.

_____. 1984. *Implanting strategic management.* Englewood Cliffs, NJ: Prentice Hall.

Argyris, C. 1984. Double loop learning in organizations. In *Organizational Psychology—Readings on Human Behavior and Communications.* Edited by D.A. Kolb, I.M. Rubin, and McIntyre, J. M. Englewood Cliffs, NJ: Prentice Hall: 45-58.

_____. 1990. *Overcoming organizational defenses.* London: Allyn and Bacon.

Aspery, J. 1993. The media: friend or foe? *Administrator* 2(2): 17-19.

Barlow, J. 1999. Laing: Rooted in the past planning for the future. *Construction Manager* April: 22-24.

Barnes, M. 1991. Risk sharing in contracts. In *Civil Engineering Project Procedure in the EC.* Proceedings of the conference organized by the Institution of Civil Engineers, Heathrow, London, January 24-25.

Barrett, P.S. (Ed.) 1995. Facilities management—towards best practice. London: Blackwell Science.

Bavelas, A. 1950. Communication patterns in task orientated groups. *Acoustical Society of America Journal* 22: 727-30.

Bax, E.H.; B.J. Steijn; and M.C. DeWitte. 1998. Risk management at the shop floor: The perception of formal rules in high-risk work situations. *Journal of Contingencies and Crisis Management* 6(4): 177-88.

Baxendale, A.T. 1991. Management information systems: The use of work breakdown structure in the integration of time and cost. In *Management, Quality, and Economics in Building.* Edited by A. Bezelga and P. Brandon. Transactions of

CIB Symposium on management, quality and economics in housing and other building sectors, Lisbon, September 30 – October 4: 4-23

Bea, R.G. 1994. *The role of human error in design, construction, and reliability of marine structures*. Ship Structure Committee SSC-378, U.S. Coastguard, Washington, DC.

Benini, A.A. and Benini, J.B. 1996. Ebola virus: from medical emergency to complex disaster. *Journal of Contingencies and Crisis Management* 4(1): 10-20.

Bennis, W. 1996. *Facing the challenge: Peter Drucker in conversation with Warren Bennis*. BBC Enterprises, London.

Benson, J. A. 1988. Crisis revisited: an analysis of strategies used by Tylenol in the second tampering episode. *Central States Speech Journal* 39(1): 49-66.

Best, R. L. 1977. *Reconstruction of a tragedy: The Beverly Hills Supper Club Fire*. Southgate, KY: National Fire Protection Association.

Bignell, V. 1977. The West Gate bridge collapse. In *Catastrophic Failures*, edited by V. Bignell, G. Peters, and C. Pym. Milton Keines, UK: The Open University Press, 127-66.

Blockley, D. I. 1996. Hazard engineering, In *Accident and Design: Contemporary Debates in Risk Management*. Edited by C. Hood and D.K. C. Jones. UCL Press, London, 31-38.

Bobo, C. 1997. Hitachi faces crisis with textbook response. *Public Relations Quarterly* 42(2): 18-21.

Booth, S. A. 1993. *Crisis management strategy—competition and change in modern enterprises*. London: Routledge.

Bovens, M. 1996. The integrity of the managerial state. *Journal of Contingencies and Crisis Management* 4(3): 125-33.

British Property Federation. 1983. *Manual of the BPF system—The British Property Federation System for building design and construction*. London: The British Property Federation Ltd.

Brecher, M. 1977. Toward a theory of international crisis behaviour—A preliminary report. *International Studies Quarterly* 21(1): 39-74.

Building. 1997. Image building. *Building* September 19: 18-23.

Bullock, C. 1999. *Killology*. A discussion on Australian Broadcasting Corporation. Sunday, June 2. http://www.abc.net.au/rn/talks/bbing/stories/s23921.htm.

Burns, T. and G. Stalker. 1961. *The management of innovation*. London: Tavistock.

Butterfield, H. 1975. Introduction. In *The Sleepwalkers: A history of man's changing vision of the universe*, edited by A. Koestler. Harmondsworth, UK: Penguin Books.

Camp, R. C. 1989. *Benchmarking: The search for industry best practices that lead to superior performance*. Milwaukee, WI: ASQC Quality Press.

Carmichael, D. 1999. Gurus of faddish management. In *Proceedings of the international conference on construction process re-engineering*, edited by K. Karim, et al. Construction Process Re-engineering, University of New South Wales, Sydney, Australia, July 12-13: 365-74.

Carper, K. L. 1989. What is forensic engineering? In *Forensic Engineering*, edited by K.L. Carper. New York: Elsevier Science Publishing, 1-12.

Cavill, N. 1999. Purging the industry of racism. *Building* 14 May: 20-22.

Cherns, A. B. and D. T. Bryant. 1984. Studying the client's role in construction management. *Construction Management and Economics* 1(2): 177-84.

Cisin, I. H. and W. B. Clark. 1962. The methodological challenge of disaster research. In *Man and society in disaster*, edited by G.W. Baker G W and D.W. Chapman. New York: Basic Books Inc, 23-49.

Clennell, A. 1999. Storm bill biggest in Australia. *The Sydney Herald*, May 8, p. 5.

Comfort, L. K. 1993. Integrating information technology in to international crisis management and policy. *Journal of Contingencies and Crisis Management* 1(1): 15-27.

Commonwealth of Australia. 1999. *Building for growth—An analysis of the Australian building and construction industries*. Canberra, Australia: Australian Government Printing Service.

Construction Management and Economics.1997. Special edition on law and dispute resolution in construction. *Construction Management and Economics* 15(6): 501-75.

Cooper, D. F. and C. B. Chapman. 1987. *Risk analysis for large projects—Models, methods, and cases*. New York: John Wiley and Sons.

Craig, R. 1996. Manslaughter as a result of a workplace fatality. In *ARCOM 96, Proceedings of 12th Annual ARCOM Conference*, September 11-13. Edited by A.Thorpe. Sheffield Hallam University, UK, Volume 1: 1-11.

Daft, R. L. 1983. *Organizational theory and design*. St. Paul, MN: West Publishing Company.

Davis, S. M. 1987. Future perfect New York: Addison Wesley.

Davis, D. T. 1995. Harzardous materials contingency planning. In *Proceedings of 2nd International Conference on Loss Prevention and Safety*, October 16-18. Edited by F. Bushehri. Bahrain Society of Engineers, Bahrain, pp. 503-13.

DeMichiei, J., J. Langton, K. Bullock, and T. Wiles. 1982. Factors associated with disabling injuries in underground coalmines. *Mine Safety and Health Administration* June: 72.

Department of Energy. 1990. The public inquiry into the Piper Alpha disaster. The Honourable Lord Cullen, Volume 1 and Volume 2. London: HMSO.
Department of Public Works. 1999. *Creating an enabling environment for reconstruction, growth and development in the construction industry*. Pretoria, South Africa: Department of Public Works Government Printer.

Dixon, N. F. 1988. *On the psychology of military incompetence*. San Francisco: Cape.

Egelhoff, W. G. and F. Senn. 1992. An information processing model of crisis management. *Management Communication* 5(4): 443-84.

Eldukair, Z. A. and B. M. Ayyub. 1991. Analysis of recent U.S. structural and construction failures. *Journal of Performance of Constructed Facilities* 5(1), 57-73.

Engineering and Construction Contract. 1995. *The engineering and construction contract*. London: Thomas Telford.

Feature. 1999. Lagging funds delay Las Vegas Flood Control Project. *Civil Engineering*, April: 18-19.

Fennelle, C. 1996. The response to TWA Flight 800: Lessons learned. *Risk Management* 43(11): 58-69.

Fink, S. L.; J. Beak; and K. Taddeo. 1971. Organizational crisis and change. *Journal of Applied Behavioral Science* 7(1): 15-37.

Forman, D. 1993. Emergency plans and the mini-crisis. *Business Review Weekly* March 12: 72-73.

Freeman, L. C. 1979. Centrality in social networks conceptual clarification. *Social Networks* 1: 215-39.

Gablentz, O. H. 1972. Responsibility. In *The encyclopaedia of the social sciences,* volumes 13 and 14. Edited by D. L. Sills. New York: The Macmillan and Company and Free Press, 496-500.

Gambatese, J. A. 2000 Safety in a designer's hands, *Civil Engineering*, June: 5659.

Gay, A. 1998. Why trophy winners lose. *Building* October 30: 29.

George, A. L. 1991. Strategies for crisis management. In *Avoiding War—Problems of crisis management*. Edited by A.L. George. San Francisco: Westview Press.

Glackin, M. and G. Barrie. 1998. Jubilee Line strike set to end after last-ditch talks. *Building*. November 27: 12.

Glackin, M. 2000. Wembley row threatens to put back stadium a year. *Building,* 14 April: 10.

Goldberg, S. D. and B. B. Harzog. 1996. Oil spill: Management crisis or crisis management? *Journal of Contingencies and Crisis Management* 4(1): 1-10.

Gonzalez-Herrero, A. and C. B Pratt. 1995. How to manage a crisis before—or whenever—it hits. *Public Relations Quarterly* 40(1): 25-29.

Gray, C.; W. P. Hughes; and J. Bennett. 1994. *The successful management of design—A handbook of building design management*. Reading, U.K.: University of Reading, Center for Strategic Studies.

Green, S. 1998. The technocratic totalitarianism of construction process improvement: a critical perspective. *Engineering, Construction, and Architectural Management* 5(4): 376-86.

Hall, G; J. Rosenthal; and J. Wade. 1993. How to make reengineering really work *Harvard Business Review* November-December: 119-31.

Haroon, S. 1999. *Engineering disaster, the Ford Pinto case: A study in applied ethics, business, and technology.* http://www.uoguelph.ca/ca/~sharoon/a1/A1disaste.htm.

Hatush, Z. and M. Skitmore. 1997. Evaluating contractor prequalification data: selection criteria and project success factors. *Construction Management and Economics* 15(3): 129-47.

Heller, R. 1993. TQM – Not a panacea but a pilgrimage. *Management Today* January: 37-40.

Hemsley, A. 1998. Nightmares of recession. *Building* November 20: 33.

Hendry, R. 1989. Industrial accidents. In *Forensic Engineering*. Edited by K. L. Carper. New York: Elsevier Science Publishing, 56-80.

Health and Safety Commission. 1994. Health and safety statistics: statistical supplement to 1993/94 Annual Report. Sudbury, U.K.: HSE Books.

Hermann, C. F. 1963. Some consequences of crisis which limit the viability of organizations. *Administrative Science Quarterly* 8(25): 61-82.

Hilmer, F. G. and L. Donaldson. 1996. *Management redeemed—Debunking the fads that undermine corporate performance.* London: The Free Press.

Hindle, R. D. and M. H. Muller. 1996. The role of education as an agent of change: A two-fold effect. *Journal of Construction Procurement* 3(1): 56-66.

Horlick-Jones, T. 1996. The problem of blame. In *Accident and design: Contemporary debates in risk management.* Edited by C. Hood and D.K.C. Jones. UCL Press, London, 61-70.

Hornstein, H. A. 1986. *Managerial courage.* New York: John Wiley and Sons.

Irvine, R. B. 1997. *What's a crisis anyway? Surviving a business crisis.* Glanbridge Publishing Ltd, Urbana, Illinois.

Janis, I. L. 1988. Groupthink. In *Behavior in organizations—An experiential approach.* 4th edition. Edited by J. B. Lau and A. B. Shani., Irwin Homewood, Urbana, Illinois, 162 - 69.

Jarman, A. and A. Kouzmin. 1990. Decision pathways from crisis—a contingency theory simulation heuristic for the challenger space disaster (1983-1988). In *Contemporary Crisis –Law, Crime and Social Policy.* Edited by A. Block. Netherlands: Kluwer Academic Press, 399-433.

Johns, J. N. 1999. Letter to editor. *Civil Engineering* May 6, 37.

Kanter, E. 1983. *The change masters.* London,: Allen and Unwin.

Kelly, J.; S. MacPherson; and S. Male. 1992. *The briefing process: A review and critique*. Paper Number 12, The Royal Institution of Chartered Surveyors.

Kelman, H. C. 1997. Social-psychological dimensions of international conflict, In

Khosrowshahi, F. 1996. A neural network model for bankruptcy prediction of contracting organizations. In *ARCOM 96, Proceedings of 12th Annual ARCOM Conference*, September 11-13. Edited by A. Thorpe. Sheffield Hallam University, UK, p. 200-09.

Knight, K. E. and R. R. McDaniel, Jr. 1979. *Organizations—An information systems perspective* London: Wadsworth.
Knutt, E. 1998. Countdown to the millennium. *Building* June 19.

_____. 1998. The troubleshooter. *Building* June 19.

_____. 2000. Are we safer now? *Building* April 7.

Koestler, A. 1975. *The Sleepwalkers: A history of man's changing vision of the universe*. Harmondsworth, UK: Penguin Books.

Kumaraswamy, M. M.   1996. Construction dispute minimisation. In *The Organization and Management of Constructio*. Edited by D.A. Langford, A. Retik. London: E and F N Spon, 447-57.

Kutner, M. 1996. Coping with crisis. *Occupational Health and Safety* 65(2): 22-24.

Latham, M. 1994. *Construction the team*. Final Report of the Government/Industry Review of Procurement and Contractual Arrangements in the UK Construction Industry. London: HMSO.

Leavitt, H. J. 1951. Some effects of certain communication patterns on group performance. *Journal of Abnormal Social Psychology* 46(1): 38-50.

Leavitt, H. J. and H. Bahrami. 1988. *Managerial psychology—managing behavior in organizations* 5th ed. Chicago: The University of Chicago Press.

Likert, R. 1961. *New patterns of management*. New York: McGraw-Hill.

Loosemore, M. 1999. The problem with business fads. In *Proceedings of the international conference on construction process re-engineering*. Edited by K. Karim, et al. Construction Process Re-engineering. University of New South Wales, Sydney, Australia, July 12-13: 355-63.

Loosemore, M. and K. Hughes. 1998. Emergency systems in construction contracts. *Engineering, Construction, and Architectural Management* 5(2):189-99.

Loosemore, M. and T. Chin Chin. 2000. Occupational stereotypes in the construction industry. *Construction Management and Economics*. 18 (5), 559-567.

Loosemore, M.; B. T. Nguyen; N. Dennis. 1999 An investigation into the merits of encouraging conflict in the construction industry. *Construction Management and Economics*, 18 (4), 447-457.

Marsh, P.; E. Roser; and R. Harre'. 1978. *The rules of disorder*. London: Routledge.

Marshall, J. 1997. The professionals. *Building*. December 5: 22-23.

Mazur, L. 1996. Confidence in crisis. *Marketing* R24-R25, June 6.

Miles, L 1967. *Techniques of value analysis and engineering*. New York: McGraw Hill Book Company.

Mincks, W.R. 1996.Construction waste management: reducing and recycling construction and demolition waste. http://www.arch.wsu.edu/bminks/cons.htm.

Mintzberg, H. 1976. Planning on the left side and managing on the right side. *Harvard Business Review* 54(2): 49-58.

Mintzberg, H. 1979. *The structuring of organizations*. Englewood Cliffs, NJ: Prentice-Hall.

Mitroff, I. and C. Pearson. 1993. *Crisis management: A diagnostic guide for improving your organization's crisis preparedness*. San Francisco: Jossey-Bass Publishers.

Moodley, K and C.N. Preece. 1996. Implementing community policies in the construction industry. In *The Organization and Management of Construction*. Edited by D.A. Langford and A. Retik. London: E and F N Spon: 178-86.

Morley, I. E. 1981. Bargaining and negotiation. In *Psychology and Management*. Edited by C. L. Cooper. Macmillan Press Ltd, New York, 95-127.

Morris, P. 1998. Warnings for designers. *Building* April 9: 32-33.

Morris, P and G. H. Hough. 1987. *The anatomy of major projects—A study of the reality of project management*. Chicester, UK: John Wiley and Sons.

Munns A. K. 1996. Measuring mutual confidence in UK construction projects. *ASCE Journal of Management in Engineering* 12 (1): 26- 33.

National Bureau of Standards. May 1982. *Investigation of the Kansas City Hyatt Regency walkways collapse*. Building Science Series 143. Washington, DC: National Bureau of Standards, U S Department of Commerce.

National Economic Development Council. 1983. *Faster building for industry*.HMSO: London.

Nicodemus, J. 1997. Operational crisis management. *Secured Lender* 53(6): 84-90.

Oberlender, G. D. 1993. *Project management for engineering and construction*. New York: McGraw-Hill, Inc.

Oliver, J. 1993. Shocking to the core *Management Today* August: 18-22.

O'Rouke, J. 1998. *Union's plea: racism not all right on site*. Syendy Herald Sun, October 11, 19-20.

Pascale, R. T. 1991. *Managing on the edge*. Harmondsworth, UK: Penguin Books.

Pearson, C. M. and J. A. Clair. 1998. Reframing crisis management. *Academy of Management Review* 23(1): 59-76.

Pearson, C. M.; S. K. Misra; J. A. Clair; and I. Mitroff. 1997. Managing the unthinkable. *Organizational Dynamics* 26(2): 51-64.

Perry, J. G. and R. W. Hayes. 1985. *Risk and its management in construction projects*. Proceedings of Institute of Civil Engineers 1(78): 499-521.

Philips, R. C. 1988 Managing changes before they destroy your business: A non-traditional approach, *Training and Development Journal* 42(9): 66-71.

Pinnell, S. 1999. Resolution solutions. *Civil Engineering* June: 62-63.

Pritzker, P. E. 1989. Fire investigation. In *Forensic Engineering*. Edited by K. L. Carper. New York: Elsevier Science Publishing, 32-53.

Quarantelli, E. L. 1993. Community crises: An exploratory comparison of the characteristics and consequences of disasters and riots. *Journal of Contingencies and Crisis Management* 1(2): 167-79.
Reid, J. 1999. Engineers' top 10 crises. *Civil Engineering* April: 27.

Richardson, W. 1996. Modern management's role in the demise of a sustainable society. *Journal of Contingencies and Crisis Management* 4(1): 20-31.

_____. 1993. Identifying the cultural causes of disaster: An analysis of the Hillsborough Football Stadium Disaster. *Journal of Contingencies and Crisis Management* 1(1): 27-36.

Robertson, I. T. and C. L. Cooper. 1983. *Human behavior in organizations.* London: MacDonald and Evans.

Rochlin, G. I., ed. 1996. New directions in reliable organization research. *Journal of Contingencies and Crisis Management* 4(2).

Rogers, E. M. and D. L. Kincaid. 1981. *Communication networks. Toward a new paradigm for research.* London: The Free Press.

Rogers, J. P. 1991. Crisis bargaining codes and crisis management. In *Avoiding War—Problems of crisis management.* Edited by A. L. George. San Fransisco: Westview Press, 413-42.

Rosenthal, U. and A. Kouzmin. 1993. Globalization: An addenda for contingencies and crisis management—An editorial statement. *Journal of Contingencies and Crisis Management* 1(1): 1-11.

Ryan, K. D. and D. K. Oestreich. 1998. *Driving fear out of the workplace,* 2nd ed. San Francisco: Jossey-Bass Publishers.

Sagan, S. D. 1993. *The limits of safety: Organizations, accidents and nuclear weapons.* Princeton, NJ: Princeton University Press.

_____. 1991. Rules of engagement. In *Avoiding war— Problems of crisis management.* Edited by A. L. George. San Francisco: Westview Press, 443-70.

Scott, J. 1991. *Social network analysis—A handbook.* London:Sage Publications, Ltd.

Sfiligoj, E. 1997. In the midst of a crisis. *Beverage World* 116(1): 92-107.

Shaw, M. E. 1954. Group structure and the behavior of individuals in small groups. *Journal of Psychology* 38: 139-49.

Sheaffer Z.; B. Richardson and Z. Rosenblatt. 1998. Early warning signals management: A lesson from the bearings crisis. *Journal of Contingencies and Crisis Management* 6(1): 1-23.

Sheldrake, J. 1996. *Management theory—From Taylorism to Japanization.* London: Thompson Business Press.

Shrivastava, P. 1992. *Bhopal: Anatomy of a crisis.* London: Paul Chapman Publishing.

Sipika, C. and D. Smith. 1993. Back from the brink—post crisis management. *Long Range Planning* 1(1): 28-38.

Sinclair, A. and F. Haines. 1993. Deaths in the workplace and the dynamics of response. *Journal of Contingencies and Crisis Management* 1(3): 125-38.

Smith, C. 1996. High risk business. *Airline Business* November: 88-89.

Smith, N. J. 1999. *Managing risk in construction projects*. Oxford, UK: Blackwell Science.

Snyder, G. H. 1972. Crisis bargaining. In *International crisis—Insights from behavioral research*. Edited by C.F. Hermann. London: The Free Press, Collier-Macmillan Ltd, 217-56.

Spring, M. 1998. Gentle Giant *Building* October 31: 41-45.

Stacey, R. 1992. *Managing chaos*. London: Kogan Page.

Stewart, V. 1983. *Change—The challenge of management*. New York: McGraw-Hill.

Teo, M. M. M. 1998. *An investigation of the crisis-preparedness of Australian Construction Companies*. Unpublished BSc Thesis, University of New South Wales, Sydney, Australia.

t'Hart, P. 1993. Symbols, rituals and power: The lost dimensions of crisis management. *Journal of Contingencies and Crisis management* 1(1): 36-51.

Theodore, J. 1975. *The Empire State Building*. New York: Harper and Row.

Tichy, N. M.; M.L. Tushman; and C. Fombrun. 1979. Social network analysis for organizations. *Academy of Management Review* 4(4): 507-19.

Toffler, A. 1970. *Future Shock— A study of mass bewilderment in the face of accelerating change*. London: The Bodley Head.

Tsoukas, H. 1995. *New thinking in organizational behavior*. Oxford, UK: Butterworth-Heinnemann.

Tsurumi, R. 1982. American origins of Japanese productivity: The Hawthorne Experiment rejected. *Pacific Basin Quarterly* 7(1): 14-15.

Turner, B. A. and N F. Pigeon. 1997. *Man-made Disasters*, 2nd ed. Oxford, UK: Butterworth Heinemann.

Uff, J. 1995. Contract documents and the division of risk. In *Risk Management and Procurement in Construction*. Edited by J. Uff and A. M. Odams. London: Centre for Construction Law and Management, Kings College, 49-69

Wagenaar, W. A. 1996. Profiling crisis management. *Journal of Contingencies and Crisis Management* 4(3): 169-74.

Watson, T. J. 1994. *In search of management*. London: Routledge.

Weyer, M. V. 1994. When the wheels come off. *Management Today* July: 30-37.

Wildavsky, A. 1988. *Searching for safety*. New Brunswick: Transaction.

Wills, J. A. 1996. Enhancing disaster planning and management: The 1990 Nyngan flood in Australia. *Journal of Contingencies and Crisis Management* 4(1): 32-39.

Wire Headlines. 1999. *Long prison terms given in South Korean Mall Collapse.* http://sddt.com/files/librarywire/96wireheadlines/08-96/DN96-08-23/DN96-08-23-1html.

Zartman, I. W. and J. L. Rasmussen. 1997. *Peace making in international conflict: Methods and techniques*. Washington, DC: United States Institute of Peace.

INDEX